Treadway Inns

3-4-58

By Ann Roe Robbins

HOW TO COOK WELL
TREADWAY INNS COOK BOOK

By Dione Lucas and Ann Roe Robbins

THE DIONE LUCAS MEAT AND POULTRY COOK BOOK

Treadway Inns Cook Book

TREADWAY INNS COOK BOOK

by Ann Roe Robbins

Illustrations by John V. Morris

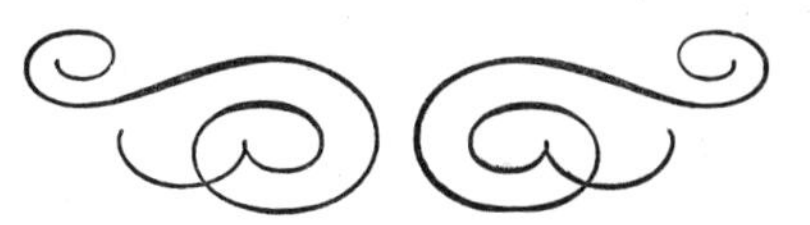

Boston · Little, Brown and Company · *Toronto*

LIBRARY OF CONGRESS CATALOG CARD NO. 57-9324

FIRST EDITION

Published simultaneously in Canada
by Little, Brown & Company (Canada) Limited

PRINTED IN THE UNITED STATES OF AMERICA

Preface

EVERY recipe in this book has been tested and worked out for family-size use. I first visited the chefs and pastry cooks in all the Treadway Inns, watching them work and securing their recipes, and then reduced the recipes to home proportions in my own kitchen. Chefs obviously work in terms of 10 pounds of flour for cakes and 20 gallons of water for beef stock, and cutting down their recipes is a little more involved than mere simple arithmetic – you can multiply, but you cannot always divide. However, I think that home cooks can use these recipes with confidence. I would add that since all chefs do not cook exactly alike, there will doubtless be some minor variations between some of these recipes and the actual dishes served at the inns. All the recipes of all the inns could not be included, for reasons of space. If any reader cannot find a particular recipe for a dish enjoyed at an inn, I shall be glad to send it.

I do want to extend general and individual thanks to the many chefs who were so kind to me. Contrary to all the theories of how temperamental and volatile chefs are, without exception they could not have been more cooperative and helpful, and they are the ones who really made this book possible.

ANN ROE ROBBINS

Contents

Introduction

THE Treadway Inns are a Yankee business and a family business. The well-known trademark, a colonial watchman, is intended to signify old-fashioned hospitality, and each Treadway Inn offers the warm welcome, comfort, and good food of the inns of earlier days.

The beginning was in 1912 when Mr. L. G. Treadway, who had worked his way through Dartmouth by waiting on table in a restaurant, took over the management of the Williams Inn in Williamstown. He became a management consultant of great independence and with very definite ideas on inn and restaurant operation. Over the years he has managed and owned a variety of inns, accepting the responsibility only when his methods were adopted. (Today the organization turns down about one new management offer every week.) Mr. Treadway has three sons, and at one time he tried going into big hotel business with an eye to establishing a business foundation for them. But he didn't find big business or board-of-directors meetings to his liking at all; in fact, they drove him mad. What he wanted to do, and has done, was to manage attractive homelike inns.

Mr. L. G. Treadway has retired from active participation in the business, and his three sons are now successfully carrying on. Richard Treadway, the eldest, is president; John Treadway manages the Williams Inn and is advertising manager; and David Treadway is in charge of sales promotion. At the time of writing, there are eighteen inns under the Treadway management, in Massachusetts, Vermont, Connecticut, New York, Pennsylvania, North Carolina – and New England hospitality even extends to Florida at the Royal Park Inn in Vero Beach and The Sea Garden in Pompano Beach. Fifteen of these inns are discussed separately in this book. The others – the Treadway Inn in Canandaigua, New York (George R. Jones, innkeeper), Treadway Manor in Asheville, North Carolina (Michael A. Byrne, innkeeper), and The Sea Garden in Pompano Beach, Florida (Warren R. Swift, innkeeper) – were acquired too late to be included.

There are several characteristic features of a Treadway Inn: the location, the furnishings and décor, the housekeeping, and the food. The inns are all strategically located in attractive surroundings, most of them either in school or college towns or in resorts. Even the new city Treadway Inns in Rochester, New York, Norwalk, Connecticut, and Meadville, Pennsylvania, are on spacious grounds in residential neighborhoods. The locations are actually so advantageous from every standpoint that any one could be picked blindfold for a vacation. Mr. L. G. Treadway's love of gardening is reflected in the well-landscaped grounds of the inns and the many lovely gardens. A guest in a Treadway Inn can take it for granted that the public rooms will be large, comfortable, and furnished with the utmost taste, usually in colonial style, much more like a fine home than a hotel; that the tables will be set with carefully chosen china and glassware; and that the service will be efficient and courteous. Bedrooms and bathrooms reflect the same care. The bedrooms will be spotlessly clean with comfortable beds and chairs, reading lights, and luggage racks. The bathrooms will even have cleansing tissues, a cloth for wiping shoes, cakes of a special lemon soap, and – it may seem like a small thing, but it is seldom found in hotels – washcloths.

The food has the same Treadway attention. Because so many people are conservative in their food preferences, standard restaurant favorites are always served, such as roast beef, steaks, roast turkey, broiled lobster, and swordfish. However, New England dishes, like Indian pudding, blueberry grunt, and codfish cakes, are featured, and there are famous Treadway Inn specialties, such as lobster pie, baked stuffed shrimp, frogs' legs sautéed in Chablis, caviar omelet, and Rock Cornish game hens (the Publick House in Sturbridge, Massachusetts, was the first restaurant to serve them). Regional foods are added to the menus of individual inns, as well as the chefs' specialties and Continental touches. So the menus have a wide variety; in fact, when a list was compiled of all the dishes on menus from all the inns, there were over seven hundred dishes. To enhance the food, most of the inns offer a carefully chosen wine list at very reasonable prices.

So whenever you see the familiar black-figured colonial watchman, you can be sure of good food, and a good place to relax and lay your head. Singly, or in combination, the Treadway Inns offer the traveler or vacationist an impressive variety of history, scenery, recreation, and good eating.

Treadway Inns Cook Book

TREADWAY INN

Norwalk, Connecticut

THE Treadway Inn in Norwalk, which opened in February 1957, is the second Treadway Inn built on the motel-hotel principle of a country inn in the city, the first being the extremely successful one in Rochester, New York.

This Norwalk inn is a community venture supported by two thousand residents, most of whom own one share each in the corporation. The inn is a pink-brick V-shaped two-story building standing on eleven acres of ground. The amount of ground is important because it eliminates parking problems. Although the inn is right in town, on 99 East Avenue just to the right of the rotary at the top of the hill on Wall Street, the neighborhood is residential and quiet. There is ample free parking space, with easy access to the rooms, informal direct registration, and optional bellboy service. The rooms are the last word in modern comfort. There are four different decorative schemes in the seventy-four rooms, all harmonious and pleasing. Every room has an extra full-size studio couch with box springs and foam-rubber mattress. Each room has a free 21-inch television set and individually controlled air-conditioning. The bathrooms are fully tiled, have combination tubs and showers, and electric radiant heat. There is twenty-four-hour room and switchboard service.

At present there are two dining rooms. The main dining room seats forty-eight people and there is a dining room for private parties which will seat thirty people. Until a planned large dining room is added, it is best to make reservations in advance to prevent waiting. The food, needless to say, is typical excellent Treadway food, and features such specialties as fried breast of chicken with supreme sauce, broiled Eastern swordfish, and lobster pie Treadway Inn style, as well as regional specialties.

Norwalk is situated on Long Island Sound only forty-one miles from Forty-second Street in New York. The inn is three quarters of a mile from the new Connecticut Turnpike and two miles from the Merritt Parkway; driving west toward New York, the exit is No. 40, Route 7; driving east from New York, the exit is No. 39.

The city is over three hundred years old. In 1640 a Puritan, Roger Ludlow, the first formally trained lawyer in the colonies at that time, purchased 15,777 acres from the Indian owners, who received "wampum, coates, hatchets, hoes, knives, scissors, jewes-harpes, tabachoe, kettles and looking glasses" worth about $60. This legal bargain was the beginning of Norwalk. By 1678 Norwalk had a schoolmaster and in 1699 the first school was built. The town was large enough by 1708 for a doctor, who charged 12¢ for a regular visit and 24¢ if bloodletting was required. A plaque in front of the inn marks an event in colonial history. There on a Sunday in July 1799 the British General Tryon watched his Redcoats destroy by fire 135 houses, 2 churches, 89 barns, and 29 shops, while the enraged Norwalk patriots inflicted sizable casualties on the British troops.

Today Norwalk is a city with a population of sixty thousand. It has many miles of shore front and is flanked on two sides with rolling hills which develop into high ridges. The inn is only a ten- to fifteen-minute walk from the business center, where there are all sorts of shops and first-run movie houses. Although much of the shore front is private property, there is a public beach – Calf Pasture – with swimming, picnic tables, and fireplaces; another beach a few miles away in Westport, Sherwood Island, has the same facilities. There is plenty of sailing, boating, and fresh- and salt-water fishing; a license is required for fresh-water fishing. For $1 you can even get a permit from the health officer to dig clams and oysters, which are abundant along the Norwalk shore.

It is a beautiful part of the country with its wooded ridges and many running brooks and small lakes, and a fine place to take leisurely drives. Fairfield County is one of the wealthiest sections per capita of the United States, and there are many interesting contemporary houses. You can see the oldest lumber mill in the United States, which is still in operation. Route 7 is loaded with antique shops. The Silvermine Guild of Artists is only a few miles away; it is the largest community art center in the East and has exhibitions all year as well as a thriving school. The Westport Country Playhouse has a long summer-theater season with professional productions and famous stars. Norwalk also has a zoo, which was photographed in *Look* magazine in 1957 when the mother kangaroo had a baby.

The inn is open all year. Mr. Francis J. Power, Jr., is the innkeeper.

THE DAVID MEAD

Meadville, Pennsylvania

A FIRE which destroyed the main hotel in Meadville ignited the sparks which set off this particular Treadway Inn. The public-minded citizens wanted a fine hotel worthy of their city, so about twelve hundred local stockholders united in this community effort, and the Treadway organization is managing another of its "country inns in the city."

Meadville was settled in 1788 by David Mead and seven companions, and the inn is named for him. Opening in 1958, it has the popular motel-hotel setup. The building is a colonial type, with seventy rooms for guests, complete with television sets, and excellent dining-room, banquet, and conference-room facilities. There are a main dining room, three private dining rooms which can be opened up to one large room seating seventy-five people, and a banquet hall or ballroom which will accommodate at least two hundred and twenty-five people. The lounge is an attractive living room; there are conference rooms, a gift shop, and a cocktail lounge. All these public rooms are air-conditioned. There is plenty of free parking.

Meadville, with a population of twenty thousand, is an interesting city, combining agriculture, industry, and culture. It surrounds French Creek, which flows through the city, and is itself surrounded by gently rolling countryside. Agriculture thrives in the country, while in the city proper there are several prosperous industries, including the Talon Zipper Company. Meadville is also the seat of Allegheny College, which was founded in 1815 and has some fascinating old buildings.

Meadville is really a semiresort. There are two nearby lakes, Lake Conneaut and Lake Pymatuning, to provide the usual water sports and picnic grounds. The state fish hatcheries keep the area's lakes and streams well stocked, and muskellunge up to 30 to 40 pounds are caught in French Creek in considerable quantity. There are two public golf courses at Lake Conneaut as well as one right in Meadville. The state game farm stocks the fields and woods with wild fowl for hunters, and there are deer and bear. Visitors will enjoy visiting the thrice-weekly farmer's market.

The David Mead is a five-minute walk from the heart of the city but in a completely residential district. It is easily accessible to major traffic routes, since Meadville is at the junction of United States routes 6, 19, and 32. The inn is open all year. Mr. Parry C. Benton is the innkeeper.

BEVERAGES

THIS collection of beverages represents a few of the specialties of the Treadway Inns. The inns, of course, serve all the standard drinks, long and short, hard and soft. But since this book is not in any sense a manual, we are assuming that most readers know how to make drinks like Manhattans and Martinis, and we have skipped them in preference to more unusual drinks. So here are some special cocktails, toddys, party punches, drinks to cool you in the summer, and drinks to warm and comfort you in the winter.

COCKTAILS

HONEYBEE SPECIAL

1 *teaspoon honey* — 1 *tablespoon lemon juice*
1½ *ounces applejack*

Warm the honey until it runs freely. Warm a cocktail glass like a Daiquiri glass. Mix the honey and lemon juice in the glass and add the applejack.

SAP BUCKET SPECIAL

The Williams Inn in the Berkshires, the foothills of Vermont's Green Mountains, is in the heart of the maple sugar country. The Sap Bucket Special uses fresh maple syrup from the surrounding countryside, old New England rum, and lemon juice. The proportions are the same as those of the Honeybee Special.

DEERSLAYER COCKTAIL

¼ *grapefruit juice*
1 *dash Heering cherry brandy*
¾ *Bacardi rum*

Shake well with cracked ice and strain into a cocktail glass.

PIONEER COCKTAIL

juice of ½ lime
1 *dash grenadine*
1 *dash orange curaçao*
1½ *ounces Jamaica rum*

Combine, shake well with cracked ice, and strain into a cocktail glass.

HIT AND RUN COCKTAIL

¼ *port wine*
¾ *Seagram's gin*
1 *dash anisette*
twist of lemon peel

Stir the wine, gin, and anisette with ice and pour into a cocktail glass. Garnish with a twist of lemon peel.

COOPERSTOWN COCKTAIL

½ *ounce Italian vermouth*
½ *ounce French vermouth*
½ *ounce gin*
sprig of fresh mint

Combine the two vermouths and the gin and stir them with ice. Pour into a cocktail glass and garnish with fresh mint.

FLYER

juice of ½ lime
1 *jigger Bacardi rum (white* or *silver label)*
½ *teaspoon sugar*
dry champagne

Shake well the lime juice, rum, and sugar with cracked ice, strain, and pour into a champagne glass. Fill the glass with chilled dry champagne.

AIRMAIL SPECIAL

juice of ½ lime
1 *jigger Bacardi rum (gold* or *amber label)*
1 *teaspoon honey*
dry champagne

Mix thoroughly the lime juice, rum, and honey, shake well with cracked ice, and strain into a highball glass. Fill the glass with chilled dry champagne.

BRANDY FLIP

1 *egg*
1½ *ounces brandy*
2 *teaspoons sweet cream*
nutmeg

Combine the egg, brandy, and cream, shake well with cracked ice, and strain into a four-ounce flip glass. Grate a little nutmeg on the top.

BRANDY STINGER

1 *ounce brandy*
½ *ounce white crème de menthe*
twist of lemon peel

Shake the brandy and créme de menthe thoroughly with cracked ice. Serve in a cocktail glass with a twist of lemon peel.

PUNCHES—ALCOHOLIC

CHAMPAGNE PUNCH

lemon milk sherbet or *orange ice* *champagne*

Use 1 quart of lemon milk sherbet or orange ice for each bottle of champagne. Place the sherbet in a large chilled punch bowl, add the chilled champagne, and blend. The sherbet keeps the champagne cold, so no ice need be added and the wine does not become watery.

CHAMPAGNE COCKTAIL PUNCH

¼ *cup sugar*
1½ *cups brandy*
juice of 2 lemons
1 *lemon, sliced thin*
½ *orange, sliced thin*
1 *pineapple, cut in small pieces,* or 1 *package frozen pineapple*
2 *bottles champagne*

Blend the sugar and brandy in a bowl. Add the lemon juice and the fruits. Chill for several hours in the refrigerator. Just before serving, pour over a large piece of ice in a large punch bowl. Add the champagne, which should be well chilled, stir, and serve.

EGGNOG

1 *dozen egg yolks*
12 *scant tablespoons sugar*
1 *cup Jamaica rum*
1 *bottle rye* or *bourbon*
1 *pint thick cream*
1 *quart vanilla ice cream*

Beat the yolks until light, then add 12 scant tablespoons of sugar. Beat the mixture until it begins to get light (about 10 to 15 minutes). Add the rum and let stand for an hour or so. Then add slightly less than 1 bottle of good rye or bourbon. Just before serving, add the cream, well beaten, and the vanilla ice cream. The ice cream will chill the eggnog. Serves 15 to 17. If there is any left over, place it in a covered jar in a cool place and use the next day.

THE BISHOP

2 *oranges*
cloves
2 *quarts good red port*
small piece of cinnamon stick
small piece of whole nutmeg
small piece of ginger root or *pinch of powdered ginger*
¼ *cup brandy*

Stud the oranges with as many cloves as will fit and bake them in a moderate oven at 350° until the cloves start to turn white and powdery, about 30 to 40 minutes. Meanwhile heat the port with a small piece of cinnamon stick, a small piece of whole nutmeg, and a small piece of ginger root or a pinch of powdered ginger. When the oranges are done, place them in a flameproof punch bowl and strain the port over them. Carefully pour on the brandy, slightly heated, and ignite it. If the flame does not die down in a few seconds, extinguish it by covering the bowl. Serve immediately. The bowl may be refilled with more hot spiced wine. Makes about 16 four-ounce servings.

SWEDISH GLÜG

1½ *cups dry red wine*
2 *cups brandy*
6 *whole cloves*
3 *cardamon seeds*
2-*inch cinnamon stick*
⅓ *cup seedless raisins*
10 or 12 *blanched almonds*
¾ *cup sugar*
about 1 *teaspoon sugar*

Put into a large saucepan all but the 1 teaspoon of sugar (the cardamon seeds should have the shells cracked, but not enough for the seeds to come out). Bring slowly to a boil and ignite, immediately sprinkling about a teaspoon of sugar into the burning liquid. Extinguish the flame by covering the pan after 15 seconds. Serve hot in small glasses, with a few raisins or almonds in each. The burning sugar is the secret for the flavor of this drink. Makes 12 to 14 servings.

BRIDE'S BOWL

½ *pineapple* or 1 *package frozen pineapple chunks*
1 *cup sugar*
1 *cup water*
1 *cup lemon juice*
2 *cups pineapple juice*
1½ *fifths gold Puerto Rican rum*
2 *quarts soda water*
1 *pint strawberries, sliced*

Cube the pineapple or defrost the frozen chunks. Make a simple syrup by boiling 1 cup of sugar and 1 cup of water together for 5 minutes. In a large pitcher place the pineapple, syrup, lemon juice, and pineapple juice. Add the rum and chill in a refrigerator for at least 2 hours. To serve, pour over a block of ice in a punch bowl and add 2 quarts of soda water and the sliced strawberries. Makes about 25 servings.

WHISKEY SOUR PUNCH

2 *cups sugar*
2 *cups water*
2½ *pints bourbon*
2½ *pints rye*
1 *cup lemon juice*
2 *teaspoons angostura bitters*
1½ *pints soda*

Make a simple syrup by boiling the sugar and water together for 5 minutes. Cool the syrup and mix with the whiskeys, lemon juice, and bitters. Place in a punch bowl with a large piece of ice. Just before serving, add 1½ pints of soda. Makes 20 to 25 servings.

FISH HOUSE PUNCH

- ¾ *pound sugar*
- 1 *quart water*
- 1 *pint lemon juice*
- 2 *quarts Jamaica rum*
- 1 *quart cognac*
- ½ *cup peach brandy*

Dissolve ¾ pound of sugar in part of 1 quart of water in a punch bowl. Add the rest of the water and 1 pint of lemon juice and stir well. Then add 2 quarts of rum, 1 quart of cognac, and ½ cup of peach brandy and allow the mixture to stand for 2 to 3 hours to blend, stirring slightly from time to time. Before serving, put a large block of ice in the punch bowl and stir to cool. Serves 20.

STRAWBERRY BOWL

- 2 *quarts strawberries*
- 1 *cup sugar*
- ½ *bottle claret*
- 2 *bottles champagne*

Hull the strawberries, cut in half, and put into a punch bowl with the sugar and claret. Rest the bowl over ice for an hour or more. When ready to serve, add 2 bottles of thoroughly chilled champagne. Serves 8 to 10.

PUNCHES—NONALCOHOLIC

CRANBERRY PUNCH

- ¾ *cup brown sugar*
- 4 *cups water*
- ¾ *teaspoon cloves*
- ½ *teaspoon cinnamon*
- ½ *teaspoon allspice*
- ¼ *teaspoon nutmeg*
- ¼ *teaspoon salt*
- 4 *cups pineapple juice*
- 2 1-*pound cans jellied cranberry sauce*
- *few drops red food coloring*
- *few bits butter*
- *cinnamon sticks*

Combine in a saucepan the brown sugar, 1 cup of water, cloves, cinnamon, allspice, nutmeg, and salt. Bring slowly to a boil. Add the pineapple juice and 3 cups of water. Crush the cranberry sauce with a fork and add. Bring to a boil again and simmer for 5 minutes. Add a few drops of red coloring. Pour into a heated punch bowl. Add a few bits of butter. Serve in mugs with cinnamon sticks as stirrers. Makes about 10 one-cup servings.

PILGRIM PUNCH

1 *cup water*
2 *cups sugar*
juice of 1 *quart strawberries*
1 *cup strong tea*
juice of 4 *oranges*
juice of 2 *lemons*
2 *cups grated pineapple* or *pineapple juice*
1 *quart shaved ice* or *lemon sherbet*
1 *quart cold water*
1 *quart carbonated water*
few strawberries
mint leaves

Stir 1 cup of water and 2 cups of sugar over a medium fire until the sugar is dissolved, then boil for 5 minutes. Press 1 quart of strawberries, fresh or frozen, through a sieve to extract the juice. Combine the sugar syrup, strawberry juice, 1 cup of strong tea, juice of 4 oranges, juice of 2 lemons, and 2 cups of grated pineapple or pineapple juice. Let stand. Strain over shaved ice or lemon sherbet in a punch bowl. Add 1 quart of cold water and 1 quart of carbonated water. Garnish with a few strawberries and mint leaves. Serves 15 to 20.

COLD CRANBERRY PUNCH

1 *quart ginger ale*
1 *No.* 2 *can pineapple juice*
1 *bottle cranberry juice*
1 *pint pineapple* or *lemon sherbet*

Chill the ginger ale and the fruit juices well. Also chill a punch bowl. Just before serving, combine the liquids and pour over the sherbet in the punch bowl. Makes 15 to 18 punch-cup servings.

GARDEN PARTY PUNCH

3 *cups boiling water*
2 *tablespoons tea*
1 *cup sugar*
1 *cup orange juice*
½ *cup lemon juice*
1 *cup pineapple juice*
1 *pint ginger ale*
1 *pint soda water*
orange slices
mint leaves

Combine the water and tea. Let steep for 5 minutes, then strain out the tea leaves. Add the sugar, stir until dissolved, and cool. Combine and chill the fruit juices. When ready to serve, place a block of ice in a punch bowl and pour in the tea and fruit juices. Add the ginger ale and soda water and decorate with orange slices and mint leaves. Makes 2½ quarts.

SUMMER BEVERAGES

SHANDYGAFF

This refreshing light drink is made by mixing equal parts of well-chilled beer and ginger beer in a tall glass. Light ale may be used in place of the beer, or lemonade in place of the ginger beer.

RASPBERRY SHRUB

1 *cup raspberries*
½ *cup sugar*
2 *cups water*
2 *tablespoons vinegar*
few raspberries

Crush the raspberries with the sugar. Add the water and vinegar. Serve very cold with a few raspberries.

EMERALD FROST

½ *cup mint jelly*
½ *cup water*
3 *teaspoons lime juice*
lemon sherbet
lemon-lime carbonated beverage
lime slices

Heat the mint jelly and water to make a syrup. Cool, then add the lime juice. Fill 8 tall glasses with scoops of lemon sherbet; top with 2 teaspoons of the mint syrup. Fill each glass with lemon-lime carbonated beverage and garnish with a slice of lime.

FROSTED PINEAPPLE AND BANANA

1 *cup pineapple juice*
½ *small ripe banana*
½ *teaspoon lemon juice*

Freeze the pineapple juice until it is hard. Purée the banana. Whip them together with ½ teaspoon of lemon juice in an electric blender or with a rotary beater until thick. Serve immediately. Serves 1.

WINTER BEVERAGES

NEW ENGLAND HOT BUTTERED RUM

5 *ounces Vermont maple syrup* or ½ *cup maple sugar*
¾ *cup butter*
1 *teaspoon ground cinnamon*
½ *teaspoon ground cloves*
2 *quarts cider (on the hard side but not sour)*
1 *pint New England rum (amber), Caldwell's Old Newburyport*
½ *pint Demarara rum (dark,* 150 *proof)* or *Jamaica rum*

Put the syrup or sugar, butter, cinnamon, and cloves into a heavy pot and heat until it bubbles. Stir, then add the cider. Heat again to a simmer, remove from the fire, and add the rum. Stir again with a heavy red-hot poker. Makes 6 five-ounce portions.

WHALER'S TODDY

1 *teaspoon brown sugar* or *molasses*
1 *slice lemon*
3 *cloves*
1 *cinnamon stick*
2 *ounces dark Carioca rum*
boiling water

In a heavy mug, blend the brown sugar or molasses, lemon, cloves, cinnamon stick, and rum. Add enough boiling water to fill the mug. Heat the mug by standing it in a pan of water as it comes to a boil over a slow fire. Makes 1 serving.

HOT SPICED TEA

6 *cups water*
1 *teaspoon whole cloves*
1-*inch cinnamon stick*
2½ *tablespoons black tea*
¾ *cup orange juice*
2 *tablespoons lemon juice*
½ *cup sugar*

Put the water in a saucepan and add cloves and cinnamon stick. Bring to the boiling point. Add the tea, remove from the fire, and steep for 5 minutes. Strain. Meanwhile heat the orange and lemon juice and sugar. Bring to a boil, stirring to dissolve the sugar, and add to the hot tea. Makes 6 to 8 servings.

MULLED CIDER

2 *quarts cider*
1 *cinnamon stick*
½ *teaspoon whole cloves*
¼ *teaspoon nutmeg*
16 *small crab apples*

Pour the cider into a saucepan and add the cinnamon stick, cloves, and nutmeg. Simmer for 10 minutes. Strain and reheat to the boiling point. Meanwhile roast the crab apples in their skins for 15 minutes in a moderate oven at 350°. Pour the hot cider into mugs and stir with a red-hot poker. Quickly drop 2 apples into each mug. The apples will split open, giving the drink a distinctive flavor. Makes 8 servings.

TOM AND JERRY

6 *eggs*
½ *cup sugar*
½ *teaspoon grated nutmeg*
Jamaica rum
brandy
hot water or *milk*

Separate the eggs and beat the yolks until thick and light. Gradually add the sugar and nutmeg. Beat until very thick. Beat the egg whites until stiff and fold them into the yolks. Chill the mixture until you are ready to serve. To serve, put a heaping teaspoon of the egg mixture into a warm mug, add 1 jigger of Jamaica rum and 1 jigger of brandy, and fill the mug with hot water or milk. Dust the top with grated nutmeg.

SYLLABUB

Syllabub is a traditional drink. One recipe, from an old New England cook book published in 1808, reads: "Sweeten a quart of cider with double-refined sugar. Grate nutmeg into it. Then milk your cow into your liquor. When you have thus added what quantity of milk you think proper, pour half a pint or more in proportion to the quantity of syllabub you make of the sweetest cream you can get all over it."

PUBLICK HOUSE RECIPE

1 *cup sherry*
1 *cup port*
½ *cup brandy*
1 *quart rich milk*
sugar to taste
1 *cup heavy cream*
nutmeg

Mix the sherry, port, and brandy. Pour into a punch bowl. Add 1 quart of rich milk and sugar to taste, and mix well. Pour 1 cup of thick cream over it all and dust with nutmeg. Serve at room temperature. Makes 10 to 12 servings.

ROYAL PARK INN

Vero Beach, Florida

THE town of Vero Beach is on the east coast of Florida, about halfway between Jacksonville and Miami, right in the middle of the Indian River country. The Treadway Inn there is the Royal Park, well named for the royal palms growing on the property. The inn is set on six acres of ground which are conveniently located near the town and yet well protected by landscaping.

There is a main stucco building of Spanish-style architecture which has guest rooms, large lounges and a cocktail lounge, and a spacious, attractively decorated dining room. There are also cottages, which have unusually large bedrooms and nice porches. The Royal Park is Mr. L. G. Treadway's winter home, which is significant because he is a keen gardener. The result is that the grounds are full of shrubs, trees, and flowers, with all the gay, brilliantly colored native flowers blooming in abundance. Bougainvillaea, hibiscus, oleanders, and crimson poinsettias are some of the flowering plants, and there are many fragrant citrus trees. So the grounds are like a tropical garden, and the porches a fine place to sit and enjoy them. There are also a swimming pool and three excellent shuffleboard courts. There are good tennis courts close to the inn, while three blocks away there is a golf course with all grass greens which is considered one of the best in Florida, with locker rooms and showers available to the hotel guests.

One of the chief attractions of Vero Beach is the beach itself, about two miles from the hotel. It is a fine stretch of white sand many miles long and never crowded. A beach wagon from the inn makes several trips a day and you could hardly ask for a better place to swim. The inn is also about a mile from the Indian River fishing dock, where there are guides, boats, and equipment for surf casting and deep-sea fishing.

Vero Beach is the winter headquarters of the Los Angeles Dodgers, and there are exhibition games at the baseball field with other major-league teams.

The keynote at the Royal Park is informality. The point of going to Florida is to be able to take it easy, and here you can wear comfortable sport clothes and feel right at home. Another special feature is the food. The same good chef has been there for several years, and since he is also the chef at one of the Treadway Inn summer resorts in the North, he is used to cooking all the regular Treadway specialties. However, he also makes use of the native foods and fruits, and cooks the local fish extremely well.

For sight-seers, cars may be rented right in town if needed. Just south of Vero Beach are the McKee Jungle Gardens, one of the famous Florida attractions. Here are one hundred and eighteen acres of native jungle. There are thousands of spectacular exotic plants and trees, half from Florida and the rest from all over the world, a native wild-animal zoo, a tropical water garden, and a stand of almost three hundred royal palms about one hundred feet tall which is considered the most beautiful stand in the world. There are continuous guided tours on the 1¼-mile trail, and the gardens are really fun to visit. For orchid lovers there is an orchid nursery where blooming orchids may be purchased for a very moderate price. Palm Beach is about sixty miles away to the south. Fifty miles inland are the Cypress Gardens, a tropical wonderland where all the native plants – azaleas, camellias, gardenias, and such – bloom along the banks of canals and lagoons. Electric boats guide the tourists around, and there are exhibitions of water skiing.

Vero Beach is readily accessible by train or plane. There is direct train service to all the Eastern and Middle Western states, and Eastern Air Lines has its own terminal in Vero Beach with regular scheduled daily flights. The beach wagon at the inn will meet either train or plane.

The rates at the Royal Park are reasonable. We haven't discussed the rates at any of the other Treadway Inns because they are never high. But Florida is so often associated with exorbitant costs that rates seem worth mentioning here. The main season is from around the middle of December to April, with a twenty-five per cent discount before January 25 and after March 25. Rooms for guests are available the rest of the year at special low rates, and Florida is becoming a year-round vacation spot. Mr. Kenneth E. Cellarius is the innkeeper.

APPETIZERS

WEBSTER defines an appetizer as "Something that excites the appetite . . . a small portion of food or drink before, or as the first course of, a meal." In the Treadway Inns, as in most restaurant menus, appetizers are the first course, and since they precede a substantial meal, the purpose is to excite rather than satiate the appetite. They should not only be light but also have a definite appeal to the palate – be cool or savory or spicy or even heady, but not too rich and not too bland.

Some appetizers can be purchased ready to serve, and need little or no additional preparation. No appetizers require meticulous care or much time, and they certainly make a pleasant start for luncheon or a special dinner. They fall into three main groups – fruit, juices, and fish – and a few miscellaneous ones.

FRUIT

FRUIT CUPS

An old stand-by and always delightful if the fruit is fresh, well chilled, and attractively served with an eye on color combinations. Any combination of fresh fruits may be used, depending of course on what is in season. Some canned or frozen fruits may be used when fresh fruits are not available. Usual fruits are: orange and grapefruit sections (or canned mandarin orange sections, which are small and sweet), any fresh berries, little white seedless grapes, red or black cherries, pineapple, sliced pears, diced apples (nice and crisp), and melon balls (your fruit cup will be especially colorful if you use watermelon). At the Treadway Inns, fruit cups are usually served topped with a small scoop of sherbet. They may be garnished with a few mint leaves, and at home you might want to add a dash of rum, brandy, or kirsch, or a little shaved dark sweet chocolate.

CHILLED FRESH MELON

Melons, of course, are seasonal. Cantaloupe and honeydew are the ones most often used, but there are several others, such as honeyball, Persian, Cassava, Cranshaw, and in New York State the delicious Irondiquoit. They may be served with a scoop of sherbet – lime, lemon, orange, or cranberry; or a wedge of lemon; or at home the melon may be pierced in several places with a fork and port poured into these openings.

MELON BALLS IN CHAMPAGNE

Any seasonal melon may be used, or a combination of melons for color contrast. Scoop the balls out with a special ball cutter, available at any hardware store. Chill them thoroughly, and just before serving, cover them with chilled champagne.

CHILLED MELON WITH PROSCIUTTO

Prosciutto is a specially cured Italian ham, available wherever there are Italian stores or in some specialty shops. It is expensive but always sliced paper-thin, so a little goes a long way. A slice or two is ample as an appetizer, delicious served either with chilled honeydew melon or with fresh figs when they are in season.

GRAPEFRUIT

This has a nice sharp, clean taste, and gets the meal off to a pleasant low-calorie start. Halve the fruit, and allow one half to each serving. Separate the sections with a short, sharp knife or with a special curved grapefruit knife, cut around the edges, and remove the center membrane. Instead of the inevitable cherry in the middle, try a small scoop of cranberry or any fruit sherbet; mixed diced candied fruit peel (available in small cans), moistened with a little rum or lemon juice; 1 to 2 tablespoons of curaçao; or remove a few sections and substitute fresh orange sections.

BROILED GRAPEFRUIT

This is served hot, and it can be alcoholic or not, as you wish. After the sections are loosened, sprinkle the whole surface with brown or white sugar and a dash of cinnamon or nutmeg, dot with butter, and broil slowly until nicely browned, about 15 to 20 minutes. Honey or maple syrup may be used in place of sugar, and rum or sherry may be added. Or grapefruit halves can be sprinkled with finely crushed peppermint-stick candy, placed under the broiler until the candy is melted and the grapefruit golden brown, and served warm.

MINTED FRESH PINEAPPLE

Either diced fresh pineapple may be used or the excellent frozen pineapple, defrosted just until it is separated but still is a little icy. Garnish with fresh mint leaves, and if you wish, pour a little rum over it.

AVOCADO COCKTAIL

SAUCE

½ *cup mayonnaise*
3 *tablespoons light cream*
2 *teaspoons tomato paste*
½ *cup finely chopped celery*
1 *tablespoon finely chopped green pepper*
3 or 4 *drops Tabasco*
salt

Combine ½ cup mayonnaise, 3 tablespoons of light cream, 2 teaspoons of tomato paste, ½ cup of finely chopped celery, 1 tablespoon of finely chopped green pepper, 3 or 4 drops of Tabasco, and salt.

Before serving, peel and dice a large ripe avocado and sprinkle it with salt and about 1 tablespoon of lemon juice. Fold gently into the sauce.

Notes. If the sauce is made several hours ahead of time, the flavors will have a chance to blend well and the sauce will have a chance to chill.

Avocados should always be seasoned separately, since they don't absorb much seasoning from the sauce, and if unseasoned, will taste flat no matter how good the sauce is.

The lemon juice prevents the avocado turning brown. If left in a covered bowl in the refrigerator, avocados in this cocktail sauce stay green for two or three days.

GINGER ALE COCKTAIL

Arrange alternate layers of well-chilled grapefruit sections and pineapple tidbits in sherbet glasses. If fresh fruit is used, sprinkle each layer lightly with powdered sugar; if canned fruit is used, no additional sugar will be necessary. Let stand in the refrigerator until just before serving. Then fill the glasses with very cold ginger ale, and top with a small scoop of lemon sherbet.

JUICES

These should just be chilled for several hours in the refrigerator, and are always refreshing. Any are good – tomato, mixed vegetable, pineapple, grapefruit, apple, cranberry. A popular appetizer at the Treadway Inns is mixed fruit juices, such as orange and pineapple, topped with a small scoop of sherbet – lime, lemon, or orange, or a mixture of two kinds in one scoop.

SARATOGA COCKTAIL

1 *quart tomato juice*
½ *cup fresh horse-radish*
1 *teaspoon Worcestershire sauce*
chopped fresh chives

Chill 1 quart of tomato juice almost to the freezing point, then stir in ½ cup of fresh horse-radish and 1 teaspoon of Worcestershire sauce. Pour into tall glasses and sprinkle with a pinch of finely chopped fresh chives. This is a man's appetizer. Serves 4 to 6.

SPICED PINEAPPLE JUICE

3 *cups unsweetened pineapple juice*
small piece stick cinnamon
2 *tablespoons honey*
2 *tablespoons lemon juice*

Simmer 3 cups of pineapple juice with a small piece of stick cinnamon for 10 to 15 minutes. Add 2 tablespoons of honey and 2 tablespoons of lemon juice and stir until they combine with the pineapple juice. Remove the cinnamon, and chill the juice. Serves 4.

FISH

Fish makes an excellent appetizer, especially when it is served with a tart sauce; in fact, the American public likes its sauces so "flavorful" that they often overpower the delicate flavor of the fish. The classic example is shrimp cocktail, which is usually served with a cocktail sauce loaded with spicy horse-radish – and if the chefs use horse-radish with a light hand, the guests complain.

Many of the fish appetizers are purchased all ready to use.

SMOKED FISH

Smoked salmon heads this list, and is a great delicacy. There are two types of smoked salmon on the market, the so-called Nova Scotia salmon, and lox, which comes from West Coast salmon. Nova Scotia salmon is preferred, since it is not salted and is paler and more subtle in color than the very salty lox. The term "Nova Scotia" is broadly used, since the fish may have come from the waters off Labrador, Newfoundland, or Maine. The fish is cut into very thin slices, with about two allowed for each serving, and the traditional accompaniment is capers, a small carafe of olive oil, and a pepper mill for freshly ground black pepper.

Other smoked fish which can be used as appetizers are smoked whitefish, smoked sturgeon, smoked fillet of brook trout, smoked oysters, and anchovies.

FILLET OF HERRING WITH SOUR CREAM

This comes already prepared in glass jars, is very good, and is far simpler than tackling the entire preparation at home.

FRESH SHRIMP COCKTAIL

Always a great favorite. The Treadway Inns use the following cocktail sauce. The shrimp is cooked according to the directions on page 97. Other shellfish are also used for cocktails, such as lobster or crab. If a less pungent sauce is desired, try blending half mayonnaise and half chili sauce.

COCKTAIL SAUCE

1 *cup chili sauce*
½ *cup tomato purée*
¼ *cup fresh horse-radish*
2 *dashes Tabasco*
juice of 1 *lemon*

Combine all the ingredients and allow to stand for 1 hour before using, to blend the flavors. Thin, if desired, with a little tomato juice. Makes 1 pint of sauce.

SHRIMP REMOULADE

There probably aren't two identical recipes for a remoulade sauce. This is a New Orleans one, using a special Creole mustard which is highly seasoned, horse-radish being one of the ingredients. If unavailable locally, it can be ordered from Solari's in New Orleans.

SAUCE

½ *cup mayonnaise*
½ *cup Creole mustard*
1 *tablespoon lemon juice*
pinch sugar
salt
1 *small clove garlic*
1 *teaspoon celery*
1 *tablespoon scraped onion*

Blend together ½ cup of mayonnaise, ½ cup of Creole mustard, 1 tablespoon of lemon juice, a pinch of sugar, and a little salt. Add 1 small clove of garlic, put through a press, about 1 teaspoon of celery, also put through a press, and 1 tablespoon of scraped onion. Let stand for at least an hour before using.

To serve as an appetizer, put 4 to 6 cooked shrimp in a cocktail glass and cover with 2 generous tablespoons of the sauce. This is sufficient sauce for about 6 cocktails. Cooked shrimp can also be marinated in the sauce to be served with cocktails. See page 97 for instructions on cooking shrimp. This sauce is also delicious with celeriac, cooked and cut into julienne strips.

SEAFOOD COCKTAIL

SAUCE

- ½ *cup mayonnaise*
- ½ *cup commercial sour cream*
- 1 *teaspoon lemon juice*
- 1 *small clove garlic, crushed*
- 1 *teaspoon salt*
- *white pepper*
- 2 or 3 *drops Tabasco*
- ¼ *cup chopped water cress* or 1 *to* 2 *tablespoons chopped parsley* or *chives* or 1 *finely diced tomato*

Blend together ½ cup of mayonnaise, ½ cup of commercial sour cream, 1 teaspoon of lemon juice, 1 small clove of garlic, crushed, a teaspoon of salt, a little white pepper, and 2 or 3 drops of Tabasco. Depending upon the season or what is on hand, also add one of the following: ¼ cup of chopped water cress, 1 to 2 tablespoons of chopped parsley or chives, or a fresh tomato which has been skinned, freed of its seedy pulp, and finely diced.

Let stand in the refrigerator at least an hour before serving. Use as an appetizer with any cooked seafood, such as crabmeat, shrimp, or lobster. Put the seafood in a cocktail glass and cover it with 2 generous tablespoons of the sauce. This is sufficient sauce for about 6 cocktails. Cooked seafood can also be marinated in the sauce to be used as a canapé.

STEAMED CLAMS

Allow 1 quart of soft-shell clams for 2 people with modest appetites, and 1 quart per person if the appetites are lusty. Scrub them well and rinse in several changes of cold water to get out all the sand possible. Put them in a large deep saucepan with 1 cup of water for each quart and a very little pepper. Cover and cook over a slow fire until all the shells are open, 15 to 20 minutes. Lift the clams out. Let the broth settle for a minute or two, then scoop it out with a ladle, leaving any silt or sand where it belongs – in the bottom. Serve the clams either on a large platter or divided into individual portions; if they are wrapped in a napkin, they stay hot longer. Have a saucer of melted butter for each person. Serve the broth, seasoned with a little celery salt or thyme, in a cup, with the clams.

MISCELLANEOUS

EGGS MAYONNAISE

This is one of the favorite French appetizers. To make it, just cut a hard-cooked egg in half lengthwise, place it on a plate cut side down, and cover with mayonnaise – simple, but fine if the mayonnaise is a good homemade one (*see* page 214).

CHOPPED CHICKEN LIVERS

½ *pound chicken livers*
3 *tablespoons butter*
¼ *pound mushrooms, finely chopped*
salt, pepper
1 *teaspoon grated onion*
1½ *teaspoons lemon juice*
1 *hard-cooked egg*

Sauté ½ pound of chicken livers in 1½ tablespoons of butter for 5 to 10 minutes, or until just tender. Remove them from the pan and chop them fine, mashing them slightly. Sauté ¼ pound of finely chopped mushrooms in the same pan with the remaining 1½ tablespoons of butter for about 5 minutes. Mix the mushrooms with the livers, and season with salt, pepper, 1 teaspoon of grated onion, and 1½ teaspoons of lemon juice. Finely chop 1 hard-cooked egg and mix it in gently. Serve warm or chilled.

When served as a first course (on lettuce, with pieces of crisp toast), serves 4 to 6. This spread is also good for sandwiches, especially on dark bread. If you wish, it may be moistened with a little brandy or sherry before serving.

STUFFED CELERY

6-*ounce package cream cheese*
1 *teaspoon white vinegar*
1 *tablespoon light cream*
1 *teaspoon curry powder*
5 *tablespoons chutney, finely chopped*

Soften a 6-ounce package of cream cheese to room temperature. Blend together 1 teaspoon of white vinegar, 1 tablespoon of light cream, and 1 teaspoon of curry powder. Add the cream cheese and work into a smooth paste. Stir in 5 tablespoons of finely chopped chutney and refrigerate for several hours, overnight if possible. About 1 hour before serving, fill into celery stalks and cut them into 1-inch pieces.

BLUE CHEESE SPREAD

½ *pound cream cheese*
½ *cup blue cheese*
¼ *to* ⅓ *cup coffee cream*
salt, cayenne
2 *tablespoons finely chopped chives*
few drops Tabasco

Soften ½ pound of cream cheese to room temperature and beat it until fluffy with an electric blender or a rotary beater. Add ½ cup of blue cheese, crumbled into small bits. Continue beating until the cheeses are blended. Then beat in ¼ to ⅓ cup of coffee cream, a little at a time, until you reach the consistency you want. This may be used to stuff celery; in that case, use the smaller amount of cream. Season with a few drops of Tabasco, salt, cayenne, and 2 tablespoons of finely chopped chives. Serve at room temperature with crisp crackers.

MARINATED ARTICHOKE HEARTS

1-pound can artichoke hearts
3 tablespoons olive oil
1 tablespoon lemon juice
salt, pepper, cayenne
pinch thyme
1 slice onion

Drain the contents of a 1-pound can of artichoke hearts well, and place them in a deep narrow dish. Combine 3 tablespoons of olive oil, 1 tablespoon of lemon juice, salt, pepper, cayenne, and a pinch of thyme, and beat well with a fork. Pour this mixture over the artichokes. Add 1 slice of onion. Refrigerate for at least 2 hours, overnight if possible, stirring gently or turning the artichokes occasionally. Remove the onion before serving. Serve on lettuce. Serves 5 to 8, depending on how many hearts the can contains.

HAM AND OLIVE CANAPÉ

¾ cup ground cooked ham
¼ cup finely chopped stuffed olives
2 to 3 tablespoons mayonnaise
unsliced white bread
stuffed olives for garnish

Blend together ¾ cup of ground ham, ¼ cup of finely chopped stuffed olives, and 2 to 3 tablespoons of mayonnaise. Slice an unsliced loaf of white bread, at least a day old, into ½-inch slices, and cut rounds out of them. Either toast the rounds or, better still, fry them in butter until golden brown on both sides. Spread rather thickly with the ham mixture and serve immediately, while the bread is still crisp. Garnish with slices of stuffed olive. If served as an appetizer, have the rounds 2 to 2½ inches in diameter, and allow one to a serving. For canapés, use smaller rounds about 1 inch across.

THE LORD JEFFERY

Amherst, Massachusetts

THE Treadway Inn in Amherst is The Lord Jeffery, an attractive whitewashed brick building facing the common. Although the inn was built in 1926 and therefore is comparatively new, it was designed in the style of an old English inn, and has the characteristic large common rooms, spacious dining rooms (air-conditioned, however), and a lovely elm-shaded old-fashioned garden in the rear. Elms, which are still so much a part of the New England landscape, line and beautify the streets and common in this two-hundred-year-old town.

The dining room is considered to be one of the most distinguished and beautiful of all the Treadway Inns – and since so much care and taste are lavished on the interiors of the inns, this is a significant statement. The soft blue-green walls with maple beams and sills, the glowing brass candelabra and lamps, the handsome flowered linen draperies, the maple Windsor chairs, and the paintings, including Gainsborough's portrait of Lord Jeffery Amherst, combine to make a room of rare charm and peace. And the excellent food sustains this feeling.

A feature in one drawing room is a fireplace with a window – a "Believe It or Not" item by Ripley. The idea, from medieval England, is that travelers can see the fireside through the window and realize that hospitality and cheer are waiting for them.

The walls of the various public rooms are lined with the famous George A. Plimpton collection of Revolutionary and pre-Revolutionary documents – French and Indian War prints, maps, autographed letters, and other papers of Lord Jeffery Amherst, George Washington, William Pitt, General Wolfe, King George III, and Louis XV.

During the French and Indian War in the colonial period, William Pitt sent some of his most promising young officers in the Army of Great Britain to this country, and one was General Amherst, who became commander in chief in New England. On July 26, 1758, he captured the French fortress of Louisburg on Cape Breton Island, the first British victory in the Seven Years' War, and to commemorate the great rejoicing, several towns were named after him in Massachusetts, New Hampshire, and Virginia. As the pamphlet called *Who Was Lord Jeffery?* – distributed at the inn – reads: "So here in this busy New England college town the gratitude of our forefathers to an English General, who saved them from invasion and conquest, is perpetuated not only in the name they gave so many years ago to what was then a hamlet, but also in an institution always dear to the English heart, a village inn."

His name was also given to Amherst College when it was founded in 1821 to train young men for the Congregational ministry. Today approximately one thousand students of the college live in the dormitories and fraternity houses on both sides of the common. The college has a number of museums and collections open to the general public: fine arts, geological, zoological; the Pratt butterfly collection, the Hitchcock collection of minerals, the Mead Art Museum, and a wildlife sanctuary.

The University of Massachusetts is also situated in Amherst. This began, as most state universities did, as an agricultural college in 1867, with four teachers, thirty-three students, and four wooden buildings. Today the attractive 700-acre campus has seventy-five major buildings and about four thousand students. Exhibits of general interest there include the nutritional laboratories, an insect collection, many interesting and rare native and tropical plants, a state-forest nursery, a poultry plant, and farm animals, including horses, cattle, and sheep.

There are several old houses in Amherst dating back to the beginning and middle of the eighteenth century. A complete list can be found in a booklet called *Amherst, Mass.* Of special interest is the first brick building in Amherst, built by Emily Dickinson's grandfather in 1813 and in which she was born in 1830; it is privately owned now but may be seen by appointment. The Strong House is the oldest house of the mansion type in the town, built in 1744, and is the home of the Amherst Historical Society. The Clark House has an exhibition of two hundred clocks dating from 1775–1850, mostly made in New England; they may be seen by appointment. The Jones Memorial Library has one of the most complete collections of Robert Frost available and a comprehensive collection of Emily Dickinson, containing all her books in all the editions, some original manuscripts, and material on her family and life.

The surrounding country is lovely, with its rolling hills of the Connecticut River valley, and nearby Mt. Sugarloaf with its tremendous view. The Pioneer Valley Association has a list of points of interest.

Five miles away is Deerfield, which has a restoration similar to those of Old Sturbridge Village and the Farmers' Museum in Cooperstown. In this case it is a prosperous eighteenth-century village.

Smith College, in Northampton, and Mount Holyoke College are about ten miles away from Amherst.

Mr. Norman M. Enman is innkeeper at The Lord Jeffery.

SOUP

SOUPS form an integral part of the Treadway Inns' meals, and they are listed on all the luncheon and dinner menus. They are, of course, all homemade, and since the chefs always have good stock on hand, the soups are excellent. Many homemakers consider making soup a chore and rely a great deal on canned soups. Now, canned soups are all right, but they have shortcomings. The high heat necessary to process them has an inevitable effect on their flavor. More important than that, since these soups aim to appeal to millions of people, seasonings are kept to a minimum, and the soups have a rather flat, lifeless taste. They have their uses, but are better in combination with other foods than alone.

One use for canned soup is substituting consommé or bouillon for basic beef stock. The inns serve so much roast beef that they have plenty of bones, and huge soup kettles are simmering on the range all the time, making consommé, stock for onion soup, and so on. Some of the chefs believe that you can extract all the flavor from bones in 3 to 4 hours; other chefs cook bones as long as 36 hours; since the fire is never out in their ranges, this is no problem. You can make fine stock in the shorter time, and directions will be found on page 40 in the beef vegetable soup recipe. Stock has so many uses, and enhances so many dishes, that it is sound culinary practice to have it on hand, especially if you have a freezer. But canned bouillon is an adequate substitute, or a good beef extract, such as B–V, dissolved in boiling water.

Chicken stock is also an essential ingredient, not only in the following poultry soups and many of the cream soups, but also in many recipes in other chapters of this book. The Treadway Inns feature many recipes with stewed chicken as a base, so they never lack chicken stock. A housewife who is not necessarily in the same fortunate position can do one of two things. She can make her own stock. This is easy and inexpensive if there is a convenient market which sells chicken parts; a large package of necks, back, and gizzards, costing about a quarter, will make at least 2 quarts of stock. It will keep in the refrigerator up to a week, or it can be frozen. Or she can use a good brand of clear chicken soup, Westchester being one of the best.

Cream soups can be made with practically any vegetable on the market. The basic method given here purées the vegetables, since the inns find that the most attractive way to serve cream soups. The chefs often garnish them with julienne of freshly cooked vegetables. Electric blenders or Foley food mills make puréeing a simple operation. For home use, whether or not you purée is a personal matter; if the vegetables are finely diced, many people like their flavor and texture in a soup. Cream soups can be made with freshly cooked vegetables, and are also a fine way of using small amounts of leftover vegetables. They can be thickened with sliced potatoes for a nourishing dish. Cook sliced potatoes and a slice or two of onion in a little boiling water and butter until soft. Add the vegetables, season, heat, then purée the whole business and reheat with milk and, if you wish, a little light cream.

Servings. Judging the number of servings of soup is always tricky, since so much depends on the rest of the meal. At the inns, soup is always a preliminary to what is often a substantial meal, so soup is served in standard soup cups, which hold relatively small amounts. At home, soup is often used with a sandwich or salad as a whole lunch or supper, so naturally the servings are larger. The servings given in this chapter are geared for home use.

Garnishes. Many soups do not need any garnish at all. Chowders, bisques, vegetable soups are so full of a variety of flavors that they are self-sufficient. Simpler soups may be garnished if you wish, and here are a few suggestions – use one, not all.

1. Salted whipped cream for cream soups and for clear soups which contain clam juice or chicken broth.
2. Finely minced parsley.
3. Finely minced chives.
4. Popcorn, plain or cheese, heated for a few minutes in the oven.
5. Chopped fresh celery leaves or crumbled dry ones.
6. Paprika.
7. Thinly sliced radishes; leave the skin on for color.
8. Grated cheese, with onion soup especially, and for added flavor and richness in many other soups.
9. Celery salt or celery seed.
10. Sherry – about a teaspoonful per serving. Do not overdo it, because a little will enhance the flavor of many soups, while too much overpowers and ruins the flavor.
11. Croutons.
12. Cheese croutons (*see* page 48).

BEEF VEGETABLE SOUP

1½ *pounds marrow bone*
2 *to* 2½ *pounds shin of beef*
3 *carrots, sliced*
1 *medium-size onion, sliced*
3 *stalks celery, sliced*
1 or 2 *sprigs parsley*
4 *quarts water*
salt, pepper, thyme
assorted vegetables

Basic Stock. Have the marrow bone cut in 3 or 4 pieces and the shin of beef in 1½-inch cubes in order to extract the maximum flavor. Try out some of the beef fat in a large skillet and brown the cubed beef all over. When it is browned, put it in a large deep saucepan with the bones. Bring 2 cups of water to a boil in the skillet to dissolve the glaze and add it to the meat with 3½ quarts of cold water. Bring slowly to a boil and skim. Add 3 sliced carrots, a sliced onion, 3 stalks of sliced celery, and 1 or 2 sprigs of parsley. Simmer covered for 3 to 4 hours. Season with salt, pepper, and thyme after the first 2 hours; adding salt at the beginning hardens the fibers of the meat and prevents the proper flow of juices. Strain the stock into a large bowl and let stand in the refrigerator for several hours or overnight so that the fat can harden on top and be easily removed.

This basic stock can be used in any recipe calling for beef stock or bouillon. If you wish it absolutely clear, clarify it following the directions below. It may be cooked with barley to make a pleasant beef barley soup often featured on the Treadway Inns' menus.

Vegetable Soup. Reheat the stock and add vegetables. There is nothing arbitrary about the choice – almost any vegetable can be used except beets, because of their harsh color. I personally like tomatoes, so suggest using 5 or 6 fresh tomatoes or a large can, coarsely chopped. The following vegetables are also often used: peas or green beans or both, for the color; 2 or 3 sliced carrots; 2 or 3 stalks of celery; leek or onion; and white turnips. They should all be cut into small pieces, about the size of peas. Some optional vegetables are lima beans, green pepper, corn, and cabbage. Cook until the vegetables are tender and the soup is ready. Just before serving, add some of the diced cooked beef and sliced marrow from the bones. Makes about 12 generous servings, 15 to 20 smaller ones.

To Clarify Stock. Clarify stock after it has been chilled and the fat has been removed. For each quart of stock allow the white and shell of 1 egg. Beat the white slightly with a fork and add to the cold stock with the crushed egg shell and 1 tablespoon of cold water. Stir over a slow fire until it comes to a full boil. Remove and let stand for 20 minutes without stirring. Then strain through a double thickness of cheesecloth.

CLEAR TOMATO SOUP

4 *cups fresh* or *canned tomatoes*
1 *cup water*
1 *small onion, sliced*
½ *cup chopped celery leaves*
1 *tablespoon lemon juice*
3 *whole cloves*
salt, pepper
pinch of sugar
sour cream for garnish

Put the tomatoes into a saucepan with the water, onion, celery leaves, lemon juice, cloves, salt, pepper, and a pinch of sugar. Bring slowly to a boil and simmer for 15 to 20 minutes. Then put through a sieve. Reheat. Serve with a generous teaspoon of sour cream on each portion. Serves 4 to 6.

Jellied Tomato Soup. Soak 1 tablespoon of gelatin in ¼ cup of cold water for 5 minutes and add it to the hot soup after it has been strained, stirring until it is dissolved. Chill in the refrigerator for several hours or overnight. Serve sprinkled with finely chopped mint or parsley and a wedge of lemon or lime, or with a teaspoon of sour cream topped with a little black or red caviar. Two tablespoons of very slim slices of celery may be added to the soup after it has been strained and before the gelatin is added; the celery stays crisp and gives the soup a nice texture.

To make the soup transparently clear, follow the directions in the preceding recipe.

AVOCADO BROTH

2 *cups chicken stock*
1 *cup clam juice*
salt to taste
½ *small ripe avocado*
whipped cream, lightly salted
chopped pistachio nuts, optional

Heat together the chicken stock and clam juice. Taste for seasoning; it may need a little salt. Strain the avocado into the hot soup and the pleasant-looking green soup is ready; it can also be kept waiting over a low fire. Garnish with lightly salted whipped cream and, if you like, a few chopped pistachio nuts. Serves 4 to 6.

OXTAIL SOUP

1 *oxtail, about* 2½ *pounds*
1 *large carrot, diced*
1 *medium-size onion, sliced*
2 *stalks celery, sliced*
1 *sprig fresh thyme* or ½ *teaspoon powdered thyme*
1 *bay leaf*
8 *to* 10 *peppercorns*
slice lemon stuck with 3 *cloves*
½ *cup canned tomatoes*
salt
2 *quarts water*
½ *cup sherry*

The oxtail should be cut in pieces. Wash them in cold water. Put into a large saucepan with the carrot, onion, celery, sprig of thyme or ½ teaspoon powdered thyme, 1 bay leaf, 8 to 10 peppercorns, a slice of lemon stuck with 3 cloves, ½ cup canned tomatoes (use only the solid part), plenty of salt, and 2 quarts of water. Bring slowly to a boil, skim, then simmer about 3 hours, until the meat is ready to fall away from the bones. Let stand until cool and take off the fat which collects in a layer on the top. Strain and reheat the soup. Add the diced cooked meat and ½ cup sherry. Serves 8 to 10.

Note. The soup can be clarified, following the directions on page 41.

BOULA

1 *large can green turtle soup*
2 *pounds peas* or 1 *package frozen peas*
2 *to* 3 *tablespoons dry sherry*
6 *tablespoons whipped cream, lightly salted*

The most inexperienced cook can make this foolproof soup although it is a credit to the most experienced. Green turtle soup with sherry is a deservedly popular first course, and boula is a slightly dressed-up version.

Cook the peas in boiling salted water until tender, 5 minutes for the frozen peas and 10 to 15 minutes for fresh ones. Drain and put through a food mill or strainer. Blend the pea purée with a large can of green turtle soup and bring slowly to a boil. Taste for seasoning and add 2 to 3 tablespoons of dry sherry.

Ideally the soup is served in individual ovenproof soup bowls. Top each serving with a tablespoon of lightly salted whipped cream, place the bowls on a cookie sheet and under the broiler until the cream starts to turn color. It may also be served in hot soup plates with the cream not browned. Serves 5 or 6.

GAZPACHO

(Iced tomato soup, Spanish style)

¼ *cup olive oil*
½ *cup cracker crumbs*
2 *cups tomato juice*
2 *cups beef stock*
1 *green pepper*
3 *stalks celery*
1 *small onion*
1 *cucumber*
2 or 3 *tomatoes*
2 *tablespoons lemon juice*
½ *teaspoon Tabasco*
1 *tablespoon chopped parsley*

Put ¼ cup of olive oil in a mixing bowl. Add ½ cup of cracker crumbs made by rolling crisp crackers like Ritz not too finely, 2 cups of tomato juice, and 2 cups of beef stock. Finely chop a green pepper, 3 stalks of celery, and a small onion and blend with the tomato mixture. Chill thoroughly in the refrigerator for several hours or overnight. Half an hour before serving cut a peeled cucumber into very thin slices and put in salted ice water to get crisp. Skin 2 or 3 tomatoes, chop very fine, and drain off the watery juice. To serve, add the drained cucumber slices, chopped tomatoes, 2 tablespoons of lemon juice, ½ teaspoon Tabasco, and 1 tablespoon of chopped parsley. Quickly stir 3 or 4 ice cubes through the soup to make sure it is very cold, take them out, and serve the soup immediately in chilled bowls. Serves 6 to 8.

BRUNSWICK STEW

- *5-pound chicken*
- 3 *large onions, sliced*
- 4 *to* 5 *tablespoons butter* or *bacon fat*
- *salt*
- *pepper*
- 2 *cups fresh* or *canned tomatoes*
- 2 *cups fresh cut* or *frozen corn*
- 2 *to* 3 *cups fresh* or *frozen lima beans*
- ½ *cup sherry*

The chicken should be cut up as for fried chicken. Slowly brown 3 large sliced onions in 2 to 3 tablespoons of butter or bacon fat, using a large skillet and a gentle fire. Remove the onions and brown the chicken, using more fat as needed. When all the chicken is browned, put it into a large saucepan with the onions. Add 8 cups of boiling water, bring to a boil, and simmer for 1 hour; season with plenty of salt and some pepper and simmer for another hour, or until the chicken is tender and falling off the bones. Strain off the stock and bring it to a boil. Add 2 cups of tomatoes, 2 cups of corn, and 2 to 3 cups of lima beans. Season and cook at a brisk boil until the vegetables are tender — 10 minutes or so if they are frozen, 20 to 30 minutes if they are fresh. Meanwhile take the chicken meat off the bones and cut it in small pieces. Add it to the stew after the vegetables are cooked, with ½ cup of sherry. The stew is now ready or can be kept waiting over a very slow fire; it can also be made ahead of time and reheated. This will make at least 12 soup servings, and serve 5 or 6 as a main course.

CORN AND CHICKEN CHOWDER

- ¼ *pound salt pork*
- 2 *tablespoons finely chopped onion*
- 2 *tablespoons finely chopped celery*
- 2 *tablespoons flour*
- 2 *cups chicken stock*
- 2 *medium-size potatoes*
- 1 *can cream-style corn*
- 1 *cup diced cooked chicken*
- 1 *cup rich milk* or *light cream*
- 1 *tablespoon chopped parsley*

Cut the salt pork into very small dice and cook slowly in a medium-size saucepan until lightly browned. Remove the pork bits with a slotted spoon and drain them on absorbent paper. Leave 3 tablespoons of pork fat in the pan and in it cook 2 tablespoons of chopped onion and 2 tablespoons of chopped celery until soft but not brown. Blend in 2 tablespoons of flour. Add 2 cups of chicken stock and stir over the fire until the mixture comes to a boil. Simmer for about 10 minutes.

Meanwhile peel and dice 2 medium-size potatoes and cook them in boiling salted water until tender, 10 to 15 minutes. Add them with any cooking water to the first mixture. Also add 1 can of cream-style corn, 1 cup of diced chicken, and 1 cup of rich milk or light cream. Simmer for at least 5 minutes, or until ready to use. Sprinkle a little chopped parsley or a few pork bits on each serving. Serves 6 to 8. For a main course will make 4 large servings.

MULLIGATAWNY

3 *tablespoons butter*
1 *medium-size onion, sliced*
2 *medium-size carrots, sliced*
1 *stalk celery, sliced*
1 *tablespoon curry powder*
3 *tablespoons flour*
8 *cups chicken stock*
2 *cloves*
pinch of mace
1/8 *teaspoon dried thyme*
1 *cup light cream*
1 *cup diced cooked chicken*
chopped parsley

Melt 3 tablespoons of butter in a large saucepan. Add 1 medium-size onion, 2 carrots, and 1 stalk of celery, all cut in very thin slices. Cook over a slow fire about 15 minutes. Blend in 1 tablespoon of curry powder and 3 tablespoons of flour and cook for 5 minutes. Pour on 8 cups of chicken stock and stir until the mixture comes to a boil. Add 2 cloves, a pinch of mace, and 1/8 teaspoon of powdered thyme. Taste to see if salt and pepper are needed – it will depend on how well seasoned the chicken stock is. Simmer covered for 30 to 40 minutes. Put through a strainer or food mill. Add 1 cup of light cream, 1 cup of diced cooked chicken, reheat, and the soup is ready. Serve garnished with chopped parsley. Serves 8 to 10.

TURKEY SOUP

turkey carcass
3 *stalks celery, sliced*
1 *large onion, sliced*
1 *large carrot, sliced*
salt
peppercorns
½ *bay leaf*
½ *teaspoon dried thyme*
½ *cup rice*
1 *cup thinly sliced celery*
2 *tablespoons chopped parsley*

Remove all the scraps of meat from the bones that you can, and break up the carcass. Put it into a large deep saucepan with all the bones — legs, wings, and so on — and the neck. Add enough cold water to completely cover the bones, 2 to 3 quarts, depending upon the size of the turkey. Bring slowly to a boil and skim. Add 3 sliced celery stalks, a sliced onion and carrot, and simmer covered for an hour. Season well with salt and a few peppercorns, half a bay leaf, and ½ teaspoon of thyme, and continue simmering another 1 to 2 hours. Strain the stock and let it stand until cool so that any fat can rise to the top and be removed. Pick any meat off the bones and save it.

Reheat the soup, and cook ½ cup of rice and 1 cup of sliced celery in it for 15 to 20 minutes. Add all the turkey bits, cut into neat dice or julienne strips, and 2 tablespoons of chopped parsley. Makes 8 to 10 servings.

FRENCH ONION SOUP

The success of a good onion soup is simple — good stock. Either chicken or beef stock can be used, making either a light or a dark soup. Browning the onions gives the soup a distinct flavor that matches the robustness of beef stock; the more delicate chicken stock blends better with unbrowned onions. Either Parmesan or Gruyère cheese is added to the soup. Their flavors are different, and Gruyère has a thicker, slightly ropy consistency which is nice.

Some form of bread is served right in the soup. In the Treadway Inns it is either specially prepared French bread or cheese croutons. It is important not to add the bread to the soup until just before it is served, so that the bread will be crisp rather than soggy.

French Bread. Use the long thin type and it should be at least a day old. Cut it in thin slices and let them stand for several hours to dry out. Butter the slices and sprinkle them with grated Parmesan cheese and a little paprika. Place on an ungreased cookie sheet in a moderately hot oven at 400° for maybe 10 minutes, until lightly browned. Use 1 or 2 slices for each serving.

Cheese Croutons. Lightly toast white bread. Spread with butter and sprinkle with Parmesan cheese. Put in a slow oven at 300° for about 10 minutes to bake the flavor in. Cut into squares.

FRENCH ONION SOUP I

1 *pound yellow onions – about 2 medium-size*
3 *tablespoons butter*
1 *tablespoon flour*
6 *cups strong chicken stock*
salt, pepper
½ *to* ¾ *cup grated Parmesan* or *Gruyère cheese*
¼ *to* ½ *cup dry white wine, optional*

Peel the onions, cut them in half, then in very thin slices. Melt 3 tablespoons of butter in a heavy saucepan. Add the onions and cook them very slowly for about 15 to 20 minutes, until soft and yellow but not browned. Blend in 1 tablespoon of flour. Pour on 6 cups of chicken stock and stir until the soup comes to a boil. Then simmer for 20 to 30 minutes or until ready to use. Just before serving, add ½ to ¾ cup grated cheese and stir until it is melted; ¼ to ½ cup of dry white wine may be added also. Serve with prepared French bread or cheese croutons (*see* preceding section), and pass a bowl of grated cheese. Serves 6 to 8.

FRENCH ONION SOUP II

This is the dark version. Follow the preceding recipe, substituting good strong beef stock for the chicken stock. This time the onions should be cooked very slowly until well browned, which will take at least 30 to 40 minutes. If wine is added, it should be red.

CORN CHOWDER

4 *slices bacon*
1 *medium-size onion, thinly sliced*
2 *cups water*
2 *cups diced potatoes*
salt, pepper
2 *cups cream-style corn*
2 *cups rich milk*
1 *tablespoon butter*

Cook 4 slices of bacon in a saucepan until some of the fat is tried out. Add the onion and cook until the bacon is crisp and the onions lightly browned. Take out the bacon and drain it on absorbent paper. Put 2 cups of water and 2 cups of diced potatoes into the pan with salt and pepper. Simmer covered for about 20 minutes. Add 2 cups of cream-style corn and 2 cups of milk and simmer another 5 minutes. Just before serving, add a tablespoon of butter and the bacon crumbled into bits. Serves 6 to 8.

CHEDDAR CHEESE SOUP

½ *cup diced carrots*
½ *cup diced celery*
½ *cup diced green pepper*
½ *cup diced onion*
4 *cups chicken stock*
4 *tablespoons butter*
4 *tablespoons flour*
2 *cups rich milk*
1 *to* 2 *cups grated Cheddar cheese*
salt, pepper

The better the Cheddar, the better the soup. This cheese soup is featured at the Toy Town Tavern, Winchendon, Mass., and a good well-aged Vermont Cheddar is used.

Cook the diced carrots, celery, green pepper, and onion in 4 cups of chicken stock over a slow fire for 20 to 30 minutes. Strain, reserving the stock. Melt 4 tablespoons of butter. Blend in 4 tablespoons of flour. Slowly add the vegetable stock and 2 cups of rich milk. Bring to a boil, stirring constantly. Simmer for 5 minutes. Add 1 to 2 cups of grated cheese and stir until the cheese is melted. Taste for seasoning; the soup will probably need a little salt and pepper. Serves 6 to 8.

NEW ENGLAND CLAM CHOWDER

- 1/4 *pound salt pork*
- 1 *tablespoon butter*
- 3 *small white onions, finely chopped*
- 3 *cups diced raw potatoes*
- *salt, pepper*
- 3 *cups boiling water*
- 1 *quart shucked clams, chopped,* or 2 *cans minced clams*
- 3 *cups milk, scalded*
- 1 *cup cream*

Clam chowder is one of New England's traditional and most famous dishes, and is featured in all the Treadway Inns. The ingredients are always the same, except that sometimes the chowder is thickened with a little flour, sometimes not. Unthickened chowder is perhaps more authentic, and is the way Mr. Treadway prefers it. Regular chowder clams are slightly larger than cherrystones, and need only to be chopped, although the squeamish may want to remove the bellies. If steamers are used, they are first steamed, then the necks are usually cut off and the rest of the clam is chopped. Canned minced clams are excellent, available anywhere, and of course less trouble. They are generally a special deep-sea clam, much larger than ordinary chowder clams. It is important not to overcook the clams you use; 5 minutes is ample actual cooking time.

Dice 1/4 pound of salt pork into small 1/4-inch cubes and cook them slowly in a heavy saucepan or large skillet until lightly browned. Add 1 tablespoon of butter and 3 small chopped onions and cook slowly until soft but not brown. Add 3 cups of diced raw potatoes, salt and pepper, and 3 cups of boiling water and cook until the potatoes are done but not too soft, about 10 minutes. Meanwhile strain the clam liquor, then bring the chopped clams slowly to a boil in it. Add to the potatoes with 3 cups of scalded milk and set aside for an hour to ripen. Add 1 cup of cream, bring slowly to a boil again, taste for seasoning, and the chowder is ready. Serve with split pilot or common crackers. This substantial soup is a suitable main-course meal, and this amount will make 8 to 10 large servings.

BOSTON FISH CHOWDER

- 1 *pound haddock fillet* or *piece of haddock*
- 2 *cups salted water*
- 1 *large onion, sliced*
- ¼ *pound salt pork*
- 4 *medium-size potatoes, diced*
- 2 *tablespoons flour*
- 4 *cups rich milk*
- 1 *to* 2 *tablespoons chopped parsley*

Cook the fish in 2 cups of salted water with a slice of onion until it flakes easily – less than 10 minutes. Drain, reserving the stock. Dice the salt pork and cook in a large skillet until some of the fat is tried out. Add the sliced onion and sauté until the onion is soft but not brown. Meanwhile cook the peeled diced potatoes in boiling salted water until tender, then drain them.

Blend 2 tablespoons of flour into the pork fat. Add the fish stock and bring to a boil, stirring constantly. Add 4 cups of milk and bring to a boil again. Put the fish and potatoes into the skillet and simmer for at least 10 minutes, or until ready to use. Sprinkle each serving with a little chopped parsley. Serves 6 to 8 or makes 4 large main-course servings.

OYSTER STEW

- 6 *oysters*
- 2 *tablespoons butter*
- ½ *cup milk*
- ½ *cup cream*
- *salt, paprika*

Simmer the oysters in their own juice until the edges begin to curl, about 5 minutes. Skim. Add 1 tablespoon of butter, ½ cup of milk, ½ cup of cream, salt, and a little paprika. Bring slowly to the boiling point. Just before serving, add another tablespoon of butter. Makes 1 serving, as a main course.

VARIATIONS

The Publick House in Sturbridge, Mass., sautés the oysters in butter with salt and pepper, then adds half milk, half cream, and a little Chablis. At the Williams Inn in Williamstown, Mass., the oysters are brought to a boil in their own liquor, then straight cream is added with butter, salt, pepper, a little Worcestershire and Tabasco. The famous oyster bar in Grand Central Station (New York City) for each serving uses ½ cup of clam broth and 1 cup of rich milk as well as butter, Worcestershire, paprika, and celery salt.

LOBSTER STEW

1 *quart milk*
1 *live lobster,* 1½ *to* 2 *pounds*
2 *to* 3 *tablespoons butter*
1 *cup clam juice, optional*
1 *cup heavy cream*

Bring 1 quart of milk to a boil in a large saucepan. Put the lobster into the milk and cook covered over a gentle fire: 15 minutes after the lobster has come to a boil for a 1½-pound lobster, 20 minutes for a 2-pound one. Remove the lobster, reserving the milk. When the lobster is cool enough to handle, remove the meat from the tail and claws and cut it into ½-inch dice. Save the tomalley, or liver, coral, and the thick white substance inside the shell.

Sauté the meat in 2 to 3 tablespoons of butter over a slow fire for about 10 minutes, using a large heavy saucepan. Add the liver, white substance, and coral (sieved). Slowly stir in the milk the lobster was cooked in, then 1 cup of clam juice and 1 cup of cream. The clam juice is not traditional in an authentic New England lobster stew, but it gives the stew an excellent flavor. Bring to a boil.

If there is time, let the stew ripen, or age; that is, just let it stand for several hours while the flavor gradually improves. Reheat before serving. Serves 6 to 8.

LOBSTER BISQUE

- 4 *tablespoons butter*
- 1 *small onion, sliced*
- 1 *carrot, sliced*
- 1 *stalk celery, sliced*
- 1 *live lobster, 1 to 1¼ pounds*
- 2 *cups Chablis*
- 1½ *cups chicken stock*
- 2 *tablespoons flour*
- 1 *cup rich milk*
- 1 *cup light cream*

Melt 2 tablespoons of butter in a deep heavy saucepan. Put in the sliced onion, carrot, and celery and sauté over a slow fire for about 5 minutes; do not let them brown. Kill the lobster instantly by cutting across its body just below the head. Cut the tail into 3 or 4 pieces, break off the claws, and put into the pan with any of the green liver. Sauté another 5 minutes. Pour on 2 cups of Chablis (it can be an inexpensive domestic wine) and 1½ cups of chicken stock. Bring to a boil, cover, and cook over a low fire for 15 minutes. Remove the lobster and when it is cool enough to handle, take out the meat and cut it into small dice. Melt 2 tablespoons of butter. Blend in 2 tablespoons of flour. Pour on the strained stock and stir until the mixture comes to a boil. Add 1 cup of milk and 1 cup of cream and bring to a boil again. Taste for seasoning and simmer for 5 minutes. Add the lobster and cook until thoroughly heated, or until ready to serve. If the bisque is to stand, it is best to keep it in a double boiler. Makes about 10 to 12 moderate servings.

LEGUME SOUPS

Legumes are dried beans, and from the soup point of view include green and yellow split peas, lentils, black beans, red beans, and pea or navy beans. They are usually cooked with a ham bone for flavor, making fine use of the tag end of a baked ham. One of the Treadway Inn chefs introduced me to an effective and very easy way to make these soups. Instead of cooking the beans and the ham bone together, a stock is made first with the bone, and then the beans are cooked in this stock. The cooking time is a little longer, the work time far less, since it can be a tedious business separating beans and bones. You also have a stock that can be used for more than one kind of soup. The following basic recipe yields about 10 cups of stock, the right amount in which to cook 2 cups of beans, making 10 to 12 generous servings. Small families can use half the stock and one type of bean, store or freeze the rest of the stock to use later with another type of bean.

Although a ham bone is traditional and adds a flavor all its own, more than adequate soups can be made by substituting for the ham bone 2 pounds of soup meat (shin bone of beef); the cooking water from any kind of pork, such as a pork tenderloin or spareribs; the cooking water from a smoked tongue; or a piece of bacon rind.

BASIC STOCK

Put a ham bone or one of the substitutes into a large saucepan with 3 quarts of cold water. Bring slowly to a boil and skim. Add a large sliced onion, a sliced carrot, 2 or 3 stalks sliced celery, and a few peppercorns. Simmer covered for at least 2 hours, skimming occasionally if necessary. Strain. Pick all the bits of meat off the bone and save, discarding the bone. Yields about 10 cups of stock.

GREEN OR YELLOW SPLIT PEA SOUP

Follow the directions on the box about soaking the beans; some beans require overnight soaking, others do not. Put 1 pound (2 cups) of peas into a large saucepan with 10 cups of ham stock (*see* preceding recipe). Bring slowly to a boil and simmer until the peas are very soft, usually about an hour. Some peas (Smith's, for example) dissolve so completely no straining is necessary. If skins are visible, put the soup through a strainer or food mill.

Reheat and taste for seasoning. No salt was used in the stock because ham bones are often salty enough. Finely dice the ham bits and add them. The soup can be seasoned with a little ground ginger, as it is in Sweden, where it is a national dish. It can be served with croutons. Another nice garnish is braised finely chopped onion, carrots and tomatoes, and diced crisp bacon.

CREAM OF SPLIT PEA SOUP

Add heavy cream to the preceding split pea soup, about 1 cup of cream to 4 or 5 cups of soup.

PURÉE MONGOLE

Equal parts of split pea soup and cream of tomato soup or thick tomato juice. Nice served with croutons. Adding flaked crabmeat to purée Mongole makes a fine main-course soup.

LENTIL SOUP

Follow the directions for split pea soup. Add half a pound of peeled cubed potatoes (about 3 medium-size potatoes) to the lentils and purée the soup. Can be served with a few slices of cooked skinned frankfurter in each bowl. It can also be creamed by adding 1 cup of cream to each 4 or 5 cups of soup.

BLACK BEAN SOUP

Follow the directions for split pea soup. Serve laced with a little sherry and with a thin slice of lemon topped with a slice of hard-boiled egg on each serving.

RED BEAN SOUP

Follow the directions for split pea soup. Garnish: Chop 3 hard-boiled eggs and some pieces of ham very fine. Put a teaspoon in each serving, a teaspoon of sherry (optional), and a thin slice of lemon. This soup has an attractive color.

NAVY BEAN SOUP

Follow the directions for split pea soup. Either navy or pea beans can be used; the only difference is size. Cook the beans with 3 medium-size cubed potatoes and purée the soup. Add thick tomato juice to the soup, about 1 cup to 4 or 5 cups of soup, and season with a little thyme.

BASIC CREAM SOUP

2 *cups finely chopped raw vegetable*
3 *tablespoons butter*
2 *tablespoons flour*
4 *cups chicken stock,* or 2 *cups chicken stock and* 2 *cups water*
salt, white pepper
1 *cup light cream*

Melt 3 tablespoons of butter in a medium-size saucepan. Sauté the chopped vegetables about 5 minutes over a gentle fire, so that the butter will not brown. Blend in 2 tablespoons of flour. Pour on 4 cups of chicken stock, or 2 cups of chicken stock and 2 cups of water, and stir until the mixture comes to a boil. Season and let simmer until the vegetable is very tender, usually about 20 to 30 minutes. Put the whole mixture through a strainer or food mill, pushing through as much of the vegetable as possible. Or purée the vegetable in an electric blender. Add 1 cup of light cream and reheat. Serve immediately or keep hot over boiling water. Garnish with lightly salted whipped cream or with croutons. Serves 6 to 7.

Note. Any vegetable can be used and it is a good way to use leftovers. Since vegetables vary in consistency, some being much starchier than others, the actual thickness of the soup will not always be the same. This recipe should make a thick enough soup for any vegetable; if any particular soup is too thick, it can be thinned with milk, cream, or chicken stock.

Creamed soups may be thickened with potato instead of flour. Just cook a peeled sliced medium-size potato with the vegetable.

SUGGESTED VARIATIONS

Cream of Asparagus. Garnish with cooked asparagus tips.

Cream of Beet. Season with rosemary.

Cream of Broccoli. Cook with a small onion and a stalk of celery, both chopped.

Cream of Brussels Sprouts. Cook with a small chopped onion and stalk of celery. Garnish with chopped chervil.

Cream of Carrot. Cook with a small chopped onion. Season with nutmeg. Garnish with cooked julienne of carrots.

Cream of Cauliflower. Cook with a small chopped onion and a piece of bay leaf. Garnish with crisp bacon or salt pork bits. Tomato juice can be substituted for half of the chicken stock.

Cream of Celery. Season with marjoram. Garnish with cooked diced celery.

Cream of Corn. Cook with a small chopped onion and garnish with crisp bacon bits.

Cream of Cucumber. Season with freshly ground black pepper and garnish with chopped parsley.

Cream of Lima Bean. Season with celery salt.

Cream of Onion. Season with mace or nutmeg. Garnish with chopped peanuts.

Cream of Pea. Cook with a small chopped onion or 1 or 2 leeks. Garnish with chopped mint.

Cream of Spinach. Cook with a small chopped onion and season with cloves or nutmeg.

Cream of Squash. Use yellow summer squash, small tender ones if possible. Season with nutmeg and garnish with crisp bacon bits or julienne of cooked ham.

Cream of Succotash. Season with celery salt. Best made in the summer with fresh vegetables.

The method of making the following cream soups varies a little from the preceding basic recipe.

CREAM OF CHICKEN SOUP

3 *tablespoons butter*	*salt, white pepper*
3 *tablespoons flour*	⅛ *teaspoon onion juice*
3 *cups chicken stock*	½ *teaspoon celery salt*
2 *cups rich milk*	1 *cup light cream*

½ *to* 1 *cup julienne of cooked white chicken*

Melt 3 tablespoons of butter in a good-sized saucepan. Blend in 3 tablespoons of flour. Add 3 cups of chicken stock and 2 cups of rich milk and bring to a boil, stirring constantly. Season with salt, white pepper, ⅛ teaspoon onion juice, and ½ teaspoon celery salt; simmer at least 10 minutes. Just before serving, add 1 cup of light cream and ½ to 1 cup of julienne of cooked white chicken meat. Serves 6 to 8.

Note. This soup is nice garnished with blanched shredded browned almonds, added at the last minute, so that they will be crisp.

CREAM OF LETTUCE SOUP

3 *tablespoons butter*	3 *cups chicken stock*
2 *tablespoons flour*	*salt, white pepper*
1 *cup light cream*	1 *small head lettuce*

Melt 3 tablespoons of butter. Blend in 2 tablespoons of flour. When that is smooth, slowly add 1 cup of light cream. Bring to a boil, stirring constantly. Add 3 cups of chicken stock, season, and bring to a boil again. Simmer for 10 minutes or so.

Remove the core of the lettuce and chop the leaves quite fine. Add to the hot soup and cook over a moderate fire for about 10 minutes, until the lettuce is wilted. It is important to have the soup actually boiling when you add the lettuce, so that it will stay green. Nice served with crisp buttered croutons. Serves 4 to 6.

CREAM OF CLAM SOUP

1 *pint fresh clams* or
  1 *7-ounce can chopped clams*
2 *tablespoons butter*
1 *small onion, minced*
¼ *teaspoon celery salt*
  salt, pepper
2 *cups milk*
1 *egg yolk*
1 *cup light cream*
parsley or *chives*

If fresh clams are used, chop them finely, saving all the juice. Put the clams and juice into a saucepan with 2 tablespoons of butter, a small minced onion, ¼ teaspoon celery salt, a little salt, and some freshly ground black pepper. Bring to a boil and simmer 10 to 15 minutes. Add 2 cups of milk and cook until the mixture comes to a boil again. Just before serving, beat an egg yolk lightly with a fork and beat in 1 cup of light cream. Blend a little of the hot soup into the egg yolk and cream, then slowly add the egg and cream mixture to the hot soup. Stir while the soup thickens, but do not let it boil. Serve sprinkled with a little chopped parsley or chives. Serves 4 or 5.

CREAM OF MUSHROOM SOUP

½ *pound mushrooms*
½ *small white onion*
½ *stalk celery*
4 *cups chicken stock*
2 *tablespoons butter*
2 *tablespoons flour*
1 *cup light cream*
2 *to* 3 *tablespoons dry sherry*
6 *teaspoons whipped cream, lightly salted*

Put the mushrooms, stems and all, onion, and celery through the fine cutter of a meat grinder. Simmer them in 4 cups of well-seasoned chicken stock for 15 to 20 minutes.

Blend together 2 tablespoons of butter and 2 tablespoons of flour, add to the mushroom mixture, and stir until it has thickened and come to a boil. Then strain and reheat. Add 1 cup of light cream and taste for seasoning. The soup is now ready to be served, but can be kept waiting in a double boiler. Just before serving, add 2 to 3 tablespoons of dry sherry and, if you wish, some sliced mushrooms which have been sautéed in butter and lemon juice to keep them white. Top each serving with a spoonful of lightly salted whipped cream. Serves 5 or 6.

MUSHROOM AND CLAM SOUP

½ *pound mushrooms*
3 *tablespoons butter*
3 *tablespoons flour*
3 *cups clam juice*
1 *cup heavy cream*
white pepper

Remove the mushroom stems and thinly slice the caps. Sauté them in 3 tablespoons of butter until lightly browned, using a medium-size saucepan. Blend in 3 tablespoons of flour, off the fire. Add 3 cups of clam juice and stir over the fire until the mixture comes to a boil. Simmer for at least 15 minutes, and it can be kept waiting indefinitely in a double boiler. Just before serving, add 1 cup of cream and heat thoroughly, but do not let the soup boil. Taste for seasoning. A little white pepper will be needed, but the clam juice may take care of the salt. Serves 4 or 5.

ONE OF EACH
(Iced summer soup)

1 *medium-size potato*
1 *medium-size onion*
1 *celery stalk with leaves*
1 *apple*
1 *banana*
2 *tablespoons butter*
1 *generous teaspoon curry powder*
2 *cups chicken stock*
salt, pepper
1 *cup light cream*
chives or *peanuts*

Peel the vegetables and fruit and cut them into large dice. Melt 2 tablespoons of butter in a medium-size saucepan. Blend in a generous teaspoon of curry powder. Add the vegetables and fruit and cook over a slow fire for 7 to 8 minutes. Pour on 2 cups of chicken stock and bring to a boil. Season with salt and pepper and cook gently for about 30 minutes, until the vegetables are very tender. Put through a strainer or food mill. Add 1 cup of light cream and taste for seasoning. Chill in the refrigerator for several hours or overnight. Serve in chilled soup bowls, garnished with chopped chives or chopped peanuts. Serves 4 to 6.

POTATO AND WATER CRESS SOUP

1 *medium-size onion*
3 *large potatoes*
3 *tablespoons butter*
½ *cup water*
salt, pepper
1 *bunch water cress*
2 *cups chicken stock*
1 *cup light cream*

Peel and thinly slice the onion and potatoes. Melt 3 tablespoons of butter in a medium-size saucepan. Add the sliced vegetables, ½ cup of water, salt, and pepper. Cover and cook very slowly until the vegetables are soft and mushy, 20 to 30 minutes. Roughly cut up the bottom half of the water cress (the stems) and add it to the vegetables with 2 cups of chicken stock. Stir over the fire until the soup comes to a boil. Then put it through a strainer or food mill. Reheat, add 1 cup of cream, and just before serving, add the water cress leaves finely chopped. This soup is also excellent ice cold. Serves 5 or 6.

Note. Parsley may be used instead of water cress.

VICHYSSOISE

This famous soup was introduced at the Ritz Hotel in New York by Louis Diat, who was chef there for many years. His mother in France used to nourish her family with a plain leek and potato soup, and that is what a true Vichyssoise is. As usually happens, people think they can improve on the original and you will find recipes with all sorts of added ingredients. But it is fine as it is in its simplest form – a delicate velvety-smooth soup, usually served ice cold.

4 *leeks*	1 *cup light cream*
3 *medium-size potatoes*	1 *cup heavy cream*
4 *cups strong chicken stock*	*chopped chives*

Finely slice the white part of the leeks and an inch of the green part. Pare and thinly slice the potatoes. Simmer the leeks and potatoes in 4 cups of chicken stock until very soft, about 40 minutes. The stock should be fat free if the soup is to be served cold; otherwise the fat will rise to the top and look unappetizing. If the soup is to be served hot, it doesn't matter; in fact, you can add 2 tablespoons of butter to the stock. When the vegetables are cooked, put them through a coarse strainer or food mill, pushing through all the vegetables possible, then put them through a fine strainer. Better still, put them in an electric blender with the stock; then you won't lose any of the vegetables and the soup will be truly smooth. Blend in 1 cup of light cream with the puréed vegetables and stock and taste for seasoning. Chill for several hours in the refrigerator in a china bowl — a metal bowl will flavor the soup. Before serving, add 1 cup of heavy cream. If the soup is too thick, it can be thinned with milk. Serve in chilled soup bowls and garnish each serving with a few chopped chives. Serves 8 to 10.

TOMATO BISQUE

1 *large can tomatoes*	*salt, pepper*
pinch baking soda	1 *cup light cream*
1 *small onion*	1 *to* 2 *tablespoons butter*

The chef of the Williams Inn, Williamstown, Mass., finds this soup a boon, since it can be made in 5 minutes if he runs short of other soups and it is always well liked.

Bring the canned tomatoes to a boil with a pinch of soda to cut the acidity and a small onion for flavor. Season with salt and pepper, add 1 cup of light cream, heat thoroughly, and the soup is ready. Break up the tomatoes a little if you wish, but don't strain them. Just before serving, remove the onion and add 1 to 2 tablespoons of butter. Serves 4 to 6.

CREAM OF TOMATO SOUP

3 *tablespoons butter*
1 *small onion, sliced*
1 *stalk celery, sliced*
1 *sprig parsley* or *thyme*
1 *large can tomatoes or* 5 or 6 *fresh tomatoes, sliced*
salt, pepper
1½ *cups chicken stock*
3 *tablespoons flour*
1½ *cups milk*
1 *cup cream*
1 *fresh tomato*
parsley, basil, or *chives for garnish*

Melt 3 tablespoons of butter in a saucepan. Add the onion, celery, parsley or thyme and cook slowly about 5 minutes. Add the tomatoes, salt and pepper, and 1½ cups of chicken stock and simmer covered for 15 minutes. Blend together 3 tablespoons of flour and 1½ cups of cold milk, and stir until the mixture comes to a boil. Simmer for 5 minutes, then strain. Add 1 cup of cream and reheat. Taste for seasoning. Skin 1 fresh tomato, quarter, remove the seedy pulp, and shred the rest. Add to the soup just before serving and sprinkle with chopped parsley, basil, or chives. Serves 6.

TOY TOWN TAVERN

Winchendon, Massachusetts

THE Toy Town Tavern is a Treadway Inn in central Massachusetts just south of the New Hampshire border. The tavern is interesting from several standpoints – the location, the inn itself, all that it has to offer in the way of sports and entertainment, and its proximity to the famed Cathedral of the Pines.

The Toy Town Tavern sits on a hill about twelve hundred feet high, almost completely surrounded by its own Donald Ross Golf Course, facing a sweep of fairway, Lake Watotick, and in the far distance Mount Monadnock. The tavern is a long, rambling, gray-shingle building with white trim and black shutters. It has the real feeling of a comfortable old-fashioned country inn, complete with wide verandas and rocking chairs. Old-fashioned may not be exactly the right word, however, since it has a modern cocktail lounge in a separate building a few yards from the inn and its own clear, blue swimming pool. There is also a playhouse for indoor games and television.

Ample entertainment is at hand for anyone who wants it. The tavern is also the local golf club, with a golf shop and pro on the grounds. In addition to golf, there are tennis, shuffleboard, croquet, riding, and swimming to choose from in the daytime, and horse races, bingo, occasional dances, and other activities at night. There is a social hostess who arranges bridge and canasta parties and other gatherings. But the tavern is so roomy and the grounds so spacious that anyone who wants to be alone can be. The flowers are beautiful – geraniums and petunias in pots on the verandas, shrubs and flowers all over the grounds, and a lovely white-picket-fenced colonial garden in the rear. There is a guest house down the road a bit for anyone who prefers uninterrupted quiet.

The name "Toy Town" is a curious one, although easily explained. At one time Winchendon was the center of wooden toy manufacture in the country. A former owner of the house was the rocking-horse king, and the large wooden rocking horse now on the grounds used to stand at the railroad station as a symbol of the town's interest. In the early 1920's the market for wooden toys declined and Winchendon switched to the manufacture of other products – particularly wooden buckets. However, a few small wooden toys, such as doll furniture and Noah's arks, are still being made and are sold in the tavern's gift shop. The toy motif is used in large gay, colorful murals on the dining-room walls. The paintings were executed by Mrs. Hershey, who at one time decorated nurseries for Jordan Marsh.

The tavern is partly old, dating to around 1786, and partly new. When it was converted to a hotel in 1912, there were extensive alterations and expansion. The main lounge has a stairway taken from the Bradley Fuller House which stood on Hawley Street in Boston. The stairs are the identical ones down which several members of the Boston Tea Party, dressed as Indians, ran to escape British officers on December 16, 1773. The original newel post was stolen or lost, but the historic John Hancock newel post from his Beacon Street house, which had been stored in the attic for many years, was secured to take its place.

The finely wooded, hilly countryside around Winchendon is perfect for motoring any time of the year, and is especially beautiful in the early fall. The foliage starts turning that far north at the beginning of September. About twenty miles away around the mountains is the old car museum in Princeton. But the spot that has brought eight hundred thousand visitors to this vicinity in the last seven seasons — the Cathedral of the Pines, at Rindge, New Hampshire — is only a twenty-minute drive. This place of worship was erected in memory of Lieutenant Sanderson Sloane, who was killed in action in World War II, by his parents, Douglas and Sibyl Sanderson Sloane. The "cathedral" is at once simple and almost heartbreaking in its beauty — a grove of towering pines perched on a hillside, with a view for miles of woods, lakes, and mountains. The altar is a memorial to all war dead, built with stones from every state in the Union. There is a simple log altar rail, a stone pulpit, and wooden benches which will seat fifteen hundred people. Several services a week are scheduled all during the summer, of all faiths and creeds. Every Sunday morning at eight o'clock during July and August there is an Episcopal communion service.

The Toy Town Tavern is sixty-five miles from Boston on Route 2 and just a short drive through the pines up Route 202. The season is from the middle of May to late October. Mr. John A. McIlhenny is the innkeeper.

FISH

THE oceans, gulfs, lakes, and streams around and in the United States swarm with a vast number of fish and shellfish. Although there are about one hundred and sixty different kinds, the following twelve fish represent eighty per cent of the total sales: salmon, pilchard (sardines), haddock, sea herring, cod, tuna, shrimp, oysters, crabs, flounder, mackerel, and halibut. Some varieties of fish are indigenous to one locality and can be found only there. Others, especially shellfish, while found only in certain local waters — Louisiana shrimp, for example, and lobsters from the icy waters of Maine — are shipped thousands of miles to markets all over the country.

At the Treadway Inns some fish are great favorites. This is particularly true of shellfish, and the inns have many interesting ways of using the ever-popular lobsters, shrimp, crabs, scallops, and clams. The number of actual fish dishes is more limited. When people dine out, it is an occasion, and the tendency is to order either dishes that are prime favorites at home, or ones that are not usually served at home. Swordfish belongs in the first group: the manager of the Toy Town Tavern in Winchendon, Mass., told me that the tavern has the largest number of guests for Sunday dinner, and that eighty per cent of them order either turkey or swordfish. Sole Marguery belongs in the second group: not that it is a difficult dish to make, but it does have rather special ingredients. Another requisite for restaurants is that a dish be easy to eat in public, which eliminates fish full of bones. So the following group of Treadway Inn fish recipes is quite selective. A brief discussion of cooking methods follows, and can be used for many fish not mentioned specifically in this book. If any readers want individual recipes for almost one hundred varieties of fish and shellfish, I recommend *James Beard's Fish Cookery.*

BUYING FISH

Fish is highly perishable, so it should be purchased from a reliable fishmonger who keeps it on ice, and it should be eaten within twenty-four hours after you bring it home. Wash it in cold water, dry, wrap well in wax paper, and store in the refrigerator.

How much to buy:

Whole fish: 3/4 pound per serving.

Drawn fish – cleaned and scaled: 1 pound for 2 servings.

Dressed fish – drawn fish with head removed: 1 pound for 2 or 3 servings.

Fillets or steaks: 1 pound for 2 or 3 servings.

TYPES OF FISH

In general there are two types of fish – lean and fat.

Lean fish have five per cent or less fat, for the most part have white flesh, and are less flavorful than fat fish. Since the flesh is more or less firm, it holds together better than that of fat fish. Therefore, lean fish is better for boiling. It can be fried, of course, and broiled or baked if plenty of additional fat is used to ensure a brown crust. Because of its lack of flavor and low calorie content, lean fish should be served either with a rich sauce, drenched in melted butter, or stuffed. Boiled white fish should always be served with a sauce to supply color and make the fish look more appetizing. Some lean fish are: cod, haddock, halibut, swordfish, and scrod.

Fat fish may have from five to twenty per cent fat, but even a fat fish is low in fat compared to meat. A fat fish usually has colored flesh and tends to fall apart quickly when boiled; salmon is an exception to this rule. It lends itself readily to broiling and baking since it browns well with only a little additional fat; in fact it is possible to cook it without using any fat at all, but the flavor will not be quite as good. Because fat fish is comparatively rich, serve it with a tart sauce or relish. Some fat fish are: mackerel, salmon, trout, and whitefish.

GENERAL COOKING INSTRUCTIONS

The principal concern in cooking fish is to retain flavor and to keep the fish intact. Overcooking defeats this aim, so it is of prime importance to cook fish in as short a time as possible, although at moderate, not high, heat. Unlike meat, fish has very little connective tissue and the little it does have softens quickly, so tough fish is never a problem. (The only exceptions are a few shellfish, like clams and oysters, which toughen if overcooked at high temperatures.) As the Fishery Council puts it, "Fish is cooked to develop flavor, not to make it tender." When fish is done, it loses its semi-transparent look and will flake easily if pierced with a sharp pointed knife or skewer. Cooking time may be less than 10 minutes with a small fillet or trout, only 15 minutes for a thick swordfish steak. When overcooked, fish falls apart, and tends to be tasteless.

Although the flavor of fish is distinctive, it is mild, and so it should be prepared to bring out the flavor. Acids go well with fish, which accounts for the prevalent use of lemon as a garnish or an integral part of a sauce. Dry white wine is excellent with fish, and is used in many of the following recipes. Sauces add substance and eye appeal as well as flavor; they are almost imperative with a bland white poached fish, and are pleasant with any kind.

Fish is cooked in several ways: broiling, pan and deep-fat frying, baking, and poaching.

BROILING

This is an excellent way to cook fish, giving it an appetizing brown crust and retaining all the natural flavor of the fish. The technique of broiling fish differs from that of broiling meat. Fish has to be handled more carefully because of its tendency to fall apart, and it is not nearly as fat as most meat. To keep it intact, it is best not to try to turn it, but to brown only the top crust. It is also a good idea to broil it right in an ovenproof serving dish so that it will not have to be transferred to another dish. Because it lacks natural fat, additional fat should be used, even with the so-called fat fish, unless they are very oily, like mackerel.

Standard Method. Recent tests have proved that broiling at 350° rather than at a higher temperature results in a more moist fish. Preheat the broiler for 10 minutes. Put the fish in a buttered dish or grease the grids of a broiling pan well. Brush the top of the fish well with softened butter, season with salt and pepper, and sprinkle with a little lemon juice. Have the fish about 2 inches from the flame. Broil until the top is nicely browned, basting once or twice. The time depends on the thickness of the fish; 5 minutes is usually sufficient for fillets, 10 to 15 minutes for a steak 1 to 1½ inches thick. Remember, *don't overcook.*

The fish that are usually broiled at the Treadway Inns are: steaks – salmon, scrod, and swordfish; fillets – mackerel, New York State whitefish, and many of the wonderful Florida fish, such as red snapper and pompano. Specific directions for all these fish follow.

Suitable Sauces. Since the flavor of broiled fish is so good, elaborate sauces are not at all necessary. A little lemon juice will do, or any of the fish butters, such as chive, water cress, cucumber, or maître d'hôtel. Frozen white relish is also suggested, or lemon fish sauce (*see* page 87).

BROILED SWORDFISH

Use a center cut at least ¾ to 1 inch thick. One reason swordfish sometimes seems dry is that it is too thin, and so dries out quickly. It is a firm-fleshed, lean fish which holds together better than most fish and needs plenty of additional fat. It can be broiled with just butter and lemon juice. Or it can be brushed with an egg slightly beaten with 1 tablespoon of water, coated with bread crumbs, and then dotted well with butter. Broil for 15 minutes at 350°, or brown the top under a hotter flame and finish cooking in a 400° oven, with a total cooking time of 15 minutes.

BROILED SCROD

Scrod is a small young cod or haddock, weighing 1 to 2½ pounds, and broiling is the accepted way of cooking it. It is often called Boston scrod, because of Boston's association with "the bean and the cod"; the sacred cod, on a six-foot plaque, is the emblem of the Commonwealth of Massachusetts, and hangs in the Spectators' Lobby of the Boston State House.

The fish is split and the backbone removed. Then it is either left whole or cut into serving-size pieces about 6 ounces each, across the grain. Scrod is firm-fleshed and lean, and needs plenty of fat. It can be cooked just like swordfish in the preceding recipe, or it can be dipped in melted butter, sprinkled with bread crumbs, and brushed with butter again. At the Treadway Inn in Rochester, N.Y., broiled scrod is topped with Welsh rabbit (*see* page 205) held together with a little cream sauce, then browned again under the broiler.

BROILED SALMON

Salmon has a lovely delicate flavor and an attractive color, ranging from light pink to a deeper coral red. For broiling, it is cut into steaks. Salmon is a fat fish and needs less butter than swordfish or scrod, but otherwise it is cooked just like swordfish.

BROILED FILLET OF MACKEREL

The fish is dipped in melted butter, bread crumbs are sprinkled over the top, and it is seasoned with a little lemon juice and Worcestershire sauce. Mackerel is a fat fish, so it does not need much additional fat. It is broiled for exactly 10 minutes.

BROILED FILLET OF WHITEFISH

Whitefish comes from the local Great Lake in Rochester, N.Y., and is served at the Treadway Inn there. It is a fat fish, so it is just dipped in melted butter and sprinkled with crumbs. Then it is browned under the broiler, and finished off in a 400° oven. The fillets are served with lobster sauce.

FLORIDA FILLETS

The warm-water fish in the southern waters of Florida are quite bland and delicately flavored. The chef at the Royal Park Inn uses fillets of native fish, such as red (St. Lucie) snapper, pompano, bluefish, kingfish, king mackerel, sea bass, and grouper. He has a special way of doing them. He uses individual sizzling platters made of a nonporous metal. The fish fillets are coated with melted butter and crumbs, browned under the broiler, and finished off in a moderately hot oven at 400°. At the very end he pours on a little Chablis. The fish is, of course, served in the same platter. A 5 to 7-ounce fillet is cooked exactly 12 minutes. Because these fish are bland, sauces are used, such as lemon, lobster, and maître d'hôtel butter; Béarnaise, Hollandaise, and Montpelier sauce.

FRYING

There are two methods of frying fish: pan frying (in a skillet in a little fat at a moderate heat) and deep-fat frying (in a deep pan in a lot of fat at a high temperature). With deep-fat frying you can be assured of even browning with less absorption of fat, so it is the preferred method for such staple restaurant dishes as fried oysters, scallops, and so on. It is easy in the Treadway Inns because they have special deep-fat fryers going all the time. It may seem like a nuisance to the homemaker, however, unless she has the right equipment and does a lot of frying, and pan frying can give fine results. Whatever method you use, fry the fish just before serving and rush it to the table, so that it will be hot and crisp. It can be kept warm in a very slow oven, but it will lose some of its crispness.

Fat. For *pan frying,* the fat can be butter, a peanut or corn oil, or a hydrogenated fat such as Crisco or Spry. The flavor of butter is best, but butter breaks down and burns at a lower temperature than the other fats, so it has to be cooked at a moderate heat. The high temperature used in *deep-fat frying* automatically rules out butter, and one of the other fats must be used; the best is oil.

Coating. When fish is fried, it needs some kind of coating to hold it together and keep it moist. For *pan frying,* the fish can be just lightly dusted with flour, it can be dipped in milk and then in corn meal, or it can have a regular breading. **Breading:** Dust the fish lightly with flour, dip into egg wash (1 egg beaten with 1 tablespoon of water), then completely cover with either dry bread crumbs or corn flour (available in some parts of the country and finer and therefore less gritty than bread crumbs). Restaurants use a product called ready breader, which can be found in a few retail markets. After the fish is breaded, if it is allowed to stand for at least 15 minutes on wax paper, turning once or twice, the coating dries out and sticks better. For *deep-fat frying,* breading the fish is essential to hold it together.

Pan Frying. Heat enough butter or oil in a skillet to cover the bottom of the pan ½ inch deep. The fat should be hot but not smoking; if it is not hot enough, the fish soaks up too much fat before it is browned. If it is too hot, the fish browns too much before it is cooked. Put the prepared fish (*see* preceding section on coating) into the pan without crowding; they should be in a single layer and far enough apart to turn easily with a spatula. Cook over a moderate heat. Turn the fish with a wide spatula when the bottom is nicely browned, and brown the other side. When both sides are browned, the fish will be done; this will take about 7 to 10 minutes, depending upon the thickness of the fish. Some fish that are pan fried are fillets of sole, shad roe, and frogs' legs.

Deep-fat Frying. The fish must be breaded. Have the fat deep enough to completely cover the fish. The fat is heated to between 350° and 375°, depending on the thickness of the fish or seafood. Do not overcrowd the pan since it lowers the temperature, causing the fish to absorb more fat than is necessary. The fish will be done when it is browned. A frying basket is the simplest way to remove the fish, but a slotted spoon will do. Drain the fish on absorbent paper to remove any excess fat. Some fish that are fried in deep fat are sole, codfish cakes, and shellfish such as soft-shell crabs, oysters, shrimp, and scallops.

Suitable Sauces. Fried fish is quite rich, so any sauce should add tartness or flavor rather than substance, such as: tartar sauce, Montpelier, or any of the butter sauces.

FRIED SOLE

Fillets of sole are generally used for frying, allowing about 6 ounces per serving. This would be either 2 small fillets or 1 large one cut in half.

DEEP–FAT FRIED SOLE

Bread the sole (*see* page 73) and fry in deep fat at 375°. Fried sole is often served with tartar sauce, but other sauces which are just as acceptable are: Hollandaise, Béarnaise, or any of the butter sauces (*see* page 86).

PAN–FRIED OR SAUTÉED SOLE

If sautéing sole for individual servings, it is nice to use a pan that can be used for serving, such as a small copper sauté pan. Bread the fillets or just coat them lightly with flour. Sauté in butter or oil over a moderate fire until golden brown on both sides. Sprinkle with a few drops of lemon juice before serving.

With Chablis. When the sautéed sole is nicely browned, pour a little Chablis into the pan and cook for just a few seconds to heat the wine. Omit the lemon juice. When serving, sprinkle with a little chopped parsley.

À la Meunière. This is one of the classic French ways of preparing fish, simple but perfect. Lightly flour the sole and sauté it in butter. Serve on a platter surrounded with thin slices of lemon, and sprinkle lightly with lemon juice and coarsely chopped parsley. If you wish, some browned butter may be poured over it.

Amandine. Serve sautéed fish or shellfish with a sauce made of butter and blanched browned slivered almonds, with a little lemon juice or white wine. The following recipe for sole amandine gives the basic proportions.

SOLE AMANDINE

4 *fillets of sole,* 4 *to* 5 *ounces each*
seasoned flour
3 *tablespoons butter*
½ *cup blanched almonds*
¼ *cup melted butter*
1 *tablespoon lemon juice* or ¼ *cup dry white wine*

Dip the sole fillets into flour seasoned with salt and pepper, and sauté them in 3 tablespoons of butter until they are nicely browned. Meanwhile sliver ½ cup of blanched almonds and brown them in ¼ cup of melted butter. Remove the fillets to a hot platter. Add the almonds and butter to the pan, and pour on 1 tablespoon of lemon juice or ¼ cup of dry white wine. Heat through, stirring to combine the liquids, and pour over the fillets. Serves 4.

SHAD ROE

Shad roe is a seasonal delicacy of delicious flavor. Roes come in pairs, and half a pair is allowed for each serving. They should be sautéed, but the one problem in cooking them is to keep them from getting too dry. To prevent this, place them in a skillet with a little water and lemon juice or white wine, enough to cover the bottom of the pan ½ inch deep. Bring to a boil, cover, and steam for 10 minutes. Then drain and dry thoroughly. Coat lightly with seasoned flour. Sauté them in butter, or half butter and half oil, over a gentle fire until browned on both sides, 10 to 15 minutes. Sprinkle a little lemon juice or white wine over the roes just before serving, or serve them amandine. Garnish with crisp bacon strips.

FROGS' LEGS CHABLIS

8 *pairs large frogs' legs*
seasoned flour
about ½ cup butter
½ *cup Chablis*
lemon

Frogs' legs are raised especially for our markets, and the meat is tender and delicate, as white as chicken breasts and a lot like them in flavor. There are three sizes, small, large, and jumbo, and the first two are perhaps more desirable than the jumbo ones. One pair of jumbo is allowed for each serving, 2 large, and 4 to 6 small. They are available fresh and frozen. The frozen ones thaw very quickly; letting them stand in cold water for 1½ minutes is long enough for them to be handled easily.

Soak the frogs' legs in milk for 1 hour, or just dip them in milk. Dust lightly with seasoned flour. Heat ½ cup of butter in a large skillet. Put in the frogs' legs and cook quickly until nicely browned on both sides; they take only about 8 to 10 minutes and tend to fall apart if overcooked. When browned, pour in ½ cup of Chablis, cook another minute, then serve immediately, with lemon wedges. Serves 4.

GREEN SPRING MOUNTAIN TROUT

These trout are a specialty at several of the Treadway Inns. They are frozen as soon as they are caught, so they are very fresh.

To sauté, flour them while they are still frozen, and brown fairly fast in about 5 minutes on top of the stove in a mixture of butter and oil. Finish off in a 350° oven for 20 minutes. They are served à la meunière (*see* page 75), or with a sauce of melted butter and white wine. At the Long Trail Lodge in Rutland, Vt., the chef arranges the cooked trout on water cress and spreads them with almond butter, which is a paste made of ground blanched almonds and soft butter. Garnish with 3 or 4 almond halves, and a thin strip of pimento across the gill.

SPOON–DROPPED CODFISH BALLS

1 *box Gorton's fibered codfish* (4-*ounce*)
3 *medium-size potatoes*
1 *tablespoon butter*
1 *egg*
dash pepper

In *The Yankee Cook Book,* edited by Imogene Wolcott (an excellent book, by the way), she says: "Codfish is one of the oldest of American foods. The Pilgrim fathers subsisted largely on it. Each year, as cold weather approached, they put away stores of meaty cod, carefully preserved with salt. . . . eating fish balls for Sunday morning breakfast is part of Boston's tradition, like reading the *Transcript* or taking visitors to see the glass flowers."

Dried codfish used to be a nuisance to prepare. It was so salty and dried that it had to be "freshened," which meant adding cold water and bringing the fish slowly to a boil and draining three times before it was ready to use. This packaged fibered codfish is a cinch to use. It is all flaked and very lightly salted, so that all you do is put it in a piece of cheesecloth over a large strainer, run cold water over it for a minute, then squeeze the water out.

Pare 3 medium-size potatoes, cut them in half or quarters, and cook until tender in boiling salted water, 10 to 15 minutes. Drain well and put through a ricer into a large mixing bowl. Beat in 1 tablespoon of butter, 1 egg yolk, and a dash of pepper. Add the prepared codfish and mix thoroughly. Fold in the stiffly beaten egg white. Drop by rounded teaspoons into hot fat at 350° to

360° and cook until golden brown, 2 to 3 minutes. These fish balls will be smooth and moist inside with a wonderfully crisp crust. Folding in the beaten egg white, rather than beating in a whole egg, as many recipes advise, helps keep them light. Serve immediately. Makes about 20.

POACHED FISH

Poached fish is cooked in a liquid which covers it and which is simmering – in other words, barely trembling. Although it is sometimes called "boiled" fish, the word boil is a misnomer. The purpose is to cook the fish slowly, so that it will retain moisture, flavor, and shape; boiling fish will break it up and make it dry.

A firm, dry-fleshed fish should be used since oily fishes break apart easily. Because poaching tends to leave the fish with a bland look and taste, its use is limited. The two most common uses are for large pieces of fish, such as salmon and cod, which have a positive flavor of their own, and for fillets, which are often poached in a combination of wine and water, giving a stock which is an excellent base for sauces. Poached fish should always be served masked with a sauce to step up the looks and taste. A typical way to poach fillets is given in the following recipe for sole bonne femme. Poaching a large piece of fish is described in the traditional New England Fourth of July dish, salmon with green peas, on page 81.

Cooking Liquid. There is quite a diversity of opinion about seasoning the liquid fish is poached in. The minimum seasonings are simple – salt and some sort of acid to help keep the fish firm and retain the color: it may be lemon juice, vinegar, or wine. Regular seasoning vegetables (carrots, onions, and celery) are all right too. From here on, the sky is often the limit; recipes for court bouillon (seasoned liquid for poaching fish) vary widely and may include up to fifteen various ingredients. Treadway Inn chefs believe that too much fancy seasoning offers too much competition with the flavor of the fish, and use only plain salted water with lemon juice or vinegar, and maybe a little sliced onion and a piece of bay leaf.

Suitable Sauces. For hot fish: egg, egg and wine, Hollandaise, Béarnaise, velouté, and poulette. For cold fish: mayonnaise or curry mayonnaise.

FILLET OF SOLE BONNE FEMME

- 6 *fillets of sole (about 2 pounds)*
- 2 *tablespoons chopped parsley*
- *salt, white pepper*
- 2 *shallots* or 1 *small onion, sliced*
- 1 *cup dry white wine*
- ½ *cup water*
- ½ *pound mushrooms, sliced*
- 5 *tablespoons butter*
- 2 *tablespoons flour*
- 1 *cup fish stock*
- 1 *cup heavy cream*
- 1 *egg yolk*

Place the fillets in a lightly greased ovenproof baking dish that can be used for serving. Sprinkle with 2 tablespoons of chopped parsley, salt, and white pepper, and put in the pan 2 sliced shallots or 1 small sliced onion, 1 cup of dry white wine, and ½ cup of water. Cover with wax paper and poach in a moderate oven at 350° for 15 minutes. Drain off the stock, remove the shallots or onion, and keep the fish warm in the oven with the heat off. If there is more than 1 cup of fish stock, reduce it to that amount. Meanwhile sauté ½ pound of sliced mushrooms in 2 tablespoons of butter. Make the following sauce: Melt 2 tablespoons of butter. Blend in 2 tablespoons of flour. Pour on the fish stock and stir until the mixture comes to a boil. Add ½ cup of heavy cream and the sautéed mushrooms. Beat 1 egg yolk lightly with a fork. Beat in ½ cup of cream. Add a little of the hot sauce, then add the egg mixture to the sauce. Stir over heat until it thickens, but do not let it boil. Off the fire beat in another tablespoon of butter. Spoon carefully over the fish, and glaze under the broiler. Serves 6.

FILLET OF SOLE MARGUERY

- 2 *pounds fillet of sole*
- *small piece bay leaf*
- *about* 1 *cup dry white wine*
- ½ *pound small shrimp, shelled*
- 1 *pound mussels, steamed,* or 12 *oysters*
- 6 *medium-size mushroom caps*
- 6 *tablespoons butter*
- 3 *tablespoons flour*
- 1 *cup fish stock*
- ½ *cup light cream*
- *salt, cayenne*
- *parsley potato balls*

Place the fillets in a shallow baking dish with a small piece of bay leaf and add enough dry white wine to just cover them. Cover with wax paper and bake in a moderate over at 350° for 15 minutes. Drain the liquid off into a saucepan and bring it to a boil. Shell and devein ½ pound of small shrimp and cook them in the liquid at a gentle boil for 5 minutes. Remove the shrimp and measure the fish stock. If there is more than 1 cup of it, reduce it to that amount. In the meantime steam 1 pound of mussels, or cook 12 oysters in their own liquor until the edges curl. Sauté 6 mushroom caps in 1 tablespoon of butter until lightly browned. Melt 3 tablespoons of butter, and blend in 3 tablespoons of flour. Pour on the cup of fish stock, strained, and stir until the mixture comes to a boil. Add ½ cup of light cream, season with salt and cayenne, and simmer for 5 minutes. Beat in 2 tablespoons of butter, bit by bit. Place the sole on an ovenproof serving dish or individual dishes, and spoon the sauce carefully over the fish. Arrange the shrimp, mussels, and mushrooms on top, and place under the broiler until lightly glazed. Garnish with steamed parsley potato balls. Serves 6 to 8.

CREAMED FINNAN HADDIE AU GRATIN

- 1½ *pounds finnan haddie*
- *milk to cover fish*
- 4 *tablespoons butter*
- 3 *tablespoons flour*
- 2 *cups light cream*
- *salt, pepper*
- 4 *hard-cooked eggs, sliced*
- *grated Parmesan cheese*

Place the fish in a shallow skillet. Just cover with milk, and simmer covered for 15 minutes. Drain, cool, remove the skin and bones, and flake the fish into good-sized pieces. Make the following cream sauce: Melt 4 tablespoons of butter. Blend in 3 tablespoons of flour. Pour on 2 cups of cream, season, and stir until the sauce comes to a boil. Simmer for 5 minutes. Carefully add the fish and the sliced hard-cooked eggs. Place in a shallow casserole or baking dish, top generously with grated Parmesan cheese, and bake in a hot over at 400° until the top is golden brown, or brown under the broiler. A border of duchess potatoes may be piped around the fish before it is browned. Serves 4.

POACHED SALMON

Use either a small whole salmon, which is very impressive for a cold buffet, or a thick slice of salmon steak. Allow about 6 ounces per serving. Tie the fish up in a piece of cheesecloth so that it will keep its shape. Bring enough water to a boil to cover the fish well. Season with salt, pepper, and a bit of bay leaf, and add 2 tablespoons of lemon juice or white wine for each quart of water. Drop the fish into the water, preferably on a rack, and cook it at a simmering temperature for 6 to 8 minutes to the pound. Remove and drain for 5 minutes; otherwise the fish will be watery when it is served. Take off the skin. Cover hot salmon with egg sauce, egg and wine sauce, Hollandaise, Béarnaise, or velouté sauce, or sauce aurore. For the Fourth of July, serve it with fresh green peas and, if you can get them, small boiled new potatoes, both well lubricated with butter. Serve cold salmon with mayonnaise or curry mayonnaise (*see* page 214).

BAKED FISH

Fish are often stuffed and baked whole. Or thick steaks can be baked. It is an easy way to cook fish since it requires no attention except an occasional basting. Unless the fish is thick and firm-fleshed, it is best to bake it in an ovenproof dish that can be used for serving, so that it will not have to be moved. Brush the fish with melted butter or use salt pork or bacon fat. Bake at 375°, allowing 10 minutes to the pound; for fish over 5 pounds, allow only 5 minutes for each additional pound. The following recipe for stuffed bass illustrates the method to be used when baking a whole fish, and the crusty baked halibut is typical of fish steaks.

BAKED BASS STUFFED WITH CRABMEAT

1 *striped bass,* 3 *to* 5 *pounds*
salt, pepper
2 *tablespoons chopped onion*
¼ *cup chopped celery*
½ *cup butter*
2 *cups soft bread crumbs*
1 *cup flaked crabmeat*
1 *tablespoon chopped parsley*
2 *cups milk*
1 *large onion, sliced*
parsley and lemon

Wash the bass and sprinkle it inside and out with salt and pepper. Sauté 2 tablespoons of chopped onion and ¼ cup of chopped celery in ¼ cup of butter until lightly browned. Mix together the sautéed vegetables, 2 cups of soft bread crumbs, 1 cup of crabmeat, 1 tablespoon of chopped parsley, salt and pepper. Fill into the fish and secure with skewers, or sew it together. Place the fish in a shallow baking dish, and put 2 cups of milk and a sliced onion in the pan. Pour ¼ cup of melted butter over the fish. Bake uncovered in a moderate oven at 350° for about 45 minutes. Garnish the top of the fish with thin slices of lemon dipped in chopped parsley. Serves 4 to 6.

CRUSTY BAKED HALIBUT

12 *paper-thin slices salt pork, about* 2½ *inches square*
1 *small onion, thinly sliced*
2 *pounds halibut steak,* 1½ *inches thick*
3 *tablespoons butter*
3 *tablespoons flour*
½ *cup buttered bread crumbs*
salt, pepper
lemon wedges

Arrange half the slices of salt pork and the sliced onion in the bottom of an ovenproof serving dish. Place the halibut in the dish and put the rest of the salt pork over it, with the slices slightly overlapping. Cream together 3 tablespoons of butter and 3 tablespoons of flour and spread over the salt pork. Season and sprinkle with ½ cup of buttered bread crumbs. Bake uncovered in a moderate oven at 350° for 30 to 40 minutes, until the top is nicely browned and the fish is tender. Serve in the baking dish, and garnish with lemon wedges. Serves 6.

BAKED HALIBUT CASSEROLE AU GRATIN

2 *pounds halibut*
salt
5 *tablespoons butter*
4 *tablespoons flour*
2 *cups milk*
1 *teaspoon salt*
¼ *teaspoon pepper*
2 *tablespoons lemon juice*
¾ *cup grated American cheese*
2 *tablespoons grated Parmesan cheese*

Wash and dry the halibut, and cut it into serving pieces. Place them on a well-greased flat pan, sprinkle with salt, and broil under a moderate flame for 12 to 15 minutes, with the fish 2 inches from the flame. Meanwhile melt 4 tablespoons of butter, and blend in 4 tablespoons of flour. Slowly pour on 2 cups of milk, and stir until the sauce comes to a boil. Season with 1 teaspoon of salt and ¼ teaspoon of pepper, and simmer for 5 minutes. When the fish is cooked, place it in a buttered 2-quart casserole, and brush with 2 tablespoons of lemon juice. Pour the sauce over the fish, and top with ¾ cup of grated American cheese and 2 tablespoons of grated Parmesan cheese, combined. Dot with 1 tablespoon of butter. Bake in a moderate oven at 350° for 20 to 25 minutes. If the top is not brown at the end of the cooking time, run the casserole under the broiler for a minute or two, watching carefully to make sure the cheese does not burn. Serves 6.

SALMON BAKED IN SOUR CREAM

1½ pounds salmon fillet
1½ teaspoons salt
1 cup thick sour cream
¼ teaspoon celery salt
1 tablespoon grated onion
dash cayenne
1 tablespoon white vinegar

Remove the skin from the salmon fillet and sprinkle with 1 teaspoon of salt. Place it in a shallow well-greased baking dish or casserole. Combine 1 cup of sour cream, ½ teaspoon of salt, ¼ teaspoon of celery salt, 1 tablespoon of grated onion, a dash of cayenne, and 1 tablespoon of white vinegar. Pour this mixture over the salmon. Bake in a moderate oven at 350° for 30 to 35 minutes. Serves 6.

CURRIED TUNA

¼ pound butter
1 large clove garlic
3 cloves
1 large stalk celery
1 medium-size onion
2 tablespoons curry powder
2 tablespoons lemon juice
1 cup chicken stock
1 can condensed mushroom soup
salt, pepper
about 6 green onions
1 to 2 tablespoons chopped parsley
2 cans tuna (7-ounce)
½ cup dry white wine

Melt the butter slowly in a large heavy saucepan or casserole. Add 1 whole clove of garlic and 3 cloves and cook very slowly while you finely chop a large stalk of celery and a medium-size onion. Put them in the pan, cover, and cook for 10 to 15 minutes, until soft but not brown. Remove the garlic and cloves.

Blend together 2 tablespoons of curry powder, 2 tablespoons of lemon juice, and 1 cup of chicken stock. Add the mushroom soup. Slowly stir into the vegetables and bring to a boil, still stirring. Season with salt and pepper. Simmer covered for about 30 minutes to cook the curry powder. Chop the green onions, using all of the white part and about half the green. Add with 1 to 2 tablespoons of chopped parsley and cook for at least 15 minutes in the sauce. Drain the oil from the tuna, mash 1 can quite finely with a fork, leave the second can in rather large pieces. Add with ½ cup of white wine and heat thoroughly. Serve immediately or keep hot as long as you like over a low fire. Serve with chutney and boiled rice, noodles, or Chinese noodles. Also with condiments if you wish (*see* page 166). Serves 5 or 6.

Note. It is almost impossible to be dogmatic about the amount of curry powder to use, since curry powders vary tremendously in strength, and people's tastes vary. Two tablespoons of a good curry powder will give this dish a decided curry flavor but not a "hot" one. Start with less if you are dubious, but don't add more at the last minute since curry always tastes raw unless well cooked.

FISH SAUCES

TARTAR SAUCE

This is the sauce most frequently served with fish and shellfish. The base is mayonnaise, and if it is a good homemade one, your sauce will be good. It is blended with two sorts of ingredients – something green and something tart. The green is usually chopped parsley or chives or both. The tart ingredients can be finely chopped sour pickles, chopped capers or olives, or lemon juice. A little scraped onion may also be added. Do not use all these, and be sure the chopped ingredients are finely chopped, since coarse pieces are unappetizing. The proportions are about 1 tablespoon of chopped parsley, 1 tablespoon of chopped pickles, capers, or olives, and 1 teaspoon each of lemon juice and onion to 1 cup of mayonnaise. Blend well, and let stand for at least an hour before serving.

CUCUMBER BUTTER

¼ *cup butter*
1 *small cucumber* or ½ *large cucumber*
1 *teaspoon minced parsley*
1 *teaspoon lemon juice*
salt

Cream the butter until it is soft. Peel the cucumber, chop it up very fine, drain, and add to the creamed butter. Also add 1 teaspoon minced parsley, 1 teaspoon lemon juice, and a little salt. Chill and use on hot fish.

CHIVE BUTTER

Substitute 1 to 2 tablespoons of finely chopped chives for the cucumber in the above recipe.

WATER CRESS BUTTER

Substitute 2 tablespoons of finely chopped water cress for the cucumber in the above recipe, and omit the teaspoon of minced parsley.

MAÎTRE D'HÔTEL BUTTER

(*See* page 123.)

MONTPELIER SAUCE

¼ *pound drawn butter*
1 *hard-cooked egg, finely chopped*
1 *to* 2 *tablespoons chopped parsley*
1 *teaspoon lemon juice*

Combine all the ingredients and serve hot with broiled or fried fish.

LOBSTER BUTTER

Substitute 1 to 2 tablespoons of finely chopped cooked lobster meat for the hard-cooked egg in the preceding recipe.

LOBSTER SAUCE

Thin lobster Newburg (*see* page 94) with light cream, and finely chop the lobster meat.

HOLLANDAISE SAUCE

(*See* page 202.)

BÉARNAISE SAUCE

(*See* page 123.)

LEMON FISH SAUCE

1 teaspoon vinegar
1 teaspoon lemon juice
½ cup melted butter
1 teaspoon Worcestershire sauce
salt, pepper

Combine all the ingredients, stir well, and serve hot with broiled or baked fish.

VELOUTÉ SAUCE

2 tablespoons butter
2 tablespoons flour
1 cup fish stock
½ cup light cream
salt, pepper

Melt 2 tablespoons of butter, blend in 2 tablespoons of flour, and, when that is smooth, slowly add 1 cup of fish stock. Bring to a boil, stirring constantly. Taste for seasoning; the fish stock may have sufficient seasoning for the sauce. Simmer for 5 minutes. Just before serving, add ½ cup of light cream and heat to the boiling point.

SAUCE AURORE

Add ½ cup of tomato purée to the above velouté sauce just before serving.

EGG SAUCE

Add 2 sliced hard-cooked eggs to the above velouté sauce.

EGG AND WINE SAUCE

Add ½ cup of dry white wine to the above egg sauce.

DILL SAUCE

- 2 *eggs*
- ¼ *cup olive oil*
- 1 *tablespoon minced dill*
- 1 *tablespoon lemon juice*
- ½ *cup cream*

Beat 2 eggs thoroughly with a rotary beater. Add ¼ cup of olive oil, a little at a time, continuing beating. Then add 1 tablespoon of minced dill, 1 tablespoon of lemon juice, and ½ cup of cream and stir until blended. Serve with any kind of fish, hot or cold.

FROZEN WHITE RELISH

- 1 *cup heavy cream, whipped*
- ½ *cup grated horse-radish*
- 1 *teaspoon lemon juice*
- ½ *teaspoon salt*
- 2 *tablespoons parsley, finely chopped*
- 1 *tablespoon pimento, finely chopped*

The cream should be whipped until it is stiff. Add the rest of the ingredients, blend thoroughly, and put into a tray in the refrigerator. Freeze for 2 to 3 hours, stirring once.

SHELLFISH

SAUTÉED LOBSTER, SHRIMP, OR CRAB

Sautéing these shellfish is a quick, easy way to make a delightful meal. Try it instead of the more commonplace method of deep-fat frying. The same technique is used for these three shellfish, except that the lobster meat and crab meat are cooked beforehand, but the shrimp is raw. Allow 1 pound of cooked lobster or crab meat for 4 servings, 1 pound of raw shrimp for 2 or 3 servings. Shell and devein the shrimp. Melt butter in a skillet, using 3 to 4 tablespoons for each pound of shellfish. Add the meat – diced lobster, picked crab, or cleaned shrimp (leave small ones whole and cut up large ones). Cook over a moderate fire until the meat is heated through. Stir lightly with a fork from time to time. When well heated, in about 5 minutes, season with salt, sprinkle with a little lemon juice and chopped parsley, and the dish is ready to serve. A little white wine, such as Chablis, may be added at the end of the cooking period.

FRIED SCALLOPS, OYSTERS, OR SHRIMP

This, of course, is the way most guests at any inn or restaurant choose to eat these shellfish. The raw shellfish are breaded (*see* page 73) or dipped in the following batter: Sift together ½ cup sifted flour, ¼ teaspoon baking powder, and 1 teaspoon salt. Combine ½ cup of milk and 1 beaten egg, and blend into the flour mixture. This is sufficient for 4 or 5 servings of shellfish. Cook in deep fat at 365° until golden brown. When shellfish is breaded, a little paprika is sometimes mixed with the crumbs for added color. Because scallops are wet, some chefs break an egg right in with them, sift flour over them, and mix thoroughly with their hands. Then they roll the scallops in cracker meal. The traditional accompaniment to this rather traditional dish is tartar sauce, and the shellfish is usually garnished with lemon wedges.

SHELLFISH SALAD

Use cooked shellfish for this salad. Clean and cut in small pieces; pick through crab meat carefully to remove all bits of shell, and flake the meat. Marinate in a small amount of French dressing for several hours, either at room temperature or in the refrigerator. Just before serving, drain and add 1 cup of finely chopped celery for every 1½ to 2 pounds of shellfish, chopped parsley, and enough mayonnaise to moisten well. The mayonnaise may be mixed half and half with sour cream if you wish.

FISHERMAN'S PLATTER

Mixed seafood platters are always a favorite, both at restaurants and at home. An attractive and succulent platter can be made by using half a boiled lobster, fried shrimp, fried scallops, and a clam fritter or a crab cake. Serve with lemon wedges, parsley, melted butter for the lobster, and tartar sauce.

LOBSTERS

Lobsters from the cold northern Atlantic waters are one of the true gastronomical delights. The size and actual shape of lobsters vary in different parts of the world. The lobsters served at the Treadway Inns are usually Maine lobsters, shipped alive in ice. They weigh from 1 to 2 pounds, have a solid piece of meat in the tail and good meat in the two large claws. The meat in the body and small claws surrounding it is negligible unless the lobster is a big one. Just below the head is a small sac which is the stomach, easily pulled out in one piece. Along the tail is a thin black intestinal vein which should be removed. That is all there is to cleaning a lobster. The green material in the body is the liver, or tomalley, which is delicious. In female lobsters there is sometimes a section of red roe, called the coral, which is also not only edible but delectable.

Whole lobsters are served boiled, steamed, or broiled. Lobster meat is used in some very fine dishes. A pound of meat makes about 2½ cups of diced meat. Handle cooked meat gently, stirring it as little as possible, so as not to toughen it.

SOME USES FOR COOKED MEAT

Lobster Salad. Use the basic seafood salad recipe on page 90.

Lobster Salad Roll. Fill a long buttered toasted roll, like the ones used for frankfurters, with lobster salad. Serve with potato chips, sliced tomatoes, and pickles if you wish.

Lobster Club Sandwich. A 3-decker sandwich with sliced lobster meat and mayonnaise in one deck and bacon, lettuce, and tomato in the other. Cut into 4 wedges.

Lobster Shortcake. Sandwich hot baking-powder-biscuit shortcakes with lobster Newburg (*see* page 94).

Lobster Sautéed with Chablis. *See* basic sautéed shellfish recipe on page 89.

BROILED OR BAKED LIVE LOBSTER

Baked lobster is really preferable to broiled because the intense heat of a broiler dries the meat too much. If you do wish to use a broiler, have the temperature only about 350° and place the lobster 3 to 4 inches from the flame.

Place a lobster of about 1¼ pounds on its back and, with a sharp knife or kitchen shears, cut down the lobster from head to tail but not through the end of the tail. Be careful not to cut through the bottom shell or you will lose juice. Pull out the stomach – a little sac right under the head – and the intestinal vein. Gently open the lobster with your hands. Cut off the large claws and crack them in several places. Put the lobster on a pie plate with a little water in the bottom. Place the claws over the end of the tail to hold it down; otherwise it will curl up when cooked. Brush well with melted butter and season. Cook in a hot oven at 400° for 10 minutes, then reduce the heat to 350° and cook another 10 to 15 minutes. Turn the claws once to cook and color evenly. The lobster may be put under the broiler for a few seconds to char the tail.

STUFFED BROILED LOBSTER

The Treadway Inns usually stuff broiled lobsters unless the guests request them not to. The lobster pie topping (*see* page 93) is generally used, and the amount in the recipe is enough to stuff two lobsters. Place it in the body cavity and down the tail, and dot with a little additional butter. A few chopped raw scallops and sautéed sliced mushrooms may be added to the stuffing.

Cheese Stuffing. Use two parts of Ritz crackers to one part of potato chips. Crush them well, and add paprika, grated Vermont cheese, a little powdered garlic, a generous dash of sherry, melted butter, and enough coffee cream to make a good wet mixture. Fill into the lobster and cover with the small claws to keep from burning while the lobster is broiled.

BOILED OR STEAMED LOBSTER

This is the easiest way to cook lobster, and a good one. There are definite schools of thought about whether boiling or steaming is better. Steamed lobster is not submerged in a quantity of water, so maybe more flavor is retained. I would suggest trying both to see which method you prefer.

Allow a 1¼ to 1½-pound live lobster for each serving.

BOILED LOBSTER

A really large saucepan is needed to cook lobsters. You need enough boiling water to cover the lobsters, with some head room or the water will boil over. Sea water is best, if available. Otherwise use heavily salted water—no other seasoning is needed. Pick the lobsters up by their backs, just below the head, and put them into the boiling water head first. They die instantly. Cook at a gentle boil, covered, 18 minutes for a 1¼-pound lobster, 20 minutes for a 1½-pound one. Drain.

To Serve Hot. When the lobster is cool enough to handle, split down the middle from end to end. Remove the stomach sac (below the head) and the intestinal vein, and crack the claws. Serve with melted butter, with a little added lemon juice or vinegar if you wish.

To Serve Cold. Let stand until cold before cutting open – less juice is lost then. Serve with mayonnaise or curry mayonnaise.

STEAMED LOBSTER

Bring not more than 1½ to 2 inches of salted water to a boil in a large saucepan. Put in the lobsters – the same amount of water is used regardless of the number of lobsters – and cook covered over a gentle fire for 20 minutes for lobsters up to 2 pounds, 25 minutes for large 2 pounds or more lobsters. Open just before serving, which should be as soon as they are cool enough to handle. The flavor of steamed lobster is excellent, the meat juicy and moist.

TREADWAY INN LOBSTER PIE

FILLING: LOBSTER NEWBURG

4 *tablespoons butter*
½ *cup sherry*
1 *pound lobster meat, coarsely chopped*
2 *tablespoons flour*
1½ *cups light cream*
salt, white pepper
2 *egg yolks*

TOPPING

4 *tablespoons butter*
½ *teaspoon paprika*
½ *cup cracker meal* or *finely crumbled stale bread crumbs*
2 *tablespoons crushed potato chips*
1 *tablespoon grated Parmesan cheese*
¼ *cup sherry*

Filling: Lobster Newburg. A true Newburg is thickened only with egg yolks, but it is a tricky sauce to make and to keep from curdling, so a little flour is added in this recipe to stabilize the sauce. Melt 2 tablespoons of butter in the top of a double boiler. Add ½ cup of sherry and 1 pound of lobster meat, coarsely chopped. Let stand over simmering water while you make the sauce. Melt 2 tablespoons of butter. Blend in 2 tablespoons of flour, pour on 1 cup of cream, and stir until the mixture comes to a boil. Season with salt and white pepper and simmer for 5 minutes to cook the flour. Beat 2 egg yolks with a fork. Beat in ½ cup of cream. Pour a little of the hot sauce over the yolks, stir, and blend the egg-cream mixture into the sauce. Stir until the sauce thickens, but do not let it boil. Add it to the lobster, blend lightly (stir lobster meat as little as possible to keep it from getting tough), and let stand over simmering water at least 10 minutes to blend the flavors. Remove from the fire. Put into 4 small deep individual casseroles or 1 larger one. Sprinkle with the following lobster pie topping. Bake for 15 to 20 minutes in a moderate oven at 350°, or brown immediately under the broiler. Serves 4.

Lobster Pie Topping. Melt 4 tablespoons of butter with ½ teaspoon of paprika and let stand over a very low fire for about 5 minutes to cook the paprika a little. Blend with ½ cup of cracker meal or finely crumbled stale white bread crumbs, 2 tablespoons of crushed potato chips, 1 tablespoon of grated Parmesan cheese, and ¼ cup of sherry. It will not need any salt; the potato chips will supply this.

Note. Newburg can be made with any shellfish. The ones most commonly used are crab and shrimp.

LOBSTER SAVANNAH

Sautéed diced green pepper and sliced mushrooms are added to the above recipe for lobster Newburg, and the Newburg is garnished with strips of pimento.

LOBSTER THERMIDOR

4 1-*pound live lobsters*
1 *cup salad oil*
3 *sliced shallots* or 1 *small onion*
1 *cup dry white wine*
6 *tablespoons butter*
4 *tablespoons flour*
½ *teaspoon dry mustard*
1 *cup rich milk*
1 *cup light cream*
salt, pepper
½ *pound sliced sautéed mushrooms*
about ½ cup grated Parmesan cheese

If the lobsters are cooked in oil, rather than boiled, there is less chance of the shell's breaking and the flavor will be better. Heat 1 cup of salad oil in a heavy saucepan. Add the lobsters and cook covered for 15 to 20 minutes. When the lobster is cool enough to handle, cut the shell along each side of the tail with kitchen shears or strong scissors. Remove the top shell and then the tail meat in one piece. Place one hand firmly over the head and with a quick twist of your other hand, pull out the whole body. You now have a clean empty shell. Dice all the meat from the tail and claws.

Meanwhile simmer 3 sliced shallots or 1 small onion in 1 cup of dry white wine until the wine is reduced to about ¼ cup. Melt 4 tablespoons of butter, and blend in 4 tablespoons of flour and ½ teaspoon of dry mustard. Pour on 1 cup of milk and 1 cup of cream and stir until the sauce comes to a boil. Season with salt and pepper and simmer for 5 minutes. Add the lobster meat, ½ pound of sliced sautéed mushrooms, the strained wine, and 1 tablespoon of grated Parmesan cheese. Cook until thoroughly heated. Divide evenly into the 4 shells, sprinkle lightly with the remaining cheese, and dot with 2 tablespoons of butter. Place in a baking dish and cook in a moderate oven at 375° about 15 to 20 minutes. Finish off under the broiler if the top is not lightly browned. Serves 4.

Note. Larger lobsters may be used, allowing half a lobster for each serving. It is quite an art to split the larger shells and keep them neat, and it is also tricky to stuff half a shell and keep the filling where it belongs. The sauce may be thickened with 2 tablespoons of flour and 2 egg yolks, rather than 4 tablespoons of flour.

CREAMED LOBSTER AND MUSHROOMS WITH NOODLES IN CASSEROLE

- 1 *pound mushrooms*
- *about* ½ *pound butter*
- *salt, white pepper*
- ¾ *pound medium noodles*
- 2 *pounds lobster meat*
- ½ *cup sweet sherry*
- 1 *teaspoon lemon juice*
- ¾ *cup flour*
- ½ *teaspoon paprika*
- 3 *cups creamy milk*
- 1 *cup heavy cream*
- *about* 12 *Ritz crackers*

Slice the mushroom caps and sauté them in ¼ pound of butter over a gentle fire until very lightly browned. Meanwhile bring about 6 quarts of water to a boil, salt it well, and cook the noodles for 10 minutes, stirring them occasionally with a long fork to keep them from sticking to the bottom of the pan. When done, rinse with warm water and drain them thoroughly in a colander. Also meanwhile cut the lobster meat into large dice, discarding the black intestinal vein. Put it into a double boiler with 2 tablespoons of butter, ½ cup of sherry, and 1 teaspoon of lemon juice to get thoroughly heated.

Make the following sauce: Drain the butter from the mushrooms and add enough additional butter to make ¾ cup. Blend in ¾ cup of flour and ½ teaspoon of paprika. Pour on 3 cups of milk, season with salt and white pepper, and stir until the sauce comes to a boil. Then add 1 cup of cream and bring to a boil again. Simmer for about 5 minutes. Then add the mushrooms and the lobster with all the juices. Stir only until blended, as too much stirring can toughen the lobster. Taste for seasoning.

Make 3 alternate layers of the noodles and lobster mixture in a buttered 4-quart casserole. Coarsely crush about 12 Ritz crackers, mix them with 3 tablespoons of melted butter, and sprinkle them over the top. Bake uncovered in a moderate oven at 350° for 20 to 30 minutes, until thoroughly heated and the top is lightly browned. Longer doesn't matter, just cover it so that the top won't get too brown. Serves 10 to 12.

LOBSTER MOUSSE

1 *tablespoon gelatin*
¼ *cup cold water*
¾ *cup celery, finely chopped*
1½ *cups cooked lobster meat*
3 *tablespoons lemon juice*
¾ *cup mayonnaise*
salt, paprika
⅓ *cup heavy cream*
water cress

Soak 1 tablespoon of gelatin in ¼ cup of cold water for about 5 minutes, then dissolve it over boiling water. Combine ¾ cup of finely chopped celery, 1½ cups of cooked lobster meat, 3 tablespoons of lemon juice, and ¾ cup of mayonnaise. Season to taste with salt and paprika. Add the gelatin. Whip ⅓ cup of heavy cream until it is stiff and fold it into the lobster mixture. Rinse a mold in cold water, and pour in the mousse while the mold is still wet. Chill for several hours in the refrigerator, until set. When ready to serve, unmold the mousse on a platter and garnish with water cress. Serves 6.

BOILED SHRIMP

Shrimp can be peeled before or after they are cooked. The yield is the same in either case, 1½ pounds of shrimp yielding ¾ pound of cooked, peeled, cleaned shrimp. The shells have flavor, so if the cooking water is to be used in a sauce, it is best to cook the shrimp with their shells on. Otherwise, since they are a little easier to shell uncooked, shell them first. To devein, run a sharp knife down the upper side of each shrimp. If you are cooking the shrimp already shelled, put them into the water after you have cut them and most or all of the vein will come out in the cooking water. Or you can rinse it out under the cold-water tap.

This vein often is white, not black—since it is an intestinal vein, I guess the reason is obvious—and then doesn't need removing.

The shrimp should be put into enough boiling water so that they can circulate freely. The best seasoning is the simplest, a little lemon juice or vinegar, plenty of salt, and a bit of bay leaf. After all, you want the flavor of the shrimp, not the flavor of numerous spices. Simmer for 5 to 10 minutes after the water has come to a boil again, depending on the size. The usual advice about fish applies to shrimp: don't overcook.

BAKED STUFFED SHRIMP

12 *jumbo shrimp*
½ *pound scallops*
4 *tablespoons butter*
¼ *teaspoon paprika*
2 *tablespoons crushed potato chips*
¼ *cup cracker meal*
3 *tablespoons grated Parmesan cheese*
1 *to* 2 *tablespoons Chablis, optional*
lemon wedges

With a sharp knife cut the shrimp from the underside through the meat but not through the shell. Wash and devein them. Put a toothpick under the meat but over the shell at both ends to keep the shrimp flat; otherwise they will curl when they are baked. Chop ½ pound of raw scallops and fill into the shrimp. Melt 4 tablespoons of butter in a small saucepan, add ¼ teaspoon of paprika, and cook over a very slow fire for 10 minutes or so to take the raw taste out of the paprika. Combine with 2 tablespoons of crushed potato chips, ¼ cup of cracker meal, and 3 tablespoons of grated Parmesan cheese. Cover the shrimp with this mixture and place them in a shallow baking dish with a little water in the bottom. Bake for about 20 minutes in a moderate over at 350°; 1 to 2 tablespoons of Chablis may be sprinkled over the shrimp if desired just before removing them from the oven. Serve with lemon wedges. Shrimp baked this way have a lovely fresh flavor and a nice moist texture. Serves 4.

BROILED SHRIMP

2 *pounds shrimp*
2 *teaspoons lemon juice*
1½ *teaspoons dry mustard*
2 *tablespoons milk*
½ *to* 1 *cup dry bread crumbs*
½ *cup melted butter*

Shell and devein the shrimp, which should be large ones. Put them into a mixing bowl and sprinkle with 2 teaspoons of lemon juice and 1½ teaspoons of dry mustard. Mix gently to distribute the seasonings and let stand about 30 minutes. Add 2 tablespoons of milk and again stir gently. Coat each shrimp with dry bread crumbs, using ½ to 1 cup of crumbs in all. Place the shrimp on a cookie sheet and pour ½ cup of melted butter over them. Broil about 5 minutes on each side, until golden brown, using a moderately hot fire – if the fire is very hot, there is a chance the shrimp will dry out. Serve on toast or bread that has been fried in butter. The shrimp may also be served with a velouté sauce if you wish (*see* page 87). Serves 5 or 6.

SHRIMP IN WHITE WINE SAUCE

3 *pounds shrimp*
2 *shallots* or 1 *small onion, sliced*
1 *cup chicken stock*
1 *cup dry white wine*
salt
4 *tablespoons butter*
5 *tablespoons flour*
1 *to* 2 *tablespoons chopped celery leaves*
1 *cup light cream*
parsley, optional

Shell and devein the raw shrimp. Put into a saucepan with 2 sliced shallots or a small sliced onion, 1 cup of chicken stock, 1 cup of white wine, and a little salt. Bring to a boil and simmer for 8 minutes. Drain, reserving the stock.

Melt 4 tablespoons of butter in the top of a double boiler over direct heat. Blend in 5 tablespoons of flour. Slowly add the strained stock and bring to a boil, stirring constantly. Add 1 to 2 tablespoons of chopped celery leaves and 1 cup of light cream and bring to a boil again. Add the shrimp, removing any of the sliced shallots or onion that have stuck to them. Taste for seasoning; you will probably need salt. Put over gently boiling water and leave until well heated or ready to serve; this can be kept waiting almost indefinitely. Serve in a rice ring or with wild rice, or garnished with steamed potato balls or noisette potatoes. A little chopped parsley may be sprinkled over the shrimp. Serves 6 to 8.

INDIVIDUAL SHRIMP CASSEROLE

- ½ *pound mushrooms, sliced*
- 1 *tablespoon minced onion*
- 4 *tablespoons butter*
- 1½ *cups canned tomatoes*
- ½ *cup light cream*
- 2 *tablespoons flour*
- 3 *pounds shrimp, cooked*
- 1 *tablespoon chopped parsley*
- ¼ *cup sherry*
- *dash angostura bitters*
- ¼ *teaspoon paprika*
- *dash Tabasco*
- *salt, pepper*
- ½ *cup dry bread crumbs*

Sauté the mushrooms, thinly sliced, and 1 tablespoon of minced onion in 2 tablespoons of butter until the onion is soft but not browned. Add 1½ cups of canned tomatoes and simmer for 15 minutes. Blend ½ cup of cream with 2 tablespoons of flour. Pour into the tomato mixture, stirring all the while. Add the shrimp, 1 tablespoon of chopped parsley, ¼ cup of sherry, a dash of angostura bitters, ¼ teaspoon of paprika, a dash of Tabasco, salt and pepper.

Simmer about 5 minutes. Put into individual casseroles (or 1 large casserole), sprinkle with bread crumbs, and dot with the remaining 2 tablespoons of butter. Bake in a moderate oven at 375° for about 15 minutes. Serves 6 to 8.

OPEN SHRIMP RAREBIT SANDWICH

- 24 *small raw shrimp*
- 5 *tablespoons butter*
- 1 *tablespoon minced green pepper*
- 1 *tablespoon minced onion*
- 3 *tablespoons flour*
- 3 *cups milk*
- 1½ *cups shredded Cheddar cheese*
- *salt, pepper*
- 12 *slices toast*

Shell and devein 24 small raw shrimp. Sauté them gently in 2 tablespoons of butter with 1 tablespoon of minced green pepper and 1 tablespoon of minced onion for about 5 minutes. Meanwhile melt 3 tablespoons of butter in a saucepan and blend in 3 tablespoons of flour. Pour on 3 cups of milk slowly, and stir until it reaches the boiling point. Simmer for 5 minutes, then add 1½ cups of shredded Cheddar cheese and stir until the cheese melts. Season with salt and pepper. For each serving, place 2 slices of toast on a plate and cover with the rarebit sauce. Arrange the shrimp and the butter sauce on top. Serves 6.

SHRIMP AND DEVILED EGG CASSEROLE

- 6 *hard-cooked eggs*
- 2 *tablespoons mayonnaise*
- 1 *teaspoon mustard*
- *salt*
- *pepper*
- 1 *pound cooked shelled shrimp*
- 3 *tablespoons butter*
- 3 *tablespoons flour*
- 1½ *cups milk*
- ½ *teaspoon salt*
- ¼ *cup sherry*
- ½ *cup grated Cheddar* or *Swiss cheese*

Cut 6 hard-cooked eggs in half lengthwise and remove the yolks. Sieve them, and mix them well with 2 tablespoons of mayonnaise, 1 teaspoon of mustard, salt and pepper. Fill this mixture into the whites, and place the stuffed eggs on the bottom of a large, shallow, greased baking dish. Cover with 1 pound of cooked shelled shrimp. Melt 3 tablespoons of butter, blend in 3 tablespoons of flour, add 1½ cups of milk, and stir until the sauce comes to a boil. Season with ½ teaspoon of salt and simmer for 5 minutes. Then add ¼ cup of sherry and ½ cup of grated Cheddar or Swiss cheese, and stir until the cheese is melted. Pour the sauce over the shrimp and eggs, and bake in a moderate oven at 350° for 20 to 30 minutes. If the top is not brown at the end of this time, run the casserole under the broiler for a minute or two. Serves 6.

SHRIMP CREOLE

- 2 *pounds shrimp*
- 3 *slices bacon, diced*
- 1 *large onion, finely chopped*
- 1 *clove garlic, crushed*
- ½ *green pepper, finely chopped*
- ¼ *teaspoon dried thyme*
- ½ *bay leaf*
- *salt, pepper*
- *dash Tabasco* or *chili powder*
- 3 *tablespoons flour*
- 1 *cup shrimp stock*
- 1 *large can tomatoes*
- 1 *teaspoon Worcestershire sauce*
- 2 *tablespoons chopped parsley*
- 2 *tablespoons minced celery*

The ingredients look complicated, but this is an easy dish to prepare and exceedingly good. Shell and devein the shrimp. Put the shells into a saucepan with water to cover, simmer for 15 to 20 minutes, then drain, reserving the stock. Meanwhile dice 3 slices of bacon and cook until crisp in a large, heavy, deep saucepan. Cook a large chopped onion and a clove of crushed garlic in the bacon fat slowly for 5 minutes. Add half a chopped green pepper and cook another 5 minutes. Put in the raw shrimp and cook until they turn pink, 5 minutes or so, stirring frequently. Season with ¼ teaspoon of thyme, ½ bay leaf, salt, pepper, and a dash of Tabasco or chili powder. Blend in 3 tablespoons of flour. Pour on 1 cup of the shrimp stock and stir until the mixture thickens and is smooth. Then stir in 1 large can of tomatoes, 1 teaspoon of Worcestershire sauce, 2 tablespoons of chopped parsley, and

2 tablespoons of minced celery. Simmer uncovered for 30 to 40 minutes. Serve with wild rice or white rice. Serves 6 to 8.

SHRIMP SALAD IN TOMATO ASPIC RINGS

Using 2 pounds of shrimp, make a shrimp salad according to the recipe given for shellfish salad (*see* page 90). Fill into individual tomato aspic rings or 1 large ring, and garnish with water cress and sliced hard-cooked eggs. Serves 6.

TOMATO ASPIC RINGS

3½ *cups tomato juice*
2 *stalks celery, sliced*
2 *slices onion*
small piece bay leaf
1 *slice lemon*
salt, pepper
pinch sugar
2 *tablespoons gelatin*

Bring 3 cups of tomato juice, 2 sliced celery stalks, 2 slices of onion, a small piece of bay leaf, and 1 slice of lemon slowly to a boil. Season with salt, pepper, and a pinch of sugar. Simmer for 15 minutes, then strain. Meanwhile soften 2 tablespoons of gelatin in ½ cup of cold tomato juice. Add to the hot tomato mixture and stir until dissolved. Pour into 6 individual ring molds (or a 1-quart mold) that have been rinsed in cold water, and put in the refrigerator until set and chilled.

CRAB PIE

1 *pound crab meat*
2 *tablespoons butter*
½ *cup Chablis* or *any dry white wine*
1 *recipe lobster pie topping* (see *page* 93)

Several of the Treadway Inns feature this dish. In the inns in the North, Alaskan king crab meat is often used. At the Royal Park Inn in Florida, they use the Indian River crabs which have two large edible claws, and the only other meat is a small piece on the back fin like the oysters on a chicken. Their flavor is delicious.

Pick 1 pound of crab meat over to remove any bits of shell. Put into a double boiler with 2 tablespoons of butter and ½ cup of Chablis or any dry white wine until thoroughly heated. Place in 4 individual casseroles or 1 large casserole. Sprinkle the topping over the crab meat. Bake in a moderate oven at 350° for about 20 minutes. If you wish, ¼ cup of sherry, ¼ cup of finely chopped sautéed mushrooms, and 1 tablespoon of chopped sautéed celery can be added to the topping. Serves 4.

FRIED SOFT-SHELL CRABS

Soft-shell crabs can be either deep-fat fried or sautéed. In either case, have the crabs cleaned and dressed, and wipe them with a damp cloth.

Deep-fat Fried. For 12 crabs, blend together 2 well-beaten eggs and 3 tablespoons of water. Combine 1 cup of bread crumbs and ½ cup of corn meal. Coat the crabs lightly with flour, dip them into the egg mixture, then into the crumbs. Heat peanut or corn oil in a deep pan until very hot, 375°. Fry the crabs two at a time for 3 to 4 minutes, until golden brown. Do not overfry. Drain and serve very hot with tartar sauce (*see* page 85). Serves 6.

Sautéed. Heat enough oil in a frying pan to cover the bottom about ½ inch deep. Dip the crabs into seasoned flour, and sauté them quickly until brown. Drain and serve immediately with lemon wedges. These can also be served à la meunière (*see* page 75) or amandine (*see* page 75).

CRAB MEAT AU GRATIN

1 *pound crab meat*
3 *tablespoons butter*
3 *tablespoons flour*
1 *cup chicken stock*
1½ *cups light cream* or *rich milk*
salt, paprika
½ *pound American cheese, grated*

Pick the crab meat carefully to remove all pieces of shell. Melt 3 tablespoons of butter in a medium-size saucepan. Blend in 3 tablespoons of flour. Add 1 cup of chicken stock and 1½ cups of light cream or rich milk and bring to a boil, stirring constantly. Season with salt and a little paprika and simmer for 5 minutes or so. Add the crab meat. Put into a buttered 1½ or 2-quart casserole or 6 individual casseroles. Sprinkle the cheese over the top. Bake in a moderate oven at 375°, uncovered, for about half an hour, or until the cheese is melted and the top lightly browned. If the service is to be delayed, lower the heat to 300° and cover. Serve in the casserole. Serves 5 or 6.

Note. Four chopped hard-boiled eggs can be substituted for half the crab meat.

CRAB MEAT CAKES

2 *slices white bread*
¼ *cup olive oil*
⅛ *teaspoon dry mustard*
½ *teaspoon salt*
½ *teaspoon Worcestershire sauce*
dash paprika
2 *eggs, separated*
1 *tablespoon chopped parsley*
1 *pound crab meat*
about 2 tablespoons butter

Take the crusts off the bread, put it in a mixing bowl, pour ¼ cup of olive oil over it, and let it stand for 1 hour. Then pull it apart lightly with two forks. Add ⅛ teaspoon of dry mustard, ½ teaspoon of salt, ½ teaspoon of Worcestershire sauce, a dash of paprika, and the yolks of 2 eggs, and blend lightly with a fork. Pick over the crab meat carefully to remove all bits of shell, and quickly mix into the bread mixture. Fold in the 2 egg whites, stiffly beaten. Form into cakes. Brown on both sides in a heavy skillet in a small amount of hot butter. This recipe has been handed down in one family for five generations, and the instructions say that if the cakes are carefully mixed, they will be light and fluffy – which is true. Makes about 12 cakes, or 6 servings. The cakes may be served with tartar sauce with a little grated horse-radish in it.

BAKED CRAB–STUFFED AVOCADOS

3 *avocados*
salt
2 *tablespoons butter*
2 *tablespoons flour*
1 *cup milk*
1 *cup cooked crab meat*
½ *cup grated Parmesan cheese*
paprika

This is a delicious luncheon or supper dish. Split 3 avocados but do not peel them. Sprinkle lightly with salt. Melt 2 tablespoons of butter in a saucepan and blend in 2 tablespoons of flour. Slowly pour on 1 cup of milk, and stir until it comes to a boil. Season and simmer for 5 minutes. Add 1 cup of crab meat. Blend well and put the mixture into the avocados, spreading it over the entire tops. Sprinkle with ½ cup of grated Parmesan cheese and a dash of paprika, and bake about 15 minutes in a moderate oven at 350°, until the tops are lightly browned. Serve at once. Serves 6.

AVOCADOS STUFFED WITH CRAB SALAD

Prepare 3 avocados, following the directions above. Allowing about 1½ pounds of crab meat for 6 servings, make crab salad (*see* basic shellfish salad recipe, page 90). Stuff the avocados with the salad and serve on beds of lettuce leaves, with quartered tomatoes, if desired.

SCALLOPED OYSTERS

1 *pint oysters*
6 *tablespoons butter*
4 *cups soft bread crumbs*
1 *tablespoon lemon juice*
salt, pepper

Drain the oysters. Grease a baking dish or casserole that can be used for serving. Mix together the melted butter, bread crumbs, lemon juice, about 1 teaspoon of salt, and some pepper. Put ⅓ of this mixture in the bottom of the dish, cover with half the oysters, repeat the layers, and top with the remaining bread crumbs. Bake about 20 minutes in a hot oven at 450°, just long enough to heat the ingredients thoroughly and brown the top a little. Serves 4.

FRIED OYSTERS

(*See* page 89.)

OYSTERS POULETTE

- 2 *dozen oysters*
- ½ *pound mushrooms, sliced*
- 2 *tablespoons butter*
- ¼ *teaspoon chopped shallot*
- ½ *teaspoon chopped parsley*
- 1 *cup heavy cream*
- 2 *egg yolks*
- ½ *tablespoon cream*
- *salt, pepper*
- *lemon juice*

Heat 2 dozen oysters in their own liquor until they reach the boiling point. Remove from the fire and let stand. Sauté ½ pound of sliced mushrooms in 2 tablespoons of butter. When they are soft but not brown, add ¼ teaspoon of chopped shallot, ½ teaspoon of chopped parsley, and 1 cup of heavy cream. Let it come to a boil, remove from the fire, and add 2 egg yolks that have been beaten lightly with ½ tablespoon of cream. Add the oyster liquor, season with salt, pepper, and a little lemon juice, and return to the fire. Stir until the sauce thickens. Just before serving, add the oysters and cook only until thoroughly heated. Serves 4.

SCALLOPS IN CASSEROLE

- 2 *pounds scallops*
- ¼ *pound butter*
- 1 *cup dry bread crumbs*
- 2 *tablespoons chopped parsley* or *chives*
- 1 *to* 2 *teaspoons lemon juice*
- *paprika, optional*

Either the small Cape scallops may be used or the larger sea scallops – if they are too big for an easy mouthful, cut them in half. Melt 1/4 pound of butter and lightly grease a 2-quart casserole or 6 individual casseroles. Have ready 1 cup of dry bread crumbs and 2 tablespoons of finely chopped parsley or chives. Make 3 layers of scallops, bread crumbs, parsley or chives, and melted butter. Sprinkle the scallops lightly with lemon juice each time, using 1 to 2 teaspoons in all. Dust the top lightly with paprika if you wish. Bake uncovered for 20 to 25 minutes in a moderate oven at 350°. Serves 6.

FRIED SCALLOPS

(*See* page 89.)

COQUILLES ST. JACQUES

- 1 1/2 *pounds scallops*
- 3 *shallots* or 1 *small onion, sliced*
- 1 1/2 *cups dry white wine*
- *salt*
- *about 7 tablespoons butter*
- 1/2 *pound mushrooms, thinly sliced*
- 1 *teaspoon lemon juice*
- 2 *tablespoons chopped parsley*
- 4 *tablespoons flour*
- 1/2 *cup heavy cream*
- *bread crumbs*

The scallops can be any size since they are going to be sliced anyway. Put them into a saucepan with 3 sliced shallots or 1 small sliced onion, 1 1/2 cups of dry white wine, and a little salt. Bring to a boil and simmer for 20 minutes. Drain, reserving the stock. When the scallops are cool enough to handle, slice them. Heat 2 tablespoons of butter in a small skillet. Put in 1/2 pound of thinly sliced mushrooms, 1 teaspoon of lemon juice, and 2 tablespoons of chopped parsley. Cook over a low fire for 5 minutes. In another pan melt 4 tablespoons of butter. Blend in 4 tablespoons of flour, and add 1 cup of the strained scallop stock. Stir until the mixture comes to a boil; it will be quite thick and should be. Then blend in 1/2 cup of heavy cream and all of the contents of the mushroom pan. Taste for seasoning and simmer for 2 to 3 minutes. Add the scallops and cook until well heated. Fill into buttered scallop shells. Sprinkle the tops lightly with bread crumbs and dot with small bits of butter. Put under the broiler until golden brown. This makes enough filling for 7 or 8 shells.

CLAMBAKE

The Toy Town Tavern in Winchendon, Mass., the Treadway Inn in Rochester, New York, and the Harbor View Hotel in Martha's Vineyard all have occasional clambakes during the summer. The clambake is prepared in the classic manner. In a shallow pit, a bed is made of stones topped with layers of hardwood logs until the pile is 4 feet high. The logs are lighted and burn for 4 hours. Then any unburned logs are raked away, leaving the rocks white with heat. Covering these with seaweed produces the steam necessary to bake the food – potatoes, clams, corn, lobsters, frankfurters, and sausages. A tarpaulin over all, 1¼ hours' gentle steaming, and the clambake is ready.

Home clambakes are not only feasible but simple. An outdoor wood or charcoal fire can be used, or the kitchen range. Clambakes make easy entertaining, since you can leave the whole thing alone while it cooks. A large enamel can for steamed clams is the best container since it has a spout on the bottom for pouring off the broth and a perforated upper section so that the food can actually steam. Have about 2 inches of boiling water in the bottom. If you have seaweed (or rockweed) available – in other words if you live near the sea, or if you can get some from your fishmonger – use it in layers between the food, but it isn't necessary. These cans make a clambake for 4 or 5 people, so judge amounts that way. First layer, potatoes, white or sweet, about the size of tennis balls, scrubbed but unpeeled. Put them in a cheesecloth bag for easy removal. Next layer, soft-shell clams, also in a bag. Next, corn; husk all but the last layer, pull off the silk, and wet the corn well. Then, 1-pound lobsters; and finally, individual packages each containing a frankfurter, a sausage, and 2 small parboiled onions; these can be wrapped in cheesecloth or aluminum foil punctured with a fork. Steam for 35 minutes. Then eat the mouth-watering food in courses, starting from the top.

Have beer and plenty of melted butter on hand. The inn has platters of sliced tomatoes and cucumbers, bread, salt, pepper, and vinegar. Fall to and count your blessings.

CLAM FRITTERS

1 *dozen littleneck clams, shucked*
⅞ *cup sifted flour*
½ *teaspoon baking powder*
¼ *teaspoon nutmeg*
1 *teaspoon salt*
1 *egg*
½ *cup milk*
1 *teaspoon grated onion*
1 *tablespoon salad oil*

Drain the clams, push out the black bellies if you wish, and chop the clams coarsely. Sift together into a mixing bowl ⅞ cup of flour, ½ teaspoon of baking powder, ¼ teaspoon of nutmeg, and 1 teaspoon of salt. Beat 1 egg well. Beat in ½ cup of milk, 1 teaspoon of grated onion, and 1 tablespoon of salad oil. Blend in the clams. Pour into the dry ingredients and stir quickly until smooth. Drop by spoonfuls into hot deep fat at 350° and cook until golden brown, turning once, about 3 minutes. Drain on absorbent paper. Serves 4.

SEAFOOD CASSEROLE

12 *oysters*
½ *pound mushrooms, sliced*
8 *tablespoons butter*
1 *pound cooked shrimp*
1 *cup cooked lobster meat, diced*
¼ *cup sherry*
4 *tablespoons flour*
2 *cups rich milk* or *light cream*
salt, pepper
¾ *cup fine bread crumbs*

Heat 12 oysters in their own liquor until the edges curl, then drain and chop them coarsely. Sauté ½ pound of sliced mushrooms gently in 2 tablespoons of butter for 10 minutes, until soft but not brown. Place the chopped oysters, 1 pound of cooked shrimp, and 1 cup of cooked diced lobster meat in the top of a double boiler with 1 tablespoon of butter and ¼ cup of sherry.

Heat over boiling water for 10 to 15 minutes. Meanwhile make the sauce. Melt 4 tablespoons of butter, blend in 4 tablespoons of flour, and, when it is smooth, slowly pour on 2 cups of milk or cream. Bring to a boil, stirring constantly. Season with salt and pepper and simmer for 5 minutes. Combine the mushrooms, the seafood mixture, and the sauce. Put into a greased casserole or baking dish that can be used for serving. Cover with 3/4 cup of bread crumbs and dot with 1 tablespoon of butter. Bake in a moderate oven at 375° for 20 to 30 minutes, until the top is brown. Serves 9 or 10.

DEVILED SEAFOOD CASSEROLE

11 *tablespoons butter*
2 *pounds haddock fillets*
9 *tablespoons flour*
2 1/2 *cups rich milk*
1 *tablespoon lemon juice*
1 *tablespoon Worcestershire sauce*
4 *tablespoons catsup*
1 *tablespoon horse-radish*
1 *teaspoon prepared mustard*
salt
4 *tablespoons chopped parsley*
1/4 *cup sherry*
1 *pound cooked diced lobster meat*
1 *cup bread crumbs*

Grease the top of a double boiler with 1 tablespoon of butter. Put in 2 pounds of haddock fillets and steam them for about 20 minutes over boiling water. Remove and, when cool enough to handle, separate into flakes. Melt 8 tablespoons of butter. Blend in 9 tablespoons of flour, pour on 2 1/2 cups of milk, and stir until the mixture comes to a boil. Season with 1 tablespoon of lemon juice, 1 tablespoon of Worcestershire sauce, 4 tablespoons of catsup, 1 tablespoon of horse-radish, 1 teaspoon of prepared mustard, salt, and 4 tablespoons of chopped parsley. Blend well and simmer for 10 to 15 minutes. Add 1/4 cup of sherry, the haddock flakes, and 1 pound of cooked diced lobster meat. Put into a large greased casserole, sprinkle with 1 cup of bread crumbs, dot with 2 tablespoons of butter, and bake for about 30 minutes in a moderately hot oven at 400°. Serve in the casserole. Serves 10 to 12.

WILLIAMS INN

Williamstown, Massachusetts

THE Treadways choose the locations of their inns judiciously, but certainly no place is lovelier than Williamstown, where Mr. L. G. Treadway first started his operation of inns in 1912. It is set on a 1200-foot plateau in the heart of the Berkshires with mountains surrounding but not crowding the town. The main street is a series of sweeping hills, with rows and rows of towering elms, wide lawns, handsome churches, and old colonial houses.

The Williams Inn is right on the college campus. It is a low, rambling white building. The center section is interesting architecturally with a Swiss-chalet motif in front – a gingerbread balcony. The inn was at one time a private school, then a Williams alumni house, which is what it was called when Mr. Treadway took over. A Mr. H. L. Bemis had a store in town and there was a sign upstairs reading THE WILLIAMS INN. Mr. Treadway bought the sign for $5 and this became the final name.

Mr. Treadway loves gardening and his son John, who is the innkeeper, is an ornithologist. The inn has the largest garden of any of the Treadway Inns, with three acres of beautiful lawns and gardens and many tall shade trees. The garden is also a bird sanctuary. It is bordered with trees and shrubs which have berries for the birds but which also flower. There are specially built birdhouses of various sizes and shapes, and even an electrically heated bird bath for the birds in the winter.

Williamstown was founded in 1749, but not with that name. Colonel Ephraim Williams, Jr., a man of wide cultural interests, made a will leaving most of his money to establish a free school in West Hoosac with the provision that the name be changed to Williamstown. He was killed in the French and Indian War and in 1791 the building called "West College" opened its doors and is still standing. In 1793 the name was changed to Williams College.

Today the college with its thousand or so students dominates or, maybe more accurately, is an integral part of the town. There are college buildings on both sides of the wide main street. The Thompson Memorial Chapel, which is the college chapel, is considered one of the best examples of Gothic architecture in America, and is famous for its magnificent stained-glass windows. Close to it but set apart on a spacious lawn is the Congregational Church, a typical colonial, spired, white-clapboard building, copied from a Christopher Wren design and considered a fine example of the Wren style.

A landmark of historical importance is the Haystack Monument, commemorating the origin of the American Foreign Mission Movement. Walk a few hundred yards down the road leading to the inn and you will see it. "On this site in the shelter of a haystack during a summer storm in 1806, five Williams College students dedicated their lives to the service of the Church around the globe." The Hopkins Observatory is the oldest college astronomical facility in the country. There are guided tours of the college every day but Sunday for anyone who wants to see its many points of interest.

Williamstown can fill almost any need — sports, cultural, or sight-seeing.

The inn is adjacent to eighteen college tennis courts which the guests are free to use. The Taconic Golf Club in town has a championship eighteen-hole golf course which is considered the finest in the state. For hikers there are twelve marked trails covering the mountains in every direction in the immediate vicinity of Williamstown. There are short trails for the uninitiated, long trails for the old hands. For instance, a two-hour walk will take you to the 1894-foot top of Pine Cobble Mountain, where you will get one of the finest panoramic views of the Williamstown Valley. The Williams Outing Club has a booklet describing these trails which can be obtained at the inn. You don't have to be ambitious, though, since any walk around Williamstown is lovely. The Outing Club also operates two ski tows at Sheep Hill, which is three minutes from the inn and is considered one of the finest open slopes in New England. It is eleven miles from Jiminy Peak and fourteen miles from Dutch Hill.

An increasingly important attraction in Williamstown is the new Sterling and Francine Clark Art Institute, which was built to house the pictures and other art treasures which the Clarks collected for about four decades. It is an imposing low, white, classically simple, marble museum, described in *Art News* as "very likely the best organized and most highly functional museum structure yet erected anywhere." It was opened in 1955, and although as this is written the exhibition is not complete, there are several rooms open with exhibits of beautiful old silver, Continental and English porcelain, furniture, books, sculpture, and paintings. Some thirty-two Renoirs are on exhibition and many, many other artists are represented.

Williamstown is only twenty-eight miles from Tanglewood, where the famous summer music festival is held. Right in town, at the Adams Memorial Theatre, one of the finest theater plants in the country, during the summer a different play is given each week by graduate students of the Yale School of Drama.

Williamstown is a paradise for sight-seers with a car. It joins the Mohawk Trail and the Taconic Trail, two roads with spectacularly beautiful mountain scenery. From the summit of the Taconic Trail, just a few miles from town, three states can be seen with views of the Green Mountains, the Berkshires, and the mountains along the Hudson. The sixty miles or so of the Mohawk Trail are all through magnificent country, and there are frequent stopping places to see the view; at one lookout tower you can see four states. There are many points of interest, such as the famous bridge of flowers at Shelburne Point, and there is a pamphlet at the desk at the inn describing them. The foliage starts turning in September and is at its height in early October.

The Williams Inn is open all year. Mr. Howard Wooster is the resident manager.

MEAT

Here are a few general instructions which may or may not be self-evident:

You will find wine as an ingredient in some of the recipes, and its use is sometimes misunderstood. It is used for its flavor, not for its alcoholic content, which vaporizes below the boiling point and completely disappears by the time the meat is done. You can smell it as it evaporates. Wine does add immeasurably to the ultimate flavor of many dishes. It is a subtle addition, however. Try tasting a beef Bourguignon when the sauce is first made and see how different it is when it is finished, all the taste of the wine now blended with the other flavors into a smooth, mellow sauce.

Stock is another common ingredient. Stock is a simple matter for the Treadway Inns' chefs, who cook dozens of chickens and have so many beef bones they always have huge stock pots on the range. If home cooks have a deep freeze, it is well worth while making up a quantity of beef stock (*see* beef vegetable soup on page 40) and chicken stock (*see* page 162). But a good beef extract, such as B–V, and hot water is an acceptable substitute, or a good canned chicken soup.

When browning meat, use a hot pan, a brisk heat, and not too much fat. If the pan is cold, the heat too low, and there is too much fat, there is a risk of stewing, and the meat may be gray rather than brown.

It is difficult to be precise about the amount of thickening in sauces and gravies because of certain variables. For example, if a sauce is made in a wide shallow pan, there will be more evaporation than in a narrow deep pan, and therefore the sauce will be thicker. Or if a dish which requires long cooking is thickened in the beginning, the sauce will get thinner as it cooks, since the meat will lose some of its juices. That is, if the meat is simmered as it should be and is not boiled; in rapid boiling, there is considerable evaporation, which would thicken the sauce.

Simmering means *simmering*, too, not boiling. To tenderize tough cuts of meat, a low, gentle heat is needed to soften the connective tissues. Boiling dissolves them, leaving only the muscle fibers, and the meat will be stringy and tasteless.

There is an expression used frequently in these recipes – "dissolve the glaze." When meat cooks, some of the valuable flavoring extracts are transferred from the meat to the pan in the form of a dark substance. This should not be wasted because of the concentration of flavor and color. Pouring a little water or stock in the pan and bringing it to a boil will dissolve this glaze, which should be added to any gravy or sauce. Incidentally, it will also help clean the pan.

Veal and pork should always be well done.

Roasts. Shallow roasting pans will permit a darker, crisper roast than a deep pan, and since that is the aim, they are therefore better. The only accurate way to time a roast is with a meat thermometer. The usual method of so many minutes per pound is, at best, only an approximation. The time varies according to the age of the roast, the thickness, the amount of bone, and other factors. Meat thermometers register the internal temperature and afford the only precise way of finding that out. They should be inserted in the thickest part of the roast, not touching any bone. A roast should stand at least 20 minutes before it is carved; then the juices have a chance to solidify a little, and it will be easier to carve the meat and more juices will stay in it.

BEEF

ROAST PRIME RIBS OF BEEF AU JUS

Roast beef, of course, is a standard restaurant dish, and the Treadway Inns' chefs have a way of cooking it that is useful for the home cook. Sometimes the prime ribs are left as a standing roast with the bone in; sometimes the roast is boned. It is easier to carve when boned, but the bones are full of flavor, which they give to the meat. Because it is a thick cut, the outside can be well seasoned with salt and pepper; the little juice the salt may draw will be just surface juice. Place in a shallow roasting pan fat side up. Insert a meat thermometer in the thickest part of the meat, not touching any bone. Do not add any water. Roast uncovered in a moderate oven at 325° to 350° until the thermometer registers 140° for a rare roast, 150° to 160° for medium rare. The inns cook it to 140° and then the inside is rare, the outside pieces are medium rare. As for the time, you really cannot figure it on a so-many-minutes-per-pound basis because large roasts do not take a proportionately longer time than a small one. My notes read: Toy Town Tavern, 7 ribs 3 hours; the Treadway Inn at Rochester, 20 to 22 pounds 2½ to 3 hours; the Publick House roasts a boned and rolled piece at least 18 inches long exactly 2 hours; and so on. Most of us at home cook only a 2 to 3-rib roast which seldom weighs more than 8 to 10 pounds, and that will also take about 2 to 2½ hours.

Here is the chefs' trick: The timing is planned so that the meat will be done an hour before it is to be served. It is removed from the oven and left standing in the roasting pan on top of the oven. The meat does not cook any more, but will stay warm. It also becomes firmer, so that it is easier to carve, and when it is cut, the juice stays in the meat and does not follow the knife into the pan or serving platter. For the *au jus* natural gravy, after the meat is removed, pour boiling water into the roasting pan, about 2 cups for each cup of pan juices, and bring to a boil. Season and skim off the fat. Roast beef can be served with horse-radish sauce (*see* page 128). Yorkshire pudding is a traditional accompaniment. It is the same batter as for popovers on page 279, but at home is baked in a baking pan in a hot oven in hot beef fat. At the Treadway Inns it is cooked as popovers so that it can be served in individual portions.

ROAST BEEF HASH

Substitute roast beef for corned beef in the corned beef hash recipe on page 132.

TENDERLOIN OF BEEF

This is the most expensive cut of beef and rightly named tenderloin since it is also the most tender cut. Although the price per pound may seem prohibitive, there is no bone and not much waste in the form of fat and tissue, and there are several ways of using it, so that buying a whole tenderloin can provide several excellent meals. It is a long narrow strip weighing 4 to 6 pounds. The center is the most uniform and thickest and is used for fillets mignons or is roasted. The ends have the same delicious meat, but they are tapered, so are generally used for sautéed slices, en brochette, or in beef Stroganoff. Recipes for all of these dishes follow.

ROAST TENDERLOIN OF BEEF

Use a whole tenderloin or the center 2 to 3 pounds. Tenderloin is lean, so add fat by having it completely surrounded by thin slices of beef suet tied at 1½-inch intervals. Season with salt and pepper. This is one roast which should be cooked at high heat and for a short time, since the only way to do justice to its flavor and texture is to have it rare. Place the tenderloin in a shallow roasting pan in a preheated oven at 450°. Use a meat thermometer and remove the meat when it registers 140°. Follow the general directions for roast beef in the preceding recipe. Like roast beef, you cannot reliably time it on a number-of-minutes-per-pound basis. It will probably be cooked in 45 to 60 minutes regardless of the weight.

This is a party dish and deserves party garnishes. Slice the beef and arrange the slices slightly overlapping down a hot platter. Garnish with such vegetables as sautéed mushroom caps, tiny stuffed tomatoes, asparagus tips with Hollandaise, and noisette potatoes. Bring 1 cup of beef stock and ½ cup of Madeira or red wine to a boil in the roasting pan and serve this gravy in a separate bowl. Allow about ½ pound per serving. This may also be served with Bordelaise sauce (*see* page 129).

SAUTÉED TENDERLOIN SLICES WITH MUSHROOMS IN CASSEROLE

Cut 8 to 12 slices about ½ inch thick from either end of a tenderloin of beef. Sauté them in hot butter in a heavy skillet, using a moderate fire. Brown both sides; since the meat is very tender, 2 to 3 minutes on each side is sufficient. In another pan sauté ½ pound of sliced mushrooms in 3 tablespoons of butter until lightly browned. Blend in 2 tablespoons of flour and cook slowly until the flour starts to brown. Add ¾ cup of Burgundy and ¾ cup of beef stock and stir until the mixture comes to a boil. Taste for seasoning and simmer for 5 to 10 minutes. Just before serving, add the beef slices with any pan juice and cook until they are heated through. A little kitchen bouquet may be added for color, if you wish. Serve in individual casseroles or 1 large casserole, garnished with toast points. Serves 4. The meat may also be cubed.

TENDERLOIN TIPS EN BROCHETTE

Cut tenderloin from either end into cubes a scant 1½ inches square. Dip into seasoned oil to which a little crushed garlic may be added. Place on skewers, allowing 3 or 4 pieces for each serving, and put a sautéed mushroom cap on the end. Place the skewers on a pie plate so that the meat is suspended. Broil until well browned all over, turning once. The total cooking time will be about 10 to 15 minutes, depending on the distance the meat is from the fire. Serve on a bed of rice pilaff to which a little fresh tomato may be added. At the Andover Inn in Andover, Mass., this dish is second in popularity to the boneless fried breast of chicken. There it is served with a mushroom sauce made with a little grated onion, chicken stock, and sherry, and thickened with a white roux.

BEEF STROGANOFF

- 2 *pounds fillet* or *tenderloin of beef*
- ½ *pound mushrooms, sliced*
- 4 *tablespoons butter*
- 4 *tablespoons flour*
- 2 *cups beef stock* or *water*
- 1 *teaspoon meat glaze*
- ½ *teaspoon dry mustard*
- *salt*
- 3 *to* 4 *tablespoons sour cream*
- 1 *small onion*

The beef should be cut into finger-size pieces, about 2 inches long and ½ inch thick, against the grain. Sauté the mushrooms in 2 tablespoons of butter, using a large heavy skillet. Remove the mushrooms. Put another tablespoon of butter in the pan, turn up the heat, and quickly brown the meat all over. Have only as many pieces in the pan at one time as will fit in a single layer without touching. When all the meat is browned, remove it from the pan. Melt the last tablespoon of butter in the skillet. Blend in 4 tablespoons of flour. Add 2 cups of stock or water and stir until it comes to a boil. Add 1 teaspoon of meat glaze, ½ teaspoon of dry mustard dissolved in 1 tablespoon of water, and salt. With a wire whisk blend in 3 to 4 tablespoons of sour cream, a little at a time, starting in the center of the sauce. Put back the beef and mushrooms with a small onion. Simmer until the meat is tender; fillet of beef needs only reheating; tenderloin, 10 to 15 minutes. Before serving, take out the onion. Serve in a casserole with wild rice, rice pilaff, or mashed potatoes. Serves 6.

Note. Round steak may be used. It is less expensive and not as tender as fillet or tenderloin, and therefore should simmer at least 20 to 30 minutes.

BROILED STEAK

Steak is just as popular at the Treadway Inns as it is everywhere else. Many people, no matter how adventuresome they are in their eating habits, often order and enjoy steak when they are dining out.

Since steak is a tender cut, it can be broiled quickly at a high heat. The steak should be cut at least an inch thick for broiling. Have it at room temperature. Preheat the broiling unit and pan. Grease the rack lightly so that the steak will not stick. Do not season the steak before starting to cook it, because salt tends to draw out juice. The steak may be brushed with garlic oil or butter. The steak should be placed about 3 inches from the flame. The broiling time varies with the thickness and age of the meat, the heat of the fire, and the distance from the fire. The minimum time would be about 8 to 10 minutes on each side for a rare 1½-inch steak, maybe up to 15 minutes for a very thick steak. For medium-rare steak the steak should be browned close to the flame and then either placed farther away from it, or the heat should be reduced.

Broil until the top side is well browned. This side can now be seasoned, since the heat has sealed the surface. Turn and brown the other side. Test for doneness by inserting a small sharp knife near the bone or in the center of a boneless steak. Serve with melted butter and, if you like, the pan juices. Or serve with one of the following sauces.

The French fried onions on page 235 are excellent with steak. So are sautéed mushroom caps.

STEAK SAUCES

GARLIC BUTTER

Coarsely chop 2 or 3 cloves of garlic. Put into a saucepan with ¼ pound of butter and heat very slowly until the butter is melted.

Keep over a slow fire for 5 to 10 minutes, then strain. Pour over broiled steak.

Or add 1 or 2 cloves of crushed garlic to ¼ pound of well-creamed butter and spread over broiled steak just before serving.

SOUR CREAM HORSE-RADISH SAUCE

Blend together 1 cup of sour cream, about ¼ cup of freshly grated horse-radish, and a little salt.

MAÎTRE D'HÔTEL BUTTER

Let ¼ pound of butter, preferably sweet butter, soften at room temperature for about ½ hour. Cream it thoroughly with 1 to 1½ tablespoons of finely chopped parsley and about ½ teaspoon of lemon juice. Form into a roll about the size of a silver dollar, cover with wax paper, and chill thoroughly in the refrigerator. To serve, cut into slices a scant ½ inch thick and place on hot steak. Also good with broiled fish.

BÉARNAISE SAUCE

½ *cup tarragon vinegar*
1 *minced shallot* or 1 *teaspoon grated onion*
sprig of parsley
3 or 4 *peppercorns*
little salt
3 *egg yolks*
¼ *pound butter*
chopped tarragon, chervil, or *parsley*

Into a small saucepan put ½ cup of tarragon vinegar, 1 minced shallot or 1 teaspoon of grated onion, a sprig of parsley, 3 or 4 peppercorns, and a little salt. Bring to a boil slowly and simmer until the liquid has reduced to ¼ cup. Put 3 egg yolks in a china or glass mixing bowl and place the bowl in a skillet with an inch of simmering water in the bottom. Strain the liquid slowly over the egg yolks, beating constantly with a wire whisk. Beat until the yolks thicken, then beat in ¼ pound of butter, a little at a time. As soon as all the butter is added, take the bowl out of the water. A little chopped tarragon, chervil, or parsley may be added before serving.

MUSHROOM SAUCE

(*See* page 170.)

BORDELAISE SAUCE

(*See* page 129.)

BRAISED SHORT RIBS JARDINIÈRE

3 *to* 4 *pounds short ribs*
2 *cups beef stock,* or 2 *cups hot water with* 1 *teaspoon beef extract*
salt, pepper, small bay leaf
3 *medium-size carrots*
12 *small white onions*
2 *tablespoons butter*
3 *medium-size potatoes*
1 *to* 2 *tablespoons chopped parsley*
3 *tablespoons flour*
½ *cup cold water*
1 *teaspoon tomato paste*

Short ribs can be delicious – juicy meat with bones to add flavor and some fat – but buy them from a good butcher so that you don't get too much fat. Cut into serving pieces. Place them in a large shallow baking pan and cook in a hot oven at 400° until well browned. Add 2 cups of beef stock or 2 cups of hot water with 1 teaspoon of beef extract and season with salt, pepper, and a small bay leaf. Cook covered at 350° for about 1½ hours. In the meantime halve 3 medium-size carrots crosswise and parboil them with 12 peeled small white onions in boiling salted water for 10 minutes. Drain and brown them lightly in 2 tablespoons of butter. Put them in with the meat after it has cooked an hour. Boil 3 potatoes until tender, cut into quarters, and put them in with the meat for 5 to 10 minutes. (The vegetables can be cooked entirely with the meat, but the risk is overcooking and a resultant loss of flavor and texture.) To serve, place the meat on a hot platter surrounded with the vegetables. Sprinkle with 1 or 2 tablespoons of chopped parsley. Thicken the pan juices with 3 tablespoons of flour blended with ½ cup of cold water. Bring to a boil, add 1 teaspoon of tomato paste, and taste for seasoning. Spoon the gravy over the meat, or serve it separately. Serves 4 to 6.

STEAK AND KIDNEY PIE

- 2 *pounds round steak, cubed*
- 6 *to 8 lamb kidneys*
- 3 *to 4 tablespoons beef suet*
- 3 *tablespoons flour*
- *about 2 cups beef stock*
- *salt, pepper*
- ¼ *teaspoon thyme*
- 1 *small onion*
- 1 *stalk celery*
- *recipe flaky pastry*

Cut the beef into 1-inch cubes. Quarter the kidneys and remove the white core. Melt 1 tablespoon of beef suet in a large skillet and quickly brown the meat all over. Have only a single layer in the pan at one time and add more fat as necessary. After the meat is browned, place it in a deep heavy saucepan. Sprinkle with 3 tablespoons of flour, shaking the pan to distribute it evenly. Pour on enough beef stock or water to just cover the meat. The glaze in the pan can be lifted with a little stock and added to the meat if the fat did not get burned. Season with salt, pepper, ¼ teaspoon of thyme, an onion, and a stalk of celery. Simmer covered until the meat is tender, about 1½ hours. Place the meat in a 2-quart casserole and strain the gravy over it. Put a custard cup, jelly glass, or pie bird in the center to hold up the crust. Brush the edge of the dish with slightly beaten egg to anchor the crust, and cover with flaky pastry rolled rather thickly. Slit the crust several places for steam to escape. Bake in a hot oven at 450° for 10 minutes, then at 350° until the crust is nicely browned, about 30 minutes longer. Serves 5 or 6.

BROWN BEEF STEW WITH VEGETABLES

2 *pounds round steak, cubed*
4 *tablespoons butter*
12 *small white onions*
3 or 4 *medium-size carrots*
4 *tablespoons flour*
2 *cups beef stock*, or 2 *cups water and* 1 *teaspoon beef extract*
1-*pound can tomatoes*
thyme or *oregano*
1 *cup cooked peas*
4 *medium-size potatoes, cubed* (*optional*)

Have the beef cut into 1-inch cubes and remove any excess fat. Brown quickly all over in 2 tablespoons of hot butter in a large skillet, a single layer at a time. When the beef is browned, put it into a deep casserole. Melt another 2 tablespoons of butter in the skillet. Brown 12 small onions, then 3 or 4 carrots cut into ½-inch slices. Add the vegetables to the beef. Sprinkle 4 tablespoons of flour over all.

Bring 2 cups of beef stock or water and 1 teaspoon of beef extract to a boil in the skillet to dissolve the glaze, and pour over the meat. Stir until the boiling point is reached. Season with salt and pepper, add the contents of a 1-pound can of tomatoes, and simmer covered until the meat is tender, about 1½ hours. Season with a little thyme or oregano after the first hour. Cook 1 cup of peas separately and sprinkle over the stew just before serving; 4 peeled, cubed potatoes can either be cooked with the stew for ½ hour, or cooked separately and added to the stew before serving. Serves 6 to 8.

BAKED BEEFSTEAK PIE, COUNTRY STYLE

Put the preceding beef stew into individual casseroles, cover with pie crust (*see* page 293), and bake in a hot oven at 425° until golden brown, about 20 minutes.

BEEF BOURGUIGNON

3 *pounds cubed beef*
1 *to* 2 *tablespoons salad oil*
½ *cup flour*
1 *pound mushrooms, sliced*
2 *to* 3 *tablespoons butter*
18 *to* 24 *baby white onions*
1½ *cups beef stock* or *water*
1½ *cups Burgundy*
salt, pepper
¼ *teaspoon dried thyme* or *oregano*
1 *to* 2 *tablespoons chopped parsley* or *chives*

Use 3 pounds of round or chuck steak cut into 1-inch squares. Heat a large heavy skillet. Put in 1 tablespoon of salad oil and quickly brown the beef on all sides. Have only as many pieces in the pan at one time as will fit in a single layer without touching, and add more oil if necessary. When the beef is browned, put it in a deep heavy casserole or saucepan. Sprinkle it with ½ cup of flour, moving the pieces around with a large spoon to distribute the flour evenly.

Sauté 1 pound of sliced mushrooms in 2 tablespoons of butter, using the same skillet the beef was browned in. Remove the mushrooms and brown 18 to 24 small onions, adding more butter if needed. Put the mushrooms and onions in with the beef. Bring 1½ cups of beef stock or water to a boil in the skillet to lift the glaze and pour it over the beef. Also pour on 1½ cups of Burgundy. Season with salt and pepper and ¼ teaspoon of dried thyme or oregano. Stir until it comes to a boil, then cover and simmer until the meat is tender, 1½ to 2 hours.

Beef Bourguignon can be kept waiting over a very low fire as long as you wish. It can also be made ahead of time and reheated, and taste better than ever. Usually served in a casserole, it can be the one it was cooked in. Just before serving, sprinkle with 1 to 2 tablespoons of chopped parsley or chives. Serves 6 to 8.

BOILED BEEF WITH HORSE-RADISH SAUCE

1 *piece cross ribs beef, about 3½ pounds*
3 *quarts water*
1 *to 2 pounds beef* or *veal bones*
2 *sliced carrots*
1 *medium-size onion, sliced*
1 *stalk celery, sliced*
1 *small bay leaf*
¼ *teaspoon dried thyme*
salt, pepper

Boiled beef should be started several hours before it is to be served, or, even better, the day before.

Put the beef into a large heavy saucepan with 3 quarts of cold water and 1 to 2 pounds of beef or veal bones. Bring slowly to a boil and simmer for 2 hours. Add 2 sliced carrots, 1 sliced onion, 1 sliced celery stalk, 1 small bay leaf, ¼ teaspoon of dried thyme, plenty of salt, and some pepper. Continue simmering for another hour.

Let the whole thing stand until cool, then place in the refrigerator for 1 to 2 hours or overnight. Remove all the fat which has solidified on the top of the stock. Bring slowly to a boil again and simmer 30 to 45 minutes. The beef is now ready to be served, cut into thin slices across the grain and with the following horse-radish sauce in a separate sauce boat. The excellent stock can be served as a soup, or used in any recipe calling for beef stock. In either case, strain it.

The beef serves 6 to 8, and you will have 2 to 3 quarts of bouillon.

CREAM HORSE-RADISH SAUCE

3-*ounce cream cheese*
1 *cup heavy cream*
2 *to* 3 *tablespoons horse-radish*
salt

Beat a 3-ounce cream cheese until well softened. Beat in 1 cup of heavy cream, a little at a time. When thick and smooth, blend in 2 to 3 tablespoons of well-drained horse-radish and season with salt.

LONDON BROIL

London broil is made with a relatively inexpensive cut of beef, the flank. Flank to be broiled must come from top-quality beef, otherwise it will be tough. Top beef properly cooked and carved is excellent. The flank is a long, wide, thin piece of meat which contracts when it cooks, so that it becomes shorter and thicker. Use a piece weighing 2 to 2½ pounds. The meat may be brushed with melted butter, although it has a certain amount of fat of its own. Place it in a greased broiler pan in a preheated broiler, about 1½ to 2 inches from the heat. Broil for 5 minutes on each side. Remove and place on a wooden board. Cut with a long sharp knife into very thin slices across the grain and at a 45° angle. This is important, or the meat will be tough. Allow 2 or 3 slices per serving. It may be served with a mushroom sauce (page 170), horse-radish sauce (page 128), any of the steak sauces (page 122), or with the following Bordelaise sauce.

BORDELAISE SAUCE

2 *shallots* or 1 *small white onion, finely chopped*
2 or 3 *medium-size mushrooms, finely chopped*
1 *tablespoon butter*
1 *cup red wine*
pinch of thyme
1 *cup brown sauce*
few slices cooked marrow
1 *teaspoon finely chopped parsley*

Finely chop 2 shallots or 1 small white onion and 2 or 3 medium-size mushrooms. Sauté in 1 tablespoon of butter until soft but not brown. Add 1 cup of red wine and a pinch of thyme and cook until it is reduced ½. Add 1 cup of brown sauce. (This can be made with 1 tablespoon of butter, 1 tablespoon of flour, and 1 cup of beef stock.) Taste for seasoning and simmer for about 10 minutes. Just before serving, add a few slices of cooked marrow and 1 teaspoon of finely chopped parsley.

Note. To get the marrow, ask your butcher for a marrow bone and simmer it in seasoned water for about 30 minutes.

BAKED MEAT LOAF

- ½ *cup finely chopped onion*
- 1 *green pepper, finely chopped*
- 2 *tablespoons butter* or *bacon fat*
- 3 *thin slices white bread*
- ½ *pint light cream*
- 1 *pound ground round beef*
- 1 *pound ground lean pork*
- 1 *egg*
- *salt, pepper*
- ¼ *teaspoon oregano*
- 1 *large can tomatoes*

Sauté the chopped onion and green pepper in 2 tablespoons of butter or bacon fat until soft but not brown. Meanwhile cut the crusts off 3 slices of bread and put them to soak in ½ pint (1 cup) of light cream in a large mixing bowl for about 5 minutes. Add the beef, pork, 1 egg, salt, pepper, ¼ teaspoon of oregano, the sautéed onion and pepper, and ¼ cup of the liquid from the canned tomatoes. Work with one hand until thoroughly blended. Place in a large buttered loaf pan, forming the meat so that there is a little space on each side. Pour the canned tomatoes and the rest of the juice over the top and sides. Bake uncovered in a moderate oven at 350° for 1 hour, basting several times. Serve hot or cold, with mushroom sauce (*see* page 170). Serves 6 to 8.

Note. Meat loaf may be baked in individual portions in greased muffin tins with 3-inch wells.

SWEDISH MEAT BALLS

- 1 *pound beef, ground twice,* or ¾ *pound beef and* ¼ *pound pork,* or ½ *pound beef and* ½ *pound veal*
- 3 *slices white bread*
- ½ *cup cream*
- ½ *cup finely chopped onions*
- 5 *tablespoons butter*
- 1 *egg*
- *salt, pepper*
- ½ *teaspoon nutmeg*
- 2 *tablespoons chopped parsley*
- 2 *tablespoons flour*
- 1 *cup beef stock,* or 1 *cup water with* 1 *teaspoon meat glaze*
- 1 *cup sweet* or *sour cream*

The meat should be put through a grinder at least twice. Trim the crusts off 3 slices of bread and soak them in ½ cup of cream about 5 minutes in a large mixing bowl. Meanwhile sauté ½ cup of chopped onions in 2 tablespoons of butter until soft but not brown. Put the meat into the mixing bowl with the onions, 1 egg, salt, pepper, a scant ½ teaspoon of nutmeg, and 1 tablespoon of chopped parsley. Work until thoroughly blended, preferably with your hand. Form into small round balls. Brown them rather slowly in about 2 tablespoons of butter, shaking the pan occasionally to brown them evenly. Have only a single layer in the pan at one time. When they are all browned, remove them from the pan and make the gravy. There should be at least 2 tablespoons of butter, so add more if needed. Blend in 2 tablespoons of flour. Pour on 1 cup of beef stock (or water with 1 teaspoon of meat glaze) and bring to a boil, stirring constantly. Slowly add 1 cup of sweet or thick sour cream. Taste for seasoning. Put back the meat balls and simmer for 15 to 20 minutes or until ready to use; waiting doesn't hurt this dish at all. Sprinkle with parsley before serving. Good with buttered noodles or mashed potatoes. Makes about 25 meat balls to serve 6 to 8 people.

NEW ENGLAND BOILED DINNER

This truly typical old New England dish goes back to the days when beef was corned (kept in salt brine) to preserve it, and the only vegetables families had in the late winter were the ones which could be stored in a root cellar, such as potatoes, carrots, parsnips, cabbages, and beets. Because some people do not like turnips and parsnips, they are not included in the following recipe, but add them by all means if you wish.

piece corned brisket of beef, 5 to 6 pounds
6 *peppercorns*
½ *pound salt pork*
6 *whole medium-size carrots*
1 *small green cabbage*
6 *medium-size potatoes*
6 *to* 10 *small beets*

Wash the meat well. Most meat really doesn't need washing, but in this case you want to wash off the brine the meat has been soaking in. Place it in a large heavy saucepan and add enough cold water to cover the meat well. Bring slowly to a boil and skim. Put in 6 peppercorns and let the meat simmer covered until tender, about 4 hours. After it has cooked for 2 hours, add the salt pork. After 3½ hours, add 6 whole scraped carrots and a cored and quartered cabbage, turn the heat up a little, and do not cover. The potatoes are best cooked separately, although they can be cooked with the meat. The beets should be cooked separately because they bleed.

To serve, cut the beef and salt pork in thin slices and arrange them on a hot serving dish, surrounded by the vegetables, well drained. The vegetables will serve 6 people, and there should be plenty of beef left for hash for another 4 to 6 servings. Serve with mustard, horse-radish, or the following horse-radish sauce.

HORSE-RADISH SAUCE

Melt 2 tablespoons of butter. Blend in 3 tablespoons of flour. Add 1¼ cups of the stock the beef was cooked in and stir until the mixture comes to a boil. Add 3 teaspoons of prepared horse-radish, ½ teaspoon of dry mustard, and season. Simmer until ready to serve, then add ½ cup of sweet or sour cream. Serves 6.

CORNED BEEF HASH

Either finely chop or put through the coarse blade of a meat chopper equal parts of trimmed cooked corned beef and boiled potatoes. There can be more beef than potatoes, but not the other way around. For each 2 cups of beef and 2 cups of potatoes grind a medium-size onion and, if you like, a raw carrot, half a green pepper, and 2 or 3 cooked beets (their color will make it a red-flannel hash). Season with salt and pepper and blend lightly with a fork. Heat 2 to 3 tablespoons of beef drippings or butter in a heavy skillet. Put the hash in the pan and smooth it with a spatula. Pour about ½ cup of cream over it all. Cook covered slowly, without stirring, until a crust is formed on the bottom, about 20 minutes. If the hash is thin, it can be folded over and served. A thick hash should be turned and the other side browned, or the top can be browned under the broiler.

For individual service the hash can be cooked in small metal serving dishes in a reasonably hot oven at 425°.

The hash may be served topped with a poached egg; also with horse-radish sauce made by adding 1 to 2 tablespoons of grated horse-radish to 1 cup of salted whipped cream.

BAKED CORNED BEEF

Cut cooked corned beef in ½-inch-thick slices. Dip in egg wash and coat with crushed corn flakes. Put in shirred-egg dishes, sprinkle with brown sugar, and top with a pineapple ring for each serving. Bake in a hot oven at 425° until the sugar is melted and glazed, about 10 to 15 minutes.

VEAL

ROAST MILK-FED VEAL

1 *piece rump of veal, about 4 pounds*
1 *clove garlic*
2 *teaspoons salt*
½ *teaspoon pepper*
1 *teaspoon oregano*
2 *tablespoons chopped parsley*
½ *cup melted butter*
1 *cup stock,* or ½ *cup stock and* ½ *cup dry white wine*
2 *tablespoons flour*

The meat can be boned or not, as you wish, or part of the bone can be removed; a little gives it a better flavor. Rub it all over with a cut clove of garlic, then with 2 teaspoons of salt mixed with ½ teaspoon of pepper. Mix together 1 teaspoon of oregano and 2 tablespoons of chopped parsley and sprinkle over the top of the meat. Place in a shallow roasting pan and pour over ¼ cup of melted butter. Roast for about 35 minutes to the pound in a moderate oven at 325°, or until a meat thermometer registers 170°. Baste every 15 to 20 minutes, first with the remaining ½ cup of melted butter and then with 1 cup of stock, or ½ cup of stock and ½ cup of dry white wine. Remove and let stand for about 20 minutes in a warm place before serving or carving. Thicken the pan juices with 2 tablespoons of flour blended with 4 tablespoons of cold water and serve in a separate sauce bowl. Serves 8 to 10.

STUFFED SHOULDER OF VEAL

shoulder of veal, about 4 pounds
2 *slices white bread*
½ *cup milk*
½ *pound ground pork*
1 *teaspoon salt*
½ *teaspoon pepper*
⅛ *teaspoon cinnamon*
⅛ *teaspoon thyme*
2 *tablespoons chopped parsley*
2 *eggs*
2 *tablespoons butter*
2 *tablespoons olive oil*
½ *large onion*
4 *slices bacon*
½ *cup dry white wine*

Have the veal boned so that there is a large pocket in the center. Soak 2 slices of bread in ½ cup of milk for about 5 minutes, then squeeze out. In a large mixing bowl blend together the bread, pork, 1 teaspoon of salt, ½ teaspoon of pepper, ⅛ teaspoon of cinnamon, ⅛ teaspoon of thyme, and 2 tablespoons of chopped parsley. Beat 2 eggs well, add to the stuffing, and mix well. Fill into the veal and secure the end with small skewers.

Heat 2 tablespoons of butter and 2 tablespoons of olive oil in a heavy deep saucepan. Season the veal and brown slowly on both sides with half an onion in the pan for flavor. When browned, put 4 slices of bacon over the top, cover, and simmer for 1 hour. Add ½ cup of wine and cook another 1 to 1½ hours — veal needs long, slow cooking, especially when it is stuffed. To serve, discard the bacon and cut the veal in thin slices across the grain. The pan juices should be served separately, either as they are or slightly thickened. Serves 8 to 10.

SAUTÉED VEAL CUTLETS WITH MUSHROOM SAUCE

6 *thin individual cutlets, cut from the leg*
egg wash
seasoned flour
butter, butter and oil, or *chicken fat*

MUSHROOM SAUCE

½ *pound mushrooms*
3 *tablespoons chicken fat* or *butter*
2 *cups beef stock*
2 *tablespoons flour*
½ *teaspoon tomato paste*
1 *to* 2 *tablespoons dry sherry*

The Treadway Inns use individual cutlets so that they can be cooked separately to order. Dip them first in egg wash, then in seasoned flour. Sauté them gently in a generous amount of butter, a mixture of butter and oil, or chicken fat. Turn once to brown both sides and cook about 15 to 20 minutes. Meanwhile prepare the sauce. Slice the caps of ½ pound of mushrooms and sauté them in 3 tablespoons of chicken fat or butter. Put the stems in 2 cups of beef stock and simmer for 10 minutes or so. Blend 2 tablespoons of flour and ½ teaspoon of tomato paste into the mushroom caps. Pour on the strained stock and stir until the sauce comes to a boil. Taste for seasoning and simmer for at least 5 minutes. Before serving, add 1 to 2 tablespoons of sherry. A little kitchen bouquet may be added, if you wish, for color. Serves 6.

FRICASSEE OF VEAL

2 *pounds leg of veal*
12 *small white onions*
1 *medium-size carrot, sliced*
1 *stalk celery, sliced*
salt, pepper
4 *tablespoons butter*
4 *tablespoons flour*
2 *cups veal stock*
1 *egg yolk*
1 *tablespoon lemon juice*
½ *cup cream*
little chopped parsley, optional

Trim any fat off the meat and cut it into small cubes, a scant 3/4 inch. Peel the onions; they should be baby ones. Put the veal, onions, a sliced carrot, and a sliced celery stalk into a saucepan with cold water to cover. Bring slowly to a boil. Skim. Season with salt and pepper and simmer covered for about an hour; longer won't do any harm.

Melt 4 tablespoons of butter. Blend in 4 tablespoons of flour. Slowly pour on 2 cups of strained veal stock and bring to a boil, stirring constantly. Beat 1 egg yolk and 1 tablespoon of lemon juice with a fork. Blend in 1/2 cup of cream. Add the hot sauce to the egg yolk-cream mixture, stirring all the while. Cook until the sauce thickens, but do not let it boil. Add the veal and onions, drained of any stock, and heat thoroughly. Serve immediately or keep hot over simmering water. A little chopped parsley may be sprinkled over the top for color. Serve with boiled rice or a rice pilaff. Serves 5 or 6.

VEAL PARMESAN

- 4 *pieces of leg of veal*
- *seasoned flour*
- *oregano*
- 1 *egg*
- 1/4 *cup light cream*
- *about 1/2 cup dry bread crumbs*
- *about 1/2 cup grated Parmesan cheese*
- 2 *tablespoons chopped parsley*
- 2 *tablespoons butter*
- 1 *small clove garlic, crushed*
- 1 *cup tomato sauce*
- 1/4 *cup dry white wine*
- 4 *slices Mozzarella cheese*

The veal should be cut into pieces large enough for individual servings, 3 to 4 inches square and about 1/2 inch thick. Season flour with salt, pepper, and oregano. Beat 1 egg until blended, then beat in 1/4 cup of cream. Combine 1/2 cup of bread crumbs, 1/2 cup of grated Parmesan cheese, and 2 tablespoons of chopped parsley. Dust the pieces of veal lightly with flour, dip in the egg wash, then coat with the cheese mixture. Brown slowly on both sides in a large heavy skillet in 2 tablespoons of hot butter with a crushed clove of garlic. When browned, pour 1 cup of tomato sauce and ¼ cup of dry white wine around the veal (not over the top), and put a slice of Mozzarella cheese on top of each piece. Bake in a slow oven at 325° until the veal is tender and the cheese lightly browned, 30 to 40 minutes. Serves 4.

BRAISED VEAL CHOPS IN CASSEROLE, COUNTRY STYLE

- 6 *large veal chops*
- 2 *tablespoons butter*
- 1 *cup water* or *dry white wine*
- 1 *medium-size yellow onion, sliced*
- 2 *medium-size carrots, sliced*
- 2 *medium-size potatoes, sliced*
- 2 *cups canned* or *fresh tomatoes*
- *salt*
- *pepper*
- 1 *teaspoon potato flour, optional*

Brown the chops slowly on both sides in 2 tablespoons of butter in a heavy skillet, which will take 15 to 20 minutes. Put them into a large casserole or 6 individual ones. Lift the glaze in the skillet with 1 cup of water or white wine and pour it over the chops. Cover them with the sliced onion, carrots, and potatoes, then with the tomatoes. Season with salt and pepper. Simmer covered for 30 to 40 minutes. By then both the chops and vegetables should be cooked; however, longer will do no harm, since it is almost impossible to overcook veal as long as it is kept moist. The pan juices may be thickened with 1 teaspoon of potato flour dissolved in ¼ cup of water. Serve in the casserole. Serves 6.

SCALLOPINI WITH MARSALA

- 12 *scallopini*
- *scant ½ cup seasoned flour*
- 4 *to* 5 *tablespoons butter*
- ¼ *to* ½ *cup Marsala* or *sherry*

Scallopini are thin slices of veal cut from the choicest part of the leg. Have the butcher prepare the scallopini, or, better still, do it yourself. Buy a slice of the leg about 1½ inches thick. One side has a large oval section that is free of tissue, and that is the part to use. The rest can be used for fricassee of veal (*see* page 135) or curried veal. Use a large well-sharpened knife and cut crosswise in slices about ¼ inch thick. Cut each slice in half. Put the slices between pieces of wax paper and pound them out to make them thinner and help tenderize the meat.

Dust each slice lightly with seasoned flour. Melt 2 tablespoons of butter in a large hot skillet and brown the slices about 3 minutes on each side. Brown only a single layer at a time, adding more butter as needed. When all the slices are browned, put them back in the pan with ¼ to ½ cup of Marsala or sherry and cook another 3 to 4 minutes until well heated. Serve overlapping on a hot platter with any pan juices. Serves 4.

VEAL CUTLET WITH SOUR CREAM SAUCE

1 *veal cutlet, about 1½ pounds*
3 *tablespoons flour*
salt, pepper
4 *tablespoons butter*
2 *medium-size yellow onions, sliced*
1 *teaspoon paprika*
1 *cup sour cream*
1 *cup tomato juice*

Coat both sides of the veal with seasoned flour. Melt 2 tablespoons of butter in a large skillet. Slowly cook the onions until they are light brown. Remove the onions. Melt another 2 tablespoons of butter in the same pan and cook the veal until it is golden brown on both sides, using a moderate fire. When the veal is browned, put the onions on top of the meat and sprinkle them both with 1 teaspoon of paprika. Blend 1 cup of sour cream with 1 cup of tomato juice and pour into the pan. Cover and simmer about 1 hour. Lift up the meat every 15 minutes or so to let the gravy run under it. Serve on a hot platter with the pan gravy poured over the meat. Serves 6.

STUFFED VEAL BIRDS

- 8 *thin slices leg of veal*
- *salt, pepper*
- 1 *small tin liver pâté* or ¼ *pound liverwurst*
- 2 *tablespoons finely chopped celery*
- 4 *tablespoons butter*
- 1 *tablespoon flour*
- 1 *cup veal* or *chicken stock*
- ¼ *cup dry white wine*
- 1 *tablespoon chopped parsley*

The veal should be cut very thin, as for scallopini. Season lightly with salt and pepper. Blend together the liver pâté or sieved liverwurst and 2 tablespoons of finely chopped celery. Spread over the center of each piece of veal. Roll up and tie each end with string. Melt 3 tablespoons of butter in a large skillet. When it starts to turn color, brown the veal birds all over, using a moderate fire. Remove the birds. Melt another tablespoon of butter in the skillet. Blend in 1 tablespoon of flour. Pour on 1 cup of stock and ¼ cup of dry white wine and stir until the sauce comes to a boil. Put back the birds and simmer covered for 20 to 30 minutes. Cut off the strings before serving and sprinkle with 1 tablespoon of chopped parsley. Serves 4.

SWEETBREADS

Sweetbreads have a delicious delicate flavor which is good by itself and which blends well with other mild-flavored foods. Sweetbreads are soft in texture, so are always given some preliminary cooking to stiffen them. Soak them in cold water. Bring enough fresh water to a boil to well cover the sweetbreads and add 1 teaspoon of salt and 1 tablespoon of lemon juice or vinegar for each quart of water; the acid will keep them white. Simmer for 15 minutes, then drain and place them right into a bowl of ice water. When cool, remove the outside membrane, tubes, and sinews. They are now thoroughly cooked and any additional cooking is just to improve the flavor. Keep in the refrigerator until ready to use.

Sautéed sweetbreads is a popular way of cooking them. Leave small ones whole, and cut large ones in half lengthwise. Dust lightly with seasoned flour. Sauté in butter, or half butter and oil, until golden brown on both sides, using a gentle fire. They are nice served on a round of fried bread topped with a thin slice of cooked ham, a sweetbread, and a sautéed mushroom cap. Serve with mushroom sauce (*see* page 170) or Bordelaise sauce (*see* page 129).

CREAMED SWEETBREADS, HAM AND ALMONDS

1 *pair sweetbreads*
4 *tablespoons butter*
4 *tablespoons flour*
1 *cup chicken stock*
1 *cup light cream*
2 *tablespoons sherry*
½ *cup diced cooked ham*
⅓ *cup slivered browned almonds*
4 *to* 6 *patty shells*

The sweetbreads should have the preliminary cooking described in the preceding section. When cool, cut them in cubes. Melt 4 tablespoons of butter. Blend in 4 tablespoons of flour. Add 1 cup of chicken stock and 1 cup of light cream and stir until the sauce comes to a boil. Add 2 tablespoons of sherry and taste for seasoning. Then add the cubed sweetbreads and ½ cup of diced ham. Let simmer until ready to serve, in a double boiler if it is going to be more than 10 minutes or so. Add ⅓ cup of slivered browned almonds just before serving. Serve in hot patty shells. Serves 4 to 6.

CREAMED VEAL KIDNEYS

2 *veal kidneys*
4 *tablespoons olive oil*
1 *tablespoon finely chopped onion*
1 *tablespoon brandy*
½ *cup heavy cream*
salt, pepper
½ *pound mushrooms, thinly sliced*
1 *tablespoon lemon juice*

Wash and dry the kidneys and cut them into 1-inch cubes, removing the center fatty part. Heat 4 tablespoons of olive oil in a heavy skillet or casserole and slowly cook 1 tablespoon of chopped onion until golden brown. Turn up the heat and quickly brown the diced kidneys. Remove them from the pan with a slotted spoon. Lift the glaze in the pan with 1 tablespoon of brandy, and add ½ cup of heavy cream. Season with salt and pepper and cook slowly for 5 minutes or so to reduce the sauce, stirring occasionally. Add the sliced mushrooms and cook for 5 minutes. Put back the kidneys with any juice, and 1 tablespoon of lemon juice, and cook just until the kidneys are thoroughly heated. Serves 3 or 4.

LAMB

ROAST LEG OF LAMB

Lamb is easy to roast. For a plain roast, first season the meat with salt and pepper. Place it fat side up in a shallow roasting pan. Cook it uncovered in a moderate oven at 350°. Place a meat thermometer in the thickest part, not touching any bone. No additional liquid or basting is necessary. In America lamb is usually cooked well done, which is 180° on the thermometer, or about 25 to 30 minutes to the pound. However, many people find the flavor better and the meat juicier if the lamb still shows a little pink, which it will at 165°.

For a more flavorful lamb, cook it with garlic and red wine. Cut a clove of garlic in half, score it, and rub it over the whole lamb. Then cut maybe 2 more large cloves in 3 or 4 pieces, insert 2 pieces around the end bone, and the rest in little slits at strategic points. If you put toothpicks in them, you will be able to remove the garlic before the lamb is served; otherwise it is hard to find. Rub the lamb with 1 tablespoon of softened butter and season with salt and pepper. When the lamb has cooked for 45 minutes, pour ½ cup of red wine in the roasting pan. Then baste it every 15 minutes or so, using an additional ½ cup of wine, ¼ cup at a time, and then the pan juices. For the gravy, bring 1 cup of water to a boil with the pan juices to dissolve the glaze. Spoon a little over the meat and serve the rest in a gravy bowl.

BONED STUFFED LEG OF LAMB

1 *leg of lamb, 7 to 8 pounds*
1 *tablespoon tomato paste*
1 *cup dry white wine*

STUFFING

2 *slices white bread*
½ *cup light cream*
½ *pound mushrooms*
1 *small onion*
2 *tablespoons butter*
½ *pound ground veal*
¼ *pound sausage meat*
1 *egg*
1 *teaspoon grated lemon rind*
¼ *teaspoon ground nutmeg*
salt, pepper

Leave the chop end of the lamb intact and remove the leg bone. A good butcher or anyone with a sharp knife can do it. Slit below the chops across the direction of the bone, and work from both ends, leaving the sides uncut and a pocket the length of the leg.

Stuffing. Soak 2 slices of white bread in ½ cup of light cream in a large mixing bowl. Chop the mushrooms and a small onion and sauté them in 2 tablespoons of butter until golden brown. Add to the bread with the ground veal and sausage, 1 egg, 1 teaspoon of grated lemon rind, ¼ teaspoon of ground nutmeg, salt and pepper. Blend thoroughly. Fill into the pocket and close both ends with small skewers.

Place the lamb in a roasting pan. Blend 1 tablespoon of tomato paste with 1 cup of dry white wine and pour around the lamb. Bake in a moderate oven at 350° for about 45 minutes to the pound, or until a meat thermometer registers 185°; boned meat takes longer to cook than meat with the bone in, and stuffing also lengthens the cooking time. Baste several times with the pan juices. Remove the meat and let stand for 10 to 15 minutes before carving. Add 1 cup of water to the pan juices, bring to a boil, and serve as gravy. Serves at least 8 to 10.

LAMB CHOPS WITH WHITE WINE IN CASSEROLE

- 4 *shoulder lamb chops*
- 3 *tablespoons butter*
- 1 *medium-size yellow onion*
- ¼ *pound mushrooms*
- 2 *tablespoons flour*
- ½ *teaspoon tomato paste*
- ½ *cup dry white wine*
- ¾ *cup chicken stock* or *water*
- *salt, pepper*

Heat 1 tablespoon of butter in a heavy skillet and when it starts to turn color, quickly brown the chops on both sides. Thinly slice the onion and cut the mushrooms into rather thick slices. Sauté them in 2 tablespoons of butter in a heavy casserole until the onions are golden brown. Blend in 2 tablespoons of flour and ½ teaspoon of tomato paste. Pour on ½ cup of wine and ¾ cup of stock or water and stir until the mixture comes to a boil. Season with salt and pepper. Put the browned chops in the sauce, cover, and simmer until they are tender, about 40 minutes, or until ready to serve. Serve in the casserole. Serves 4

LAMB STEW WITH PARSLEY DUMPLINGS

- 2½ *pounds shoulder lamb, cut in ¾-inch cubes*
- 3 *tablespoons seasoned flour*
- 5 *tablespoons butter*
- 2 *medium-size yellow onions, sliced*
- 1 *can tomatoes* (1 *lb.* 4 *oz.*)
- 4 *large carrots, diced*
- 12 *whole baby onions*
- 4 *large potatoes, cut into balls*
- *salt, pepper, thyme*
- 1 *pound peas*

Coat the meat with the seasoned flour. Melt 3 tablespoons of butter in a large skillet and sauté the 2 sliced onions until soft and yellow. Remove the onions, add 2 more tablespoons of butter, turn up the heat, and brown the lamb. Put the onions and lamb into a heavy casserole with the can of tomatoes and season with salt, pepper, and a little dried thyme. Cover and simmer for about 1 hour. Add the carrots, baby onions, and potato balls. Cook still covered for another hour in a moderate oven at 375°. Cook the peas separately and put them on top of the stew just before serving. If you are having dumplings, they should be put in the stew 20 minutes before the cooking time is up. Serve in the casserole. Serves 4 to 6.

PARSLEY DUMPLINGS

1½ cups flour
3 teaspoons baking powder
scant teaspoon salt
2 tablespoons vegetable shortening
¾ cup milk
1 to 2 tablespoons chopped parsley

Sift 1½ cups of flour, 3 teaspoons of baking powder, and a scant teaspoon of salt into a medium-size mixing bowl. Cut in 2 tablespoons of vegetable shortening. Add ¾ cup of milk and 1 to 2 tablespoons of chopped parsley and stir quickly with a fork until just blended. Drop by tablespoons on top of the stew and cook covered for 20 minutes. Makes 8 dumplings. Allow 1 or 2 for each serving.

SHASHLIK

Shashlik is a Caucasian way of broiling lamb on a skewer. Although the meat does not have to be marinated, it adds considerably to the flavor. Since the meat is to be broiled, it should be a tender cut, and the best is the leg. Cut it into 1½-inch cubes, removing any excess fat. Place the meat in a mixing bowl with a sliced onion, a few celery leaves, and, if you wish, a whole clove of garlic. Make a marinade of equal parts of lemon juice, sherry or red wine, and olive oil. Season with salt, a few peppercorns, and a little thyme or oregano. Add enough of this marinade to the bowl to just cover the meat, and let it stand at least an hour, or overnight if possible. Place the meat on skewers and broil until well browned, turning once; it will take about 10 minutes with a hot fire. Allow 4 or 5 pieces for each serving. Shashlik is always served with rice; either place the whole skewer on a bed of rice or gently push the meat off the skewer on top of the rice.

KIDNEYS AND MUSHROOMS IN CASSEROLE

1 *pound mushrooms, thickly sliced*
3 *tablespoons butter*
1 *teaspoon lemon juice*
2 *tablespoons flour*
1 *cup beef* or *chicken stock*
¼ *cup cream*
salt, pepper
9 or 10 *lamb kidneys*
2 *tablespoons brandy*
about 1 *tablespoon chopped parsley*

Sauté the mushrooms gently in 2 tablespoons of butter with 1 teaspoon of lemon juice until lightly browned. Blend in 2 tablespoons of flour. Add 1 cup of stock and stir until the mixture comes to a boil. Blend in ¼ cup of cream, season with salt and pepper, and simmer for 5 to 10 minutes. Meanwhile cut 9 or 10 lamb kidneys in half, remove the white cores, and cut each half in thick slices. Heat 1 tablespoon of butter in a skillet and when it starts to turn color, quickly brown the kidneys all over, starting with the cut side down. Remove with a slotted spoon and add to the sauce with 2 tablespoons of brandy. Simmer until the kidneys are piping hot. Sprinkle with about 1 tablespoon of chopped parsley just before serving. Serves 4 to 6.

LAMB KIDNEYS AND BACON EN BROCHETTE

Remove any membrane on the kidneys, cut them in half, and cut out the center white core. Cut strips of sliced bacon in half crosswise and flatten them a little with a knife. Roll each half kidney with a piece of bacon and thread on skewers. Place the skewers on a pie plate so that the bottom of the meat is not resting on anything. Broil until the bacon is nicely browned, turning once to brown both sides. Kidneys cook quickly, so the whole process will take only about 4 to 5 minutes on each side. Vegetables such as sautéed mushroom caps or tiny parboiled white onions may alternate with the kidneys on the skewer. Serve on a bed of rice pilaff and pour over the pan juices mixed with a little butter. Garnish with water cress or chopped parsley. Allow 2 to 3 kidneys per serving.

HAM AND PORK

BAKED HAM

Baking a ham presents no problems. Most of the hams on the market today are tenderized, which means that they have been precooked and need very little additional cooking at home. Shop for brands rather carefully, as there is quite a lot of difference. Morrell hams are excellent and so are Ferris. If there is a rind, leave it on the ham, because it will cook more quickly and shrink less. Place the ham, fat side up, in a shallow roasting pan and bake just as it is in a moderate oven at 350°. The fat on the ham makes it self-basting. The time is usually given on the wrapper and it averages about 10 to 15 minutes per pound; a meat thermometer will register 150° to 155°. Half an hour before the cooking time is up remove the pan from the oven. Pour off the drippings. Take off the rind, if any. Score the top with a sharp knife, making diagonal crisscross lines 1/4 inch deep to form diamonds. Stud each diamond with a whole clove. Cover with one of the following glazes: 1 cup of brown sugar mixed with 2 tablespoons of flour, 1/2 teaspoon of dry mustard, and 1/4 cup of honey or orange marmalade; 1 cup of brown sugar mixed with 1/2 teaspoon of dry mustard, 1/2 cup of honey, and 1/2 cup of orange juice. Return to the oven for about 30 minutes until the glaze is nicely browned. Let stand for 20 minutes before carving.

Ham may be served with one of the following sauces.

SAUCES FOR HAM

FRUIT SAUCE

Citrus fruits, such as oranges, grapefruits, and kumquats, make nice sauces for ham, and so do crushed pineapple and sour red cherries (color this sauce with a few drops of vegetable coloring). The basic sauce is the same for all, except that the sugar is variable, depending on the sweetness of the fruit, and kumquats should be first sliced and stewed with a little sugar. Kumquats are often used at the Royal Park Inn in Vero Beach, Florida.

Blend together 2 to 4 tablespoons of sugar, 1 tablespoon of cornstarch, and a dash of salt. Pour on 1½ cups of fruit juice and stir well. Bring to a boil, stirring until the sauce thickens, then simmer for 5 to 10 minutes. Remove and add 1 tablespoon of butter, 1 teaspoon of lemon juice, and about 1 cup of diced or crushed fruit. A little white wine or ginger ale may be added for flavor, or a little grated orange or lemon rind, or a little cinnamon or nutmeg. This sauce is usually served hot with hot baked ham.

SHERRY SAUCE

1 *teaspoon cornstarch*
3 *tablespoons cold water*
¼ *cup sherry*
½ *cup red currant jelly*
1 *tablespoon butter*

Blend 1 teaspoon of cornstarch with 3 tablespoons of cold water. Add ¼ cup of sherry and ½ cup of red currant jelly and cook until the sauce is thick and clear, stirring constantly. Remove and add 1 tablespoon of butter.

ORANGE RAISIN SAUCE

¼ *cup seedless raisins*
2 *cups orange juice*
⅓ *cup sugar*
1 *tablespoon cornstarch*
dash of salt
1 *teaspoon lemon juice*

Soak ¼ cup of seedless raisins in 1 cup of orange juice for 1 hour. Then bring them slowly to a boil and simmer for 15 minutes. Blend together ⅓ cup of sugar, 1 tablespoon of constarch, and a dash of salt. Blend in 1 cup of orange juice. Add to the raisins and stir until the mixture thickens; then simmer for 5 to 10 minutes, stirring occasionally. Before serving, add 1 teaspoon of lemon juice.

RAISIN SAUCE

¼ *cup brown sugar*
1 *tablespoon flour*
½ *teaspoon salt*
½ *teaspoon dry mustard*
2 *cups cider,* or 1¾ *cups water and* ¼ *cup cider vinegar*
¼ *cup seedless raisins*
1 *tablespoon butter*
small piece stick cinnamon, 2 or 3 *cloves, optional*

In a saucepan blend together ¼ cup of brown sugar, 1 tablespoon of flour, ½ teaspoon of salt, and ½ teaspoon of dry mustard. Slowly stir in 2 cups of cider, or 1¾ cups of water and ¼ cup of cider vinegar. Bring to a boil, stirring constantly, and simmer for 5 minutes. Add ¼ cup of seedless raisins and simmer another 5 to 10 minutes. Before serving, add 1 tablespoon of butter. A small piece of stick cinnamon and 2 or 3 cloves may be cooked with the sauce and then strained out.

CHAMPAGNE SAUCE

½ *cup currant jelly*
½ *teaspoon grated orange rind*
½ *teaspoon grated lemon rind*
dash of cinnamon
dash of cloves
1 *cup champagne*

Blend together in a saucepan ½ cup of currant jelly, ½ teaspoon each of grated orange and lemon rind, a dash of cinnamon and a dash of cloves, and 1 cup of champagne. Bring slowly to a boil. Serve hot or cold.

MUSTARD SAUCE

1 tablespoon butter
1 tablespoon flour
½ teaspoon English mustard
1 cup chicken stock
1 teaspoon finely chopped parsley

Melt 1 tablespoon of butter. Blend in 1 tablespoon of flour and about ½ teaspoon of English mustard. Pour on 1 cup of chicken stock and stir until the mixture comes to a boil. Taste for seasoning and simmer for 5 to 10 minutes. Before serving, add 1 teaspoon of finely chopped parsley.

CREAMY MUSTARD SAUCE

¼ cup cider vinegar
¼ cup water
1 cup brown sugar
½ pint heavy cream
about 1 tablespoon Bahamian mustard

Bring ¼ cup of cider vinegar, ¼ cup of water, and 1 cup of brown sugar slowly to a boil and cook until it forms a syrup. Whip ½ pint of heavy cream until it is stiff. Whip in 1 tablespoon more or less of Bahamian mustard. Carefully fold in the cooled syrup.

CURRANT AND WINE SAUCE

½ cup dried currants
½ cup water
¾ cup Burgundy
½ cup sugar
1 teaspoon dry mustard
6 to 8 gingersnaps
½ teaspoon cloves
¼ cup wine vinegar
1 stick cinnamon

Soak ½ cup of dried currants overnight in ½ cup of water and ¾ cup of Burgundy, combined. Add ½ cup of sugar, 1 teaspoon of dry mustard, 6 to 8 gingersnaps, ½ teaspoon of cloves, ¼ cup of wine vinegar, and 1 stick of cinnamon. Simmer until thickened. Remove the cinnamon before serving. Serves 6.

GRILLED HAM

Use a center cut of a precooked ham at least ¾ to 1 inch thick. Remove most of the fat and slash the remaining fat in several places, so that it will not curl up. Preheat the broiling unit and pan. Lightly grease the rack. Place the meat about 3 inches from the fire and broil from 3 to 5 minutes on each side, until nicely browned. At the Treadway Inns broiled ham is sometimes served with brandied peaches, pineapple fritters (*see* page 357), or the following glazed pineapple, spiced apple sections, or corn fritters.

GLAZED PINEAPPLE

Use well-drained canned pineapple slices. Heat butter in a heavy skillet and when it starts to turn color, put in the pineapple. Sprinkle with sugar. Cook at a brisk heat, turning several times and sprinkling with sugar until the pineapple is well browned and glazed, which only takes a few minutes.

SPICED APPLE SECTIONS

½ cup water
1 cup sugar
¼ cup cinnamon candies
3 apples

Bring ½ cup of water, 1 cup of sugar, and ¼ cup of cinnamon candies to a boil and simmer for 5 minutes. Put 3 peeled, cored, and sliced apples in the syrup and simmer until they are tender but not too soft.

CORN FRITTERS

⅔ cup sifted flour
1 teaspoon baking powder
½ teaspoon sugar
½ teaspoon salt
⅛ teaspoon pepper
1 egg
1 cup canned cream-style corn
3 tablespoons milk

Sift ⅔ cup of sifted flour, 1 teaspoon of baking powder, ½ teaspoon of sugar, ½ teaspoon of salt, and ⅛ teaspoon of pepper into a mixing bowl. Beat 1 egg until thick. Stir in 1 cup of cream-style corn and 3 tablespoons of milk. Add to the dry ingredients and stir just until blended and the dry ingredients are dampened. Drop by rounded teaspoonfuls into hot fat at 360° and cook about 3 to 4 minutes until golden brown on both sides, turning once. Drain on absorbent paper. Makes about 20 fritters.

HAM MOUSSE

1 *cup ground cooked ham*
2 *tablespoons butter*
2 *tablespoons flour*
1 *cup milk*
2 *eggs, separated*
1 *tablespoon cream*
salt, pepper
¼ *teaspoon dry mustard*
1 *cup heavy cream, whipped*

Put cooked ham through the fine blade of a meat grinder until you have 1 cup of ground ham. Melt 2 tablespoons of butter, add 2 tablespoons of flour, and stir until smooth. Slowly pour on 1 cup of milk and cook until it comes to a boil, stirring constantly. Let simmer for 5 minutes. Meanwhile separate 2 eggs and beat the yolks with 1 tablespoon of cream. Stir in a little of the hot sauce, then add the yolks to the sauce. Stir for a minute or two and season with salt, pepper, and ¼ teaspoon of dry mustard. Remove from the heat and let stand until cold. Beat the 2 egg whites until they are stiff and fold them gently into the ground ham. Fold the ham mixture and 1 cup of heavy cream, whipped, into the cold sauce. Pour into a buttered ring mold, set in a pan of hot water, and cook in a slow oven at 325° for 25 to 30 minutes, until set. Serve hot. A nice sauce for this is made by combining well-drained crushed pineapple with stiffly whipped cream. Serves 6.

HAM EN BROCHETTE

Cut boiled ham into 1-inch cubes and spread them with prepared mustard. Roll pineapple chunks in brown sugar. Cut cooked sweet potato into pieces about the same size as the ham and wrap each piece in raw bacon. Alternate the ham, pineapple, and sweet potatoes on a skewer, allowing three pieces of each to every skewer. Broil about 5 minutes on each side, turning once, until brown.

CREAMED HAM AND MUSHROOMS IN INDIVIDUAL CASSEROLES

2 *cups diced cooked ham*
½ *pound mushrooms, sliced*
3 *tablespoons butter*
3 *tablespoons flour*
1½ *cups chicken stock*
pepper
½ *cup light cream*

Melt 2 tablespoons of butter in a large heavy skillet. Sauté the diced ham and sliced mushrooms until lightly browned, about 5 minutes. Add another tablespoon of butter. Blend in 3 tablespoons of flour. Pour on 1½ cups of chicken stock and stir until the boiling point is reached. Simmer for at least 5 minutes to cook the flour. Season with a little pepper; salt will probably not be needed. Slowly add ½ cup of light cream. Serve in individual casseroles garnished with toast points. Serves 4.

PORK LOIN

An economical way to use a loin is to buy a whole one, which is cheaper per pound than buying just the tenderloin, and have the butcher copy the chefs at the Treadway Inns: use part for tenderloin, part for chops, and grind up the end for sausage. Recipes follow for these 3 ways of using a loin of pork.

PORK TENDERLOIN

Pork tenderloin comes from the best part of a loin of pork. Cut the tenderloin into slices about 1 inch thick. Flatten them gently with a wooden mallet, or you can use just your hands. The slices may be breaded or not, as you wish. Sauté them slowly in butter until golden brown on both sides. Then cover the pan and steam them for 15 to 20 minutes. They may be served with any of the ham sauces on page 147 or the accompaniments for broiled ham on page 150.

SAUSAGE

Season each 2 pounds of ground pork with about 2 teaspoons of salt, ½ teaspoon of pepper, 1 teaspoon of oregano or ½ teaspoon of sage (the traditional pork seasoning), ½ teaspoon of thyme, ¼ teaspoon of celery salt, and ¼ teaspoon of hickory salt. Blend thoroughly and let stand in the refrigerator for the flavors to get married.

STUFFED PORK CHOPS

- 6 *thick pork chops*
- 4 *tablespoons butter*
- 1 *medium-size onion, chopped*
- ½ *cup chopped celery*
- 1½ *cups soft bread crumbs*
- ½ *teaspoon oregano*
- *about* 1 *teaspoon salt*
- ½ *teaspoon pepper*
- *about* 1¼ *cups chicken stock,* or *about* ¼ *cup chicken stock and* 1 *cup dry white wine*
- 6 *thick slices tomato*

Since pork must always be well cooked, it is quite easy to dry out pork chops. This recipe in which the chops are braised does away with that problem. Melt 3 tablespoons of butter in a large skillet. Sauté 1 chopped onion and ½ cup of chopped celery over a slow fire until soft but not brown. Put the vegetables with all the butter into a mixing bowl. Melt another tablespoon of butter in the same skillet and brown the chops on both sides over a moderate fire. Meanwhile finish the stuffing by adding to the vegetables 1½ cups of bread crumbs made with stale white bread, ½ teaspoon of oregano, about 1 teaspoon of salt, ½ teaspoon of pepper, and enough chicken stock to moisten the stuffing, maybe ¼ cup. When the chops are browned, divide the stuffing among them, piling it on top of the chops. Cover with a slice of tomato. Pour 1 cup of chicken stock (or dry white wine) in the pan. Cook covered in a moderate oven at 350° for 45 to 60 minutes. Serves 6.

TREADWAY INN

Rochester, New York

THIS inn is the result of an interesting experiment which has turned out amazingly well. The specific problem was to build a city hotel that would offer the same inducements as a country motel. The advantages of a hotel are availability, service – especially room and twenty-four-hour telephone service – and food and drink on the spot. The disadvantages are the general impersonality and formality of hotel public rooms, the complications of checking in and the feeling that you should look fresh and personable when you do it, the expense and nuisance of bellboys, and the cost and time consumed in parking a car, usually at a distant garage.

The men responsible for the construction of the inn took all these factors into consideration. The result is the first project built from scratch combining, in a city, the comforts of a hotel with the conveniences of a motel. Persuading Mr. L. G. Treadway to become associated with the venture was a great step in the right direction. His forte is hospitable country inns, and in fact he has never been associated with a city hotel; it was only after careful thought and the stipulation that a country-inn atmosphere be maintained that he agreed.

So let's examine the Rochester Treadway Inn, which was opened in 1954. Taking first things first, the approach. If you are driving west on the New York State Thruway, you turn off on Route 96 and then 31 and find yourself on East Avenue, a wide street with imposing houses on well-kept luxurious lawns, shaded with old trees. Entrances to cities are usually depressing, but in Rochester an incredible thing happens. The well-established residential section ends as though a curtain had come down at Alexander Street, and the business district of the city begins. The Treadway Inn is at a corner of this intersection. So it is both in the country and in the city.

It is a two-story red-brick colonial building with a lawn in front. A driveway runs under a porte-cochere. At the right is the main hall with the registration desk and there is a special parking space allotted for newcomers within a few feet. At the left is the dining area. The incoming guest registers, with no fuss or bother, and then parks his car in the adjacent free parking area. A bellboy can help with his luggage or not, as he wishes. The one hundred and thirty-seven bedrooms flank the parking area, so it is only a few steps from the car to the rooms.

The décor of the rooms is modern but relaxing. Each room, in addition to a single or double bed, has a comfortable studio couch; a child under fourteen may share a double room with his parents at no extra charge. Each room has a free 21-inch television set on a swivel base so that it can be seen from either the bed or the couch, a bathroom with automatic radiant heat, and many other usual Treadway comforts. The building is fully air-conditioned. There are twenty-four-hour telephone service — and, of course, a telephone in every room — room service, laundry service — in fact, full hotel services.

The public rooms include the entrance hall, a lounge, a cocktail lounge with an outdoor terrace, dining rooms, and special rooms for banquets and meetings. The lounge has a country-inn atmosphere, with a beamed ceiling, random-width pegged floor, Oriental rugs, and a huge fireplace. The furniture comprises eighteenth-century reproductions, and there are old lamps and prints. A color television set and high-fidelity record player provide modern touches.

The main dining room serves meals at stated hours. The coffee shop is open every day except Sunday from 7 A.M. until 11 P.M. Mr. J. Frank Birdsall, Jr., the innkeeper, is lucky to have a particularly good chef and pastry cook (who makes all the breads, desserts, and pastries), and they serve the full range of delicious Treadway specialties.

One innovation of Mr. Birdsall's is Les Amis du Vin et de la Viande. Once a month a special dinner is served for those who appreciate good wine and good food. The menus vary but are predominantly French, and the wines are carefully selected by experts to accompany and enhance the delicacy of each course.

The Eastman Theatre and School of Music in Rochester are well known. George Eastman of Kodak fame was a guiding factor in the development of the city. The fifty-room Georgian house Mr. Eastman built for his mother and himself in 1905 is on East Avenue on ten acres of landscaped grounds, within walking distance of the inn. It is now a photographic museum with many photographic exhibits as well as exhibitions from Mr. Eastman's collection of old masterpieces of such artists as Gainsborough, Hals, Van Dyck, and Rembrandt. The house Mr. Eastman was born and lived in is on the grounds and is furnished with contemporary furniture which has been loaned or donated, including an old 1854 Waterville kitchen. The Duran Eastman Park is about ten miles away on Lake Ontario (where the swimming is excellent and a locker costs 10¢). The Rochester Museum of Arts and Sciences is also nearby on East Avenue, with three floors comprising a Hall of Man, Hall of Optical Science, Hall of Natural History, and Hall of Cultural History, as well as special exhibits. There are two parks in the city, Kodak and Highland, which is famous for its lilac collection.

Within easy driving distance is Newark (New York), where Jackson and Perkins have one of the best-known rose gardens in the country.

A last word. The check-out time at the Treadway Inn in Rochester is 3 P.M., and not 10 in the morning as it is in so many motels.

TREADWAY INN

Niagara Falls, New York

ANOTHER of the efficient and successful Treadway hotel-motels, similar to the Treadway Inns in Rochester and Norwalk, was opened in 1957. The inn is situated on the Niagara River in Niagara Falls and adjoins Prospect Park. Of the one hundred and fifty rooms, ninety-one overlook the river and park, and the ones that don't have the compensation of a slightly lower price. It is a five- to ten-minute walk to the Falls, actually quite close enough, because if you are too near, the roar of the Falls is not exactly conducive to a sound sleep.

The motel features of the inn are free parking for two hundred cars and a marquee at the entrance where six cars can be unloaded at the same time. There is a simple motellike registration, and after that there is no need to enter the lobby again, since there are three other entrances convenient to the various sections of the inn. The guests may pay in advance. There are double, twin, and studio rooms, and about thirty of the rooms have two double beds, saving sleeping in cots for any members of the family.

The hotel services include telephones in every room, room service, and free television. All rooms have tub and shower combinations, and they are all air-conditioned with individual controls. Another hotel feature is the excellent dining-room facilities. The main dining room seats one hundred and twenty people and has an open kitchen with a hearth where chefs broil steaks and chops to order. Treadway specialties such as lobster pie, baked stuffed shrimp, and Indian pudding are also on the menu. One small dining room with a fireplace and chimney covering one wall is reserved for men at lunch. The bar has an international theme with airline posters from all parts of the world and a polar map on the ceiling.

It really goes without saying that Niagara Falls is one of the most spectacular and exciting sights in the world, beautiful at any season, and the inn is open all year. James G. Healy is the innkeeper.

POULTRY

POULTRY ranks high in popularity with diners at the Treadway Inns. Roast turkey and boneless fried chicken are special favorites. The various ways of using bits and pieces of both chicken and turkey make it possible to use every bit of the meat, and the Treadway recipes should be useful for any cook. The obvious uses for cooked chicken or turkey are in sandwiches, salads, and croquettes; more unusual recipes are given in this chapter.

ROAST CHICKEN

Any size chicken may be roasted. The baby 1-pound chickens can be roasted according to any of the recipes for Rock Cornish game hens, or just roasted plain. The larger 3½ to 6-pound chickens, sometimes used for stewing, are the usual size for roasting. Stuff them or not as you wish. You may use any of the stuffing recipes in this book, starting on page 173. Allow 1 cup of stuffing for each pound of chicken. Alternatively, the chicken can be stuffed with a few sprigs of fresh tarragon. Tie up, rub with softened butter, and place in a shallow roasting pan with sliced celery, carrot, onion, and a little dry white wine. Roast uncovered in a moderate oven at 350°, basting several times with additional melted butter. A 2½-pound chicken will take about 45 minutes, a 4-pound chicken about 1½ hours. Test for doneness by piercing the leg with a skewer; it is done when the juice runs clear, with no pink in it. Strain pan juices for gravy.

FRIED CHICKEN

The following two methods of frying chicken both produce excellent results. With **oven-fried chicken,** all the cooking is done in the oven and it requires almost no attention, just turning each piece once. There is none of the fat spluttering that goes on when chicken is fried on top of the stove. If the directions are followed accurately, the chicken will be thoroughly cooked but still nice and moist, with a delicious crisp brown crust. **Southern fried chicken** is first steamed, then batter-dipped and fried in deep fat. The steaming keeps the chicken beautifully juicy; the deep-fat frying provides a fine brown crust. Allow 2 or 3 pieces for each serving.

OVEN–FRIED CHICKEN

Preheat the oven to 450°. Put seasoned flour in a paper bag and shake 3 or 4 pieces of chicken in it at a time until evenly coated. Melt enough vegetable shortening in the broiler pan of the range (rack removed) to cover the bottom ½ inch deep. Put the chicken into the hot fat, if possible in a single layer. Cook for 20 minutes at 450°. By then the bottom of each piece should be well browned. Turn the heat down to 350°. Turn the chicken and put a small piece of butter on each piece. Continue cooking for another 25 minutes. Cream gravy may be made in the pan, allowing 2 tablespoons of the fat and 2 tablespoons of flour for each 1½ cups of rich milk or light cream.

SOUTHERN FRIED CHICKEN

Put 2 cut-up frying chickens in a heavy saucepan and add 2 cups of cold water. Bring slowly to a boil. Season with celery, sliced onion and carrot, and salt. Cover and steam for 30 minutes.

Take 1 cup of the stock and let it cool. Make the following batter: Beat together the stock, 1 egg, a generous cup of flour, 1 teaspoon of baking powder, salt and pepper. Let stand covered for ½ hour. Dip each piece in the batter and fry in deep fat at 375° until nicely browned, maybe 5 minutes. Cook only 2 or 3 pieces at one time. Keep cooked pieces hot on a cake rack in a slow oven, 275°.

STEWED CHICKEN

The Treadway Inns use cooked chicken meat in several dishes. The cooking method used may be called stewing, boiling, poaching, simmering, or whatever you wish; the important thing is never to let the liquid actually boil. Put the chicken, either whole or cut into parts, in a deep heavy saucepan. Barely cover with cold water. Bring slowly to a boil and skim. Add a sliced onion, carrot, 1 or 2 celery stalks, and a few peppercorns. These are basic. A bay leaf and 2 or 3 whole cloves are often added, although their flavor seems too pronounced to me. A sprig or two of parsley and thyme or either one may also be used. Salt may be added now or after the chicken has cooked for an hour. Simmer, covered, until the chicken is tender: 1½ hours for a young chicken, 2 to 3 hours for an older one. Cool the chicken, then let it stand in the cooking liquid until used. Refrigerate it only if it is not used the same day it was cooked. The chicken stock can be stored in the refrigerator or frozen. In either case, strain it first. Turkey is stewed in the same way. Young turkeys of 12 to 14 pounds require only 2 to 2½ hours' cooking time.

BROWN FRICASSEE OF CHICKEN

1 *4-pound roasting chicken, cut up*
salt, pepper
4 *tablespoons butter*
1 *small onion, sliced*
1 *small carrot, sliced*
4 *cups chicken stock* or *water*
1 *clove*
½ *cup flour*
1 *cup cream*
1 *tablespoon lemon juice*
2 *tablespoons chopped parsley*

Season the pieces of chicken with salt and pepper. Brown them all over slowly in 4 tablespoons of butter in a deep heavy saucepan. When they are all browned, add 1 small sliced onion and 1 small sliced carrot and sauté a minute or so. Then add 4 cups of chicken stock or water, 1 clove, and salt and pepper. If you did not use the chicken back, add it now for extra flavor. Bring to a boil and simmer covered until tender, about 1 hour. Arrange the pieces of browned chicken on a hot platter and keep warm. Remove the chicken back and strain off 3 cups of the liquid. Blend ½ cup of flour and 1 cup of cream, add to the strained liquid, and stir until it comes to a boil. Add 1 tablespoon of lemon juice and 2 tablespoons of chopped parsley, and taste for seasoning. Spoon a little of the gravy over the chicken and serve the rest separately. Serves 4 to 6.

BONELESS GOLDEN FRIED CHICKEN WITH SUPREME SAUCE

This is the best seller on many of the Treadway Inn menus. Whole 6-pound chickens are stewed, following the directions on page 162. After the chicken is cool, the skin is removed. Then the breast is taken off from each side in one piece, and each one is cut into 3 serving pieces. The thigh, or second joint, is boned (all you need do is twist the bone out) and cut into two pieces. These are either breaded with flour, egg wash, and bread crumbs, or dipped into batter (*see* Southern Fried Chicken) and fried in deep fat, allowing 2 pieces per serving.

The chicken is served with supreme sauce or Chantilly sauce, and sometimes with a banana fritter (*see* page 357).

SUPREME SAUCE

3 *to* 4 *tablespoons butter*
2 *tablespoons flour*
2 *cups chicken stock*
¼ *cup heavy cream*
few drops lemon juice

Melt 2 tablespoons of butter. Blend in 2 tablespoons of flour. Pour on 2 cups of chicken stock and stir over a gentle fire until the mixture comes to a boil. Season and simmer for at least 5 minutes. Add 1/4 cup of heavy cream and a few drops of lemon juice; then beat in 1 to 2 tablespoons of butter, bit by bit.

CHANTILLY SAUCE

Fold 1/2 cup of heavy cream, whipped until stiff, into the preceding recipe for supreme sauce.

CHICKEN BAKED IN CREAM

- 3 *large broilers, 2 1/2 to 3 pounds*
- 1/4 *pound butter*
- 1 *large yellow onion*
- *salt, pepper*
- 1 *pint heavy cream*

Have the broilers quartered. Place them, skin side up, in a large shallow roasting pan. Spread them with 1/4 pound of softened butter. Bake uncovered in a moderate oven at 350° for about 1/2 hour, until they have browned a little. Then put a thick slice of onion on each piece, and pour the cream over them. Continue cooking until the chickens are tender, another 30 to 45 minutes. Serve on a hot platter with all the pan gravy. Serves 12.

LE COQ AU VIN

- 1 *3 1/2 to 4-pound chicken*
- 4 *tablespoons butter*
- 2 *tablespoons brandy*
- 3 *tablespoons flour*
- 1 1/2 *cups red wine*
- 1/2 *cup dry white wine*
- *salt, pepper*
- 1 *small clove garlic, crushed*
- 1/4 *pound salt pork*
- 12 *small white onions*
- 1/2 *pound mushrooms, sliced*

Tie up the chicken and brown slowly all over in 3 tablespoons of hot butter. Flame with 2 tablespoons of warm brandy, then remove the chicken from the pan. Add another tablespoon of butter to the pan. Blend in 3 tablespoons of flour. Pour on 1 1/2 cups of red wine and 1/2 cup of white wine (all red wine may be used).

Stir until the sauce comes to a boil. Season and add a crushed clove of garlic. Let simmer while you cut the chicken into serving pieces. Put the chicken in the sauce and simmer covered for about 45 minutes, or until the chicken is tender.

Meanwhile cut the salt pork into small dice and cook slowly until the pork bits are brown. Remove them with a slotted spoon and drain on absorbent paper. Brown 12 small white onions in the pork fat, then put them into the pan with the chicken. Lightly brown the sliced mushrooms and add them to the chicken too.

Serve in a casserole with the browned pork bits sprinkled over the top. The chicken may be cooked in a heat-resistant casserole and served right in that. Serves 4.

CHICKEN ON BROCCOLI WITH MORNAY SAUCE

1 *cooked fowl, 5 to 6 pounds*
1 *bunch broccoli*
2 *cups strong chicken stock*
4 *tablespoons butter*
4 *tablespoons flour*
1 *cup heavy cream*
1 *cup grated Parmesan* or *Romano cheese*

Cook the chicken following the directions on page 162. Cut the stalks off the broccoli, separate it into flowerets, and cook until tender in boiling salted water, about 15 minutes. Drain well and arrange on an ovenproof serving platter or in individual dishes. Meanwhile skin and bone the chicken, slice it neatly, and place over the broccoli. Make the following sauce: Reduce 4 cups of chicken stock to 2 cups, so that it will be strong, using a large skillet. Melt 4 tablespoons of butter. Blend in 4 tablespoons of flour. Pour on the hot chicken stock and stir until the mixture comes to a boil. Add 1 cup of cream and ½ cup of grated cheese, taste for seasoning, and simmer for 4 to 5 minutes. Spoon over the chicken and broccoli, and sprinkle with the remaining ½ cup of cheese. Bake uncovered in a moderate oven at 350° for 20 to 25 minutes, until well heated and the cheese is lightly browned. Serves 6 to 8.

CHICKEN CURRY

- 1 *large frying chicken, 3½ to 4 pounds, cut up*
- 6 *tablespoons butter*
- ½ *cup chicken stock* or *water*
- 1 *small onion, sliced*
- 1 *carrot, sliced*
- 1 *stalk celery, sliced*
- 1 *apple, cored and chopped*
- 3 *to 4 tablespoons curry powder*
- ½ *teaspoon chili powder*
- 3 *tablespoons flour*
- 2 *cups coconut* or *almond milk*
- *salt*
- ⅛ *teaspoon each mace, allspice, nutmeg, cloves, cinnamon*
- 2 *teaspoons red currant jelly*
- 2 *teaspoons chutney*

Brown the chicken slowly in 3 tablespoons of hot butter. Add ½ cup of chicken stock or water, cover and steam over a slow fire until the chicken is tender, about 30 to 40 minutes. Remove the meat from the bones and dice it, cut the skin into small bits, and reserve the stock. Meanwhile prepare the following curry sauce: Cook 1 sliced onion, 1 sliced carrot, 1 sliced stalk of celery, and 1 chopped apple in 3 tablespoons of butter in a deep heavy saucepan until they are soft, about 20 minutes. Add 3 to 4 tablespoons of curry powder and ½ teaspoon of chili powder and cook another 5 minutes. Blend in 3 tablespoons of flour. Pour on 2 cups of coconut or almond milk. (If a fresh coconut is not available for coconut milk, make almond milk by pouring 2 cups of scalded milk over ¼ pound of blanched chopped almonds. Let stand for 30 minutes to infuse the milk with the almond flavor.) Stir until the mixture comes to a boil, season with salt, and simmer for about ½ hour. Curry powder needs thorough cooking or it will taste raw. Then put through a strainer or food mill. Put the sauce into a double boiler with the chicken, skin, ⅛ teaspoon each of mace, allspice, nutmeg, cloves, and cinnamon, 2 teaspoons of red currant jelly, and 2 teaspoons of chutney. Taste for seasoning and cook until thoroughly heated. Serve with boiled rice and chutney and any or all of the following condiments: chopped or whole peanuts, diced green pepper mixed with shredded orange rind, shredded coconut, chopped hard-cooked egg whites and yolks (chopped separately), diced avocado mixed with crisp bacon bits, preserved ginger, diced ripe tomato, Bombay duck, raisins soaked overnight in orange or lemon juice, bananas sliced with lemon juice.

CHICKEN À LA KING

- 3 *cups cooked chicken, preferably breast*
- 4 *tablespoons butter*
- ½ *pound mushrooms, thinly sliced*
- 1 *green pepper, diced*
- ½ *teaspoon paprika*
- 2 *tablespoons flour*
- 1 *cup chicken stock*
- 2 *egg yolks*
- 1 *cup light cream*
- ¼ *cup dry sherry*
- 1 *piece pimento, diced*

Cut the chicken into neat ½-inch dice. Melt 4 tablespoons of butter in the top of a double boiler over direct heat. Cook the mushrooms, green pepper, and ½ teaspoon of paprika over a slow fire for about 10 minutes, until soft but not brown. Blend in 2 tablespoons of flour. Add 1 cup of chicken stock and stir until the sauce comes to a boil. Simmer for 4 to 5 minutes. Beat 2 egg yolks lightly with a fork. Beat in 1 cup of cream. Add to the sauce and stir until it has thickened, but do not let it boil again. Add the chicken, place over hot water, and heat thoroughly. Just before serving, add ¼ cup of sherry and a diced pimento. Serve in a hot serving dish or individual dishes, garnished with triangles of thin toast. Serves 6.

POULET VIEILLE FRANCE
(Chicken with mushrooms and pâté)

- 1 3½ *to 4-pound chicken*
- 3 *tablespoons butter*
- *salt, pepper*
- 1 *small truffle, finely chopped, optional*
- ¼ *pound mushrooms, sliced*
- ¼ *cup sherry* or *dry white wine*
- 1½ *cups heavy cream*
- 2 *tablespoons pâté*

Cut the chicken into small serving pieces, separating the wings from the breast and the legs from the second joints. Brown slowly all over in 2 tablespoons of hot butter in a deep heavy saucepan. Season. Add another tablespoon of butter, a finely chopped truffle, if you wish, and the sliced mushrooms and cook for another 5 minutes. Pour over ¼ cup of sherry or dry white wine, being careful that each piece gets a little. Continue cooking for 3 or 4 minutes while the wine soaks in. Add 1½ cups of heavy cream and bring slowly to a boil. Cover and simmer for 30 to 40 minutes, until the chicken is tender, stirring several times.

Arrange the chicken on a hot serving dish. Blend 2 tablespoons of pâté into the sauce with a wire whisk. Spoon the sauce over the chicken. Serves 4.

Note. True pâté de foie gras is very expensive, but there are good tinned domestic pâtés, and even liverwurst can be used if necessary.

CHICKEN LEG MIXED GRILL

Use the legs of frying chickens weighing 3½ to 4 pounds. Remove the skin and cut off the end of the bone. Roll in seasoned flour. Brown slowly all over in hot butter in a heavy skillet with a little sliced carrot, onion, and celery in the pan. When well browned, add enough chicken stock to cover an inch of the bottom of the pan, and braise covered until the legs are tender, about 30 to 40 minutes. Allow 1 leg for each serving with grilled sausage, bacon, and a broiled tomato. Strain the pan juices over the chicken.

Braised chicken legs are also good served with a supreme sauce (*see* page 163).

CHICKEN PIE

1 *4-pound cooked chicken*
4 *tablespoons butter*
4 *tablespoons flour*
2 *cups chicken stock*
¼ *cup heavy cream*
nutmeg
paprika
salt, pepper
¼ *cup dry white wine*
pastry for 1-crust pie

Cook the chicken according to the directions given for stewing chicken. Let it cool in the stock, then remove the chicken and take the meat from the bones in large pieces. Melt 4 tablespoons of butter, blend in 4 tablespoons of flour, and gradually stir in 2 cups of the chicken stock (skim any fat off the top first). Cook until thickened, stirring constantly. Add 1/4 cup of heavy cream and season to taste with nutmeg, paprika, salt, and pepper. Put the pieces of chicken into a deep 9-inch pie pan, using the pieces of white meat first, then the dark meat. Pour over the sauce, adding 1/4 cup of dry white wine. Cover with pastry; cut openings for the escape of steam. Bake in a moderately hot oven at 400° for 20 to 25 minutes, until brown. Serves 6.

Note. The filling for the pie should be cold when the crust is put on, since a hot filling will melt the shortening in the crust. Baking powder biscuits (*see* page 268) may also be used as a topping – the bottoms will soak up some of the sauce and be delicious. The pie may be baked in deep individual casseroles if desired; this is the way it is served at the Treadway Inns.

CHICKEN LOAF

1 *4-pound cooked chicken*
2 *cups soft bread crumbs*
1 *cup cooked rice*
1 1/2 *teaspoons salt*
1/4 *teaspoon paprika*
1 1/2 *cups chicken stock, strained*
1 1/2 *cups light cream*
4 *eggs, well beaten*

Cook the chicken according to the directions given for stewing chicken, and reserve the stock. Remove the meat from the bones and dice it. Combine with 2 cups of soft bread crumbs, 1 cup of cooked rice, 1 1/2 teaspoons of salt, 1/4 teaspoon of paprika, 1 1/2 cups of the strained chicken stock, 1 1/2 cups of light cream, and mix well. Stir in 4 eggs, well beaten. Pour into a greased 2-quart ring mold or rectangular shallow baking dish. Bake in a slow oven at 325° for 1 hour, or until firm. Serve hot with the following mushroom sauce or with supreme sauce (*see* page 163). Serves 6.

MUSHROOM SAUCE

6 tablespoons butter
4 tablespoons flour
2 cups chicken stock
¼ cup light cream
½ pound mushrooms, sliced
¼ teaspoon paprika
½ teaspoon chopped parsley
¼ teaspoon lemon juice

Melt 4 tablespoons of butter, stir in 4 tablespoons of flour, and when smooth, add 2 cups of chicken stock and ¼ cup of light cream. Bring to a boil, stirring constantly, and add ½ pound of mushrooms, thinly sliced and sautéed in 2 tablespoons of butter. Season with ¼ teaspoon of paprika, ½ teaspoon of chopped parsley, ¼ teaspoon of lemon juice, and salt if needed. Let the sauce simmer gently for 10 to 15 minutes before serving.

CREAMED CHICKEN AND SWEETBREADS AU GRATIN

1 cup diced cooked chicken breast
1 cup diced cooked sweetbreads
1 cup heavy cream
2 tablespoons butter
2 tablespoons flour
1 cup milk
salt, white pepper
½ cup grated Parmesan cheese
duchess potatoes

Put the chicken and sweetbreads into a double boiler with the cream and cook until well heated and the cream has reduced a little. Meanwhile make the following cream sauce: Melt 2 tablespoons of butter. Blend in 2 tablespoons of flour. Add 1 cup of milk, season, and stir until the sauce comes to a boil. Blend with the chicken and sweetbreads, taste for seasoning, and simmer for 10 to 15 minutes. Put the mixture in an ovenproof serving dish or individual dishes. Sprinkle with ½ cup of grated cheese. Pipe a border of duchess potatoes around the edge. Put under the broiler until lightly browned. Serves 4.

BAKED CHICKEN AND CORN IN CASSEROLE

3 tablespoons butter
4 tablespoons flour
2 cups chicken stock
salt, pepper
1½ cups cooked corn, fresh or *frozen*
2 cups diced cooked chicken
1 cup soft bread crumbs
4 tablespoons melted butter

Melt 3 tablespoons of butter. Blend in 4 tablespoons of flour. Add 2 cups of chicken stock and stir until the sauce comes to a boil. Taste for seasoning. Put half the corn in a greased wide casserole or individual casseroles, and cover with half the chicken. Pour over half the sauce. Repeat these layers. Mix 1 cup of soft bread crumbs with 4 tablespoons of melted butter and spread over the top. Bake uncovered in a moderate oven at 350° about 25 to 30 minutes. If the crumbs are not brown enough, finish off with a minute or so under the broiler. Serves 4 to 6.

SAUTÉED CHICKEN LIVERS AND MUSHROOMS

5 tablespoons butter
½ pound small mushroom caps
1 pound chicken livers
¼ cup brandy
2 tablespoons flour
¼ teaspoon dry mustard
1½ cups chicken stock
salt, pepper
½ cup heavy cream, whipped

Melt 2 tablespoons of butter in a heavy skillet and sauté ½ pound of mushroom caps over a moderate fire until lightly browned. Remove them with a slotted spoon. Turn up the heat, add another 2 tablespoons of butter, and when it has turned color, quickly brown 1 pound of chicken livers all over. Heat ¼ cup of brandy, ignite it, and flame the livers. Add the remaining tablespoon of butter, and blend in 2 tablespoons of flour and

¼ teaspoon of dry mustard. Pour on 1½ cups of chicken stock and stir until the mixture comes to a boil. Season with salt and pepper, put back the mushrooms, and simmer for 4 to 5 minutes. Fold in ½ cup of heavy cream, whipped, and serve immediately. Serves 4.

ROAST TURKEY

Roast turkey is always a hit on restaurant menus, and the Treadway Inns are no exception. The Treadway chefs generally do not stuff their birds, because stuffing slows up the cooking a little, and because they can make more stuffing if it is baked separately. Most of us at home are used to stuffing a turkey, and we will assume that is how we will cook them.

Go over the turkey to remove any pin feathers. Feel inside to see if any of the lung remains. Cut out the oil sac in the tail if it hasn't already been done. Run cold running water quickly through the inside, and dry with paper towels. Wipe the outside with a damp cloth. Do *not* soak the turkey. Stuff the inside and the neck cavity, using one of the following stuffing recipes, and secure with skewers and string. Tie the legs to the tail. Fold the wing tips under the back. The turkey can be trussed, but it will cook more quickly if it isn't. Brush well with melted butter. Cut a double thickness of cheesecloth long enough to just cover the bird, dip in melted butter, and place it over the turkey. Place in a shallow roasting pan in a moderate oven at 325°. Every 30 minutes, brush the cheesecloth with butter or pan juices. Remove the cheesecloth about 30 minutes before the bird is done, so that it will brown well, although actually it may brown under the cheesecloth. The cloth helps keep the turkey moist, and gives it an even, crisp crust. The turkey is done when a meat thermometer placed in the leg registers 185°, or when the legs move up and down easily.

I hesitate about quoting a timetable for roasting turkeys because I disagree with most of them. They all allow too much time; that is why turkeys dry out. Roughly speaking, 20 minutes to the pound for a turkey up to 12 pounds, 15 minutes to the pound for larger ones is about right. Start testing before that, though, especially with a large 20 to 24-pound bird.

Meanwhile cook the neck and giblets in water to cover with onion, carrot, celery, and salt. Let simmer about 1½ hours and drain, reserving the stock. Chop the giblets fine.

Place the turkey on a hot platter and allow to stand for at least 15 minutes before carving. Pour the pan juices into a bowl. For gravy, allow 1 tablespoon of fat skimmed from the bowl of juices and 1 tablespoon of flour for each cup of giblet stock; make the gravy in the roasting pan to get all the glaze, and add the pan juices (with remaining fat skimmed off) and the chopped giblets. Taste for seasoning and simmer for at least 5 minutes. Allow ¾ to 1 pound of turkey, dressed weight, for each person to be served.

OYSTER STUFFING

10 *cups coarse bread crumbs*
2 *cups chicken stock*
18 *oysters*
2 *cups finely diced celery*
2 *medium onions, chopped*
1 *cup butter*
4 *tablespoons poultry seasoning*
salt, pepper

Moisten 10 cups of coarse bread crumbs with 2 cups of chicken stock and let stand. Poach 18 oysters in their own liquor until their edges curl, then drain and chop them coarsely. Add the oysters to the bread crumbs. Sauté 2 cups of finely diced celery and 2 chopped onions in 1 cup of butter over a moderate fire until soft but not brown. Add to the oysters and crumbs with 4 teaspoons of poultry seasoning, salt and pepper. Mix thoroughly and fill into the turkey. If a moister, less crumbly stuffing is desired, use more chicken stock. Enough stuffing for a 15 to 16-pound bird.

BREAD STUFFING

Omit the oysters in the preceding recipe; 2 tablespoons of dried thyme can be substituted for the poultry seasoning.

WILD RICE STUFFING
(For 14 to 16-pound turkey)

1½ *cups wild rice*
1 *cup diced celery*
1 *cup chopped onion*
1 *cup butter*
½ *pound mushrooms, sliced*
1 *cup chopped walnuts* or *pecans*
salt, pepper
2 *tablespoons chopped parsley*
about ½ teaspoon dried thyme

Wash 1½ cups of wild rice in several changes of lukewarm water. Bring 3 or 4 quarts of well-salted water to a boil. Slowly add the rice and cook until it is tender, 35 to 40 minutes. Drain into a large strainer and steam for 10 minutes or so over simmering water. Meanwhile gently cook 1 cup of diced celery and 1 cup of finely chopped onion in ½ cup of butter until soft but not brown. Add ½ pound of sliced mushrooms and cook another 2 to 3 minutes. Melt the remaining ½ cup of butter in the same pan. Blend together the rice, vegetables, and butter, 1 cup of chopped nuts, salt, pepper, 2 tablespoons of chopped parsley, and about ½ teaspoon of dried thyme. Fill into the turkey or bake separately.

CORN BREAD STUFFING WITH SAUSAGE

1 *pound sausage meat*
1 *cup finely chopped celery*
1 *cup finely chopped onion*
1 *teaspoon poultry seasoning*
salt

About 6 cups of crumbled corn bread are needed for this stuffing, and the recipe which follows provides that amount.

Cook the sausage meat slowly in a medium-size skillet. Break it up as it cooks with a fork to make small pieces and cook until nicely browned. Remove the sausage with a slotted spoon. Sauté 1 cup of chopped celery and 1 cup of chopped onion in the sausage fat until soft but not brown. Put the corn bread in a large mixing bowl with the sausage, salt, 1 teaspoon of poultry seasoning, and the onion and celery with all the sausage fat. Blend well and fill into the main cavity and neck opening of the turkey. Sufficient stuffing for an 18 to 20-pound turkey.

CORN BREAD

2 *eggs*	1 *teaspoon salt*
1 *cup sour milk*	1 *teaspoon sugar*
1½ *cups yellow corn meal*	3 *tablespoons salad oil*
½ *cup flour*	1 *teaspoon baking powder*

½ *teaspoon soda*

Beat 2 eggs well. Add 1 cup of sour milk, 1½ cups of corn meal, ½ cup of flour, 1 teaspoon of salt, 1 teaspoon of sugar, and 3 tablespoons of salad oil. Beat thoroughly. Stir in 1 teaspoon of baking powder and ½ teaspoon of soda and mix only for a few seconds to blend. Place in an oiled or greased 9 x 13-inch baking pan. Bake for 25 to 30 minutes in a moderate oven at 400°, until lightly browned.

Note. Milk can be soured by adding lemon juice or vinegar, but it is much better to let it sour naturally by standing at room temperature for several days.

CHESTNUT STUFFING
(For 20 to 22-pound turkey)

1 *pound chestnuts*	1 *pound butter*
½ *cup salad oil*	½ *pound mushrooms, chopped*
3 *cups beef stock* or *water*	*salt, pepper*
1 *loaf sliced white bread*	½ *teaspoon dried thyme*
1 *medium-size yellow onion, finely chopped*	2 *tablespoons chopped parsley*
1 *cup chopped celery*	

With a sharp knife make a slit in each chestnut all across the flat side. Heat ½ cup of salad oil in a large skillet. Add the chestnuts and cook for about 5 minutes, until the shells open around the slit, shaking the pan occasionally. Remove, and when cool enough to handle, peel off the shell and inner skin; they come off easily while the chestnuts are hot, are very difficult to remove when they are cool. Cook the nuts in 3 cups of beef stock or water until tender, 15 to 20 minutes. Drain. All this can be done a day or two ahead of time.

The bread should be firm and at least a day old. Toast until nicely browned. Run cold water over each slice and put into a large mixing bowl. Let stand for 5 to 10 minutes, then pull into small pieces, removing any crusts that are still hard. Meanwhile cook 1 finely chopped yellow onion and 1 cup of chopped celery in ½ pound of butter over a gentle fire for 15 to 20 minutes, until soft and yellow. Add ½ pound of chopped mushrooms and the remaining ½ pound of butter and cook another 5 minutes. Add to the bread with the chestnuts, coarsely chopped, plenty of salt, pepper, ½ teaspoon of dried thyme, and 2 tablespoons of chopped parsley. Blend thoroughly and either fill into the turkey or bake it separately.

CRANBERRY–ORANGE RELISH

4 *cups fresh cranberries*
2 *oranges*
2 *cups sugar*

Put 4 cups of cranberries and 2 oranges (which have been quartered and seeded) through a food chopper. Add 2 cups of sugar and mix well. This relish may also be made in an electric blender. Put the oranges and the sugar in the blender and combine at low speed. Add the cranberries gradually. When they are all added, remove from the blender. Store the relish in the refrigerator for several hours before serving to allow the flavors to mingle.

CRANBERRY SAUCE

4 *cups cranberries*
1 *cup water*
2 *cups sugar*

Wash 4 cups of cranberries and pick out any bad ones. Put the berries in a saucepan with 1 cup of water and bring to a boil. Cook for 15 minutes after it reaches the boiling point, stirring frequently to prevent sticking. Then remove from the fire, add 2 cups of sugar, and stir well. Return to the fire and cook for about 30 seconds, just to make sure all the sugar is dissolved. Pour into individual molds or 1 serving dish. This sauce stiffens quickly, so it can be made either an hour or so before serving or the day before. Place in the refrigerator to chill before serving. Serves 10.

SPICED CRANBERRY SAUCE

- 1 *cup water*
- 1¼ *cups brown sugar*
- ¾ *cup white sugar*
- ½ *cup vinegar*
- 2 *teaspoons whole cloves*
- 2 *sticks cinnamon*
- 4 *cups fresh cranberries*

Combine 1 cup of water, 1¼ cups of brown sugar, ¾ cup of white sugar, ½ cup of vinegar, 2 teaspoons of whole cloves, and 2 sticks of cinnamon in a saucepan and boil rapidly for 5 minutes. Remove the cloves and the cinnamon. Add 4 cups of cranberries and boil about 5 minutes more, or until the cranberries burst open. Cool. Makes about 3½ cups of sauce.

BARBECUED TURKEY

- 1 6 *to* 7-*pound turkey*
- 1 *cup melted butter*
- ½ *cup fresh lemon juice*
- 1 *teaspoon Tabasco sauce*
- 1 *teaspoon dried onion flakes*
- ½ *teaspoon paprika*
- ½ *teaspoon dry mustard*
- 1 *teaspoon salt*
- ¼ *teaspoon pepper*
- 1 *whole clove garlic, optional*

Have the turkey split in half and put it skin up in a shallow roasting pan. Melt butter in a saucepan over a slow fire. When you have 1 cup of melted butter in the pan, add ½ cup fresh lemon juice, 1 teaspoon Tabasco, 1 teaspoon onion flakes, ½ teaspoon paprika, ½ teaspoon dry mustard, 1 teaspoon salt, ¼ teaspoon pepper, and 1 clove of garlic, if you wish. Stir until the mixture comes to a boil. Simmer for a few minutes, then remove the garlic if it was used. Brush the turkey thoroughly with the sauce. Cook in a moderate oven at 375°, turning the turkey every 15 or 20 minutes and brushing and basting with the rest of the sauce. The turkey should be tender and beautifully browned in about 1½ hours. Serve covered with all the sauce. Serves 6 to 8.

TURKEY WINGS CREOLE

4 *uncooked turkey wings*
seasoned flour
4 *to* 6 *tablespoons butter*
1 *cup chopped onions*
1 *green pepper, diced*
1 *clove garlic, crushed*
1 *large can tomatoes*
salt, cayenne, thyme

Cut the tips off the wings, since they don't have any meat to speak of. Flatten the rest of the wings. Coat them lightly with seasoned flour, and brown them slowly on both sides in 4 tablespoons of butter. Remove the wings and put them in an ovenproof casserole. Sauté the onions, green pepper, and garlic until lightly browned, using the same pan the wings were browned in and adding more butter if necessary. Pour on the tomatoes, season with salt, cayenne, and dried thyme, and bring to a boil. Pour over the wings. Bake covered in a moderate oven at 350° until tender, about 1½ hours. Serve in the casserole. Serves 4.

FRICASSEE OF TURKEY WINGS WITH RICE

See recipe for fricassee of chicken on page 162. Turkey wings will take about as long to cook as a tender 5-pound chicken, 1½ to 2 hours.

STUFFED TURKEY LEGS

4 turkey legs, from 12 to 14-pound turkeys
1 unbeaten egg white
½ pound veal, ground three times
1½ cups light cream
salt
4 tablespoons butter
1 cup dry white wine
1 teaspoon paprika
6 slices bacon
½ cup chopped onion
1 to 2 tablespoons flour

Bone the raw turkey legs and remove the white tendons—your butcher can do all this. Spread them out flat, skin side down. Make the following stuffing: Beat the egg white into the veal. Slowly beat in ½ cup cream. Season with salt. Cover the legs with the stuffing, roll them up, and tie with string. It doesn't matter if some of the stuffing is exposed; it will set when the legs are cooked. Heat 4 tablespoons of butter in a large skillet. Brown the legs slowly all over. When browned, pour 1 cup of wine into the pan, blend in 1 teaspoon of paprika, cover, and cook over a slow fire for about an hour. Meanwhile dice 6 slices of bacon and sauté until brown and crisp. Remove with a slotted spoon and put to drain on absorbent paper. Sauté the chopped onion in the bacon fat until lightly browned, then put into the pan with the legs. To serve, place the legs on a hot serving dish and keep warm. Blend 1 to 2 tablespoons of flour into the pan juices. Add 1 cup of cream and stir until the sauce comes to a boil. Taste for seasoning and simmer for 2 to 3 minutes. Spoon over the legs and sprinkle with the bacon bits. Serves 4.

TURKEY HASH

Turkey hash can be made the same way as corned beef hash (*see* page 132), omitting the green pepper. Or the following creamed turkey hash may be used.

2 cups diced cooked turkey
1 cup heavy cream
2 tablespoons butter
2 tablespoons flour
1 cup milk
salt, white pepper
½ cup grated Swiss or *Parmesan cheese*

Put the turkey and cream into a double boiler and cook until well heated and the cream has reduced a little. Make a cup of cream sauce: Melt 2 tablespoons of butter. Blend in 2 tablespoons of flour. Add 1 cup of milk, salt, and white pepper, and stir until the sauce comes to a boil. Add to the turkey, taste for seasoning, and simmer for 10 to 15 minutes. Put the hash into an ovenproof serving dish or individual dishes. A border of duchess potatoes may be piped around the edge. Sprinkle with cheese and place under the broiler until lightly browned. Serves 4.

CREAMED TURKEY AND OYSTERS

½ pint oysters
1 cup water
salt, pepper
3 tablespoons butter
3 tablespoons flour
1 cup light cream
1½ cups cooked diced turkey
water cress for garnish

Bring the oysters slowly to a boil in 1 cup of seasoned water and simmer until their edges curl, about 2 to 3 minutes. Drain, reserving the stock. Melt 3 tablespoons of butter over a medium fire. Blend in 3 tablespoons of flour. Slowly pour on the oyster stock and 1 cup of light cream and stir until the sauce comes to a boil. Taste for seasoning and simmer for at least 5 minutes. Just before serving, add the poached oysters and the turkey, and cook until they are piping hot. Serve with slices of toast or in patty shells. Garnish with water cress. Serves 4 to 6.

SAUTÉED TURKEY STEAK, POULETTE SAUCE

Cut 4 slices of cooked turkey breast ½ inch thick and weighing about 5 ounces. Coat with seasoned flour, dip in egg wash, then in dry bread crumbs. Sauté in slightly browned butter in a large heavy skillet until golden brown on both sides. Arrange slightly overlapping down a hot platter and spoon over the following poulette sauce.

POULETTE SAUCE

3 *tablespoons butter*
½ *cup finely chopped mushrooms*
1½ *cups milk*
salt
white pepper
2 *egg yolks*
½ *cup light cream*
1 *to* 2 *teaspoons lemon juice*
1 *tablespoon finely chopped parsley*

Melt 3 tablespoons of butter. Cook in it ½ cup of finely chopped mushrooms until they just start to turn color, using a slow fire. Pour on 1½ cups of milk and stir until the mixture comes to a boil. Season with salt and white pepper and simmer for 4 to 5 minutes. Beat 2 egg yolks slightly, then beat in ½ cup of light cream. Add to the sauce and stir over a slow fire until it has thickened, but do not let it boil. Just before serving, add 1 to 2 teaspoons of lemon juice and 1 tablespoon of finely chopped parsley. Serves 4.

TURKEY PAPRIKA

1 *cooked turkey,* 8 *to* 9 *pounds*
8 *tablespoons turkey fat* or *butter*
3 *tablespoons paprika*
8 *tablespoons flour*
2½ *cups turkey stock*
1 *cup rich milk*
1½ *cups cream*
rice ring

Cook the turkey according to the directions on page 162. Make the following paprika sauce: Melt 8 tablespoons of turkey fat or butter in a large saucepan. Blend in 3 tablespoons of paprika and 8 tablespoons of flour. Pour on 2½ cups of turkey stock and 1 cup of milk and stir until the sauce comes to a boil. Add 1½ cups of cream, taste for seasoning, and bring to a boil again. Simmer for at least 30 minutes over boiling water to cook the paprika; otherwise it will taste raw. Meanwhile skin and bone the turkey and cut the meat into neat pieces. Add to the sauce and cook until the turkey is thoroughly heated, or until ready to use – it can wait almost indefinitely. Serve in a rice ring made with 2½ cups of rice, cooked, blended with at least ½ cup of melted butter, 3 cups of cooked peas, and 2 or 3 diced pimentos. Serves 10 to 12.

DEVILED TURKEY

4 *slices cooked turkey breast*
2 *tablespoons melted butter*
¾ *cup bread crumbs*
½ *teaspoon dry mustard*
salt, cayenne
½ *teaspoon curry powder*
parsley or *water cress*

Cut 4 large neat slices of turkey breast and have them at room temperature. Brush well with melted butter. Blend together ¾ cup bread crumbs, ½ teaspoon dry mustard, salt, cayenne, and ½ teaspoon of curry powder. Coat each slice on both sides with this mixture. Broil until nicely browned on both sides, either using a low flame or placing the turkey 4 to 5 inches from the flame so that it will not brown too fast. Serve the following sauce separately and garnish with parsley or water cress. Serves 4.

SAUCE DIABLE

2 *finely chopped shallots* or 1 *small white onion*
½ *cup wine vinegar*
8 *to* 10 *peppercorns*
small piece bay leaf
½ *teaspoon dry mustard*
salt
paprika
1 *cup brown* or *tomato sauce*

Into a saucepan put 2 finely chopped shallots or 1 small white onion, ½ cup vinegar, 8 to 10 peppercorns, a small piece of bay leaf, ½ teaspoon dry mustard, salt, and paprika. Simmer until reduced one half, then strain. Add to 1 cup of brown sauce (turkey gravy may be used) or tomato sauce and heat thoroughly.

TURKEY NEWBURG

4 *tablespoons butter*
½ *pound mushrooms sliced*
3 *tablespoons flour*
1 *cup chicken* or *turkey stock*
1 *cup light cream*
salt, cayenne
3 *cups diced cooked turkey*
2 *egg yolks*
2 *to* 3 *tablespoons sherry*

Melt 4 tablespoons of butter in the top of a double boiler over direct heat. Add the sliced mushrooms and cook slowly for 8 to 10 minutes. Blend in 3 tablespoons of flour. Pour on 1 cup of chicken or turkey stock and 1 cup of light cream and stir until the sauce comes to a boil. Season with salt and cayenne, and simmer for about 10 minutes over gently boiling water. Add 3 cups of diced cooked turkey and cook until the meat is thoroughly heated. Just before serving, beat 2 egg yolks slightly with 2 to 3 tablespoons of sherry. Add a little of the hot sauce, blend, then stir into the turkey mixture. Cook for a minute or two, just until the yolks have thickened the sauce. Serve in individual casseroles with toast points. Serves 4 to 6.

BROILED FRESH TOMATO WITH TURKEY, CHEESE TOPPING

Cut the top off a large firm ripe tomato and carefully spoon out the center pulp. Fill with creamed turkey, sprinkle the top well with grated mild Cheddar cheese, and dot with a little butter. Bake in a moderate oven at 350° for 15 to 20 minutes, and finish off with a minute or so under the broiler to lightly brown the cheese.

HOT TURKEY SANDWICH

Sandwich 2 slices of white bread with thinly sliced turkey breast, a thin slice of boiled ham, and a few sautéed mushrooms. Dip in egg wash and sauté in hot butter until nicely browned on both sides, as for French toast. Place on an ovenproof serving dish, cover lightly with Hollandaise sauce (*see* page 202), and glaze under the broiler.

TURKEY BREAST MORNAY

On individual ovenproof serving dishes place a piece of unsweetened corn bread. Top with a thin slice of cooked ham, a slice of cooked turkey breast, and 3 cooked jumbo asparagus spears. Cover with Mornay sauce (*see* page 165). Place in a moderate oven at 350° for 10 to 15 minutes, then glaze lightly under the broiler. At Andover they use mild Wisconsin Cheddar cheese for their Mornay sauce.

BAKED TURKEY AND CORN AU GRATIN

Mix ½ cup of grated Swiss or mild Cheddar cheese with the bread crumbs in the recipe for baked chicken and corn in casserole on page 171.

ROCK CORNISH GAME HENS

Jacques Makowsky, owner of the Idle Wild Farm, Pomfret, Conn., first introduced Rock Cornish game hens to the public in 1950; today he ships out about two million birds a year. The Publick House in Sturbridge, Mass., was one of Mr. Makowsky's first customers, and the birds now appear on the menus at all the inns. A cross between the fighting game cocks of Malaya and the domesticated chicken, they are compact, full-breasted, very meaty birds with a distinctive admirable flavor described by Mr. Makowsky as "a flavor combining the sweetness of the grouse with the white meat of the finest milk-fed chick."

ROAST ROCK CORNISH GAME HEN

Allow 1 hen weighing about 1 pound for each serving. The hens may be stuffed or not, as you wish. Either of the following stuffings is good.

WILD RICE STUFFING
(For 4 hens)

1 *cup cooked wild rice*
1 *teaspoon grated onion*
½ *teaspoon celery salt*
¼ *teaspoon dried thyme*
pepper
¼ *cup finely diced ham, optional*

Combine 1 cup of cooked wild rice, 1 teaspoon of grated onion, ½ teaspoon of celery salt, ¼ teaspoon of dried thyme, and pepper. No salt will be needed if enough was used in the cooking water for the rice; ¼ cup of finely diced ham may be added. Fill into the hens and secure with a skewer.

SAUSAGE STUFFING
(For 6 hens)

¾ *pound sausage meat*
6 *thin slices white bread*
1 *to* 2 *tablespoons sausage fat*
2 *tablespoons chopped parsley*
¼ *teaspoon dried thyme*
salt
1 *cup cream*

Cook ¾ pound of sausage meat slowly until well browned, breaking it apart with a fork into small bits. Trim the crusts off 6 thin slices of white bread and toast them. Cut the toast into small squares and combine with the sausage meat, 1 to 2 tablespoons of sausage fat, 2 tablespoons of chopped parsley, ¼ teaspoon of dried thyme, salt, and 1 cup of cream. Let the stuffing stand for 10 minutes or so, for the bread to absorb the cream. Then fill into the hens and secure with a skewer.

Season the hens lightly with salt and rub them well with softened butter, 1 to 2 tablespoons for each hen. Place in a shallow roasting pan. Thin slices of bacon or salt pork may be placed over the bird, but personally I think butter is a less pronounced and therefore better flavor for these delicate birds. Roast uncovered in a moderate oven at 375° for about 50 to 60 minutes if stuffed, 35 to 40 minutes if not. After the birds have cooked for 10 minutes, pour ¼ cup of white wine in the pan. Baste every 10 minutes, adding more butter if necessary. Serve with the pan juices and a tart jelly like wild grape. Cornish game hens may be finished off with one of the following sauces.

SOUR CREAM SAUCE
(For 4 hens)

2 *cups sour cream*
½ *teaspoon salt*
little white pepper

Bring to a boil 2 cups of sour cream seasoned with ½ teaspoon of salt and a little white pepper. After the hen has cooked for 25 minutes, pour on the sauce and cook for another 15 minutes or so, basting several times.

WINE SAUCE
(For 4 hens)

1 *tablespoon butter*
½ *cup currant jelly*
juice ½ *lemon*
pinch cayenne or *paprika*
3 *cloves*
1 *teaspoon salt*
½ *cup water*
1 *tablespoon cornstarch*
½ *cup port wine*

Bring to a slow boil 1 tablespoon of butter, ½ cup of currant jelly, the juice of half a lemon, a pinch of cayenne or paprika, 3 cloves, 1 teaspoon of salt, and ½ cup of water. Simmer for 5 minutes, then strain. Reheat and thicken with 1 tablespoon of cornstarch dissolved in ½ cup of port wine. Serve separately.

CHAMPAGNE SAUCE

Braise the hens with carrots, onion, celery, and thyme. After they are browned, in about 30 minutes, add 1 pint of champagne for each 4 birds, and cook another 15 minutes. Strain the sauce and reduce it to half. Add sautéed mushrooms, heavy cream, and chopped truffles.

BROILED ROCK CORNISH GAME HEN

Allow 1 squab hen weighing about 1 pound for each serving. Cut through the backbone with a pair of kitchen shears. Spread the hen out flat on a shallow roasting pan, skin side up. Season lightly with salt and pepper and rub the skin with about 2 tablespoons of softened butter. Place under the broiler at least 7 to 8 inches away from the fire and with a moderate heat – if your broiler is shallow and hot, it is better not to cook the hens this way because the skin will get too brown before the birds are cooked. Broil about 10 minutes, then turn over. Have ready a mixture of the juice of 1 lemon and ½ teaspoon of dry mustard melted in 1 to 2 tablespoons of butter. Pour this over the breastbones. Continue cooking for another 20 minutes, turning twice again and basting with the pan juices. To serve, place the birds on a hot serving dish, spoon over all the pan juices, dissolve the glaze in the pan with a little white wine or water, and pour it over the hens.

SAUTÉED ROCK CORNISH GAME HEN

Allow 1 squab hen of about 1½ pounds for each serving. Cut through the backbone with kitchen shears and open the hen up flat. Season lightly with salt and pepper. Melt 3 tablespoons of butter in a heavy skillet and slowly brown the hen on both sides, starting with the skin side down. The hen should be brown in about 15 or 20 minutes. Then pour ½ cup of dry white wine in the pan and continue cooking another 15 to 20 minutes. Serve with just the pan juices or make a sauce by adding to the juice a few sautéed mushrooms and ½ cup of cream, thickened either with an egg yolk or with ½ tablespoon of flour.

DUCK WITH ORANGE

- 1 5 *to 6-pound duck*
- *salt, pepper*
- 2 *large oranges*
- 1 *small onion*
- 2 *teaspoons potato flour*
- 1½ *cups orange juice*
- ½ *cup red wine* or *Grand Marnier*
- 1 *tablespoon red currant jelly*

Season the duck lightly with salt and pepper. Stuff it with a quartered orange and small onion, and tie the legs together. Place in a roasting pan breast side up, and roast in a moderate oven at 350° for 25 to 30 minutes to the pound. Keep pouring off the fat as it accumulates, so that when the duck is cooked, there are only about 2 to 3 tablespoons of fat in the pan with all the brown glaze. Meanwhile remove thin slices of the peel from an orange with a vegetable peeler and cut them in small julienne strips. Cover with cold water, bring to a boil, and drain. Section the orange.

Place the cooked duck on a hot serving platter and keep it warm. Make the following sauce in the roasting pan: Blend 2 teaspoons of potato flour into the pan juices. Pour on 1½ cups of orange juice and ½ cup of red wine or Grand Marnier and bring to a boil, stirring constantly. Add 1 tablespoon of red currant jelly and the drained rind and taste for seasoning. Simmer for a few minutes. Just before serving, add the orange sections. Spoon a little of the sauce over the duck and serve the rest separately. Serves 4.

DUCK WITH CHERRIES

Follow the preceding recipe for duck with orange. Substitute 1 cup of sour red cherries for the orange sections, cherry juice for the orange juice (or use half and half), and use red wine with a little kirsch.

COOPER INN

Cooperstown, New York

THERE are two Treadway Inns in Cooperstown, the Cooper Inn and The Otesaga. Like the locations of so many of the Treadway Inns, Cooperstown has much to offer in the way of beauty, sports, and historical interest.

In the late eighteenth century, Judge William Cooper, the father of James Fenimore Cooper, purchased about forty thousand acres along the south shore of the nine-mile Lake Otsego and built the first house in Cooperstown. Today Cooperstown is still a charming traditional town with its heavily tree-lined streets, gracious houses, and the lovely lake, set in some of the finest rolling hill country in the state.

The two inns are physically very different. The Cooper Inn is a well-designed colonial house. It was called Willow Brook when it was built in 1812, and the architect, Philip Hooker, was known for his fine interiors. The inn has hand-carved woodwork and the graceful original circle stairway. It is decorated with fine antiques, Oriental rugs, and oil paintings. Contemporary additions are the pine-paneled dining room and cocktail lounge. There are several cottages for guests on the grounds and across the street.

The sports in Cooperstown are diverse, including golf and sailing. Motorboats may be rented, and in the summer, motor launches take visitors on lake-long tours. For the fishermen, some of the local fish are lake trout, walleyes, pickerel, perch, and large- and small-mouth bass. In the winter, there are daily ski tows on nearby Mt. Otsego.

Cooperstown has a real wealth of historical interest. The New York State Historical Society has its headquarters there and has established two museums, the Farmers' Museum and Fenimore House. There are also the National Baseball Hall of Fame and Museum and Doubleday Field, which will be discussed with Fenimore House in the following section on The Otesaga.

The Farmers' Museum is a fascinating place, presenting a graphic picture of life in rural New York between 1800 and about 1870. The native-stone main building was converted from a dairy barn. In it are displays of the arts and crafts of those days. The part called "Woman's World" is a good object lesson to any woman who complains about the drudgery of housework today. It contains the equipment for butter, cheese, and candle making, old stoves and iron kitchen utensils, implements for butchering and meat preparation and for laundering, including the first clumsy washing machine, dated 1855. On the second floor, demonstrations are given of flax preparation, spinning, and weaving. There are also a model circus and a display of farm implements. In the crafts section all the contemporary crafts, such as making barrels, gloves, brooms of birch and corn, baskets, and harnesses, are demonstrated by expert craftsmen; there are also a cobbler, cabinetmaker, and leather tanner.

Outside the main building is the "Village Crossroads," a group of buildings typical of the period from 1800 to 1840, when New York was a frontier state. The buildings were all actually found in the state and set up as they were originally, and include a schoolhouse, a country store, a blacksmith shop with a demonstrating blacksmith (when he came to Cooperstown in 1903, there were eight blacksmiths in town; now there is only one itinerant one in the region), a printing office where the *Otsego Herald* is published (the wages used to be 10¢ an hour for a ten-hour day), a tavern, a homestead, a lawyer's office, and a doctor's office (with whiskey and opium as anesthetics, and a price list with items of 25¢ to pull a tooth and $1.25 to deliver a baby). The druggist sells old-fashioned pomanders and here is the recipe:

Take 3 ounces whole cloves, stick them into an orange so they will touch each other all way around. Then roll each one in 2 teaspoons orris root powder and 2 teaspoons ground cinnamon, wrap each one in tissue paper and put away for several weeks in a cool place. Will keep indefinitely. Keeps out moths.

One real curiosity is the Cardiff Giant lying peacefully on the ground. He has been described as the "most amazing of all American frauds." A Chicago stonecutter with two assistants produced this 10½-foot, 2990-pound giant and aged him with sulfuric acid. He was then carted off to Syracuse, buried, and "accidentally" discovered. He was an immediate best-seller, with six million people paying 50¢ apiece to see him before the deception was discovered. The Farmers' Museum is open daily from May 1 to October 31.

The Cooper Inn is open all year. Mr. H. J. Merrick, Jr., is the innkeeper.

THE OTESAGA

Cooperstown, New York

THE Otesaga is one of two Treadway Inns in Cooperstown. The other is the Cooper Inn, which has just been described. There you will also find a little about the history and sports of Cooperstown and a description of one of the town's points of interest – the Farmers' Museum.

The Otesaga was built in 1909 as a resort by the Clark family of Singer Sewing Machine fame. It is a large, towering brick building with tall white pillars, and it looks like a Southern mansion. The driveway to the front entrance sweeps up a wide sloping lawn dotted with stately old trees. The whole effect of the inn is one of immense size and airy spaciousness. The ceilings are high, and the rooms are built on a grand scale. There is a ballroom, for example, which will seat two hundred and fifty people.

The Otesaga is on the nine-mile Lake Otsego and has a circular porch facing it. You will find nice old-fashioned rocking chairs to sit in, too. Mr. H. J. Merrick, Jr., the innkeeper, bought new aluminum ones, but the guests objected, saying they were too hard to get out of, so he obliged them by putting back the old rockers and received a letter of thanks signed by every guest. The view from the porch is magnificent, across the length of the wooded lake to the mountain at the end popularly called the Sleeping Lion.

There is an eighteen-hole golf course right at the door and The Otesaga has a private swimming dock. It also has a billiard room, putting green, croquet, and shuffleboard. A pianist plays in the cocktail lounge; there are movies once a week, a few entertainers, and TV. One attractive feature of The Otesaga is the corridor and bar below the first floor decorated with themes from James Fenimore Cooper's *Leatherstocking Tales*. There are displays of old New York State glass, American folk arts, "froufrou," such as hats and veils, lace parasols and jewelry, and so on.

The New York State Historical Society has its headquarters in Fenimore House, which stands across the road from the Farmers' Museum. Both museums reflect the life of the community in the last century, in different ways. Fenimore House has seven folk-art galleries, exhibiting such branches as decorated tinware, goose decoys, weathervanes, figureheads, needlework, and cigar-store carvings. Other exhibitions are the famous Browere collection of life masks of many outstanding historical figures, Cooper manuscripts, documents relating to the Hamilton–Burr duel, an art gallery, a Shaker exhibit, and a photography exhibit of three hundred sepia enlargements covering many years of the work of Arthur J. "Putt" Telfer, who was credited with having the best "wet" plates anywhere. The Historical Society has an eight-thousand-volume library. There is also a lovely herb garden. Fenimore House is open daily from May 1 to October 31, and five days a week the rest of the year.

One hundred and twenty-five thousand baseball fans make a pilgrimage every year to Cooperstown to visit the National Baseball Hall of Fame and Museum and Doubleday Field. Cooperstown is officially the home of baseball. In a local cow pasture, Abner Doubleday suggested the first fundamental rules of the present sport, converting the game of "one-old-cat" (one man against the field) to a contest between two equal teams. The first traditional baseball diamond was built in 1839 and the museum was dedicated one hundred years later. It has four exhibition halls reflecting the history and development of the game. There is the famous Hall of Fame, containing plaques of great players, Babe Ruth's locker and a gallery of mementoes of him, and many, many more memorabilia. The museum is open all year, and until 9 o'clock at night in the summer.

The Otesaga is open to the public from July 1 until after Labor Day, and for conventions from May 1 to July 1 and from Labor Day until October 31.

LUNCHEON DISHES

THE trend toward lighter lunches is in evidence even at the Treadway Inns, with many people preferring them to large sleep-provoking meals in the middle of the day. The inns offer a much more varied selection than this chapter would imply, since sandwiches and some of the simpler egg and vegetable dishes have not been included.

OMELETS

There are two main types of omelets, the plain, or French, omelet and the puffy omelet.

BASIC PLAIN OR FRENCH OMELET

The ingredients are simple enough, just eggs, water, and salt. The trick is the technique. The pan should be of heavy metal, preferably aluminum, although an iron skillet will do, and at least 6 inches across for an individual omelet. It is best to use the pan only for omelets, since it should never be washed, just wiped out with a paper towel. The pan thus becomes seasoned, and the omelets will not stick to it. To season a new pan, wash well, cover the bottom with salad oil, and leave overnight. Then pour off the oil and wipe the pan.

Preheat the pan for about 10 minutes over a very low fire. For each omelet beat 3 eggs, 1 tablespoon of water, and a little salt with a fork or a rotary beater until well blended but not frothy. Strain them. When ready to make the omelet, turn up the heat under the pan. The pan should be hot enough to make butter sizzle but not brown. Put a good tablespoon of butter in the pan and when it is melted, pour in the eggs. Leave for maybe 30 seconds, until the bottom starts to set a little, then shake the pan with one hand and stir the eggs lightly with a fork with the other. While the omelet is still soft and creamy, let stand for a few seconds, then tilt the pan at right angles toward a hot plate or omelet dish, and with the same fork, fold the omelet over and turn out.

OMELET VARIATIONS

There are literally dozens of omelet variations. The following are some of the most popular ones at the Treadway Inns.

Cheese. Sprinkle ½ cup of grated Cheddar cheese over the omelet after it is cooked but before it is folded over. Let stand for a few seconds to melt the cheese.

Fines Herbes. Finely chop enough fresh herbs to make 1 to 2 tablespoons. Two or three herbs are sufficient, and with parsley and chives as a base, you may add basil, tarragon, marjoram, or thyme. Add to the beaten eggs before the omelet is cooked.

Water Cress. Add ¼ cup of chopped water cress to the beaten eggs before the omelet is cooked. Garnish with 1 tablespoon of sour cream.

Mushroom. Add ½ cup of sliced sautéed mushrooms to the beaten eggs before the omelet is cooked.

Ham. Add ½ cup of ground or finely diced cooked ham to the beaten eggs before the omelet is cooked.

Parsley and Ham. Add 1 tablespoon of finely chopped parsley to the above ham omelet.

Cheese and Ham. Add 1/4 cup of grated Cheddar cheese and 1/4 cup of ground or finely diced cooked ham to the beaten eggs before the omelet is cooked.

Parsley and Smoked Oyster. Add 1 to 2 tablespoons of finely chopped parsley to the beaten eggs before the omelet is cooked. Garnish with smoked oysters.

Western. Sauté 1 tablespoon of minced white onion and 1/2 cup of ground or finely diced cooked ham in 1 tablespoon of butter until the onion is golden brown. Add to the beaten eggs before the omelet is cooked.

Bacon. Add 1/4 cup of crisp cooked bacon bits to the beaten eggs before the omelet is cooked. Garnish with strips of cooked bacon.

Grandmère. Add 1/2 cup of tiny buttered croutons and 1 tablespoon of chopped parsley to the beaten eggs before the omelet is cooked.

Parmentier. Add 1/2 cup of tiny diced sautéed potatoes and 1 tablespoon of chopped parsley to the beaten eggs before the omelet is cooked.

Paysanne. The same as Parmentier, with 1 to 2 tablespoons of diced crisp bacon added. The potatoes may be cooked in the bacon fat.

Wild Grape Jelly. Garnish a basic omelet with wild grape jelly.

Caviar with Sour Cream. Cut a cooked omelet down the center and fill with red caviar. Garnish with 1 tablespoon of sour cream and a little chopped parsley.

Sweetbread. Cut a cooked omelet down the center and fill with sautéed cubed sweetbreads.

Cottage Cheese. Cut a cooked omelet down the center and fill with cottage cheese that has been blended with chopped chives, parsley, or ground cooked ham.

Spanish. Sauté 1 tablespoon of minced onion and 1 tablespoon of minced green pepper in 1 tablespoon of butter until soft. Add 1½ cups of chopped tomatoes (with the seedy pulp removed), season, and cook until thick and smooth. Spoon over a cooked omelet.

Lobster Newburg. Cut a cooked omelet down the center and fill with lobster Newburg.

Chicken à la King or Creamed Chicken. Cut a cooked omelet down the center and fill with chicken à la king or creamed chicken.

Shrimp Creole. Cut a cooked omelet down the center and fill with shrimp Creole.

Chicken Liver. Sauté diced chicken livers in a little butter until brown, and combine with brown sauce with a little sherry added. Cut a cooked omelet down the center and fill with this mixture.

PUFFY OMELET

1 *slice white bread*
½ *cup milk*
2 *tablespoons butter*
4 *eggs, separated*
salt, pepper

This particular recipe is a good one because the omelet is solid enough not to collapse when cut. Trim the crusts off 1 slice of white bread about ½ inch thick. Scald ½ cup of milk and pour it over the bread; let stand for 10 minutes so that the bread can absorb the milk. Meanwhile, season the egg yolks with salt and pepper and beat with a rotary beater until thick, which takes about 3 minutes. Drain any excess milk off the bread and add the bread to the yolks; beat for another minute or so to blend. Beat the egg whites until stiff and fold them into the yolk mixture. Melt 2 tablespoons of butter in a 9-inch skillet, pour in the omelet, and cook over a moderate fire for about 5 minutes. Place in a moderately hot oven at 400°. The top will puff up and brown lightly in 5 to 8 minutes. Serve immediately and cut in quarters.

This is good with cheese, mushroom or Spanish sauce, or just as it is. Serves 4.

SHIRRED EGGS

Shirred eggs are cooked in small individual dishes in the oven, and are a delicious way of cooking eggs. Like omelets, they may be given added interest by various garnishes.

Use a special shirred-egg dish or any shallow ovenproof dish large enough to hold 2 eggs and pretty enough to go to the table. Place it in a preheated oven at 375° with 1 teaspoon of butter until the butter is melted. Break 2 eggs into the dish, dot with butter, and season with salt and a little white pepper. A tablespoon of cream may be added also. Bake about 8 to 12 minutes, until the whites are set and the yolks firm but not hard.

VARIATIONS

Cooked shirred eggs may be garnished with sautéed chicken livers, country bacon, small sausage patties, sliced broiled ham, or tenderloin tips. They may also be sprinkled with grated Cheddar or Swiss cheese before they are cooked, or with a combination of grated cheese and ground cooked ham.

PIZZA EGGS

8 *eggs*
¼ *cup light cream*
salt, pepper
3 *tablespoons butter*
4 *slices tomato*
4 *rings green pepper*
8 *slices bacon, lightly cooked*
1 *cup grated Cheddar cheese*

Beat 8 eggs with ¼ cup of light cream, salt, and pepper until well blended. Melt 3 tablespoons of butter in a saucepan. Add the eggs and cook over a slow fire until they are starting to set but are still creamy, stirring constantly with a wooden spoon. Place the scrambled eggs in an ovenproof shallow baking dish. Cover with 4 slices of tomato surrounded by 4 green-pepper rings.

Put 2 slices of lightly cooked bacon on each tomato and sprinkle 1 cup of grated Cheddar cheese over all. Place under the broiler until the cheese is melted and serve immediately. Serves 4.

EGGS CREOLE

- 6 *eggs*
- 1 *green pepper, diced*
- 1 *small onion, finely chopped*
- 4 *tablespoons butter*
- 2 *tablespoons flour*
- 1 *cup beef stock*
- 1 *can cream of tomato soup*
- 3 or 4 *drops Tabasco*
- *salt*
- 1 *cup grated American cheese*
- ½ *cup bread crumbs*

Hard-cook 6 eggs on a low heat, since rapid cooking makes them tough. Sauté 1 diced green pepper and 1 chopped onion in 2 tablespoons of butter until they are soft but not brown, using a medium-size skillet. Blend in 2 tablespoons of flour. Add 1 cup of beef stock and 1 can of cream of tomato soup and stir over the fire until the mixture comes to a boil. Season with 3 or 4 drops of Tabasco and salt. Stir in 1 cup of grated cheese, and slice and add the eggs. Put into a lightly greased casserole or individual baking dishes. Top with ½ cup of bread crumbs and dot with 2 tablespoons of butter. Bake for 20 minutes in a moderate oven at 375°, until the top is nicely browned. Serves 4 or 5.

EGG CROQUETTES

- 4 *hard-cooked eggs*
- ½ *small white onion*
- 2 *tablespoons butter*
- 1 *tablespoon flour*
- ¼ *cup milk*
- *salt, pepper*
- 1 *egg, slightly beaten*
- *cracker crumbs* or *corn meal*
- 2 *tablespoons shortening*

Chop 4 hard-cooked eggs and ½ small white onion together, as fine as possible, or put them through the meat grinder. Melt 2 tablespoons of butter, blend in 1 tablespoon of flour, and, when that is smooth, slowly add ¼ cup of milk. Stir constantly until it reaches the boiling point. Be careful, because this sauce is thick enough to scorch easily. Mix the eggs with the sauce and season well with salt and pepper. Spread out on a plate and put in the refrigerator to cool and stiffen. Let stand for an hour; longer will not matter. Then shape with a spoon or your hands into 6 oval croquettes. Dip into a slightly beaten egg, then coat well with cracker crumbs or corn meal. Heat 2 tablespoons of vegetable shortening in a skillet and fry the croquettes quickly until brown on both sides. Serve immediately, while they are still piping hot, with cheese, mushroom or tomato sauce, or plain. Serves 2 or 3.

FRESH ASPARAGUS AND HAM WITH CHEESE SAUCE

24 *stalks cooked asparagus*
8 *thin slices boiled ham*

CHEESE SAUCE

2 *tablespoons butter*
1 *tablespoon flour*
1 *cup milk*
salt, pepper
1 *cup grated American* or *Swiss cheese*
1 *egg, slightly beaten*
2 *tablespoons whipped cream*

Place 3 stalks of thoroughly drained cooked asparagus on each slice of boiled ham and roll the ham around them. Place the rolls close together in a greased shallow baking dish, or put 2 rolls each on 4 individual flameproof dishes. To make the cheese sauce, melt 2 tablespoons of butter and blend in 1 tablespoon of flour. Pour on 1 cup of milk, season with salt and pepper, and stir until the mixture comes to a boil. Add ½ cup of grated American or Swiss cheese and stir until the cheese is melted. Remove the sauce from the fire and stir in 1 slightly beaten egg and 2 tablespoons of whipped cream. Spoon the sauce over the ham rolls and sprinkle with the remaining ½ cup of cheese. Bake in a moderate oven at 375° to heat the rolls thoroughly, and finish off under the broiler to brown the top lightly. Serves 4.

POACHED EGGS BENEDICT

4 *English muffins*	8 *eggs*
3 *to* 4 *tablespoons butter*	*Hollandaise sauce*
8 *slices cooked ham*	8 *slices truffles* or *black olives*

Split 4 English muffins in half by pushing a fork through each muffin all around the middle; cutting them with a knife makes them tough. Butter each half. Sauté 8 slices of ham the same size as the muffins in butter until lightly browned. Poach 8 eggs: bring salted water to the boiling point in a wide shallow saucepan or skillet, and then either turn the heat down or take the pan off the fire while you slip each egg from a custard cup into the water. Keep the water at a simmering point while the eggs poach, because if they cook briskly, the eggs will disintegrate. Remove with a slotted spoon and drain well. (Poached eggs can be kept waiting in a bowl of warm water until ready to use.) To serve, lightly brown the muffins under the broiler. Place a slice of ham and a poached egg on each half, carefully spoon Hollandaise sauce over the eggs, and glaze under the broiler. Top with a small slice of truffle or black olive. Serves 4.

HOLLANDAISE SAUCE

¼ *pound butter*	*salt*
2 *egg yolks*	*speck of cayenne*
1½ *tablespoons lemon juice*	*little light cream*

Divide ¼ pound of butter into 3 parts. Put 1 part in a double boiler with 2 unbeaten egg yolks, 1½ tablespoons of lemon juice, salt, and a speck of cayenne. Place over *very gently* boiling water. Stir with a wooden spoon until smooth and the butter is melted. Add the other 2 parts of butter, one at a time, stirring each time until the sauce is smooth and thick. Remove and thin with a little light cream. If the sauce is to stand, keep it covered in a warm bowl in a skillet with an inch or so of warm (not hot) water in the bottom.

CHEESE SOUFFLÉ

1/4 cup butter
1/4 cup flour
1 cup milk
1 teaspoon salt
1/8 teaspoon paprika
1/2 teaspoon dry mustard
1 cup grated American cheese
4 eggs, separated
grated Parmesan cheese, optional

The Cooper Inn in Cooperstown, N.Y., serves this cheese soufflé. The chef guarantees that it won't collapse as soon as it leaves the oven, but will hold up remarkably well. It does, too. The secret seems to be the long cooking time – an hour. Ordinarily, half an hour is long enough, and it is for this soufflé if it can be served immediately. But it becomes firmer the longer it cooks, and if cooked an hour, can be kept waiting after it is removed from the oven or be served at different times.

Melt 1/4 cup of butter in a medium-size saucepan. Blend in 1/4 cup of flour. Add 1 cup of milk, 1 teaspoon of salt, 1/8 teaspoon of paprika, and 1/2 teaspoon of dry mustard. Bring to a boil, stirring constantly. Add 1 cup of grated cheese and stir until the cheese is melted. Remove from the fire. Add 4 unbeaten egg yolks, one at a time, beating after each addition. Let cool. Then fold in 4 stiffly beaten egg whites. Put into a greased 2-quart soufflé dish or baking dish. Place in a pan with an inch of boiling water in the bottom. Bake for an hour in a moderate oven at 350° until brown and firm to the touch. Serves 6.

Note. A little grated Parmesan cheese may be sprinkled over the top before baking. The flavor may also be varied by using an ounce of sieved Camembert or Roquefort or an ounce of grated Gruyère as well as the American cheese.

CREAMED MACARONI, HAM AND CHEESE

1/2 pound macaroni
4 tablespoons butter
3 tablespoons flour
2 cups milk
salt, white pepper
1/2 pound Cheddar cheese, grated
1 to 2 cups diced cooked ham

Cook the macaroni in at least 3 quarts of boiling salted water until just tender, usually about 10 minutes, stirring occasionally with a long fork to keep the macaroni from sticking to the bottom of the pan. Drain well in a colander. Meanwhile make the following cream sauce: Melt 4 tablespoons of butter. Blend in 3 tablespoons of flour. Pour on 2 cups of milk, season, and stir over the fire until the sauce comes to a boil. Add half the grated cheese and continue stirring until the cheese is melted. Make alternate layers of macaroni, ham, and sauce in a greased wide casserole or in individual casseroles, having 2 or 3 layers in all. Sprinkle the top with the remaining cheese. Bake for 20 to 30 minutes in a moderate oven at 375°, until the mixture is bubbling and the cheese is melted. Finish off under the broiler if the top is not lightly browned. Serves 6.

ORANGE FRENCH TOAST

6 *slices slightly stale white bread*
marmalade
2 *eggs*
4 *tablespoons milk*
1 *teaspoon sugar*
about 1 *tablespoon butter*
sifted confectioners' sugar

Spread 3 slices of slightly stale white bread with marmalade, and sandwich with the other 3 slices. Beat together 2 eggs, 4 tablespoons of milk, and 1 teaspoon of sugar, and dip the sandwiches in this mixture. Sauté them in a hot skillet with about 1 tablespoon of butter until brown on both sides. Sprinkle with sifted confectioners' sugar and cut in half diagonally before serving. Serves 3.

WELSH RABBIT

A true Welsh rabbit (or rarebit) is made with nothing but cheese, butter, beer or ale, and a little mustard. Americans put Worcestershire sauce in it, but you will not find that in an authentic English recipe.

The secret of a successful rabbit is a well-aged cheese, and constant stirring over a very gentle heat. For 3 or 4 people, melt 1 tablespoon of butter with about ½ teaspoon of prepared mustard in a double boiler over slowly boiling water. Add 1 pound of grated sharp Cheddar or Cheshire cheese and stir slowly with a wooden spoon. When the cheese starts to melt, gradually add ½ cup of beer or ale. As soon as the cheese is melted and the mixture smooth, pour over hot toast on a hot plate and serve immediately. Sometimes a beaten egg is added after the cheese is melted; it acts as an emulsifier and will keep the cheese from possibly getting stringy.

NEVER–FAIL RABBIT

- 1½ *tablespoons butter*
- ½ *teaspoon dry mustard*
- ⅛ *teaspoon paprika*
- *salt*
- 1½ *tablespoons flour*
- 1½ *cups milk*
- 1 *cup grated Cheddar cheese*
- 1 *egg*

This is more of a rabbit sauce than a true rabbit, but it holds up well, so it is useful when it cannot be served immediately. Melt 1½ tablespoons of butter with ½ teaspoon of dry mustard, ⅛ teaspoon of paprika, and salt. Blend in 1½ tablespoons of flour. Pour on 1½ cups of milk and stir until the mixture comes to a boil. Add 1 cup of grated Cheddar cheese and stir until the cheese is melted. Beat 1 egg well. Pour the cheese mixture over the egg, return to the fire, and cook 2 minutes longer. Serve immediately on hot buttered toast, or keep hot in a double boiler over gently boiling water until ready to use. Serves 4.

FRUIT SALAD

For each serving, remove the fruit from half a pineapple, with the top leaves on, or half a cantaloupe. Cut the pineapple in chunks, or make balls out of the melon. Combine gently with honeydew and watermelon balls, sliced banana, small seedless grapes or halved seeded grapes, fresh stoned cherries, and a few mint leaves. Pile into the pineapple or melon shell and top with 2 small scoops of sherbet, using lime in combination with orange, lemon, or raspberry. This may be served with a dressing made by blending vanilla ice cream with mayonnaise.

MUSHROOMS STUFFED WITH CHICKEN LIVERS, WHITE WINE SAUCE

8 *large mushroom caps*
3 *tablespoons butter*
1 *teaspoon lemon juice*
salt, pepper
1 *pound chicken livers*
4 *thin slices white bread*

Sauté 8 large mushroom caps in 2 tablespoons of butter with 1 teaspoon of lemon juice, salt, and pepper. Cook gently just until lightly browned. In another pan, cook 1 pound of chicken livers in 1 tablespoon of hot butter over a brisk fire until well browned all over, which will take about 5 minutes. Toast 4 thin slices of white bread and cut them in half to form triangles. Place a sautéed mushroom cap on each triangle, and put a chicken liver in each cap. Arrange on a hot platter or on 4 individual dishes. Garnish with the remaining chicken livers — there are about 1 dozen whole livers to the pound. Pour over the following white wine sauce. Serves 4.

WHITE WINE SAUCE

2 *shallots* or 1 *small white onion, sliced*
½ *cup white wine*
2 *tablespoons butter*
1 *tablespoon flour*
1 *cup chicken stock*
few drops lemon juice
1 *teaspoon chopped parsley*

Simmer 2 sliced shallots or 1 small sliced white onion in ½ cup of white wine until the wine is reduced to ¼ cup. Melt 2 tablespoons of butter. Blend in 1 tablespoon of flour. Add 1 cup of chicken stock and stir until the mixture comes to a boil. Add the strained wine, a few drops of lemon juice, and taste for seasoning. Simmer for at least 5 minutes. Before serving, add 1 teaspoon of chopped parsley and the mushroom pan juices.

DELICATELY THIN FRENCH PANCAKES WITH JELLY AND BACON

2 *large eggs*
½ *cup flour*
½ *cup milk*
½ *teaspoon salt*
2 *tablespoons warm melted butter*
jelly
confectioners' sugar
crisp cooked bacon

Beat 2 large eggs with a rotary beater for about ½ minute. Add ½ cup flour, ½ cup milk, ½ teaspoon salt, and beat just until blended and smooth. Blend in 2 tablespoons of warm melted butter. Let stand covered for at least ½ hour.

Lightly grease a hot 6 or 7-inch skillet or omelet pan with butter. The butter should sizzle but not brown. Spoon in about 2 tablespoons of batter and tip the pan to distribute the batter evenly. Cook over a moderate fire until brown on one side, about 1 minute, then turn and brown the other side. To serve, spread thinly with jelly (wild grape is delicious) and roll up. Dust with confectioners' sugar, and serve with crisp bacon. Allow 3 pancakes per serving.

CHEESE BLINTZES

French pancakes
1 *cup cottage cheese*
salt
2 *to* 3 *tablespoons sugar*
grated lemon rind, optional
sour cream

Make French pancakes following the preceding recipe, but cook only on one side. Blend together 1 cup of cottage cheese, a little salt, and 2 to 3 tablespoons of sugar. A little grated lemon rind may also be added. Place a spoonful of this mixture down the center of the cooked side of the pancake, and fold two opposite sides over the filling, then roll the pancake up. Sauté in butter until lightly browned all over. Serve with sour cream and sugar.

1812 HOUSE

Framingham, Massachusetts

IN Framingham, about midway between Boston and Worcester on the Worcester Turnpike (Route 9), stands the 1812 House, more or less unchanged externally for the last one hundred and forty-five years. The turnpike has been a thoroughfare for much longer than that. Three centuries ago the Indians made a trail there over the low hills of east central Massachusetts to Connecticut, and in 1633 the first pioneers followed this path. Oxcarts were then superseded by stagecoaches, and the trail became a highway linking Boston and Worcester.

In 1812 one John Fiske purchased from one Thomas Buckingham a site overlooking this highway, and the same year he built the house which has been known through the succeeding years as the 1812 House. It is a name that seems to stick readily in the mind and on the tongue; Robie L. Faulkner, the innkeeper, says that it is now well known all over the country. Mr. Fiske's daughter married Colonel James Brown, whose son, James Watson Brown, opened a boys' boarding school in the house. It was famous for a geometrical birdhouse in the yard by which the students were taught geometry. The house remained in the same family until 1946, when Mr. Faulkner took it over.

The architecture is typically colonial: white clapboards with dark shutters, and a fine weathervane. The front entrance has a lovely wisteria-covered arch over a wide door spanned by a fanlight. Much of the interior of the house is old and unchanged. The hallway has the original and elegant staircase with fine molding, a graceful balustrade, and a famous newel post with a silver dollar minted in 1812 imbedded in it. There are also an old chandelier and wall sconces.

The drawing rooms are furnished with antiques of 1812 vintage, and the walls are covered with reproductions of old wallpapers. The windows have the original "Indian" shutters, so called for obvious reasons.

There are five separate dining rooms of individual character, which can seat two hundred and fifty people. The Hearth Room was the old kitchen and has the original great brick fireplace complete with contemporary utensils. The charming wallpaper is by Archibald Rutledge and is called the Charleston (South Carolina) rose. The Pine Room is named for its pine wainscoting, and may be used for banquets, since it will seat seventy-five people. An attractive feature of this room is the window wall on one side, lined with old glass. The main dining room is the Terrace Room, which was added in 1946. It is a most pleasant room with high ceilings, dark green walls, upholstered chairs, hurricane lamps, and a soothing indoor water-lily pool with a gentle waterfall effect. The room is surrounded on three sides with rhododendrons – each plant of a different variety – which enclose the room with a living soft gray-green wall. Since the room is soundproofed, there is an air of quiet and peace, which seems incredible in a building located on a main highway. It is a very suitable place to enjoy the inn's fine food.

The rustic cocktail lounge is another original room, actually a second kitchen with the old fireplace, a collection of old iron implements, and some of the original beams. The chairs are reproductions of captains' chairs. Upstairs there is a private room which may be used for bridge parties.

The 1812 House is twenty miles from Boston, twenty-six miles from Worcester, and about forty miles from Providence. It is one and a half miles from each of two Framingham exits on the Massachusetts Turnpike. There is ample free parking space. The inn is gastronomic and atmospheric only; it has no accommodations for overnight guests. It is open from April 1 to December 1.

SALADS

SALADS can play an important role in a meal — nutritionally, for eye appeal, and for texture. There are many sorts of salads, from the simple but excellent plain mixed green salads to ones using almost any vegetable or fruit, meat, fish, or seafood. In this chapter we are concerned primarily with salads that are used as adjuncts to meals, rather than as main courses, and we are confining our discussion to a few basic salads and salad dressings. The Treadway Inns' menus list many more salads than you will find here, but since space is always a problem, salads have been sacrificed.

One way to make a salad interesting is to try various greens. Lettuce, of course, is the staple one. Markets or gardens supply quite an assortment: head lettuce (Boston, Simpson, and iceberg), endive, chicory, escarole, romaine, and the relatively new Bibb which is a great delicacy. Other greens include spinach leaves, water cress, corn salad, and dandelions.

All greens should be washed before they are used or stored. They grow close to the ground and are necessarily quite silty. Separate into leaves without breaking them and remove the core if there is one. Always handle greens gently, since they bruise easily. Run cold water over them, and again be gentle. Then dry thoroughly, ideally in a wire salad basket. Chill in the refrigerator in a clean cloth or stockinette salad bag or a plastic bag. If you do not have time to chill them, soaking in ice water for a short time will make the greens crisp and fresh.

MIXED GREEN SALAD

A mixed green salad can be just lettuce or lettuces, or other vegetables may be added. The most frequently used vegetables are tomatoes, onions, celery, cucumbers, radishes, and carrots. Peel the tomatoes and cut them into quarters and sixths; don't slice them into the salad bowl, because the juice will make the dressing watery. Peel and thinly slice onions, and try using red ones sometimes for color. Slice celery, cucumbers, and radishes very thin and leave the skin on radishes for color. Grate carrots or cut them into julienne strips. Chill them well before using.

Making the salad should be a last-minute job. If you want to use garlic, either rub the salad bowl with a cut clove of garlic, or rub the heel of a loaf of French bread with garlic and mix it with the greens, removing it before serving the salad. Bread used this way is called a *chapon*. Break the greens into pieces and drop them into the bowl. Add any prepared vegetables. Most salads are improved by adding herbs: chives, tarragon, parsley, chervil, basil, marjoran, or summer savory all can be used, finely chopped. Then add the salad dressing, either just before the salad is brought to the table or right at the table. Add just enough dressing, preferably French dressing, to coat the leaves, and toss lightly with a salad fork and spoon.

CHEF'S SALAD

Thin julienne strips of cooked chicken, ham, tongue, and Swiss cheese are added to a mixed green salad to make it a main-course dish.

FRENCH DRESSING

Basically, French dressing is nothing but oil, vinegar, salt, pepper, and a little dry mustard. That doesn't mean that you won't find endless additions, many of them good. But the starting point is five simple ingredients. Into a screw-top jar put 1 teaspoon of salt, some black pepper, and about 1/4 teaspoon of dry mustard. The proportions of oil to vinegar are subject to great controversy, but let's be dogmatic and say it should be 1 part of vinegar to 3 to 4 parts of oil. The vinegar can be red or white wine vinegar, tarragon or other herb vinegar, cider vinegar, or whatever you like. The oil at least partly should be good olive oil, and preferably all olive oil, although some people find the taste too strong. For 1 teaspoon of salt, use 1 cup of oil and 1/4 to 1/3 cup of vinegar. Shake well, and chill in the refrigerator. Shake again before using, since it will separate. An egg added to the mixture will help emulsify it and keep it intact. A whole garlic clove may be stored with the dressing, but not for too long, since the flavor increases rather than diminishes.

ROQUEFORT DRESSING

The Treadway Inns are justly famous for their Roquefort dressing – a lovely creamy one full of small chunks of Roquefort. Roquefort dressing can also be made by just adding crumbled cheese to a French dressing; this version is good, but it lacks the smooth richness of the Treadway Inns' specialty.

1/2 *cup cider vinegar*
1 3-*ounce cream cheese*
salt
dash Tabasco
2 *cups mayonnaise*
6 *ounces Roquefort cheese*
lemon juice, optional
light cream, optional

In a mixing bowl or an electric mixer blend together 1/2 cup of vinegar, a 3-ounce cream cheese, salt, and a dash of Tabasco. Add 2 cups of mayonnaise and continue beating until smooth. Stir in 6 ounces of Roquefort cheese that has been broken into small pieces. The dressing should not be beaten after the cheese is added, since you want actual pieces of cheese. A little lemon juice may be added if you wish, and the dressing may be thinned with a little light cream.

NEVER-FAIL FIVE-MINUTE MAYONNAISE

2 *egg yolks* or 1 *whole egg*
¼ *teaspoon dry mustard*
1 *tablespoon vinegar*
¼ *teaspoon pepper*
1 *scant teaspoon salt*
1 *cup salad oil (use part olive oil)*
1 *to 2 tablespoons lemon juice*

True mayonnaise is made with just the egg yolks, but using a whole egg guarantees that it will not curdle and does not alter the flavor. Put either 2 egg yolks or 1 whole egg in a small deep mixing bowl with ¼ teaspoon dry mustard, 1 tablespoon vinegar (preferably red wine or tarragon), ¼ teaspoon pepper, and 1 scant teaspoon salt. Beat with a rotary beater or electric mixer about ½ minute. Then slowly add about 1 cup of salad oil. If all olive oil is used, be sure it is a mild one. A little more than 1 cup of oil may be needed, depending upon the size of the eggs. Lastly add 1 to 2 tablespoons of lemon juice.

RUSSIAN DRESSING

Blend equal parts of mayonnaise and chili sauce.

THOUSAND ISLAND DRESSING

1 *cup mayonnaise*
2 *tablespoons finely chopped sweet pickles*
2 *tablespoons chili sauce*
1 *tablespoon finely chopped pimento*
2 *tablespoons finely chopped green olives*
1 *tablespoon finely chopped chives*
1 *tablespoon heavy cream*
salt
dash paprika

Combine the above ingredients and blend well.

SOUR CREAM DRESSING

1 *teaspoon salt*
¼ *teaspoon mild paprika*
½ *teaspoon dry mustard*
dash cayenne
1 *tablespoon cider vinegar*
1 *tablespoon lemon juice*
1 *cup sour cream*
1 *tablespoon chopped chives*

In a small china or glass bowl blend together 1 teaspoon of salt, ¼ teaspoon of paprika, ½ teaspoon of dry mustard, a dash of cayenne, 1 tablespoon each of vinegar and lemon juice. Slowly stir in 1 cup of sour cream, then add 1 tablespoon of chopped chives. Chill well before using. This dressing has an excellent flavor and the paprika gives it a pleasing color. It is nice with mixed greens, seafood salad (*see* page 90), or raw vegetable salad.

CAESAR SALAD

½ *cup olive oil*
3 *cloves garlic*
2 *heads romaine*
2 *eggs*
1 *teaspoon pepper*
½ *teaspoon salt*
½ *teaspoon dry mustard*
1 *lemon*
1 *cup croutons*
½ *cup grated Parmesan cheese*
6 *anchovy fillets*

A vital ingredient for this recipe is garlic olive oil, which is made by letting ½ cup of olive oil stand for a day, or overnight, with 3 cloves of garlic. Remove the garlic before using the oil. Wash 2 heads of crisp romaine lettuce and dry thoroughly, since water will ruin the salad. Chill well. In a small mixing bowl drop 2 coddled eggs which have stood just 30 seconds in boiling water. Pour over them the garlic olive oil, and season with 1 teaspoon of freshly ground pepper, ½ teaspoon of salt, ½ teaspoon of dry mustard, and the juice of 1 lemon. Beat very well and pour over the lettuce. Toss lightly. Add 1 cup of croutons, ½ cup of grated Parmesan cheese, and 6 anchovy fillets cut into small pieces. Toss again and serve immediately, while the croutons are still crisp. Serves 4.

CUCUMBERS WITH SOUR CREAM DRESSING

2 *large cucumbers*
1 *medium-size yellow onion*
3 *to* 4 *tablespoons sour cream*
2 *tablespoons tarragon vinegar*
1 *teaspoon salt*
¼ *teaspoon white pepper*

Peel 2 large cucumbers and cut them into very thin slices. Thinly slice 1 medium-size yellow onion. Blend together 3 to 4 tablespoons of sour cream, 2 tablespoons of tarragon vinegar, 1 teaspoon of salt, and ¼ teaspoon of white pepper. Mix with the cucumbers and onion and chill for several hours in the refrigerator. Serves 8 to 10.

CARROT SALAD

5 *tablespoons mayonnaise*
1 *tablespoon sour cream*
1 *teaspoon prepared mustard*
1 *teaspoon lemon juice*
salt, dash paprika
1½ *cups grated carrots*

Mix together well 5 tablespoons of mayonnaise, 1 tablespoon of sour cream, 1 teaspoon of prepared mustard, 1 teaspoon of lemon juice, salt, and a dash of paprika. Add 1½ cups of grated carrots and blend well. Serve plain, on a bed of lettuce, or as a filling for stuffed tomatoes. Serves 3.

POTATO SALAD

Regular potato salad is best when made from potatoes cooked especially for the purpose. Choose old potatoes about the same size and boil them in their jackets until just tender. Drain well and cool with the skins still on. When cooled, peel off the skins and cut in slices about ¼ inch thick. Sprinkle with grated onion, allowing about ¼ teaspoon for each potato. Make a well-seasoned French dressing (*see* page 212) and add enough to coat each slice of potato well. Put in a salad bowl, cover, and chill thoroughly. Before serving, drain off any dressing that has not been absorbed, mix with mayonnaise, add some minced parsley and celery, and garnish with sliced hard-cooked eggs.

Here are two variations.

SPECIAL POTATO SALAD

- 2 *tablespoons sour cream*
- 2 *tablespoons olive oil*
- 1½ *tablespoons lemon juice*
- 2 *tablespoons minced chives*
- ½ *teaspoon prepared mustard*
- *salt*
- 3 *large cooked potatoes, peeled and sliced*

Mix together 2 tablespoons of sour cream, 2 tablespoons of olive oil, 1½ tablespoons of lemon juice, 2 tablespoons of minced chives, ½ teaspoon of prepared mustard, and season well with salt. Add 3 sliced cooked potatoes and blend gently. Chill before serving if you wish. Serves 4.

POTATO–BACON SALAD

- 3 *cups diced raw potatoes*
- 2 *small onions*
- 4 *slices cooked crisp bacon*
- ⅓ *cup French dressing*
- 2 *tablespoons hot bacon fat*
- 1 *tablespoon minced chives*

Cook 3 cups of diced raw potatoes and 2 small onions together until the potatoes are tender, which will take 15 to 20 minutes. Drain well and discard the onions. Add 4 slices of crisp bacon, crumbled, ⅓ cup of French dressing, 2 tablespoons of hot bacon fat, and 1 tablespoon of minced chives. Put in a salad bowl, cover with wax paper, and chill for several hours before serving. Serve with or without lettuce. Serves 6.

SPRING SALAD

1 cup cold boiled potatoes, diced
1 cup celery, diced
1 cup cooked peas
½ cup cucumber, diced
½ cup red radishes, thinly sliced
French dressing
mayonnaise

Toss all the vegetables lightly with a little French dressing. Chill them thoroughly. Just before serving, add enough mayonnaise to moisten and bind the mixture. Pile the salad in a mound and surround with lettuce leaves and whole radishes. Serves 6 to 8.

SPICED BEET SALAD RING

1 1-pound can diced beets
about 1 cup cider vinegar
2 packages lemon gelatin
¼ teaspoon nutmeg
¼ teaspoon ground cloves
¼ teaspoon cinnamon
rind of 1 lemon
1 cup brown sugar
½ pint heavy cream, whipped
horse-radish

Drain 1 can of diced beets and add enough vinegar, about 1 cup, to the juice to make 2 cups of liquid. Dissolve 2 packages of lemon gelatin well in 2 cups of cold water. Put the vinegar and beet juice in a saucepan and bring slowly to a boil with ¼ teaspoon each of nutmeg, cloves, and cinnamon, the rind of 1 lemon, and 1 cup of brown sugar. Stir until the sugar is dissolved, then stir occasionally. When it comes to a boil, remove the lemon peel and add the mixture to the gelatin with the drained beets. Combine, pour into a large ring mold, and chill until set. To serve, unmold on a large platter and fill the center with ½ pint of heavy cream, whipped, seasoned to taste with horse-radish. Serves 10 to 12.

ONION SALAD

2 *large Spanish onions*	2 *tablespoons cider vinegar*
½ *teaspoon salt*	1 *teaspoon lemon juice*
½ *cup olive oil*	1 *tablespoon chopped parsley*

Slice the onions thinly and sprinkle with ½ teaspoon of salt. Mix together ½ cup of olive oil, 2 tablespoons of vinegar, and 1 teaspoon of lemon juice. Pour over the onions, cover, and refrigerate for several hours before serving. Just before serving, sprinkle with 1 tablespoon of chopped parsley. Serves 4.

TOMATO AND ONION SALAD

Marinate 2 or 3 peeled sliced tomatoes with the onions in the preceding recipe.

LONG TRAIL LODGE

Rutland, Vermont

THIS Treadway Inn is right in the heart of the beautiful Green Mountains of Vermont. The Williams Inn is surrounded by mountains, but the Long Trail Lodge is *in* the mountains, at the 2200-foot highest point of Sherburne Pass with 4000-foot Pico Peak in the back yard. The lodge is set back from the road and surrounded by trees but not closed in by them. There are mountains everywhere – wonderful undeveloped forest country of the Green Mountain National Forest. Five minutes away there is a view of the Green Mountains, Taconic Range, and the peaks of the Adirondacks. The Green Mountains are well named, because there is a special beauty in the dark green evergreens, interspersed with birches and deciduous trees which color gorgeously in September and early October, making the countryside spectacular.

The weather is cool in the summer, usually in the sixties at night, guaranteeing sound sleep. The fall and spring days are pleasantly warm, with crisp nights. And the winters are cold, with heavy snowfall, but dry. The lodge is on a main paved road, Route 4, nine miles east of the active city of Rutland. Skiers should note that the main roads are kept well plowed and sanded in Vermont, for the primary reason that vast quantities of milk must get to the market, and secondly so that motorists can get around.

Long Trail Lodge has several buildings—the main house, cottages, and a ski lodge. The architecture is rustic, with the buildings made of native timbers. The main house was built by ex-Governor Mortimer R. Proctor in the early twenties as a clubhouse for a mountain club. It is called Long Trail Lodge because the well-known Long Trail goes right through the main lounge, where the trail markers may be seen at the rear corner door. The large main lounge has birch walls, a fireplace which holds four-foot logs, snowshoe chairs, and Indian rugs on the walls. The dining room is built around a boulder twenty-five feet long and fifteen feet high. One end projects into the dining room and there is a rock garden with a stream of water. The same rustic décor prevails here, with timbered walls, yellow birch tables with pine tops, and old-fashioned split-bottom chairs. Mr. Grover E. Wright, the innkeeper, has had the same good chef and pastry cook for years and the food is excellent. There is a gift shop which sells, among other things, all kinds of marble products, pottery, hand-tooled leather goods, and woolen goods hand-loomed in Canada. There is also a cocktail lounge called the "Muzzle Loader."

The cottages are spacious rustic cabins. They have living rooms, most of them with fireplaces. The Deer Leap Chalet across the road is open in the summer and used for skiers in the winter. It has a large recreation room with a steadily blazing fire, television set, and various indoor games and dancing.

There are several sports at the lodge and in the vicinity. Hiking and skiing are two prominent ones. The Long Trail and the

Appalachian Trail meet here. The Long Trail, called the "footpath in the wilderness," is a 250-mile marked footpath the full length of the Green Mountains from the Massachusetts border near Williamstown to the Canadian border. The scenery is rugged, but the trail is well marked and may be followed safely by inexperienced hikers. The Appalachian Trail starts in Georgia. The two trails follow each other from the Massachusetts border to Sherburne Pass; then the Long Trail goes north, and the Appalachian Trail turns east to the White Mountains and Maine. There are ten trails from the lodge, many of them short. For example, a walk of an hour or so goes along a native trail which starts up the stone stairway from the lounge and ascends to Pulpit Rock, where you can see the Adirondacks sixty miles away and a panorama of the whole valley. The trail descends through a cool rock-ledged canyon.

The Green Mountains have fine snow conditions for sports from mid-December into April. Long Trail Lodge is the only ski area in Vermont with a convenient airport (in Rutland) and pickup service. Pico Peak and the upper ski area are within sight of the lodge, with ski lifts and slopes for the novice as well as difficult runs. There are also skating and snowshoeing. The Deer Leap Chalet has inexpensive bunks for the winter sports.

With all the lakes and streams this is a fine fishing area. Spring and early summer are best for trout and land-locked salmon, and midsummer and fall are good for small-mouth bass, pike, pickerel, and pan fish. Hunters will find bear, deer, grouse, woodcock, and other small game. There are a tennis court on the grounds, two nearby golf courses which are seldom crowded, and nearby riding stables.

A place that draws thousands of visitors each summer is the Vermont Marble Company in Proctor, which is fourteen miles away, where there is the world's largest marble exhibit. Some of the displays are large slabs of samples of most of the marble currently available from quarries all over the world; marble carvings, including a bas-relief of the Last Supper; a chapel; memorials; altars; fireplaces; garden furniture; and bathrooms. A color and sound movie may be seen of the complete process of marble production, and the sawing, shaping, and finishing of marble may be seen on the spot. Admission is free and the exhibit is open from late May to mid-October.

The Long Trail Lodge is open from mid-June to October, and the Deer Leep Chalet from December 15 to April 1.

VEGETABLES

ALTHOUGH vegetables are important nutritionally, maybe for that very reason they are often considered merely a dull duty. So it is up to the restaurateur or housewife to make vegetables appetizing and inviting. To do this, vegetables should be fresh, properly cooked and seasoned, and sometimes dressed up a little. In this chapter we have concentrated on the dressed-up ones, since it is a more interesting phase of the Treadway Inns' menus. But vegetables don't have to be dressed up to be good. Cook them a minimum time in rapidly boiling salted water, drain them thoroughly, drench them in melted butter, and there you are.

ASPARAGUS PARMESAN

2 *pounds fresh* or 1 *package frozen asparagus*
½ *cup grated Parmesan cheese*
2 *tablespoons butter*
salt
freshly ground black pepper

Cook 2 pounds of fresh asparagus or 1 package of frozen asparagus until tender in boiling salted water. Place in a greased shallow baking dish. Sprinkle with ½ cup of grated Parmesan cheese, dot with 2 tablespoons of butter, and season with salt and freshly ground black pepper. Bake in a hot oven at 400° for 10 minutes, then finish off under the broiler until lightly browned. Serves 4.

ASPARAGUS WITH SWISS CHEESE

2 *pounds fresh* or 1 *package frozen asparagus*
½ *cup dry bread crumbs*
3 *tablespoons butter*
½ *cup grated Swiss cheese*

Cook 2 pounds of fresh asparagus or 1 package of frozen asparagus until tender in boiling salted water. Drain well. Lightly brown ½ cup of dry bread crumbs in 3 tablespoons of butter. Place the asparagus in a greased shallow baking dish. Sprinkle with the browned crumbs and ½ cup of grated Swiss cheese. Bake for 10 minutes in a hot oven at 400° and finish off under the broiler until the top is lightly browned and crusty. Serves 4.

SPICED BEETS

2 *cups cooked sliced beets*
2 *tablespoons butter*
2 *tablespoons cider vinegar*
1 *teaspoon sugar*
6 *cloves*
salt

Put 2 cups of cooked sliced beets in a saucepan with 2 tablespoons of butter, 2 tablespoons of cider vinegar, 1 teaspoon of sugar, 6 cloves, and a little salt. Cover and simmer about 10 minutes. Serves 4.

STRING BEANS AND MUSHROOMS IN CREAM

1 *pound fresh green beans*
½ *pound mushrooms, sliced*
2 *tablespoons butter*
2 *tablespoons sherry*
½ *cup light cream*
salt, pepper

Cut the ends off the beans and slice them lengthwise into thin strips. Cook them in boiling salted water until tender, about 10 to

15 minutes. While the beans are cooking, simmer ½ pound of sliced mushrooms in 2 tablespoons of butter and 2 tablespoons of sherry until soft. Combine the drained beans and the mushroom mixture, and add ½ cup of light cream. Season with salt and pepper, and place over the fire until the cream is heated through. If you wish, the sauce may be thickened by adding beurre manié, made by creaming together 1 tablespoon of butter and 1 tablespoon of flour. Add in little bits, stirring constantly. Lima beans, fresh or frozen, may also be served this way. Serves 4.

GREEN BEANS WITH ALMONDS

½ *cup slivered almonds*
3 *to* 4 *tablespoons butter*
1 *pound green beans, thinly sliced*

Blanch and sliver enough almonds to make ½ cup. Or they may be bought already prepared in a can. Sauté them gently in 3 to 4 tablespoons of butter until they are lightly browned. Cook 1 pound of green beans which have been thinly sliced lengthwise (Frenched) in boiling salted water until tender, about 15 to 20 minutes. Drain well, and combine the hot beans with the almonds and butter. Serve immediately. Serves 3 or 4.

LIMA BEANS WITH BACON

3 *pounds lima beans*
6 *slices bacon, diced*
1 *small minced onion*
½ *green pepper, finely chopped*
1 *cup chicken stock*

Cook 3 pounds of lima beans in boiling salted water for 15 minutes and drain. Meanwhile cut 6 slices of bacon into small dice and cook until lightly browned in a medium-size skillet. Remove the bacon bits with a slotted spoon. Put 1 small minced onion and ½ a green pepper, finely chopped, in the pan and cook slowly for 5 minutes. Add the drained limas and 1 cup of chicken stock and simmer for another 15 minutes or so, until the beans are perfectly tender and the liquid absorbed. Sprinkle with the bacon bits just before serving. Serves 6.

BROCCOLI WITH LEMON BUTTER

1 *bunch fresh* or 2 *packages frozen broccoli*
3 *tablespoons butter*
1 *teaspoon flour*
½ *cup water*
2 *tablespoons lemon juice*

Serve 1 bunch of cooked fresh broccoli or 2 packages of cooked frozen broccoli with the following lemon butter: Melt 3 tablespoons of butter. Blend in 1 teaspoon of flour. Add ½ cup of water and 2 tablespoons of lemon juice and stir until smooth and hot. Serves 6.

BROCCOLI WITH HORSE-RADISH CREAM

1 *bunch fresh* or 2 *packages frozen broccoli*
1 *cup commercial sour cream*
½ *teaspoon horse-radish*
½ *teaspoon prepared mustard*
¼ *teaspoon salt*

Serve cooked broccoli with the following sauce: Heat together 1 cup of commercial sour cream, ½ teaspoon of horse-radish, ½ teaspoon of prepared mustard, and about ¼ teaspoon of salt. Sufficient for 6 servings.

SAUTÉED BROCCOLI

1 *bunch broccoli*
3 *to* 4 *tablespoons butter*
1 *small chopped onion or* 1 *clove chopped garlic*

Split 1 bunch of broccoli into small sections and cook until almost tender in boiling salted water. Heat 3 to 4 tablespoons of butter in a medium-size skillet and cook 1 small chopped onion or 1 clove of chopped garlic in it for about 5 minutes, until soft but not brown. Strain the butter, discarding the onion or garlic.

Then sauté the broccoli, well drained, in this butter, until lightly browned. Serves 5 or 6.

BROCCOLI PARMESAN

Sprinkle about ½ cup of grated Parmesan cheese over the sautéed broccoli in the preceding recipe.

FRENCH FRIED BRUSSELS SPROUTS

1 *quart fresh* or 2 *packages frozen Brussels sprouts*
1 *egg*
1 *tablespoon water*
dry bread crumbs
salt, pepper
grated Parmesan cheese, optional

Cook fresh or frozen Brussels sprouts until just tender but still crisp. Drain thoroughly. Beat 1 egg well, and add 1 tablespoon of water. Season dry bread crumbs with a little salt and pepper. Coat the sprouts with crumbs, dip in beaten egg, and cover with crumbs again. Let stand for at least 15 minutes, then fry in deep fat at 375° for 2 to 3 minutes, until nicely browned. Serve at once. May be sprinkled with a little grated Parmesan cheese. Allow 3 or 4 per serving. Cooked cauliflower flowerets are also good French fried in the same way.

BRUSSELS SPROUTS AU GRATIN

1 *quart Brussels sprouts, cooked*
2 *tablespoons butter*
2 *tablespoons flour*
¾ *cup chicken stock*
¾ *cup milk*
salt, pepper, nutmeg
1 *tablespoon lemon juice*
½ *cup grated American cheese*

Make the sauce while the sprouts are cooking. Melt 2 tablespoons of butter. Blend in 2 tablespoons of flour. Add ¾ cup of chicken stock and ¾ cup of milk and stir until the mixture comes to a boil. Season with salt, pepper, and a pinch of nutmeg. Simmer for about 5 minutes. Add 1 tablespoon of lemon juice and ½ cup of grated cheese and stir until the cheese is melted. Drain the sprouts thoroughly and dry out for a minute or so over a slow fire. Add to the sauce and serve piping hot. The mixture may be put into a baking dish and under the broiler until lightly browned. Serves 6.

RED CABBAGE WITH APPLES AND RED WINE

3 slices bacon, diced
1 medium-size red cabbage
1 cup red wine
½ cup brown sugar
2 apples, peeled and diced
¼ cup cider vinegar
salt

Cook the bacon slowly in a medium-size saucepan until it is brown and crisp. Remove the bacon bits with a slotted spoon. Cut the cabbage in thin slices and put it in the pan with 1 cup of red wine, ½ cup of brown sugar, 2 diced apples, ¼ cup of vinegar and some salt. Cook uncovered over a slow fire until the cabbage is tender, about 30 minutes. This cabbage has an agreeable tart taste which is refreshing with rich meats, particularly pork. Sprinkle with the bacon bits just before serving. Serves 5 or 6.

COLE SLAW I

3 cups shredded cabbage
3 tomatoes, quartered
1 small cucumber, peeled and sliced
2 tablespoons chopped parsley
½ cup French dressing
½ cup mayonnaise
salt, pepper

Blend the French dressing and mayonnaise together and mix with the rest of the ingredients. Chill for an hour or so before serving. Serves 4 to 6.

COLE SLAW II

1 medium-size cabbage, shredded
2 large carrots, shredded
2 cups mayonnaise
½ cup sour cream
1 teaspoon celery seed
1 teaspoon mustard seed
1 small onion, finely chopped
1 teaspoon sugar
salt

Mix all the ingredients together and chill for 1 to 2 hours before serving.

BABY PARSLEY CARROTS

medium-size carrots
melted butter
lemon juice
chopped parsley
freshly cracked black pepper

Use medium-size carrots, peel them, and cut into small 1½-inch carrot-shaped pieces. Cook in boiling salted water until tender, about 15 minutes. Drain and serve with melted butter, a little lemon juice, plenty of chopped parsley, and freshly cracked black pepper.

GLAZED CARROTS

10 *to* 12 *small carrots*
2 *to* 3 *tablespoons butter*
2 *tablespoons sugar*

Use small whole carrots, allowing 2 or 3 for each serving. Peel them and cook whole in boiling salted water until just tender, about 15 to 20 minutes. Drain. For 10 to 12 carrots melt 2 to 3 tablespoons of butter in a large heavy skillet. When the butter is on the point of turning color, put in the carrots and sprinkle them with 2 tablespoons of sugar. Cook over a moderate fire, shaking the pan occasionally, until they are nicely browned and glazed all over – which will take maybe 10 minutes.

CREAMED CARROTS

8 medium-size carrots
2 cups chicken stock
2 tablespoons butter
2 tablespoons flour
½ cup light cream
cayenne, lemon juice
1 tablespoon chopped parsley

Peel the carrots and either slice or dice them. Bring 2 cups of chicken stock to a boil, add the carrots, and cook until tender, about 15 minutes. Drain, reserving the stock, and reduce the stock to ½ cup. Melt 2 tablespoons of butter. Blend in 2 tablespoons of flour. Add the chicken stock and ½ cup of cream and bring to a boil with constant stirring. Season with a little cayenne and a few drops of lemon juice. Taste to see if salt is needed. Put the carrots in the sauce and cook until well heated. Sprinkle with 1 tablespoon of chopped parsley before serving. Serves 4.

CAULIFLOWER POLONAISE

1 cooked cauliflower
½ cup butter
1 cup dry bread crumbs
1 chopped hard-cooked egg
1 tablespoon chopped parsley
salt, pepper

Cover cooked cauliflower with the following sauce: Melt ½ cup of butter. Add 1 cup of dry bread crumbs and cook until the crumbs and butter are lightly browned. Add 1 chopped hard-cooked egg, 1 tablespoon of chopped parsley, salt, and a little pepper. Serves 5 or 6.

CAULIFLOWER FRITTERS

Cook cauliflower flowerets until tender but still crisp. Drain thoroughly. Deep-fat fry either in batter (*see* French fried onions, page 235), or with egg wash and bread crumbs (*see* French fried Brussels sprouts, page 228).

CAULIFLOWER AU GRATIN

1 *medium-size cauliflower*
2 *cups chopped tomatoes*
salt, pepper
2 *tablespoons flour*
4 *tablespoons cold water*
½ *to* 1 *cup grated American cheese*
½ *cup bread crumbs*
2 *tablespoons butter*

Cook the cauliflower in boiling salted water until tender and break it into flowerets. Put the tomatoes – fresh or canned – in a small saucepan, season with salt and pepper, and simmer for 5 minutes. Blend 2 tablespoons of flour with 4 tablespoons of cold water, add to the tomatoes, and cook another 5 minutes, stirring until the boiling point is reached. Put the cauliflower in a greased shallow baking dish. Pour over the tomato mixture, sprinkle with grated cheese and ½ cup of bread crumbs, and dot with 2 tablespoons of butter. Bake uncovered in a moderate oven at 350° for about 20 minutes, until the top is lightly browned and the cheese melted. Serves 5 or 6.

BRAISED CELERY

1 *bunch celery*
4 *tablespoons butter*
few slices carrot
⅓ *cup beef stock,* or *hot water with* ½ *teaspoon beef extract*
finely chopped parsley

Cut off the stem end of a bunch of celery, wash the stalks, and cut them into 2-inch lengths. The leaves can be used if you like. Parboil the celery for 10 minutes in boiling salted water, and drain. Melt 4 tablespoons of butter in a large skillet. Put in the drained celery with a few slices of carrot for flavor and ⅓ cup of beef stock (or hot water with ½ teaspoon of beef extract). Cook over a gentle fire until the celery is golden brown, about 15 to 20 minutes, turning often. Remove the carrot slices and serve with the pan juices, which will probably be reduced to a glaze. Sprinkle with a little finely chopped parsley. Serves 4 to 6.

SAUTÉED CORN

Cook either fresh corn cut from the cob (in season) or frozen cut corn (very good) in boiling water until tender. Drain well and sauté in butter with salt and pepper until lightly browned.

SUCCOTASH

Use cooked corn and cooked lima beans in about equal proportions. Heat well with butter, salt and pepper, and a little heavy cream. Succotash makes a good stuffing for tomatoes.

CREAMED FRESH CORN

1 *cup corn*
¼ *cup cream*
pinch of sugar
salt, pepper
1 *tablespoon butter*

Put 1 cup of corn cut from the cob into a saucepan with ¼ cup of cream, a pinch of sugar, salt, pepper, and 1 tablespoon of butter. Simmer covered until tender, about 10 minutes. Serves 1 or 2.

CORN FRITTERS

(*See page* 150.)

CORN PUDDING

2 *tablespoons butter*
2 *tablespoons flour*
1½ *cups milk*
salt, pepper
3 *eggs*
2 *cups corn, cooked*

Melt 2 tablespoons of butter in a saucepan, blend in 2 tablespoons of flour, and when it is smooth, slowly add 1½ cups of milk, stirring all the while. Bring to a boil, stirring constantly, season with salt and pepper, and simmer for 5 minutes. Beat 3 eggs well, for about 2 minutes with a rotary beater; add the cream sauce and 2 cups of cooked corn and blend thoroughly. Pour into a well-buttered baking dish and bake for about 1¼ hours in a moderate oven at 375°, until the top is light brown and the pudding looks firm. Serves 6.

PARSLEY CUCUMBERS

young cucumbers
melted butter
chopped parsley
lemon juice
freshly cracked black pepper

Peel young cucumbers and cut them into neat small cubes about ¾ inch or into small olive shapes. Cook in boiling salted water until tender but still crisp, about 10 minutes. Drain thoroughly. Serve with hot melted butter, chopped parsley, a few drops of lemon juice, and plenty of freshly cracked black pepper.

EGGPLANT MILANESE

1 *medium-size eggplant*
1 *medium-size onion, finely chopped*
1 *green pepper, diced*
2 *tablespoons olive oil*
2 *fresh* or *canned tomatoes, cut up*
salt, pepper
½ *cup grated Parmesan cheese*
½ *cup bread crumbs*
1 *tablespoon chopped parsley*
1 *to* 2 *tablespoons butter*

Peel the eggplant, cut it into 1-inch cubes, and cook gently for 15 minutes in boiling salted water. Drain well. Meanwhile sauté a chopped onion and a diced green pepper in 2 tablespoons of olive oil until soft but not brown. Mix together the eggplant, onion, pepper, tomatoes, salt, and pepper. A little thyme may also be used. Place in a greased casserole or baking dish that can be used for serving. Sprinkle with ½ cup of grated Parmesan cheese, ½ cup of bread crumbs, and a tablespoon of chopped parsley. Dot with 1 to 2 tablespoons of butter. Bake in a hot oven at 400° for 20 to 30 minutes, until the top is nicely browned. Serves 4 to 6.

ONIONS

Baby whole onions are buttered, boiled, peeled, small white onions. To keep the size uniform, a layer or two of the larger ones can be removed (these bits are useful for seasoning other dishes). To prevent tears, peel onions under cold running water. Boil them in salted water until just tender, about 15 to 20 minutes. Drain well and return them to the saucepan over a slow fire for a minute or so to dry out. Then add butter and let it melt. Allow 3 or 4 onions for each serving.

PARSLEY ONIONS

Add chopped parsley and a little lemon juice to baby whole onions after the butter is melted. The parsley helps the color and tastes good.

GLAZED ONIONS

1 *dozen small white onions*
3 *tablespoons butter*
1 *tablespoon sugar*

Parboil small peeled white onions in salted water — or use drained canned cooked white onions and save yourself the nuisance of peeling. Melt butter in a heavy skillet and when it starts to turn color, put in the onions, well drained. Sprinkle with sugar. Figure on about 3 tablespoons of butter and 1 tablespoon of sugar for each dozen onions. Cook with a fairly brisk fire until well browned and glazed all over, shaking the pan often. It will take about 10 to 15 minutes. Allow 3 or 4 per serving.

FRENCH FRIED ONIONS

BATTER

1 *egg*
1 *cup sifted flour*
1 *teaspoon salt*
1 *cup beer*
1 *tablespoon salad oil*

Beat 1 egg slightly. Sift together 1 cup of sifted flour and 1 teaspoon of salt. Add the egg alternately with 1 cup of beer, stirring with a wooden spoon. Blend in 1 tablespoon of salad oil. Let stand for at least 1 hour, and it can stand for several hours. This actually is a croustade batter, which makes a perfect thin crisp crust. The carbon dioxide in the beer leavens the batter so that it rises a little, with a dry rather than a soggy coating.

Dip thin onion rings from large yellow onions in this mixture, coating them well. Fry in deep fat at 360° until golden brown, turning to brown all over. Drain on absorbent paper, and serve immediately.

PEAS À LA FRANÇAISE

8 *baby white onions*
1½ *cups salted water*
1 *package frozen* or 2 *cups fresh peas*
3 *tablespoons butter*
pinch of sugar
1 *large lettuce leaf*
2 *tablespoons flour*

The onions should really be baby ones about the size of a large marble; if they are too big, remove some of the outside layers. Parboil them for 5 minutes in 1½ cups of salted water. Add the peas, 1 tablespoon of butter, and a pinch of sugar. Cover with a large lettuce leaf and cook over a gentle fire until the peas are tender, about 10 minutes for frozen peas, 15 for fresh ones. Remove the lettuce leaf. Have ready a beurre manié made by blending together 2 tablespoons of butter and 2 tablespoons of flour. Add it in little bits to the peas and stir until the liquid has thickened. Taste for seasoning. Serves 4.

PEAS WITH HAM

2 *pounds fresh* or 1 *package frozen peas*
½ *cup stock*
2 *to* 3 *tablespoons butter*
salt, pepper
¼ *cup cooked ham, cubed*

For 4 people use 2 pounds of fresh peas or 1 package of frozen peas. Frozen peas should be put in 1 cup of boiling water and cooked for a minute or two until separated, then drained. Put the peas in a saucepan with ½ cup of stock, preferably chicken, 2 to 3 tablespoons of butter, a little salt and pepper, about ¼ cup of tiny cubes of cooked ham (less than ¼ inch). Bring to a boil and simmer until the peas are tender. Frozen peas will take about 5 minutes, fresh ones 10 to 15 depending on their age and size. If all the liquid hasn't evaporated, turn up the heat at the end.

BAKED POTATOES

Use large potatoes for baking, preferably Idaho potatoes, allowing one for each serving. Scrub them well. The skin may be greased with salad oil to make it glossy. Bake the potatoes in a moderately hot oven at 375° to 400°; if the oven is 400° and the skin starts to shrivel up, it means that they are cooking too fast, so lower the heat to 375°. The potatoes will take about 1 to 1¼ hours to cook – test by squeezing them. Do not open them until just before serving; the steam should stay in the potatoes to keep them mealy. Then make a small cross in the center, push the potatoes open with your fingers, and drop nice big pieces of butter in the centers. Serve immediately.

A problem in restaurants with baked potatoes is that they really shouldn't stand too long before they are served. At some of the Treadway Inns this is solved by baking the potatoes wrapped in aluminum foil. It takes them longer to cook, 1¼ to 1½ hours, but they will stand up for 1½ to 2 hours out of the stove, and will stay hot, too.

Instead of butter, some of the inns top baked potatoes with sour cream mixed with a little mayonnaise and some chopped chives.

DELMONICO POTATOES

6 *medium-size potatoes*
salt
2 *tablespoons butter*
2 *tablespoons flour*
2 *cups milk*
¼ *pound Cheddar cheese*
½ *cup buttered bread crumbs*
dash paprika

Cook 6 medium-size potatoes in generously salted boiling water until just tender. Drain them and cool until they can be handled easily. Then remove the skins and cut them into ½-inch cubes. Melt 2 tablespoons of butter in a saucepan, blend in 2 tablespoons of flour, and when it is smooth, slowly add 2 cups of milk and stir until it reaches the boiling point. Let it simmer while you cut ¼ pound of Cheddar cheese into small pieces. Add the cheese to the sauce, reserving about 1 tablespoon, and stir until it is melted. Place half the potato cubes in a large, shallow greased baking dish and cover with half the sauce. Repeat these two layers, and top with ½ cup of buttered bread crumbs. Dot with the tablespoon of cheese pieces, sprinkle with a dash of paprika, and bake in a moderately hot oven at 400° for 10 to 15 minutes, or until the crumbs are brown. Serves 4 to 6.

NOISETTE POTATOES

"Little nut" potatoes make an attractive garnish. Peel medium-size or large potatoes and cut them into small balls with a special ball cutter, available in any hardware or dime store. Drop them into cold water to avoid discoloration. Drain well and sauté in plenty of butter in a heavy skillet over a medium fire. Shake the pan occasionally so that they will brown evenly. They will be tender in about 30 minutes. Season with salt and pepper just before serving.

RISSOLÉ POTATOES

"Sunburned" potatoes are cooked the same way as the noisette potatoes in the preceding recipe. The shape is the only difference; rissolé potatoes are cut in olive shapes about 1½ inches long.

SCALLOPED POTATOES

5 *medium-size potatoes*
3 *tablespoons butter*
2 *tablespoons flour*
salt, pepper
about 1½ cups milk

Peel the potatoes and cut them into slices about ⅛ inch thick. Drop them into cold water as you slice them to prevent discoloration. Drain well. Butter a 1½ or 2-quart baking dish that can be used for serving. Arrange the potatoes in layers; dot each one with bits of butter the size of peas, and sprinkle with flour, salt, and pepper. Pour in milk until it just covers the potatoes, about 1½ cups. Bake covered in a moderate oven at 350°, uncover and cook an additional 30 to 40 minutes, until the potatoes are tender when pierced with a toothpick and the top lightly browned. If this recipe is increased, the cooking time will be longer. The layers may be sprinkled with grated Cheddar or Swiss cheese, using about ½ cup in all. Serves 4 to 6.

ONE-STEP CREAMED POTATOES

3 *cups diced raw potatoes*
1 *cup light cream*
salt, white pepper
2 *tablespoons butter*

Peel the potatoes and cut them into small dice — a scant ½ inch. Put them into a double boiler with 1 cup of light cream and season with salt and white pepper. Have the fire on full until the water comes to a boil, then turn it down to simmering. Cook for 35 to 40 minutes, or until the potatoes are tender. Cover for the first 30 minutes. If the sauce is too thin when the potatoes are done, put the pan over direct heat for a few minutes, stirring all the while. Before serving, add 2 tablespoons of butter. Some grated cheese may also be added, if you wish. Serves 6.

LYONNAISE POTATOES

Lyonnaise potatoes are fried potatoes cooked with onion. Peel medium-size potatoes and cut them in ¼-inch slices. Peel and thinly slice or chop medium-size onions, allowing 1 onion for every 3 or 4 potatoes. Melt butter or bacon fat in a heavy skillet. Cook the potatoes and onions covered over a slow fire for about 15 to 20 minutes to steam and get cooked through. Stir once or twice, adding more fat if the potatoes stick. Then uncover, season, and cook briskly for another 10 minutes or so, turning them often with a knife so that they will be nicely browned on both sides.

POTATOES O'BRIEN

Potatoes O'Brien are fried potatoes cut into small ½-inch cubes and cooked with minced onion and finely diced green pepper and pimento (1 tablespoon each for each 2 cups of potato cubes).

CANDIED SWEET POTATOES

- 6 *medium-size sweet potatoes, boiled*
- ¾ *cup brown sugar*
- 1 *teaspoon salt*
- 4 *tablespoons butter*
- *marshmallows, optional*

Peel 6 boiled sweet potatoes after they have cooled and cut them into slices about ½ inch thick. Butter a baking dish or casserole that can be used for serving. Place a layer of potatoes in the bottom, sprinkle with brown sugar and salt, and dot with butter. Continue these layers until you have used up all the potatoes; be sure to have some sugar and butter on top. Bake uncovered in a moderate oven at 375° for about ½ hour, or until the potatoes are glazed on top. The potatoes can also be cooked on top of the stove in a large iron skillet. A layer of marshmallows can be put on top of the potatoes just before they are taken from the oven and cooked for 5 minutes or so, or until they have melted a little and the top is lightly browned. Serves 6.

SWEET POTATOES IN ORANGE CUPS

- 2 *cups boiled mashed sweet potatoes*
- 3 *tablespoons cream*
- 3 *tablespoons butter*
- ½ *teaspoon cinnamon*
- *salt*
- 1 *tablespoon grated orange rind*
- 4 *oranges*

Beat 2 cups of mashed sweet potatoes with 3 tablespoons of cream and 2 tablespoons of butter. Add ½ teaspoon cinnamon, salt, and 1 tablespoon of grated orange rind. Cut 4 oranges in half crosswise and take out all the pulp and the white membrane. Pile the potato mixture into the orange skins and dot with the remaining tablespoon of butter. Place in a baking dish and bake in a moderate oven at 375° for about 20 minutes, or until the tops are very lightly browned. Serves 4.

BOILED RICE

There are two ways of cooking rice – in a little water and in a lot of water. Since cooking it in a little water is pretty tricky, we will just discuss the more foolproof method of using a lot of water.

Boiled Rice. Rice can be washed or not; with today's clean packaging it isn't necessary. For 1 cup of uncooked rice bring 8 cups of water to a boil with plenty of salt, about 1½ to 2 tablespoons. It takes a lot of salt to season rice. Add the rice and cook over a gentle fire for 13 to 14 minutes – it may take longer, but start testing the rice then by tasting it. It is done when there is no hardness left in the center. Drain in a large strainer, and run a little hot water over it to separate the grains and to wash off any excess starch. Then place the strainer over gently boiling water. Do not let the water touch the rice. Let stand for about 10 minutes or until ready to use, stirring occasionally lightly with a fork. Or the rice can be put into a shallow pan and placed in a warm oven at 350° for a few minutes to dry out. A cup of uncooked rice makes 3 cups of cooked rice, which will serve 4 people.

Wild Rice. Although there are recipes for wild rice which use very little water, maybe 2 or 3 cups to 1 cup of rice, I have never been able to get it tender unless I use plenty of water. Wild rice is dusty, so wash it thoroughly by putting it into a strainer and letting cold water run through it until the water is clear. Bring 8 cups of well-salted water to a boil for each cup of wild rice.

Add the rice and cook until it is tender, which will be in about 35 to 40 minutes; it takes longer than regular rice (wild rice actually isn't rice at all, but the seed of a wild grass). Skim occasionally while it is cooking, and stir once or twice with a fork. Drain in a large strainer and steam over gently boiling water for about 15 minutes or until ready to use.

Wild rice is nice sautéed in butter with a little sherry or dry white wine, to be served with Rock Cornish game hens or with poultry.

PILAFF

3 *tablespoons butter*
2 *tablespoons finely chopped onion* or *green onion tops* or *Spice Islands shredded green onions*
1 *cup rice*
3 *cups chicken* or *beef stock*
salt, pepper
sautéed sliced mushrooms and/or *browned slivered almonds, optional*

Pilaff is rice cooked in a more interesting way than just plain boiling. The flavor of rice is bland, and it can be stepped up by cooking it in a seasoned liquid such as chicken or beef stock or tomato juice, and by adding seasonings such as onions and herbs. There are many pilaff recipes, and here is a typical one.

Melt 3 tablespoons of butter in a medium-size skillet. Add 2 tablespoons of finely chopped onion, green onion tops, or Spice Islands shredded green onions. Cook over a slow fire for 2 to 3 minutes, without browning. Add 1 cup of rice (it need not be washed) and cook and stir for another 2 to 3 minutes. Pour on 3 cups of chicken or beef stock, season with salt and pepper, and simmer covered for about 20 minutes, until the rice is tender. The liquid will all be absorbed and the rice should be fluffy and dry. Stir lightly with a fork before serving.

Sautéed sliced mushrooms and/or browned slivered almonds may be added to pilaff after it is cooked.

WILD RICE WITH MUSHROOMS

½ pound mushrooms, sliced
3 to 4 tablespoons butter
1 cup wild rice, cooked
½ cup sweet or *sour cream*
salt, pepper

Sauté ½ pound of mushrooms, sliced, in 3 to 4 tablespoons of butter until lightly browned. Add to 1 cup of wild rice, cooked, with ½ cup of sweet or sour cream, salt and pepper. Let stand over hot water at least 5 minutes before serving. Serves 5 or 6.

WILD RICE CASSEROLE

6 slices bacon
1 small onion, finely chopped
1 egg yolk
½ cup light cream
1 cup wild rice, cooked
2 cups grated carrot
salt, pepper
2 to 3 tablespoons butter

Fry 6 slices of bacon until they are crisp, drain them on absorbent paper, and crumble into small bits. Sauté a small chopped onion in the bacon fat until soft and yellow. Beat 1 egg yolk lightly with ½ cup of light cream in a large mixing bowl. Add 1 cup of cooked wild rice, 2 cups of grated carrot, the onion, and the bacon bits. Season with salt and pepper. Put into a greased casserole or baking dish that can be used for serving, dot with 2 to 3 tablespoons of butter, and bake covered for 35 to 45 minutes in a moderate oven at 350°. Serves 6 to 8.

SPINACH WITH BLACK BUTTER AND NUTS

1 package frozen chopped or *1½ pounds fresh spinach*
4 tablespoons butter
pignolias or *blanched slivered almonds*

Cook 1 package of frozen chopped spinach or 1½ pounds of fresh spinach, chopped. Drain very well and keep warm. Melt

4 tablespoons of butter very slowly in a heavy skillet with a few pignolias (if available) or blanched slivered almonds. Allow to heat until the butter just starts to turn brown. Pour quickly over the spinach and serve at once. Serves 3.

SQUASH WITH PEANUT TOPPING

- 2½ *pounds summer squash*
- 2 or 3 *onions, sliced*
- *salt, pepper*
- ¼ *pound salted peanuts*
- 8 *to* 10 *Ritz crackers, crumbled*
- 3 *to* 4 *tablespoons butter*

Slice 2½ pounds of summer squash but do not peel it. Cook it for about 20 minutes with 2 or 3 sliced onions, ½ cup water, salt and pepper. Then mash it well, right in the pan, and drain off all the watery liquid. While the squash is cooking, chop ¼ pound of salted peanuts and mix them with 8 to 10 coarsely crumbled Ritz crackers. Season the drained squash generously with salt and pepper, and add 1 to 2 tablespoons of butter. Put it into a greased baking dish, top with the nut mixture, and dot with 2 tablespoons of butter. Bake about 30 minutes in a moderate oven at 350°. Serves 4.

BUTTERNUT SQUASH WITH PARMESAN

Butternut squash has sweet orange flesh. Cut the squash in serving pieces and scoop out the seeds and the stringy part. Leave the rind on. Parboil for 15 minutes in boiling salted water. Remove and drain thoroughly. Season with salt and pepper, dot with small bits of butter, and sprinkle with grated Parmesan cheese. Bake for 15 to 20 minutes in a moderate oven at 375°.

FRENCH FRIED ZUCCHINI

Slice unpeeled zucchini about ¼ inch thick, coat with the batter for French fried onions (*see* page 235), and fry in deep fat at 350° to 360°.

ZUCCHINI AU GRATIN

1 *medium-size onion, thinly sliced*
1 *tablespoon chopped celery leaves*
3 *tablespoons butter*
1 *pound zucchini*
1 *cup tomato juice*
salt, pepper, thyme
½ *to* 1 *cup grated Cheddar cheese*

Sauté 1 thinly sliced onion and 1 tablespoon of chopped celery leaves in 3 tablespoons of butter in a large skillet until soft but not brown. Wash 1 pound of zucchini and cut it into ¼-inch slices without peeling. Put them into the pan and cook about 10 minutes, until lightly browned, stirring often. Pour on 1 cup of tomato juice and season with salt, pepper, and thyme. Put into a lightly greased casserole and top with ½ to 1 cup of grated cheese – the amount depends on the width of the casserole, a shallow wide one requiring more than a deep narrow one. Bake in a moderate oven at 375° for 20 to 30 minutes, until the cheese is melted and the top is browned. Serves 4 to 6.

BAKED STUFFED TOMATOES

4 *firm ripe tomatoes*
1 *cup chopped mushrooms*
1 *tablespoon chopped onion*
1 *tablespoon chopped celery*
5 *tablespoons butter*
1 *cup cooked rice*
salt, pepper
1 *tablespoon chopped parsley*
about 1 *cup grated Cheddar cheese* or *lobster pie topping*

Cut 4 firm tomatoes in half and scoop out the centers. Chop the pulp, discarding the seeds. Sauté 1 cup of chopped mushrooms, 1 tablespoon of chopped onion, and 1 tablespoon of chopped celery gently in 3 tablespoons of butter until soft but not brown, about 10 minutes. Remove from the pan and blend in 1 cup of cooked rice, salt, pepper, and 1 tablespoon of chopped parsley. Fill into the tomatoes, and top with about 1 cup of grated Cheddar cheese or lobster pie topping (*see* page 94). Dot with the remaining 2 tablespoons of butter, and bake in a moderate oven at 375° 20 to 30 minutes, until lightly browned. Serves 4.

GRILLED TOMATOES AU GRATIN

Use large firm ripe tomatoes. Remove the core at the stem end and cut the tomatoes in half. Cover the tops with grated or thinly sliced Cheddar cheese, or with grated Parmesan. Sprinkle lightly with bread crumbs, salt, and pepper, and dot with butter. Place in a shallow flameproof baking dish and put under the broiler until the cheese is melted and the tops nicely browned.

BAKED CURRIED TOMATOES

4 *large tomatoes*
4 *tablespoons butter*
1 *tablespoon curry powder*
½ *teaspoon sugar*
½ *teaspoon salt*
pepper

Cut 4 large firm tomatoes in half, and put them in a shallow baking dish or pie plate that can be used for serving. Cream together 4 tablespoons of butter, 1 tablespoon of curry powder, ½ teaspoon of sugar, ½ teaspoon of salt, and some black pepper. Put some of this mixture on top of each halved tomato, using your fingers to make the butter pieces flat and round. Bake for 40 minutes in a moderate oven at 375°. If you like curry, you will find this a most delicious way of preparing tomatoes. Serves 4.

ANDOVER INN

Andover, Massachusetts

THE first Andover Inn was built in 1810. The present inn, built in 1930, is an imposing brick structure of Georgian architecture, mellowed by its covering of ivy and ampelopsis. It is situated on the four-hundred-acre campus of the Phillips Academy, strategically facing a wide sweep of the campus across to the Memorial Tower with its carillon of thirty-seven bells. A porch in front of the inn offers a fine place to rest and enjoy the view.

Although not old, the interior of the inn has an authentic colonial atmosphere. The spacious main lounge has genuine antiques, old portraits and prints. The high-ceilinged dining room is decorated with murals of old Boston and colleges such as Dartmouth and Yale, all conveniently labeled. There is a gift shop and among other items are locally made mahogany salad bowls.

Pleasant as the interior is, a most compelling attraction is a truly magnificent formal garden in the rear of the inn. Many of the Treadway Inns have lovely gardens, but it is probably safe to say that none of them equals this garden for the range of plant material and splendid color. With an orchard and Rabbit Pond to set it off in the background, and the vine-covered walls of the inn on the other side, the garden has an ideal setting.

Garden and bird lovers will also have a treat in store for them in the Cochran Memorial Sanctuary. Within easy walking distance of the inn about ninety acres have been devoted to a combination bird sanctuary and planting of trees and shrubs, all in a natural wild setting. There are numerous white birch and laurel, and in the spring, azaleas bloom in many colors, as well as rhododendrons, including banks of light orange and yellow ones. There are two ponds frequented by wild ducks in passage – as well as by members of the academy in swimming. Among the numerous birds are ring-necked pheasants and Chinese silver pheasants.

The Phillips Academy, usually referred to as Andover School, and Abbot Academy for girls draw many people to the town. Phillips Academy was founded in 1778 by Samuel Phillips, Jr., and was incorporated in 1780, making it the oldest incorporated boarding school in the country. It started with a one-room building and thirteen pupils. Today with its seven hundred and twenty-five students and over one hundred buildings it is one of the two or three largest schools.

For the general public, there are several school buildings of interest. The Addison Gallery of Art is right across the street from the inn. The nearly two thousand items include a wide selection of paintings, sculpture, and prints from colonial times to the twentieth century. Some of the artists represented are Edward Hopper, Winslow Homer, Childe Hassam, George Grosz, and John Marin. There is a display of models of American ships built to uniform scale, forming a comprehensive survey of shipping in the sailing era with a few present-day examples. There is, for example, a model of Robert Fulton's *Clermont,* dated 1807, with a note that it "brought steam navigation for the first time to commercial success. Passengers and freight between New York and Albany moved at the then remarkable rate of 5 miles an hour." There is a room of old furniture, one of eighteenth-century silver, and another with glass and pewter of the colonial period. The Oliver Wendell Holmes Library has many treasures. There is an exhibition of birds in the George Washington Hall. And the Georgian Cochran Chapel is lovely with its warm oak paneling and carved capitals.

The inn is only a five-minute walk from the town proper, which has many wide, spacious, tree-lined streets and impressive-looking houses. Andover is twenty-three miles from Boston on Route 28, and within easy motoring distance of historic Lexington and Concord, Newburyport, and all the north shore, including Gloucester and the beautiful seacoast village of Rockport on Cape Ann.

The inn is open all year. Mr. Robert N. Frazer is the innkeeper. Although the inn has no bar, Andover is not dry.

BREADS

IT is always a joy to watch anyone work who is completely proficient, and seeing a good pastry cook in action is a revelation to the home cook. I love to make breads and rolls, but it is a production when I do it. Working on this book, I had the privilege of being in the kitchens of most of the Treadway Inns with their pastry cooks when they started work at six o'clock in the morning, and their speed, skill, and authority were fascinating. Dozens of yeast rolls would be baked or rising by breakfast time, and other hot breads would be prepared, as well as pancake batter and often doughnuts.

Which proves that bread making isn't as hard as most of us think it is. This isn't meant to disparage the Treadway Inns' pastry cooks, but to encourage home cooks. Many of the pastry cooks at the inns have had no professional training, just experience. And with a little of that, plus an understanding of the techniques of making different kinds of breads, home cooks can easily master the art and have a fine time doing it. There is a special kind of thrill working with yeast doughs, watching them rise, and, above all, smelling them while they cook. And a good hot homemade bread of any sort can be the hallmark of an excellent meal, no matter how simple it is otherwise.

The Treadway Inns have a wide assortment of breads, varying from inn to inn, but with pecan or butterscotch rolls the most favored of all. Every one of these breads is not included in this chapter, but I hope there are enough of them to give an interested cook a good start.

Breads are roughly divided into two types – quick breads and yeast breads. Quick breads are so called because they can be baked as soon as the dough or batter is made. Yeast breads have to rise two or three times, which takes at least two hours, usually longer. But although the time lapse between the start and finish of making a yeast bread is longer than with quick breads, yeast doughs, if a few basic rules are followed, are relatively simple to handle and more foolproof than some of the quick breads, which require different techniques and skills. So don't let the time element deter you.

A few timesaving methods the pastry cooks use may be helpful to the home cook. The quickest way to grease pans is with melted shortening and a pastry brush. If you make bread regularly, you can keep one small saucepan just for this use, not cleaning it, but storing it in the refrigerator with any leftover shortening in it. Most of the pastry cooks wash their baking pans only every two weeks or so. Between washings they just wipe them out with paper towels or don't do anything at all to them. The fat that remains helps season the pans and prevents sticking. Baked-on fat eventually gets tired and develops an unpleasant taste, so it should be washed off occasionally. But as one of the cooks said, "There is no necessity to overdo it."

For sifting flour, a large strainer is simpler to use than a regular flour sifter. Sift onto wax paper to save washing any bowls.

Accurate measurements are highly important with breads. Professional cooks weigh ingredients, which is much more precise than the usual home practice of using cups and spoonfuls. However, you can get good results if you use standard measuring cups and spoons and measure carefully. Flour should be sifted once before measuring, then filled lightly into a cup that holds just 1 cup and leveled off with a spatula. Liquids are best measured in a cup with a lip for pouring that holds a little more than 1 cup, so that you can get a full cup without spilling. Spoons should be heaped full, then leveled off.

Don't have your mixing bowl more than half full, so that you can beat without concern for where the contents might go. Bowls with sloping sides and rounded bottoms are the best shapes for mixing. Wooden spoons are easier to hold than metal ones, won't scratch, and won't discolor mixtures.

YEAST BREADS

INGREDIENTS

The ingredients in basic yeast breads are simple. They may be only yeast, flour, water, and salt, as in the French bread on page 263. Generally sugar and fat are also used; the liquid may be milk or potato water; and eggs are sometimes added.

An elastic rule of thumb for proportions for a loaf of plain bread is 1 package or cake of yeast, 1 cup of liquid, 3 to 4 cups of flour, 1½ teaspoons of salt, and 2 tablespoons each of sugar and fat. The amount of yeast is variable: often 1 yeast is used for 2 loaves; conversely, sometimes more is used. The more yeast, the quicker the bread rises, and experienced pastry cooks, to save time, use more yeast than is given in most home recipes. But it requires careful handling, or the bread may have a "yeasty" flavor.

Yeast. The leavening agent in bread is yeast, a tiny live organism which under proper temperature conditions and when placed in contact with sugar or a sugar-producing substance and a liquid will multiply enormously (ferment), giving off the necessary bubbles of gas (carbon dioxide) to make bread rise. High heat kills it; cold retards its growth. It flourishes best in a warm, but not hot, temperature, growing readily at 75° to 90°, with 80° to 85° ideal. If the temperature goes much over 85°, the bread will have a "yeasty" smell and flavor, so it is important not to expose rising bread to too much heat. Temperatures lower than 75° do not harm the bread; it just takes longer to rise.

There are two types of yeasts: compressed cakes and dry, active, granular yeast in packages. The dry, active yeast has much better keeping qualities than the highly perishable cakes, so it has almost entirely supplanted cake yeast in many localities. The two types can be used interchangeably, 1 cake equaling 1 package, but dry yeast must be soaked before using, as described later. Packages are dated, so be sure to use them before the expiration date.

Flour. The flour should be all-purpose or bread flour. These flours, when kneaded or thoroughly mixed, develop the strong gluten which is necessary to produce a framework to hold the expanding gas in the rising dough.

Liquid. The liquid can be water, milk, buttermilk, the water in which potatoes have been cooked, or a mixture of these liquids. Water makes a light, white bread with a crisp crust. Bread made with milk has a creamy color, more velvety crumb, a little additional food value, and better keeping qualities. Potato-water bread is more moist, with a little more volume and slightly coarser texture.

Salt. Salt flavors, as we all know. Just don't use too much, since it may interfere with the development of the yeast.

Sugar. Sugar is used for flavor and to color the crust, since it caramelizes as it cooks, giving the bread a nice brown crust. It also acts as food for the yeast, helping it to form the ever-necessary carbon dioxide.

Fat. Fat improves the flavor, tenderness, and keeping quality, and aids in browning the crust. It can be any fat, but is usually butter or one of the vegetable shortenings. Butter is preferred, perhaps because of the flavor. The amount is small; too much slows up fermentation.

Other ingredients may be eggs, which add color and flavor and help make the bread firm, and additional flavorings such as nuts, fruits, various types of flours, herbs, flavoring extracts, and so on.

METHOD

There are two methods of making yeast breads: the sponge method and the straight dough method. In the sponge method only part of the flour is added before the first rising. In the straight dough method all of the flour is added before the dough rises. The sponge method is an old one, used when yeast was less predictable than it is now. Today the straight dough method is generally used, and is the one we are about to describe.

Bought yeast is dormant, so the first step is to renew the activity of the yeast cells. This is done by soaking the yeast in a lukewarm liquid, usually water, for about 5 minutes. Cake yeast is generally soaked in whatever liquid is used in the bread. Each package of dry yeast should be soaked in ¼ cup of warm water for 5 minutes without stirring, then stirred thoroughly before using. The temperature of the liquid is important; it should feel warm if dropped on your wrist; or a thermometer can be used, registering 95° for cake yeast, 105° for dry yeast.

Mixing. In a large mixing bowl place the salt, sugar, and softened shortening. Add the liquid, which should be warm. If raw milk is used, it should be scalded to destroy any possible bacteria. Actually, whether raw or scalded, it is usually scalded just on general principles. To these warm ingredients are added the flour and yeast, and the mixture is beaten until it is stiff enough to leave the sides of the bowl. Then it is turned out on a slightly floured board and kneaded.

Kneading. Kneading is a manipulation of the dough, usually by hand, to develop the gluten in the flour and distribute the yeast cells evenly through the dough. It is an essential part of bread making (although for a few sweet rolls and coffee cakes thorough beating takes the place of kneading). Strong electric mixers can be used. Pastry cooks often use them, but they are handling large quantities of dough. There is a risk of overmixing small home quantities, and anyway, kneading is fun. Flour your hands lightly and flatten the dough. Pick up the edge of the dough farthest from you, fold it over to the edge near you, and with your hand curved, push the dough lightly away from you with the heel of your hand, with a sort of rocking motion. Give the dough a quarter turn and push again with the heel of your hand. It isn't a heavy motion and strength isn't even wanted. Light, dexterous movements are much better. The dough will be soft in the beginning and tend to cling to the board. It should be kneaded until it stiffens and is smooth, springy, and elastic and does not stick to the board. Until you are practiced, this may take 8 to 10 minutes; later it should take about 5 minutes.

Rising. When kneaded, pat into a ball. Place in a warm greased bowl, and brush with melted fat, preferably butter, so that the top won't form a dry crust and resist ready expansion. Cover with a cloth and place to rise in a warm place, about 80° to 85°, free from drafts. It can be near a stove or radiator, but not on it – it's too hot. As we have said before, if the temperature is too high, the bread will taste of yeast. Pastry cooks have special "proving" units – covered racks lit by a very small flame. If the kitchen is warm, home cooks can place the bowl in an unheated oven with a large pan of hot water beneath it. Or the bowl can be placed in another bowl of warm (not hot) water.

The dough should rise until it is double in bulk. The first rising is the longest and will take about 1½ to 2 hours, depending on the temperature and the amount of yeast. To test, push your finger gently into about an inch of the dough and if the impression stays, the dough is light enough.

Punch down. Flour your fist and push it into the middle of the dough. The dough will collapse. Remove your fist and fold the edges of the dough over the center. The large air spaces are now broken into smaller ones. If you can afford the time, let the dough rise again before shaping. The second rising will give your bread a better grain. Excess gas is removed, new air is admitted to stimulate renewed yeast activity, and the ingredients are blended more thoroughly. But it isn't essential. The second rising will take about 40 to 50 minutes.

Shaping. After either the first or second rising, the dough is ready to be shaped. After shaping, it rises a final 30 to 40 minutes, and then is baked. Be careful that this time it does not rise more than double, or it will fall and the final product will be coarse and dry.

WHITE AND WHOLE WHEAT BREAD

White bread is made by using the rule-of-thumb proportions on page 252 for each loaf and following the preceding directions. For whole wheat bread, substitute unsifted whole wheat flour for half the white flour and substitute an equal quantity of brown sugar or molasses for the sugar.

SWEET ROLLS

1 *package dry yeast*
¼ *cup lukewarm water*
4 *tablespoons butter*
4 *tablespoons sugar*
1 *teaspoon salt*
½ *cup scalded milk*
about 3½ *cups sifted flour*
1 *egg*

Soak the yeast for 5 minutes in ¼ cup of lukewarm water without stirring. Put 4 tablespoons of butter, 4 tablespoons of sugar, and 1 teaspoon of salt in a large mixing bowl. Scald milk and put ½ cup in the mixing bowl, stirring until the butter is melted. Add 1½ cups of flour and beat about 100 strokes with a wooden spoon. Stir the yeast thoroughly and add it, removing it all with a rubber spatula. Also add 1 egg and another 1½ cups of flour and beat until smooth, about another 100 strokes. Turn out on a floured board and knead, working in about ½ cup more flour. The dough will be soft and should be, since roll dough is softer than bread dough, but enough flour should be added to keep the dough from sticking to the board. Knead about 5 minutes, until an impression left by sticking a finger in it remains. Place in a greased bowl, brush the top with melted fat (preferably butter), and let rise covered in a warm place until double, about 1½ hours. Punch down and let rise again, about 45 minutes this time.

Yeast dough can take many shapes and sizes. Some suggestions follow.

Pecan Buns. For 12 buns, use ⅔ of the above dough. Pat and roll it into a rectangle about 12 inches long and 4 to 5 inches wide. Brush with melted butter, and sprinkle with cinnamon, brown sugar, and chopped pecans. Roll lengthwise. Cut into 1-inch slices. Brush 12 3-inch muffin wells with melted butter. In each well put about 1 teaspoon of brown sugar, 1 teaspoon of dark corn syrup, and 2 or 3 pecans. Put the buns in, cut side down, and press them lightly and evenly. Cover and let rise in a warm place until double, about 30 to 40 minutes. Bake in a moderate oven at 375° until golden brown, about 20 to 25 minutes. Remove and invert, so that the syrup can drop down the buns. The buns may be baked in one baking tin instead of in a muffin pan.

Butterscotch Buns. The same as pecan buns without the nuts.

Orange Buns. Follow the directions for pecan buns but use the following orange filling instead of the cinnamon, nuts, and sugar. Spread the dough with part of the filling before rolling it up, and put the rest in the muffin wells or baking pan. Filling: Melt ½ cup of butter. Add ½ cup of orange juice, ½ cup of sugar, and 2 teaspoons of grated orange rind. Cook for 2 to 3 minutes, then cool before using.

Coffee Ring. Use the pecan bun recipe. After rolling up the dough, place it on a greased cookie sheet, curving it to form a ring, and pinch the ends together. Brush with butter and sprinkle with brown sugar and nuts. Let rise until double, about 30 to 40 minutes. Bake in a moderately hot oven at 400° about 30 minutes. Remove and glaze with apricot glaze (*see* page 295) or vanilla water icing (*see* page 261).

Bubble Bread. Take about half the sweet roll dough and form it into small balls the size of a walnut. Dip each one in melted butter. Place in a buttered 8 x 4½-inch baking dish. Let rise covered until double, about 30 to 40 minutes. Pour over a mixture of 1/4 cup melted butter, 1/2 cup brown sugar, and 1/2 cup dark corn syrup. Sprinkle with chopped nuts. Bake in a hot oven at 400° until golden brown, about 20 to 30 minutes.

PLAIN ROLLS

Basic white rolls can be made with the preceding sweet roll recipe, cutting both the sugar and butter to 4 tablespoons. Or the following white roll recipe may be used. Some suggestions for ways to cut out the dough follow. Let the dough rest after rolling and before cutting out. Place on a greased baking sheet and let rise until light, about 20 to 30 minutes. Bake in a hot oven at 400° to 425° until golden brown, 12 to 20 minutes, depending upon the size.

Cloverleaf Rolls. Shape dough into small balls and dip each one in melted butter. Place 3 in each buttered muffin well.

Parker House Rolls. Roll the dough 1/4 inch thick. Cut into rounds with a 2-inch cutter. Brush with melted butter. Lightly press across the middle of each round with the back of a knife and fold over, pinching the edges together. Brush with melted butter and place in a greased baking dish, close together.

Bowknots. Roll dough 1/4 inch thick. Cut into strips 1/2 inch wide and 6 inches long. Fold into loose single or double knots.

Butterhorns. Roll dough 1/4 inch thick and cut into a 12-inch circle. Brush with melted butter. Cut into 12 pie-shaped pieces. Starting at the wide end, pull the dough a little and roll up. Place on a greased cookie sheet with the point underneath. Curving the ends makes them crescents.

Salt Sticks. Roll dough 1/4 inch thick. Cut into 4-inch squares. Roll diagonally, starting with a corner. Brush with egg wash and sprinkle with coarse salt.

WHITE ROLLS

1 *package dry yeast*
1 *cup lukewarm water*
1½ *tablespoons sugar*
1 *egg*
3 *tablespoons cooled melted butter*
3¼ *cups sifted flour*

Place the yeast in a mixing bowl or the bowl of an electric mixer with 1 cup of lukewarm water and 1½ tablespoons of sugar. Stir until the yeast is dissolved. Add 1 egg, 3 tablespoons of cooled melted butter, and half the flour. Beat for 3 to 4 minutes, add the rest of the flour, and beat or knead another 3 to 4 minutes. This mixing can all be done in the electric mixer if it is sturdy. Place the dough in a greased bowl, cover with a dish towel, and let stand in a warm place for about 1½ hours, until double in bulk. Punch down, form into desired shapes (*see* page 258), or just place rounded balls of dough in a greased muffin tin. Cover and let rise again, which will probably take about an hour. Bake until golden brown in a hot oven at 425°. Brush with melted butter after removing from the oven. Makes 1 dozen large rolls or 2 dozen small ones.

Parsley and Onion Rolls. Brush the above rolls with melted butter and sprinkle with a mixture of ¼ cup of very finely chopped onion and ¼ cup of chopped parsley just before putting them in to bake.

DANISH PASTRY

2 *packages dry yeast*
½ *cup warm water*
5 *tablespoons sugar*
3 *eggs*
2 *ounces (half a ¼-pound stick) melted butter*
½ *cup warm milk*
1 *teaspoon salt*
½ *teaspoon grated lemon rind*
½ *teaspoon vanilla*
about 4 *cups flour*
10 *ounces butter*

So-called Danish pastry is sometimes made with a sweet yeast dough, but it is not a true Danish pastry, which is made with the following combination of yeast dough and puff paste.

Soak 2 packages of dry yeast in ½ cup of warm water for 5 minutes. Put into a large mixing bowl, scraping out all the yeast with a rubber scraper. Add 5 tablespoons of sugar and beat well with a wire whisk. Beat 3 eggs with a rotary beater and add them with 2 ounces of lukewarm melted butter, ½ cup of warm milk, 1 teaspoon of salt, ½ teaspoon of grated lemon rind, and ½ teaspoon of vanilla. Mix well with a wire whisk. Then add 3½ cups of flour and beat with a wooden spoon, scraping down the sides occasionally. You may not need the full 4 cups of flour; it is better to have the dough slightly soft than too stiff. The dough is not kneaded, just thoroughly mixed. Flour a dish towel. Place the dough on one half, and cover with the other half. Let rest ½ hour at room temperature. Roll into a rectangle 10 to 12 inches wide and about four times as long. Mark the dough lightly into 4 squares. Break 10 ounces of butter into small pieces and dot the center 2 squares with ⅔ of the butter. Fold the end squares over the center squares. Flatten with a rolling pin by pressing, not rolling. Dot one square with the remaining ⅓ of the butter, fold the other square over it and flatten again. Wrap in a damp cloth and let rest in the refrigerator for ½ hour.

Now comes the part that is similar to puff pastry. The dough should have 2 or 3 "turns," which is a process of rolling and folding the dough to seal in the butter and give the pastry many flaky layers. The dough is rolled into a neat rectangle, the same length as the first one but not quite as wide – maybe 8 to 10 inches. Fold the ends over to the middle, then fold over again. Press down the sides with a rolling pin. Wrap in a damp cloth and place in the refrigerator for ½ hour. Repeat once or twice. When rolling, roll from the end where the folds show. When all the turns are done, let the dough rest in the refrigerator for at least ½ hour; overnight is better. Always keep it wrapped in a damp cloth. The dough is now ready to be shaped, and some of the ways this can be done follow.

Custard Danish. Roll out about ⅓ of the dough ¼ inch thick and 12 to 14 inches wide. Cut crosswise into ½-inch strips with a sharp knife or wallpaper cutter. Starting at each end of the strip, with your fingers roll the ends toward the center, so that you have 2 rounds joined at the top. Place on a lightly buttered cookie sheet and brush with egg wash. Let rise in a warm place until double. Brush again with egg wash. Place about a teaspoon of custard cream (*see* pastry cream, page 296) on top of each one and sprinkle with slivered toasted almonds. Bake in a hot oven at 400° about 18 to 20 minutes. Remove, brush with hot apricot glaze (*see* page 295) and vanilla water icing (*see* below). Or the pastry may be baked with just the egg wash and a spoonful of raspberry jam, and brushed with vanilla water icing after it is cooked.

Vanilla Water Icing. Blend together ¼ cup of water, 2 cups of sifted confectioners' sugar, and a little vanilla.

Danish Coffee Rings. Roll out about ⅓ of the dough into a rectangle ¼ inch thick, about 12 inches wide, and 16 inches long. Brush with egg wash. Over half the dough sprinkle raisins which have been soaked in orange juice or rum, and sprinkle with cinnamon. Fold over the other half. Cut crosswise into strips about ¼ inch wide with a sharp knife or wallpaper cutter. Then cut down the middle of each strip but not through the ends. Place your hands on each end and roll, with your hands working in opposite directions. Pinch the ends together and turn the rings over. Place on a lightly buttered cookie sheet. Brush with egg wash. Let rise in a warm place until double and brush again. Sprinkle with sliced toasted almonds. Bake in a hot oven at 400° for 15 to 20 minutes. Remove and brush with hot apricot glaze and vanilla water icing.

Cinnamon Buns. Roll out ⅓ of the dough into a rectangle about 8 x 16 inches, ¼ inch thick. Brush with egg wash. Sprinkle with chopped walnuts, then with sugar and cinnamon, leaving a bare edge about 1 inch all around. Run a rolling pin over the filling. Roll lengthwise as for a jelly roll. Cut into ¾-inch slices and place in a buttered baking pan, cut side up. (Melted butter, brown sugar, and dark corn syrup may be put in the bottom of the pan for richer, stickier buns.) Brush with egg wash and let stand in a warm place until double. Brush again with egg wash and sprinkle with chopped nuts. Bake in a hot oven at 400° for 18 to 20 minutes. Remove. If the pan did not have the butter-sugar mixture in the bottom, brush the buns with hot apricot glaze and vanilla water icing.

Rum Bread. Roll about ⅓ of the dough into an 8-inch square about 1 inch thick. Brush with egg wash. Sprinkle with white raisins, candied citron, and candied cherries which have all been soaked in rum. Dust with cinnamon. Roll up and place sealed edge down in a buttered 9 x 4½-inch loaf pan. Brush with egg wash and let stand in a warm place until double. Brush again with egg wash and bake about 50 to 60 minutes in a hot oven at 400°. Remove and turn out. Place on a cake rack and spoon over a simple syrup flavored with rum.

HOT CROSS BUNS

1 *cake* or 1 *package yeast*
¼ *cup lukewarm water*
1 *cup scalded milk*
¼ *cup sugar*
½ *teaspoon salt*
4 *tablespoons melted butter*
1 *egg, well beaten*
3 *cups sifted flour*
½ *teaspoon cinnamon*
½ *cup currants* or *raisins*
1 *egg, slightly beaten*
3 *tablespoons confectioners' sugar*
2 *tablespoons milk*

Dissolve the yeast in ¼ cup of lukewarm water. Put 1 cup of scalded milk into a large mixing bowl with ¼ cup of sugar, ½ teaspoon of salt, and 4 tablespoons of melted butter. Stir until the sugar is dissolved, and cool to lukewarm. Then add the yeast and 1 well-beaten egg, and stir until well blended. Sift 3 cups of sifted flour and ½ teaspoon of cinnamon over the liquid mixture.

Stir until all the flour is mixed in, then knead or beat in an electric mixer for 4 to 5 minutes. Blend in ½ cup of currants or raisins. Place in a greased bowl, brush lightly with melted shortening, and let rise covered with a clean cloth in a warm place until double in bulk, about 1½ hours.

Grease a 7 x 11-inch baking pan. Punch down the dough. Pull off pieces of dough about the size of a ping-pong ball, roll until well rounded, and place them in the baking pan with the sides touching. This size pan will hold 15 rolls, 3 x 5. Cut a deep cross on each bun with a sharp knife and let rise again until double in bulk, about 45 minutes. Brush with slightly beaten egg and bake for about 15 to 20 minutes in a hot oven at 400° until nicely browned. Remove and brush with icing made by cooking 3 tablespoons of confectioners' sugar and 2 tablespoons of milk together for a minute or two with constant stirring. Makes 15 rolls.

FRENCH BREAD

1 *package dry yeast*
2½ *cups lukewarm water*
1 *tablespoon salt*
7 *cups sifted flour*
corn meal
1 *egg white*
1 *tablespoon water*

This is a true French bread, with no shortening and no sugar – nothing but yeast, flour, salt, and water, and it is delicious.

Dissolve 1 package of dry yeast in ½ cup of lukewarm water. Stir in 2 cups of lukewarm water, 1 tablespoon of salt, and 2 cups of flour. Add 4 more cups of flour and beat thoroughly. Turn out on a cloth covered with the remaining 1 cup of flour and let rest for 10 minutes. Then knead in the flour. Place the dough in a greased bowl, cover with a dish towel, and let rise in a warm place for 1½ hours. Punch down and let rise again for 1 hour. Turn out on a floured cloth and cut in half. Let rest for 10 minutes. Roll each half into a rectangle about 12 x 15 inches. Roll tightly lengthwise. Grease 2 large cookie sheets and sprinkle them with corn meal. Place a loaf on each sheet and slit crosswise every 2½ inches. Beat 1 egg white with 1 tablespoon of water lightly with a fork, and brush over the top of the loaves. Let rise for about 1½ hours. Bake at 375° for 20 minutes. Brush again with the egg mixture and bake for another 20 minutes. Makes 2 large loaves.

Garlic Bread. Soften ¼ pound of butter at room temperature. Blend in 2 or 3 crushed garlic cloves. Cut a loaf of French bread into 2-inch slices crosswise down to, but not through, the bottom crust. Spread the garlic butter between the slices and over the top. Wrap the loaf in aluminum foil, and bake for about 10 minutes in a moderate oven at 350°.

Parsley or Chive Bread. Substitute 1 to 2 tablespoons of chopped parsley or chives for the garlic in the preceding recipe.

CHEESE BREAD

1 *cake* or *package yeast*
¼ *cup warm water*
½ *cup milk*
½ *cup cold water*
1 *tablespoon sugar*
½ *teaspoon salt*
⅛ *teaspoon powdered ginger*
2 *tablespoons melted butter*
½ *cup grated Cheddar cheese*
about 3 *cups sifted flour*

Dissolve the yeast in ¼ cup of warm water in a large mixing bowl. Scald ½ cup of milk. Add ½ cup of cold water and cool to lukewarm. Add to the yeast 1 tablespoon of sugar, ½ teaspoon of salt, and ⅛ teaspoon of powdered ginger. Blend in the cooled milk, then 2 tablespoons of melted butter, ½ cup of grated Cheddar cheese, and 1 cup of the sifted flour. Beat until smooth. Let rise covered in a warm place for ½ hour. Blend in the remaining 2 cups of flour and knead, adding a little more flour if necessary to make a stiff dough. Cover and let rise in a greased bowl in a warm place, 85° to 90°, until double, about 1 hour. Knead again gently until smooth and shiny, and form into a loaf. Put in a greased large loaf pan, 9 x 5 x 3 inches. Cover and let rise about 45 to 50 minutes. Bake in a moderate oven at 375° until golden brown, about 45 to 50 minutes. If this bread is not cut for several hours or overnight, it can be sliced thinly and makes excellent toast. Makes 1 loaf.

RYE BREAD

- 1 *cup milk*
- 1 *tablespoon molasses*
- 1 *tablespoon salt*
- 1 *cake yeast*
- 1 *cup lukewarm water*
- 4 *cups sifted rye flour*
- 2 *cups sifted white flour*
- 1 *tablespoon melted shortening*
- 1 *egg white*
- 1 *teaspoon cold water*

Scald 1 cup of milk, add 1 tablespoon of molasses and 1 tablespoon of salt, and pour into a large mixing bowl. Let cool until lukewarm. Dissolve 1 cake of yeast in 1 cup of lukewarm water, and add to the cooled milk. Sift together 4 cups of sifted rye flour and 2 cups of sifted white flour, and add half to the milk mixture. Beat until smooth, and add 1 tablespoon of melted shortening and the remaining flour. Beat until it starts to leave the sides of the bowl, then turn out on a lightly floured board and knead until smooth and elastic, about 5 minutes. Place the dough in a greased bowl, cover with a damp cloth, and let rise until double in bulk, about 1½ hours. Then punch down, divide the dough in half, and let rest for 10 minutes. Shape into 2 loaves and place them in greased loaf pans. Cover and let rise about 1 hour. Brush the tops of the loaves with 1 egg white lightly beaten with 1 teaspoon of cold water. Bake in a hot oven at 400° for 25 to 35 minutes, until the tops are lightly browned. Makes 2 loaves.

WIGHT'S GRIST MILL

One of the most picturesque buildings in Old Sturbridge Village, Sturbridge, Mass., is the grist mill, where whole grain is ground on old-fashioned stone burrs. A pamphlet about the mill describes the process:

The slow-moving stones do not heat the grain. Hence its full, rich, unaltered nutriment and flavor are retained. Such meals and flours are entirely different from any commercially packaged articles. No chemical process, no bleaching, or removal of vital elements is practiced. You get the whole grain – at its absolute best.

The mill's products are white and yellow corn meal, whole wheat flour, graham flour, buckwheat flour, and rye flour. It also makes a brown bread mix. All these can be ordered by mail, and will be sent with a recipe folder. The recipes for the preceding rye bread and for Boston brown bread (page 267) are taken from this folder.

QUICK BREADS

Quick breads are leavened by fast-acting agents such as baking powder, baking soda, and steam, in contrast to slower-acting yeast. They are quite diversified; biscuits, muffins, popovers, waffles, griddlecakes, and some coffee cakes are all quick breads, as well as a number of actual breads, such as corn bread and the numerous fruit and nut breads. As with any baking, attention is needed for individual mixing methods and oven temperatures. But heeding these, and "with a little bit of luck," success should be yours.

YANKEE CORN STICKS

1⅓ *cups sifted flour*
⅔ *cup corn meal*
2 *teaspoons baking powder*
½ *teaspoon salt*
3 *tablespoons sugar*
1 *egg, well beaten*
⅔ *cup cream-style corn*
1 *cup milk*
2 *tablespoons cool melted shortening*

Sift together 1⅓ cups of sifted flour, ⅔ cup of corn meal, 2 teaspoons of baking powder, ½ teaspoon of salt, and 3 tablespoons of sugar into a large mixing bowl. Beat 1 egg well, and blend well with ⅔ cup of cream-style corn, 1 cup of milk, and 2 tablespoons of cool melted shortening. Add to the dry ingredients and stir just until all the flour is moistened – do not beat. Fill or pipe into well-greased heated corn-stick pans or muffin pans. Bake in a hot oven at 425° about 20 minutes, until golden brown. Makes 12 corn sticks or muffins.

SKILLET CORN BREAD

4 *tablespoons melted butter or bacon fat*
1 *cup corn meal*
1 *tablespoon flour*
1 *teaspoon baking powder*
¼ *teaspoon soda*
½ *teaspoon salt*
1 *egg*
1 *cup buttermilk*

Preheat a 9-inch skillet in a hot oven at 425°. Melt 2 tablespoons of fat in this hot skillet before putting the batter in. Sift together into a mixing bowl 1 cup of corn meal, 1 tablespoon of flour, 1 teaspoon of baking powder, ¼ teaspoon of soda, and ½ teaspoon of salt. Beat 1 egg. Stir in 1 cup of buttermilk. Add gradually to the dry ingredients and stir just until blended. Add 2 tablespoons of cool melted fat. Place in the hot skillet and right into the oven. Bake about 20 to 25 minutes, until golden brown. Cut into pie-shaped pieces. Serves 6 to 8.

Note. The omission of sugar is not a mistake – real Southern corn bread does not have any sugar. A tablespoon or two may be added, if you wish.

Skillet Corn Bread with Bacon. Add ¼ to ½ cup of crisp, crumbled, cooked bacon bits to the preceding batter before it is baked.

Corn Bread. Another corn bread recipe will be found on page 175, in a sausage stuffing for turkey.

BOSTON BROWN BREAD

1 *cup yellow corn meal*
1 *cup sifted graham flour*
1 *cup sifted rye flour*
1 *cup molasses*
1½ *cups sour milk*
1 *teaspoon soda*
1 *teaspoon salt*
½ *to* 1 *cup raisins, optional*

Mix all the ingredients together thoroughly, adding from ½ to 1 cup of raisins if you wish. Turn into a well-greased mold with a tight-fitting cover, or put rounds of greased paper on the bottoms of greased baking-powder tins and fill ⅔ full with the mixture. Steam for 4 hours in a covered kettle. Makes 1 large loaf or 3 small ones. Serve hot.

BAKING POWDER BISCUITS

2 *cups flour*
3 *teaspoons baking powder*
1 *teaspoon salt*
4 *heaping tablespoons vegetable shortening*
¾ *cup milk*

The secret of tender, flaky biscuits is an absolute minimum of handling, and that has to be light.

Sift 2 cups of flour, 3 teaspoons of baking powder, and 1 teaspoon of salt into a large mixing bowl. Add 4 heaping tablespoons of vegetable shortening and quickly cut it in with a fork, the edge of a large metal spoon, or a pastry blender. A fork or spoon is perhaps better than a pastry blender, since you may use too heavy a hand with a blender; the aim is just to coat the fat particles with flour, not actually mix them together. Cutting in the fat should take only about 1 minute. Add ¾ cup of milk, ¼ cup at a time, stirring lightly in one direction, which will take about another ½ minute.

Turn out on a lightly floured board. Pat into a round shape. Roll out, rolling from the center with light butterfly strokes. Do not roll over the edge of the dough. Roll ¼ inch thick, cut into rounds with a 2½-inch cutter, and fold in half like a Parker House roll. Or roll out ½ inch thick, use a 2-inch cutter, and do not fold. When cutting, do not twist the cutter, or the sides of the biscuits will be uneven. Cut close together so that there will not be much dough left. Leftover dough can be rerolled, but this additional manipulation tends to make the biscuits tough. They can be cut into squares or triangles with a sharp knife and there won't be any leftovers. Lift the biscuits with a spatula and place on an ungreased cookie sheet. Put them about 1 inch apart if you like them crusty on all sides, almost touching if you prefer the sides soft. Bake until golden brown in a hot oven at 425°, about 12 to 15 minutes. Serve hot. Makes 12 to 16 biscuits.

This makes a very short, flaky biscuit. For a higher biscuit with more and softer insides, the dough should be kneaded for 20 to 30 strokes. This develops the gluten, giving the biscuits more volume. To knead, after the dough has been patted out, fold it over and press lightly with the heel of your hand. Pick it up off the board, give it a quarter turn, and knead again, always remembering to use the lightest possible strokes.

BISCUIT VARIATIONS

Bacon Biscuits. Add ½ cup of diced crisp bacon bits to the flour and fat mixture. Or split freshly baked biscuits, butter lightly, and put a piece of crisp cooked bacon in each one.

Ham Biscuits. Add ½ cup of finely chopped cooked ham to the flour and fat mixture.

Cheese Biscuits. Add ½ cup of grated cheese to the flour and fat mixture.

Chive or Parsley Biscuits. Add 1 to 2 tablespoons of finely chopped chives or parsley to the flour and fat mixture. Good as a topping for meat pie.

Onion Biscuits. Add 1 to 2 teaspoons of grated onion to the milk. Good as a topping for meat pie.

Nut Biscuits. Add ½ cup of chopped nuts to the flour and fat mixture.

Peanut Butter Biscuits. Substitute 2 tablespoons of peanut butter for 2 tablespoons of the vegetable shortening.

Tomato Juice Biscuits. Substitute tomato juice for the milk. Good as a topping for meat pie.

Crust for Meat or Chicken Pie. Use an extra tablespoon of shortening. Roll the dough ½ inch thick and place on top of the filling either in one large round or cut into biscuits. The crust will bake better if the filling is hot.

Butterscotch Pinwheel Biscuits. Roll the dough into a rectangle ¼ inch thick. Brush with 4 tablespoons of melted butter, and sprinkle with ½ cup of brown sugar and ½ teaspoon of cinnamon. Roll lengthwise as for a jelly roll. Cut into slices about ¾ inch thick. Place cut side up in a shallow greased baking dish about ½ inch apart. Remove from the pan as soon as they are done.

Orange Pinwheel Biscuits. Follow the directions for butterscotch pinwheel biscuits and spread the dough with the following orange filling: Cook 3 tablespoons of butter, 2 tablespoons of orange juice, 1 teaspoon of grated orange rind, and 6 tablespoons of confectioners' sugar in a double boiler until thick. Remove and cool to lukewarm.

Maple Pinwheel Biscuits. Follow the directions for butterscotch pinwheel biscuits. Sprinkle the dough with ½ to ¾ cup of maple sugar and dot with 2 tablespoons of butter.

Coconut Biscuits. Sift 2 tablespoons of sugar with the dry ingredients. Add ½ cup of shredded coconut or coconut flakes to the flour and fat mixture.

Honey Biscuits. Add 2 tablespoons of honey to the milk.

Orange Biscuits. Roll the dough ¼ inch thick and cut with a 2-inch cutter. Place a small piece of lump sugar which has been dipped in orange juice in the center of one round, cover with another round, and press the edges together. Or substitute orange juice and 1 teaspoon of grated orange rind for the milk, and sift 2 tablespoons of sugar with the dry ingredients.

Shortcake. Use 6 tablespoons of shortening. Sift 2 tablespoons of sugar with the dry ingredients. Roll out ¼ inch thick and cut either in 2 or 2½-inch rounds for individual servings or in 2 9-inch rounds. Place one round on top of another, after brushing the bottom round with melted butter.

CHERRY BISCUITS

- 2 *cups sifted flour*
- 4 *teaspoons baking powder*
- 1 *teaspoon salt*
- 1 *tablespoon sugar*
- 1 *cup light cream*
- 6 *tablespoons melted butter*
- ½ *cup chopped pecans*
- ¼ *cup light brown sugar*
- 12 *maraschino cherries, quartered*

Sift together 2 cups of sifted flour, 4 teaspoons of baking powder, 1 teaspoon of salt, and 1 tablespoon of sugar. Stir in 1 cup of light cream. Roll out in a rectangle about 12 inches long and ¼ inch thick, and brush with 2 tablespoons of melted butter. Sprinkle ½ cup of chopped pecans over the top and roll lengthwise as for a jelly roll. Place 1 teaspoon of the remaining butter, 1 teaspoon of light brown sugar, and a quartered maraschino cherry in each of the 12 muffin wells. Cut the dough into 1-inch slices, and place them over the cherries, cut side up. Press them down, and bake for 12 to 15 minutes in a very hot oven at 450°. Let stand for 5 minutes, then turn out, cherry side up.

MUFFINS

Muffins are quickly assembled, quickly made, and can be varied in numerous ways. The ingredients for basic muffins are always the same. The dry ingredients are flour, baking powder, salt, and sugar; the liquid ingredients are egg, milk, and shortening. For 12 3-inch muffins the standard recipe is 2 cups of flour to 1 cup of milk and 1 egg, 3 teaspoons of baking powder, and ½ teaspoon of salt. Sugar is used to sweeten the muffins and help brown the crust, and the amount varies from 2 to 4 tablespoons. For sweet muffins, like blueberry, the maximum of 4 tablespoons is used; for unsweet muffins, like bacon, the minimum of 2 tablespoons. The shortening can be butter, vegetable shortening, or salad oil, with butter preferred, especially in plain muffins, because of the flavor.

True muffins have a low proportion of fat and sugar to flour and liquid, making them coarse and more like bread than cake in texture; they are heavier when cold, so ideally they should be eaten hot. Leftover muffins can be split, buttered, and lightly browned under the broiler. There are some cakelike muffins, such as the blueberry muffins on page 278, but these are not typical muffins.

The flour is generally all-purpose, although occasionally all or part cake flour is used for a more delicate texture.

The mixing technique is always a factor in successful bread making. With muffins, the factor of prime importance is speed. When the dry and liquid ingredients are combined, they should be stirred (not beaten) just until all the flour is dampened – scientific tests specify not more than 25 strokes, and it may be less. The mixture will, and should, look lumpy. Even a few extra strokes will make the muffins heavy and tough, and vigorous beating eliminates any chance of making good muffins. Heavy muffins are characterized by "tunnels" – long narrow strands, usually running from the bottom toward the top, which appear when overbeating so develops the gluten in the flour that the leavening gas is forced out along strands instead of rising evenly. Double-acting baking powder, because part of the action is delayed, helps prevent the formation of tunnels, and there is less danger when there is a high proportion of sugar and fat.

The batter should be put into pans as soon as it is mixed, and the muffins should be baked immediately, so be sure the oven is preheated. Fill the batter into the muffin pan with as little additional mixing as possible, and do not drop the batter from a height, but stay close to the pan. The quickest way to fill a pan is with a small ice-cream scoop. You can also use a ⅓ or ½ fraction cup. Fill the wells ⅔ full, and put hot water in any unused wells, so that the pan won't burn.

Muffins should be cooked quickly, which means a hot oven, usually at 425°. As one of the Treadway Inns' pastry cooks said, "You have to hit them with a nice hot oven or they will flatten out on you."

After the muffins are baked, remove and let stand for 5 minutes and they will come out of the pan more easily. If they have to wait, loosen them and tip on one side and leave in the oven with the heat off.

Added solid ingredients, such as berries, raisins, nuts, and so on, should be blended with the dry ingredients before any liquid is added, to prevent overmixing.

To prepare muffins ahead of time, even the night before, sift the dry ingredients and cut in the shortening. Grease the pan. At the last minute all you need do is prepare the liquid ingredients and combine with the dry ingredients, a matter of 2 or 3 minutes.

There are two methods of making muffins:

1. Sift dry ingredients into a mixing bowl. Combine slightly beaten egg, milk, and cool melted shortening. Add the liquid ingredients to the dry ones, and stir just until the flour is dampened. The easiest shortening to use is salad oil, since it is already in liquid form and at room temperature. Either butter or vegetable shortening must first be melted, then cooled.

2. Sift dry ingredients. Cut in shortening (preferably butter) with a pastry blender or two knives. Beat egg and blend with milk (the egg can be beaten in an electric mixer while you sift the dry ingredients). Add liquid ingredients to dry ones, and stir just until flour is blended.

Both methods make fine muffins. I happen to think the second method better, with a finer-textured, lighter, higher muffin, so the following recipes will use it. It is also quicker than melting shortening and then cooling it.

BASIC MUFFINS

2 *cups flour*
3 *teaspoons baking powder*
½ *teaspoon salt*
2 *to* 4 *tablespoons sugar*
3 *tablespoons shortening*
1 *egg*
1 *cup milk*

Preheat the oven to 425°. Grease a muffin tin with 12 3-inch wells. Sift 2 cups of flour, 3 teaspoons of baking powder, ½ teaspoon of salt, and 2 to 4 tablespoons of sugar into a mixing bowl. The difference in sugar depends on whether or not you like muffins sweet. Cut in 3 tablespoons of shortening with a pastry blender or two knives. Use either butter or vegetable shortening, preferably butter for flavor. Meanwhile, if you are using an electric mixer, start beating 1 egg. Otherwise, beat it well with a rotary beater after the shortening is cut in. Add 1 cup of milk to the egg. Pour in the center of the dry ingredients and mix for just a few seconds, until the dry ingredients are dampened. Fill immediately into the muffin tin, filling each well ⅔ full. Bake for 18 to 20 minutes in a hot oven, until nicely browned.

MUFFIN VARIATIONS

Whole Wheat Muffins. Substitute 1 cup of whole wheat flour for 1 cup of white flour; ½ cup of chopped dried fruit or crisp bacon may be added.

Rye Muffins. Substitute 1 cup of rye flour for 1 cup of white flour.

Rice Muffins. Substitute 1 cup of cooked rice for 1 cup of flour.

Bacon or Ham Muffins. Add ½ cup of crisp cooked bacon bits or finely chopped cooked ham to the dry ingredients.

Cheese Muffins. Add ⅔ cup of finely grated American cheese and a dash of paprika to the dry ingredients. Cut the sugar to 1 tablespoon. Sprinkle grated cheese over the top. Bake at 400°.

Cinnamon Muffins. Use 1 teaspoon of baking powder and ½ teaspoon of soda and sift 1½ teaspoons of cinnamon with the dry ingredients. Substitute 1 cup of sour milk or buttermilk for the sweet milk.

Cocoa Muffins. Substitute 2 tablespoons of cocoa for the same amount of flour. Use 4 tablespoons of sugar.

Coffee Cake Muffins. Blend together ½ cup of flour, ⅓ cup of brown sugar, ¼ teaspoon of cinnamon, and ¼ cup of melted butter. Sprinkle on top of the uncooked muffins.

Cream Muffins. Use cream instead of milk. Cut the shortening to 2 tablespoons.

Curry Muffins. Sift ½ teaspoon of curry powder and ½ teaspoon of celery salt with the dry ingredients.

Marmalade or Jelly Muffins. Half fill the muffin tins, put ½ teaspoon of marmalade or jelly in each one, then cover with a little more batter.

Nut Muffins. Add 1 cup of chopped nuts to the dry ingredients. Brazil nuts are especially good. Top with a mixture of ½ cup of chopped nuts and 2 tablespoons of sugar.

Olive Muffins. Add ½ cup of sliced stuffed olives to the dry ingredients.

Peanut Muffins. Use peanut butter instead of shortening. Add ½ cup of chopped salted peanuts to the dry ingredients.

FRUIT MUFFINS

Sprinkling the tops of fruit muffins with a little granulated sugar makes a nice crust. Half brown sugar may be used instead of all white sugar. When fruit muffins are done, they can be sprinkled with sifted confectioners' sugar or rolled in it.

Apricot Muffins. Add 1 cup of cooked, well-drained dried apricots to the dry ingredients.

Banana Muffins. Add ½ cup of mashed bananas to the dry ingredients.

Blueberry Muffins. Add 2 tablespoons of sugar to 1 cup of blueberries and let stand for at least 10 minutes. Then blend with the dry ingredients.

Cherry Muffins. Mix ¾ cup of pitted fresh cherries and 2 to 3 tablespoons of sugar. Add to the dry ingredients.

Cinnamon Apple Muffins. Sift ½ teaspoon of cinnamon with the dry ingredients, and add 1 cup of diced apples sweetened with ¼ cup of sugar. Top each muffin with a thin slice of apple, sprinkled with a little granulated sugar.

Cranberry Muffins. Add ¾ cup of chopped cranberries mixed with 3 tablespoons of sugar and 1 teaspoon of grated orange rind to the dry ingredients.

Date Muffins. Add ¾ cup of chopped dates to the dry ingredients.

Date and Nut Muffins. Add ½ cup of chopped dates and ½ cup of chopped nuts to the dry ingredients.

Orange Peel Muffins. Add 1 cup of chopped candied orange peel to the dry ingredients.

Pineapple Muffins. Add 1 cup of thoroughly drained crushed pineapple to the dry ingredients.

Raisin Muffins. Mix ¾ cup of seedless raisins with the dry ingredients.

Strawberry or Raspberry Muffins. Slice the strawberries, leave raspberries whole. Add 2 tablespoons of sugar to 1 cup of berries, and let stand for at least 10 minutes. Add to the dry ingredients.

Waikiki Muffins. Substitute ¾ cup of corn meal for 1 cup of flour. Add ½ cup of well-drained crushed pineapple and ½ teaspoon of lemon rind to the dry ingredients.

GINGER MUFFINS

2 *cups sifted flour*
3 *tablespoons sugar*
1½ *teaspoons baking powder*
½ *teaspoon soda*
½ *teaspoon salt*
¼ *teaspoon ginger*
¼ *teaspoon cinnamon*
⅛ *teaspoon nutmeg*
3 *tablespoons butter*
1 *egg*
½ *cup buttermlik*
½ *cup molasses*

Sift together into a mixing bowl 2 cups of sifted flour, 3 tablespoons of sugar, 1½ teaspoons of baking powder, ½ teaspoon of soda, ½ teaspoon of salt, ¼ teaspoon of ginger, ¼ teaspoon of cinnamon, and ⅛ teaspoon of nutmeg. Cut in 3 tablespoons of butter. Beat 1 egg lightly, and stir in ½ cup of buttermilk and ½ cup of molasses. Add to the dry ingredients and stir just until the flour is all dampened. Fill into a greased muffin tin and bake about 20 minutes in a hot oven at 425°. Makes 1 dozen 3-inch muffins.

ORANGE BRAN MUFFINS

- 4 *tablespoons honey*
- 24 *orange sections*
- 3 *maraschino cherries*
- 1 *cup bran*
- 1 *cup milk*
- 1 *cup of sifted flour*
- 3 *teaspoons baking powder*
- ½ *teaspoon salt*
- 2 *tablespoons shortening*
- ¼ *cup sugar*
- 1 *teaspoon grated orange rind*

Thoroughly grease 12 muffin wells, and place in each 1 teaspoon of honey, 2 orange sections, and a quarter of a maraschino cherry. Soak 1 cup of bran for 5 minutes in 1 cup of milk. Meanwhile sift together 1 cup of sifted flour, 3 teaspoons of baking powder, and ½ teaspoon of salt. Cream 2 tablespoons of shortening, ¼ cup of sugar, and 1 teaspoon of grated orange rind in a mixing bowl. Blend in the milk and bran. Quickly stir in the dry ingredients, and stir only until the flour is dampened. Fill into the muffin pan, and bake in a moderately hot oven at 400° for 25 minutes.

RAISIN BRAN MUFFINS

- 1½ *cups sifted flour*
- 1 *teaspoon baking powder*
- ½ *cup seedless raisins*
- 4 *tablespoons vegetable shortening*
- ¾ *cup confectioners' sugar*
- ½ *teaspoon salt*
- 1 *egg*
- 3 *tablespoons dark molasses*
- 2 *cups bran*
- 1 *teaspoon baking soda*
- 1 *cup milk*

Sift together 1½ cups of sifted flour and 1 teaspoon of baking powder and add ½ cup of seedless raisins. Cream 4 tablespoons of vegetable shortening, ¾ cup of confectioners' sugar, and ½ teaspoon of salt. Beat in 1 egg. Blend in 3 tablespoons of dark molasses and 2 cups of bran. Add 1 teaspoon of baking soda to 1 cup of milk and stir that in. Add the dry ingredients and stir only until all the flour is dampened. Fill the greased and flour-dusted wells of a muffin tin ¾ full, and bake about 15 minutes in a moderately hot oven at 400°. Makes 12 3-inch muffins.

Note. The confectioners' sugar gives these muffins an excellent light texture. They are quite sweet, and the amount of sugar can be cut down if you wish.

OATMEAL MUFFINS

- 1 *cup quick-cooking oats*
- 1 *cup buttermilk* or *sour milk*
- 2 *tablespoons sugar*
- 1 *cup sifted flour*
- ½ *teaspoon salt*
- ½ *teaspoon baking soda*
- 1 *teaspoon baking powder*
- 1 *egg, slightly beaten*
- ½ *cup sifted brown sugar*
- ½ *cup cool melted shortening*

Soak 1 cup of quick-cooking oats in 1 cup of buttermilk or sour milk for 5 minutes in a mixing bowl and sprinkle with 2 tablespoons of sugar. Meanwhile sift together 1 cup of sifted flour, ½ teaspoon of salt, ½ teaspoon of baking soda, and 1 teaspoon of baking powder. Add to the oatmeal mixture 1 slightly beaten egg, ½ cup of sifted brown sugar, and ½ cup of cool melted shortening and beat well. Add the sifted dry ingredients and stir only until the flour is dampened. Fill into a greased muffin pan, and bake in a moderately hot oven at 400° for 20 minutes. Makes 12 muffins.

SWEET BLUEBERRY MUFFINS

- ⅓ *cup shortening*
- ½ *cup sugar*
- ¼ *teaspoon salt*
- 1 *egg, well beaten*
- 1¾ *cups sifted cake flour*
- 1½ *teaspoons baking powder*
- ½ *cup milk*
- 1 *cup fresh* or *frozen blueberries*

This recipe makes a fine-textured, sweet muffin more like a tea or dessert muffin than a plain one. It is a particularly good recipe.

Cream the shortening (butter or vegetable shortening), ½ cup of sugar, and ¼ teaspoon of salt. Add 1 well-beaten egg and blend thoroughly. Sift together 1¾ cups of cake flour and 1½ teaspoons of baking powder. Add alternately with ½ cup of milk, beating for just a few seconds after each addition; better not use a machine for this step. Lastly stir in the berries, which have been dusted with a little flour – if you are using frozen berries, be sure they are well drained. Fill a greased muffin tin ⅔ full. Bake for 20 to 25 minutes in a moderately hot oven at 400°, until the tops are a nice light brown. Makes 12 3-inch muffins.

CORN MUFFINS

1 *cup corn meal*
1 *cup flour*
1 *teaspoon salt*
1 *teaspoon sugar*
2 *teaspoons baking powder*
½ *cup vegetable shortening*
1 *egg*
¼ *teaspoon baking soda*
1 *cup buttermilk* or *sour milk*

Sift together into a large mixing bowl 1 cup of corn meal, 1 cup of flour, 1 teaspoon of salt, 1 teaspoon of sugar, and 2 teaspoons of baking powder. Cut in ½ cup of vegetable shortening. Stir in 1 slightly beaten egg. Put ¼ teaspoon of soda into 1 cup of buttermilk or sour milk, add, and stir just until blended. Bake in a greased muffin pan in a hot oven at 425° for 20 to 25 minutes, until the tops are nicely browned. Yield: 12 3-inch muffins.

Note. More sugar may be added, the degree of sweetness in corn bread or corn muffins being entirely a matter of personal preference.

POPOVERS

1 *cup sifted flour*
½ *teaspoon salt*
2 *eggs*
1 *tablespoon salad oil*
1 *cup milk*

The ingredients of popovers are simple, and so is the mixing method. Yet popovers are considered tricky, and are often unsuccessful. Just remember a few simple things about popovers, and you should have excellent results. Popovers, like cream puffs, are leavened entirely by steam, and to create steam you need a hot oven. Recommended oven temperatures vary from 375° to 450°, and after numerous testings, I have found 425° best for 20 to 25 minutes until the popovers have risen and browned, then a lower temperature of about 375° for 10 to 15 minutes to dry them out and make the shells firm. The oven should be preheated and so should the baking pan, regardless of what you may have read elsewhere. The highest, crispest popovers seem to be made in individual Pyrex custard cups, but they must be deep with narrow bottoms, rather than shallow with wide bottoms. The traditional pan for popovers is an iron gem pan with eleven deep cups, and it is good; but the cups are so close together that the popovers in the middle are crowded and can't rise and spread as they should.

Preheat the oven to 425°. Lightly grease 8 Pyrex custard cups, place them on a cookie sheet, and preheat them for about 5 minutes. Sift 1 cup of sifted flour and ½ teaspoon of salt into a mixing bowl. Beat 2 eggs thoroughly. Beat in 1 tablespoon of salad oil, then 1 cup of milk. Add to the dry ingredients, blend well, then beat for 2 to 3 minutes. Fill the custard cups about ½ full. Bake for 20 to 25 minutes until golden brown and "popped," then reduce the heat to 375° and cook another 10 to 15 minutes. Serve immediately.

Cheese Popovers. Add ¼ cup of grated Cheddar cheese to the dry ingredients with the egg mixture.

COFFEE CAKE I

½ *cup brown sugar*
½ *cup chopped nuts*
1 *teaspoon cinnamon*
2 *cups sifted flour*
1 *teaspoon baking powder*
1 *teaspoon soda*
¼ *pound butter*
1 *cup sugar*
2 *eggs*
1 *cup sour cream*

First make the topping for this coffee cake by mixing together ½ cup of brown sugar, ½ cup of chopped nuts, and 1 teaspoon of cinnamon. Set aside until ready to use. Sift together 2 cups of sifted flour, 1 teaspoon of baking powder, and 1 teaspoon of soda. Cream ¼ pound of butter well, and gradually add 1 cup of sugar. Beat in 2 eggs, one at a time. Add the sifted dry ingredients alternately with 1 cup of sour cream, mixing well after each addition. Put the batter in a greased 9-inch-square baking pan, and spread it out, smoothing the top. Sprinkle the prepared topping over it, and bake for 30 to 40 minutes in a moderate oven at 350°.

COFFEE CAKE II

TOPPING

½ cup flour
½ teaspoon cinnamon
2 tablespoons sugar
3 tablespoons butter
½ cup chopped nuts
⅛ teaspoon almond extract

CAKE

½ cup butter
¾ cup sugar
2 eggs
2 cups cake flour
2 teaspoons baking powder
½ teaspoon salt
2 teaspoons soluble coffee
½ cup milk

Prepare the following topping before making the coffee cake.

Topping. Blend together in a mixing bowl ½ cup of flour, ½ teaspoon of cinnamon, 2 tablespoons of sugar, 3 tablespoons of butter, ½ cup of chopped nuts, and ⅛ teaspoon of almond extract.

Cake. Cream together ½ cup of butter and ¾ cup of sugar. Beat in 2 eggs. Sift together 2 cups of cake flour, 2 teaspoons of baking powder, ½ teaspoon of salt, and 2 teaspoons of soluble coffee. Add alternately with ½ cup of milk to the creamed mixture, blending well after each addition. Place in a greased 9-inch-square baking tin or a deep round cake tin and sprinkle the topping evenly over the top. Bake for about 30 minutes in a moderate oven at 375°.

ORANGE BREAD

2 cups flour
3 teaspoons baking powder
¾ teaspoon salt
½ cup sugar
1 egg
¾ cup orange juice
2 tablespoons lemon juice
1 teaspoon grated orange rind
½ teaspoon grated lemon rind
¼ cup melted vegetable shortening

Sift together into a large mixing bowl 2 cups of flour, 3 teaspoons of baking powder, ¾ teaspoon of salt, and ½ cup of sugar. Beat 1 egg well. Combine with ¾ cup of strained orange juice, 2 tablespoons of lemon juice, 1 teaspoon of grated orange rind, ½ teaspoon of grated lemon rind, and ¼ cup of cool melted vegetable shortening (or butter). Make a well in the center of the dry ingredients, add the liquid ones, and stir just until all the flour is dampened, about 20 strokes. Put into a greased paper-lined 8 x 4½-inch loaf pan. Let stand for 20 minutes. Then bake about 1 hour in a moderate oven at 350°. This loaf will be smaller than the following orange bread, with a coarser texture, but it has a good flavor and cuts easily.

ORANGE NUT BREAD

½ cup butter
1 cup sugar
2 eggs
3 tablespoons grated orange rind
2 tablespoons orange juice
¾ cup milk
2 cups flour
3 teaspoons baking powder
½ teaspoon salt
½ cup chopped nuts
½ cup chopped raisins

Cream ½ cup of butter, preferably in an electric mixer. Gradually add 1 cup of sugar and beat until light and fluffy. Beat in 2 eggs, one at a time, then 3 tablespoons of grated orange rind and 2 tablespoons of orange juice. Meanwhile sift together 3 times 2 cups of flour, 3 teaspoons of baking powder, and ½ teaspoon of salt.

Chop ½ cup of nuts and ½ cup of raisins and mix them with a little of the flour. Add the sifted dry ingredients to the first mixture alternately with ¾ cup of milk, using a rubber scraper rather than the mixer. Fold in the nuts and raisins. Place the batter in a greased 9 x 4½-inch loaf pan. With the scraper, push the batter around the edges of the pan, leaving the center a little lower. Let stand for 20 minutes. Then bake about 1 hour in a moderate oven at 350°. The loaf will cut more easily if it is allowed to stand overnight, although this bread is fine the first day.

NUT BREAD

2 *tablespoons shortening*
¾ *cup sugar*
¼ *teaspoon salt*
1 *egg, well beaten*
2 *cups sifted flour*
2 *teaspoons baking powder*
1 *cup milk*
½ *cup chopped walnuts* or *pecans*

Cream 2 tablespoons of shortening (butter or vegetable shortening) until it is soft. Add ¾ cup of sugar and ¼ teaspoon of salt, and cream well. Add 1 beaten egg and continue beating until the mixture is smooth and light. Sift together 2 cups of flour and 2 teaspoons of baking powder. Add alternately with 1 cup of milk, beating just for a few seconds after each addition until the mixture is smooth. Lastly stir in ½ cup of chopped nuts. Put into a greased loaf pan. Bake in a slow oven at 325° for 40 to 50 minutes, until the top is light brown and the sides start shrinking from the pan. Remove from the oven, let stand for 5 minutes, then turn out and cool on a cake rack. Makes 1 8 x 4½-inch loaf.

DATE NUT BREAD

1 8-ounce package dates
3 tablespoons butter
1 cup boiling water
2 cups sifted flour
1 teaspoon baking powder
1 teaspoon soda
1 teaspoon salt
¾ cup sugar
1 cup chopped nuts
1 egg
1 teaspoon vanilla

Pit the dates. Put them into a large mixing bowl with 3 tablespoons of butter, pour 1 cup of boiling water over them, and let stand for 20 minutes. Then mash the dates a little with a fork. Sift together 2 cups of sifted flour, 1 teaspoon of baking powder, 1 teaspoon of soda, 1 teaspoon of salt, and ¾ cup of sugar. Mix 1 cup of chopped nuts with these dry ingredients. Beat 1 egg until light and fluffy. Beat in 1 teaspoon of vanilla. Add to the dates and mix well. Then add the dry ingredients and mix just until the flour is all dampened. Place in a greased 9 x 4 x 2½-inch loaf pan. Bake for 50 to 60 minutes in a moderate oven at 350°.

DARK NUT BREAD

1½ cups whole wheat flour, sifted
¾ cup white flour, sifted
2½ teaspoons baking powder
1 teaspoon soda
¾ teaspoon salt
¾ cup brown sugar
¾ cup chopped nuts
1 egg
1½ cups buttermilk or *sour milk*

Sift together twice 1½ cups of sifted whole wheat flour, ¾ cup of sifted white flour, 2½ teaspoons of baking powder, 1 teaspoon of soda, and ¾ teaspoon of salt. Add ¾ cup of brown sugar and ¾ cup of chopped nuts. Beat 1 egg until light and fluffy, and add 1½ cups of buttermilk or sour milk. Make a well in the dry ingredients. Add the egg and milk mixture all at once, and stir only until there are no traces of flour. Pour the batter lightly into a greased 3½ x 7½ x 3-inch loaf pan. Bake 1¼ hours in a moderate oven at 350°. Remove from the oven and let stand in the pan for a few minutes. Turn out on a cake rack and let cool before cutting.

VARIATIONS

Fruit Nut Bread. Reduce the nuts to ¼ cup and add 1 cup of one or more of the following fruits: raisins, currants, chopped dates, chopped apricots, or chopped prunes.

Spice Fruit Bread. Sift the following spices with the dry ingredients: ¾ teaspoon of cinnamon, ¼ teaspoon of mace, ¼ teaspoon of cloves, ¼ teaspoon of ginger, and ¼ teaspoon of nutmeg. Add 1 cup of currants or raisins.

Banana Nut Bread. Add 1 cup of mashed bananas to the buttermilk or sour milk.

BANANA BREAD

1¾ *cups sifted flour*
2 *teaspoons baking powder*
¼ *teaspoon soda*
½ *teaspoon salt*
⅓ *cup shortening*
⅔ *cup sugar*
2 *eggs, beaten*
1 *cup mashed bananas* (2 or 3 *bananas*)

Sift together 1¾ cups of sifted flour, 2 teaspoons of baking powder, ¼ teaspoon of soda, and ½ teaspoon of salt. Beat ⅓ cup of shortening until it is creamy, then add ⅔ cup of sugar gradually. Beat until light and fluffy. Add 2 beaten eggs and beat well. Add the sifted dry ingredients alternately with 1 cup of mashed bananas, a small amount at a time. Beat until smooth after each addition. Turn into a greased loaf pan and bake about 1 hour in a moderate oven at 350°. Let the loaf cool, then wrap it tightly, and store for at least 24 hours before slicing it.

APPLESAUCE NUT BREAD

½ cup shortening
⅔ cup light brown sugar
2 eggs
1 cup applesauce
2 cups sifted flour
½ teaspoon salt
½ teaspoon soda
1 teaspoon baking powder
½ cup chopped walnuts
½ cup raisins

Cream ½ cup of shortening and add ⅔ cup of light brown sugar gradually, creaming well after each addition. Beat in 2 eggs, one at a time. Stir in 1 cup of applesauce. Sift together 2 cups of sifted flour, ½ teaspoon of salt, ½ teaspoon of soda, and 1 teaspoon of baking powder. Add half of the sifted ingredients to the first mixture and stir to blend. Add ½ cup of chopped walnuts and ½ cup of raisins to the remaining dry ingredients, and blend into the mixture. Pour the batter into a greased loaf pan and bake about 55 minutes in a moderate oven at 350°. Let the bread stand in the pan for about 10 minutes before removing to a cake rack to cool.

CRANBERRY NUT BREAD

2 cups sifted flour
1 teaspoon baking soda
1 teaspoon salt
¾ cup sugar
1 cup whole cranberry sauce
1 cup chopped nuts
1 egg
⅔ cup milk
¼ cup cool melted butter

Sift 2 cups of sifted flour, 1 teaspoon of baking soda, 1 teaspoon of salt, and ¾ cup of sugar into a large mixing bowl. Add 1 cup of whole cranberry sauce and 1 cup of chopped nuts. Slightly beat 1 egg. Blend in ⅔ cup of milk and ¼ cup of cool melted butter. Add to the rest of the ingredients and stir just until all the flour is dampened. Put into a greased 9 x 5 x 3-inch loaf pan, and bake in a moderate oven at 375° for 50 to 60 minutes. Remove from oven, let stand for 5 minutes, then turn out on a rack to cool. For easier slicing, let stand 3 to 4 hours or overnight.

PUBLICK HOUSE

Sturbridge, Massachusetts

JUST over the Massachusetts border, one half mile from the intersection of Routes 15 and 20 and the new Massachusetts Turnpike, lies the village of Sturbridge, a distinct contrast of the new and the old. The highways are the latest word in modern construction. The village is a small group of white clapboard houses facing a quiet common, all shaded with gigantic elms. One of the buildings is the Publick House, a Treadway Inn.

Publick House is saturated with old New England spirit. The oldest part was built prior to 1770. Here Ebenezer Crafts had a tavern. He was born in Pomfret, Connecticut, in 1740, graduated from Yale, and later came to Sturbridge and established himself as a storekeeper and tavern keeper. He worked hard, acquired quite an estate, was a colonel in the Revolutionary War, and a leader in every civic undertaking. The building has always been a restaurant or tavern. At one time in the nineteenth century it was called The Elms and served a full-course chicken dinner for 50¢. In 1944 it was purchased by the Treadways.

It is a typical colonial-style white wooden building with dark shutters, and the interior carries out the colonial feeling. The Publick House does a tremendous restaurant business, and both the atmosphere and the food explain why. There are four pine-paneled dining rooms with reproductions of antique furniture and old prints and an enclosed outdoor dining deck for summer use. One of the dining rooms, called the Tap Room, was the original tavern. It is a pleasant, long, rather narrow room with a 7½-foot brick fireplace complete with the old utensils. Breakfast is served here in the winter and most agreeable it is too, with a roaring fire. Another dining room is called the Pineapple Room because of the pineapple wallpaper motif, and that too has a fireplace and old wall sconces. One of the larger dining rooms was an old barn, with the hayloft and stalls still standing. Lunch and dinner are served in the regular dining rooms from noon until eight-thirty. There are two cocktail lounges, where à la carte meals are served until midnight. And there is a small well-stocked gift shop. The Publick House has a countrywide reputation for its fine food. Mrs. Louise Coggeshall, the innkeeper, and her chefs are thoroughly interested in food, and the quality is kept to a high par on all the standard dishes and Treadway specialties (many of which were first introduced here). They also offer well-tested new dishes. The menus are primarily complete table-d'hôte luncheons and dinners, with a wide choice for each course, but there are special light luncheons too.

The Publick House also has rooms for guests. The colonial furnishings include copies of old wallpapers, wide floor boards, beamed ceilings, pewter wall sconces, braided rugs, candlewick spreads, reproductions of antique maple furniture, old flower prints, and nice old-fashioned pincushions. Modern touches are comfortable armchairs, luggage racks, and fresh apples to add a fine fragrance. There is an art gallery in the former ballroom with loan exhibitions at all times. On a hill about a mile away rooms are also available in the former Treadway residence with attractive modern décor, a swimming pool, and a stunning view for miles on each side across the valley to far-off ridges.

At Christmas time the Publick House celebrates with festive decorations, parties, and candles at every window. After Christmas, in early January, ten Yankee Winter Weekends start. Old Sturbridge Village is only about a mile away and one purpose of these weekends is to study that fascinating reconstruction of an early nineteenth-century community. The weekend starts Friday evening with a syllabub party for the guests before open fires, followed by dinner and dancing. Breakfast Saturday in the Tap Room features griddle cakes, fried mush, and apple pie. The day is devoted to a leisurely visit to Old Sturbridge Village, with a break in the middle of the day for mulled cider and a fabulous buffet lunch at the tavern there. After lunch there are "sugaring off" and hay or sleigh rides, a big hit with children, who often join their families for these weekends. That evening there is a game dinner at the Publick House and square dancing in the town hall on the common. The weekend is officially over after breakfast on Sunday, and the total cost is very reasonable. In the summer, plays are given at the summer theater by college students and there is golf in nearby Southbridge.

Old Sturbridge Village represents a New England farming community about 1810. There are some fifty buildings, thirty open to visitors, on about two hundred acres of meadow, woodland, and river shore. The idea is to show how thrifty hardworking people of modest means then lived, and the exhibits reveal their home life, activities, skills, and arts. There are two covered bridges, a sawmill, general store, homes, an herb garden, an extensive selection of glassware and paperweights, one hundred and seventy-five old clocks, early wrought iron, and art works. A simple and stately white-spired meeting house dominates the green, and a recent addition is the Salem Towne House, which is a typical squire's mansion. Most of the buildings are contemporary and have been brought from adjacent parts of the country. The tavern, although a perfect reproduction, is new. What makes Old Sturbridge particularly interesting is the live demonstrations. Goods are baked in the old ovens, using old recipes. The grist mill on the Quinebaug River grinds meal between stones and the flour may be purchased. There are candlemakers, potters, a blacksmith, weavers, wood turners, and metalsmiths. The village is open daily from May through November. The rest of the year it is open on Saturdays and Sundays, but on weekdays it can be seen only by guided tours at ten and two.

The Publick House is sixty miles from Boston and one hundred and fifty miles from New York. It is the only good restaurant between Hartford and Sturbridge on Route 15, and the best restaurant for miles around. There is plenty of free parking space in the rear. It is open all year.

DESSERTS

DISCRETION usually goes with the wind when people dine out, and the most careful calorie counters splurge on nice rich desserts they wouldn't dream of eating at home. Guests also enjoy the opportunity of sampling foods they may not know how to cook themselves. The result is that desserts are a key factor in the Treadway Inns' menus. The most popular desserts are Indian pudding, deep-dish apple pie, peppermint-stick snowballs, and strawberry ice-cream pie. But they are far from the whole story. When we summarized the dishes found on the menus of all the inns, we discovered there were about 175 desserts; too many to be included in a general cook book. So if any favorites are left out, and a reader wants the recipes, please let us know.

PIES

PIE CRUST

Pie crust is a Waterloo for many otherwise good cooks. As one technical cook book says, "Pie crust has at once the simplest ingredients and the most diverse results of any baked food known.

It seems to require a light hand, a sure touch, and at least two prior generations of excellent cooks."

Regular pie crust is nothing but flour, shortening, salt, and water. Although the proportions can vary, within limits, the proportions aren't what makes a good crust. It is all in the handling. It is essential that pie crust should be handled lightly and as little as possible. Cold solid shortening is cut into flour, and the aim is not to actually mix them but just to coat the particles of fat with flour. The layers of small fat particles make a pie crust flaky and "short." If a heavy hand is used in the cutting-in process and if it goes on too long, the fat melts, forming a solid mass and a tough crust. Too much water produces the same result. Just enough cold water is used to hold the fat and flour together.

The flour is usually all-purpose flour, since pastry flour makes a rather crumbly crust. Pastry flour is sometimes used for a very thin precooked crust for chiffon and cream pies. The type of shortening is a subject of disagreement among good cooks. Some swear by lard, some by chicken fat; others like part butter for flavor; others use all vegetable shortening. Vegetable shortening is easy to handle and is perfectly satisfactory. The standard proportion of fat to flour in most technical cook books is 3 to 1. A shorter pastry can be made by increasing the fat up to 2 to 1, or even almost equal parts.

The term "prepared 9-inch pie shell" in some of the following recipes refers either to a baked regular pie crust or to a crumb crust.

PIE CRUST I

2¼ *cups flour*
¾ *cup shortening*
1 *teaspoon salt*
5 *to* 6 *tablespoons ice water*

All the ingredients should be cold. Even the flour can be chilled right in a mixing bowl in the refrigerator. The shortening can be part vegetable shortening and part butter, or all vegetable shortening. Cut half the shortening into the flour until the mixture is like coarse meal, using 2 knives. A pastry blender is sometimes recommended, but the tendency is to press down too hard with it. Cut the rest of the shortening in until the pieces are the size of small peas. Dissolve 1 teaspoon of salt in 5 tablespoons of ice water. Stir lightly into the flour mixture with a fork. If the mixture holds together, do not add any more water; you may need a little more. As soon as it holds together, wrap it in wax paper and let it rest in the refrigerator for at least half an hour; it can be overnight. It can be rolled out immediately, but is easier to handle after a rest. If it has been chilled a long time, let it stand at room temperature for a little while before rolling it out. This is enough dough for 2 9-inch crusts.

PIE CRUST II

For people who find pie crust difficult to make, I recommend the following receipe, which from my own experience is just about foolproof. There is no guesswork about the amount of water, and the crust is easy to handle and nice and flaky.

2¼ *cups flour*
5 *tablespoons cold water*
1 *teaspoon salt*
¾ *cup cold vegetable shortening*

Take ⅓ cup of the flour and blend it with 5 tablespoons of cold water to form a paste. Sift the remaining flour with 1 teaspoon of salt into a large mixing bowl. Cut half the shortening in until the mixture is like coarse meal. Cut the other half in until it is the size of small peas. Add the paste and mix lightly with a large fork. Makes 2 9-inch crusts.

FLAKY PASTRY

Roll the above pie crust out ¼ inch thick. Dot with 2 to 3 tablespoons of butter cut into small pieces. Fold in half and then in half again. Chill before using. Flaky pastry can also be made by doubling the amount of vegetable shortening.

HOT WATER PIE CRUST

¾ cup vegetable shortening
¼ cup boiling water
1 tablespoon milk
2 cups sifted flour
1 teaspoon salt

This method of making pastry produces a crumbly rather than flaky pastry. It is easy to manage and guaranteed to work. An electric mixer simplifies the task. Put ¾ cup of vegetable shortening into the bowl of the mixer or into a mixing bowl. Pour on ¼ cup of boiling water and 1 tablespoon of milk and beat or mix with a fork until the mixture is thick and smooth. Sift in 2 cups of flour and 1 teaspoon of salt. By hand stir until the dough cleans the sides of the bowl. Wrap in wax paper and place in the refrigerator for 15 minutes. Makes 2 9-inch crusts.

CRUMB PASTRY SHELL

1½ cups crumbs
¼ cup sugar
⅓ cup melted butter
½ teaspoon cinnamon, optional

The crumbs can be made with graham crackers, vanilla or chocolate wafers, or a crisp cereal such as Rice Crispies or corn flakes. Roll them very fine with a rolling pin and have enough to make 1½ cups. Blend with ¼ cup of sugar and ⅓ cup of melted butter. Cinnamon is good with some pies. Press evenly on the bottom and sides of a 9-inch pie plate. Chill for 2 to 3 hours in the refrigerator before adding the filling. The crust can also be baked for 8 to 10 minutes in a slow oven at 325° if you wish to use it quickly. Let it cool before adding the filling.

FRUIT TARTS

SWEET DOUGH

½ pound butter
2 cups flour
1 egg
¾ cup confectioners' sugar
2 tablespoons water

This is a cookielike dough which makes a nice crunchy, sweet base for fresh fruit tarts. Let ½ pound of butter stand for ½ hour at room temperature in a large mixing bowl. Add 2 cups of flour and blend them together with a large wooden spoon or your hands. Put 1 egg, ¾ cup of confectioners' sugar, and 2 tablespoons of water in another small bowl and beat hard with a wire whisk. Add to the flour and butter and mix until a smooth dough is formed. Unlike a regular flaky pie crust dough, handling does not hurt this dough unless it is done with a heavy hand. Wrap in wax paper and let rest in the refrigerator for at least an hour before rolling out. It is soft at first, but will harden in the refrigerator as the flour swells. Roll out a generous ¼ inch thick on a lightly floured board and with a plain or fluted cutter cut into the desired shapes to fit small tart pans. Place in the pans with the floured bottom side up. Put wax paper and dry beans or rice in each one to hold the pastry in place. Bake in a moderate oven at 375° for about 25 to 30 minutes, until delicately colored, removing the paper and rice after the first 20 minutes.

To serve, fill each shell with a bed of sweetened whipped cream or the following pastry cream. Dip fresh fruit in hot fruit glaze and arrange it attractively over the top. The fruit can be whole strawberries, raspberries, or blueberries, sliced peaches, sliced bananas, little seedless white grapes, pitted black cherries, sliced pineapple – any fruit that looks nice. Red fruits are glazed with a red glaze, other fruits with regular apricot glaze.

Apricot Glaze. This is the standard glaze for any fruit tarts or pies. It can be made with dried or canned fruit, or by melting a jar of apricot jam with 1 to 2 tablespoons of water and straining it. Glaze lasts indefinitely, so it is worth while to make a quantity, and it should be stored in a covered jar to prevent a crust forming.

Dried Apricots. Soak 1 pound overnight in 1 quart of water. The next day bring them slowly to a boil and cook until the apricots are soft; as one of the Treadway Inn's pastry cooks says, "stew the daylights out of them." Remove and strain. Add 1 cup of sugar for each cup of fruit, return to the fire, and stir until the boiling point is reached, then simmer for 5 to 10 minutes.

Canned Apricots. Use a large 2-pound can. Push the fruit through a colander. Simmer with the juice ¾ pound of sugar and 1 teaspoon of lemon juice (optional), stirring occasionally with a wooden spoon until the mixture is very thick and sticks to the spoon.

Red Glaze. Apricot glaze can be colored with red vegetable coloring. Or strain a jar of red currant jelly and heat it slowly with 1 tablespoon of water.

Clear Glaze. Use packaged apple gelatin, using half as much water as the directions call for. Fruit juice may be used instead, and the glaze may be colored with vegetable coloring.

PASTRY CREAM

4 egg yolks
½ cup sugar
¼ cup flour
¼ teaspoon salt
2 cups scalded milk
1 teaspoon vanilla
½ cup heavy cream, whipped

Beat 4 egg yolks with a wire whisk. Beat in ½ cup of sugar, then ¼ cup of flour and ¼ teaspoon of salt. Pour on 2 cups of scalded milk, stirring all the while. Cook over a slow fire, stirring constantly with a wire whisk until the mixture thickens. Remove, cool for a few minutes, then stir in 1 teaspoon of vanilla. Or flavor with rum. When cool, fold in ½ cup of heavy cream, whipped. Up to ½ cup of flour may be used for a stiffer pastry cream, but the consistency of this one is nice and creamy.

COBBLERS

In old New England cook books a cobbler is an alcoholic drink, usually with a sherry base. Today the term is used for a deep-dish fruit pie with a rich biscuit crust instead of a regular pie crust.

Strawberries, peaches, blueberries, and cherries are the fruits generally used, and they are prepared as they would be for any deep-dish pie. For a clear filling, cornstarch may be used instead of flour for the thickening. The following excellent crust has been worked out by the pastry cook at the Publick House, Sturbridge, Mass.

COBBLER CRUST

1¾ *cups sifted flour*
2 *teaspoons baking powder*
1 *teaspoon salt*
½ *cup shortening*
1 *egg*
½ *cup milk*

Sift 1¾ cups of sifted flour, 2 teaspoons of baking powder, and 1 teaspoon of salt into a large mixing bowl. Cut in ½ cup of shortening with 2 knives. Slightly beat 1 egg. Blend in ½ cup of milk. Stir quickly into the flour-fat mixture. Put the dough on a lightly floured board and pat it out. It is very soft, so difficult to roll. Place on the filling, which should be hot; if it is cold, it takes so long to heat that the juice soaks into the crust and makes it soggy. Bake about 25 to 30 minutes in a hot oven at 425°, until golden brown. The crust may be brushed with cream or sprinkled with sugar before it is baked.

CREAM PIES

Cream pies are thickened with a starch, either flour or cornstarch or sometimes both, and with egg yolks. The proportion of starch is rather high in the following basic recipe so that the pie will set well enough to be cut into neat pieces for restaurant serving. For home use, if a slightly runny pie is wanted, the flour can be cut to ⅓ cup, or the cornstarch to 2½ tablespoons. When thickening anything with flour or cornstarch, the starch must first be blended with a cold liquid (as in a cream pie) or with fat (as in a gravy). If it is just dumped into a hot mixture, lumps are inevitable.

Cornstarch cooks to an almost translucent paste if it is cooked in water or any other clear liquid, so it makes nice clear-looking mixtures. But it has to be handled carefully. It is unripe starch which breaks down into a sugar (corn) syrup if subjected to prolonged heat, losing its thickening action. (Acids sometimes have the same effect.) So do not overcook a cornstarch mixture, although it should continue to cook after it first thickens to obtain a maximum gel. And soon after it is removed from the fire, turn it out into a prepared pie shell or shallow wide container, since in a saucepan the mass generates heat which will break down the starch.

BASIC CREAM PIE

⅔ *cup sugar*
½ *cup flour* or 4 *tablespoons cornstarch*
½ *teaspoon salt*
2 *cups milk*
3 *egg yolks*
2 *tablespoons butter*
1 *teaspoon vanilla*
1 *prepared 9-inch pastry shell*

Blend ⅔ cup of sugar, ½ cup of flour or 4 tablespoons of cornstarch, and ½ teaspoon of salt together in a saucepan. Add ½ cup of cold milk and stir until the starch is dissolved. Slowly pour on 1½ cups of scalded milk, stirring all the while. Stir over a moderate fire until the mixture thickens. Reduce the heat and simmer about 10 minutes, stirring frequently. Slightly beat 3 egg yolks. Blend a little of the hot mixture with them, then stir them into the hot mixture. Cook with constant stirring for 2 to 3 minutes. Remove. Add 2 tablespoons of butter and cool for 5 minutes. Then add 1 teaspoon of vanilla and fill into the pastry shell. The pie may be topped with meringue, following the directions on page 306 using the 3 egg whites and 6 tablespoons of sugar. Or it may be spread with a thin layer of whipped cream just before serving. In any event, cool the pie at room temperature and then chill it for several hours in the refrigerator.

VARIATIONS

Chocolate. Melt 2 squares (ounces) of baking chocolate with the scalded milk. Increase the sugar to ¾ cup. Use 1 tablespoon less flour or ½ tablespoon less cornstarch. For *mocha* pie use half coffee and half milk.

Banana. Cover the bottom of the pie shell with sliced bananas and cover with half the filling. Use another layer of bananas and the rest of the filling.

Butterscotch. Use 1 cup of dark brown sugar in place of ⅔ cup of sugar. Increase the butter to 3 tablespoons. For **butterscotch pecan** pie, mix together 1 tablespoon of melted butter, 3 tablespoons of brown sugar, and ½ cup of chopped pecans. Sprinkle over the filling; it won't cover it all, but there will be enough for some for each serving.

Fruit. Fold 1 cup of fruit into the filling; it can be sliced berries, sliced cherries, chopped dates or raisins, blueberries, well-drained crushed pineapple – whatever you like, really.

Rum. Fold ½ cup of heavy cream which has been whipped and flavored with 2 to 3 tablespoons of Jamaica rum into the filling. Garnish with whipped cream and grated semisweet chocolate.

Coconut. Whip ½ cup of heavy cream. Blend with ½ cup of shredded coconut and fold into the filling. Garnish with plain or lightly toasted coconut.

Coffee. Use half strong coffee and half milk. Nice in a chocolate crumb crust (*see* page 294).

FRESH FRUIT PIES

3½ *cups prepared fruit*
¾ *to 1 cup sugar*
2 *tablespoons flour*
¼ *teaspoon salt*
1 *tablespoon lemon juice*
1 *to 2 tablespoons butter*
1 *recipe for double pie crust*

The basic principle for all fresh fruit pies is the same. Individual differences lie in the flavoring, as noted later. Peel fruit such as apples and peaches and thinly slice them. Slice large berries, leave small ones whole. Dice rhubarb. The amount of sugar depends on the sweetness and ripeness of the fruit. The maximum is used for tart fruits like rhubarb, while sweet fruits like ripe strawberries need less.

Blend together the sugar, 2 tablespoons of flour, ¼ teaspoon of salt, and any flavorings in a large mixing bowl. Add the fruit and mix thoroughly. Fill into a deep pastry-lined 9-inch pie plate, heaping slightly in the center. Sprinkle with 1 tablespoon of lemon juice and dot with 1 to 2 tablespoons of butter. The top crust should have slits so that steam can escape, and the pie looks attractive if the slits are cut into some sort of design. Moisten the edge of the lower crust with water, cover with the top crust, and trim, leaving a margin of ½ inch to tuck under. The top can be brushed with milk or light cream and sprinkled with sugar before baking; or after the pie is cooked, it may be brushed with melted butter, and when cool, dusted with confectioners' sugar. Bake in a hot oven at 425° for about 35 to 40 minutes, until the pastry is nicely browned.

VARIATIONS

Apple Pie. Use tart, firm apples so that they will keep their shape. Some eating apples, McIntosh, for example, have a high moisture content and get mushy when cooked. If the apples are precooked for about 10 minutes with the sugar and 1 cup of water, the pie will not shrink. Apple pie is usually flavored with spices, about 1 teaspoon of cinnamon or ¼ teaspoon of nutmeg or half and half. Half a teaspoon of grated lemon rind may also be used. The sugar may be replaced with brown or maple sugar, or ½ cup of honey.

Deep-Dish Apple Pie. This is one of the three most popular desserts at the Treadway Inns. The only difference between a regular apple pie and a deep-dish pie is that a deep-dish is baked in a rectangular baking pan about 3 inches deep and has only one crust, on top. A regular pie crust may be used, or the flaky crust on page 293. At the inns the pie is served warm, generally with vanilla ice cream. Cherries also make a nice deep-dish pie.

Blueberry Pie. Half a teaspoon of grated lemon rind may be added, and ¼ teaspoon of nutmeg, cinnamon, or ginger.

Cherry Pie. Use sour red pie cherries. Increase the flour to 3 tablespoons and add ¼ cup of cherry juice. Cherry pie may be flavored with ½ teaspoon of cinnamon and ¼ teaspoon of almond extract. A drop or two of red vegetable coloring gives it an attractive color.

Peach Pie. May be flavored with ½ teaspoon of cinnamon.

Rhubarb Pie. Mix 1 slightly beaten egg with the fruit. Nice flavored with a little grated orange rind.

Strawberry Pie. May be flavored with ½ teaspoon of cinnamon.

LEMON CHIFFON PIE

- 1 *tablespoon gelatin*
- ¼ *cup cold water*
- 4 *eggs*
- 1 *cup sugar*
- ½ *cup lemon juice*
- 1 *teaspoon grated lemon rind*
- ½ *teaspoon salt*
- 1 *prepared 9-inch pie shell*
- ½ *cup heavy cream, whipped, optional*

This recipe is for a standard lemon chiffon pie. Soften 1 tablespoon of gelatin for 5 minutes in ¼ cup of cold water. Beat 4 egg yolks until light. Blend in ½ cup of sugar and ½ cup of lemon juice. Cook in a double boiler until the mixture thickens and coats the spoon, stirring constantly. The water should boil gently and not touch the upper section. Remove, add the softened gelatin, and stir until it is dissolved. Blend in 1 teaspoon of grated lemon rind. Let stand until cool and the mixture starts to set; the consistency should be syrupy. Meanwhile beat 4 egg whites and ½ teaspoon of salt until stiff. Beat in the remaining ½ cup of sugar, a tablespoon at a time. Fold gently into the first mixture. Fill into a prepared pie shell and place in the refrigerator until set and chilled. It will set quickly, but takes 2 to 3 hours to chill.

Before serving, a thin layer of whipped cream may be spread over the top. The pie may be garnished with toasted coconut.

VARIATIONS

Lime Chiffon Pie. Follow the directions for lemon chiffon pie. Substitute lime juice for lemon juice, and 2 teaspoons of grated lime rind for 1 teaspoon of grated lemon rind. Tint it a very delicate light green with a few drops of vegetable coloring, but be careful not to overdo it.

Orange Chiffon Pie. Follow the directions for lemon chiffon pie. Substitute ½ cup of orange juice and 1 tablespoon of lemon juice for the lemon juice, and orange rind for the lemon rind.

Citrus Chiffon Pie. Follow the directions for lemon chiffon pie. Substitute ¼ cup of orange juice and ¼ cup of lemon juice for the lemon juice, and ½ teaspoon each of grated lemon and orange rind for the lemon rind.

Coffee Chiffon Pie. Follow the directions for lemon chiffon pie. Substitute ¾ cup of strong coffee for the lemon juice. Soak the gelatin in ¼ cup of cold coffee. Cook the remaining ½ cup of coffee with the egg yolks and sugar. Omit the lemon rind. Add 1 teaspoon of vanilla to the egg whites after they are beaten.

Pumpkin Chiffon Pie. Follow the directions for lemon chiffon pie. Omit the lemon juice and lemon rind. Cut the granulated sugar to ⅓ cup. With the beaten egg yolks cook 1¼ cups of cooked pumpkin, ¾ cup of brown sugar, ⅓ cup of milk, 1 teaspoon of cinnamon, and ½ teaspoon each of nutmeg and ginger. Beat ⅓ cup of sugar with the egg whites. Fold in ½ cup of heavy cream, whipped, and 1 teaspoon of grated orange rind.

Sherry Chiffon Pie. Follow the directions for lemon chiffon pie. Omit the lemon juice and rind. Cook ⅔ cup of sherry with the egg yolks and sugar. A few chopped pecans or almonds may be sprinkled over the top when serving.

Cream Chiffon Pie. Follow the directions for lemon chiffon pie. Use a chocolate wafer crust (*see* page 294). Omit the lemon juice and rind. With the beaten egg yolks cook ¼ cup of sugar, 1 cup of hot milk, and 1 teaspoon of vanilla. Beat ¼ cup of sugar with the egg whites. Fold in 1½ cups of heavy cream, whipped, then the egg whites. Garnish with grated semisweet chocolate.

Rum Chiffon Pie. Follow the directions for lemon chiffon pie. Omit the lemon juice and rind. Cook 2 cups of scalded milk and ¼ teaspoon of nutmeg with the beaten egg yolks and sugar. Fold ⅓ cup of Jamaica rum in with the beaten egg whites. The following chocolate topping is delicious with this pie. Melt ½ pound of milk chocolate with 2 tablespoons of water. Whip ¾ cup of heavy cream. Flavor half of it with 1 teaspoon of Jamaica rum and fold into the chocolate. Flavor the other half with 1 tablespoon of confectioners' sugar. Spread this over the chilled pie, and cover with the chocolate. Return to the refrigerator for further chilling.

Strawberry Chiffon Pie. Follow the directions for lemon chiffon pie. Omit all the rind and all but 1 tablespoon of lemon juice. Cook the beaten yolks with the lemon juice and sugar. After the gelatin is added, stir in 1 cup of strawberry juice and pulp. Also a drop or two of red vegetable coloring if you wish. Beat ¼ cup of sugar into the whites. Garnish with whole berries.

Berry Chiffon Pie. Substitute any berry for the strawberries in the preceding recipe.

CHOCOLATE CHIFFON PIE

1 *tablespoon gelatin*
¼ *cup cold water*
2 *squares chocolate* or 6 *tablespoons cocoa*
½ *cup boiling water*
4 *eggs*
1 *cup sugar*
¼ *tablespoon salt*
1 *teaspoon vanilla*
1½ *cups heavy cream*
baked 9-*inch pie shell*

Soak 1 tablespoon of gelatin in ¼ cup of cold water for at least 5 minutes. Put 2 squares of chocolate or 6 tablespoons of cocoa in ½ cup of boiling water and stir over a slow fire until smooth.

Remove from the fire and add the gelatin, stirring until it is dissolved. Beat 4 egg yolks slightly with ½ cup of sugar, ¼ teaspoon of salt, and 1 teaspoon of vanilla. Add the chocolate mixture and blend well. Cool until it begins to thicken. Beat the 4 egg whites until frothy, slowly add the other ½ cup of sugar, and beat until a thick meringue is formed. Fold into the chocolate mixture. Half a cup of heavy cream, stiffly beaten, can also be folded in. Put into a baked pie shell and chill for several hours in the refrigerator. To serve, spread a thin layer of whipped cream over the top and garnish with rosettes of whipped cream and a little grated chocolate.

CREAM CHIFFON PIES

These pies have a thicker, smoother, creamier texture than the more airy regular chiffon pies. The basic technique follows with a lemon pie. Any of the preceding variations of lemon chiffon pie can be made in this manner, and some other variations follow the basic recipe.

LEMON CREAM CHIFFON PIE

- 4 *eggs*
- 1 *cup sugar*
- ½ *cup lemon juice*
- *pinch of salt*
- 1 *tablespoon gelatin*
- ¼ *cup cold water*
- 1 *teaspoon grated lemon rind*
- 1 *cup heavy cream, whipped*
- *prepared 9-inch pastry shell*

Beat 4 egg yolks until light and fluffy. Gradually beat in ½ cup of sugar. Blend in ½ cup of lemon juice and a pinch of salt. Stir over gently boiling water until the mixture thickens. Meanwhile soften 1 tablespoon of gelatin in ¼ cup of cold water. Remove the egg yolk mixture from the fire and stir in the gelatin, then 1 teaspoon of grated lemon rind. Let cool, then place in the refrigerator until just set. Beat 4 egg whites until they hold their shape, then beat in the remaining ½ cup of sugar, a tablespoon at a time.

Continue beating until a thick meringue is formed. Beat in the egg yolk mixture, 1/4 at a time. Do not overbeat, but do beat until the mixture is smooth. Fold in 1 cup of heavy cream, whipped. Fill into a pastry shell and chill in the refrigerator for at least 2 hours. The pie may be covered with a thin layer of whipped cream before serving, but it really does not need it.

Butterscotch Cream Chiffon Pie. Follow the directions for lemon cream chiffon pie. Omit the lemon juice and lemon rind. Cook 1 cup of hot milk and 1/2 cup of brown (instead of white) sugar with the beaten egg yolks.

Maple Cream Chiffon Pie. Follow the directions for lemon cream chiffon pie. Omit the lemon juice and rind. Substitute 1/2 cup of maple syrup for 1/2 cup of sugar, and cook it and 1/2 cup of hot milk with the beaten egg yolks. Add 1 teaspoon of vanilla to the beaten whites.

LEMON MERINGUE PIE

1 1/2 *cups sugar*
4 *tablespoons flour*
1/8 *teaspoon salt*
1 1/2 *cups boiling water*
4 *eggs*
2 *tablespoons butter*
6 *tablespoons lemon juice*
1 *teaspoon grated lemon rind*
8 *tablespoons sugar*
prepared 9-inch pastry shell

Recipes for this pie vary in respect to the type and the amount of the thickening agent. Sometimes cornstarch is used in place of flour, sometimes both are used. Many recipes specify a larger amount than we have here. Since cornstarch is tricky to use, as explained in the basic cream pie recipe on page 297, we use only flour and not too much of it. The consistency will not be too stiff, but creamy and just set.

Blend together in a saucepan 1 1/2 cups of sugar, 4 tablespoons of flour, and 1/8 teaspoon of salt. Pour on 1 1/2 cups of boiling water. Stir over a slow fire about 5 minutes, until the mixture has thickened and no longer tastes starchy. Slightly beat 4 egg yolks. Pour the hot mixture slowly over them, stirring all the while. Return to the fire and stir and cook about 2 minutes, just until the mixture thickens. Remove and add 2 tablespoons of butter, 6 tablespoons of lemon juice, and 1 teaspoon of grated lemon rind. Cool slightly before filling into the prepared shell.

Cover with the following meringue, starting from the outside and working toward the center. Swirl it a little, but have the top fairly smooth, or it will brown unevenly. Be sure it touches the edge all around, or it may shrink, or slip when cut. Bake in a hot oven at 450° for 4 to 5 minutes, until lightly browned, and watch it carefully. Cool at room temperature, then place in the refrigerator until chilled and ready to serve.

SOFT MERINGUE

Beat 4 egg whites until stiff but not dry with a pinch of salt. Beat in 8 tablespoons of sugar, a tablespoon at a time, beating thoroughly after each addition. It takes long beating to dissolve the sugar, and when it isn't dissolved, it turns into syrup and forms bubbles.

Notes on Soft Meringues. (*See* the general discussion on meringues on page 345.) If meringues are placed on a hot filling, there is less risk of weeping. Soft meringues may be baked at a variety of temperatures, but the latest tests favor 450° for a short time, about 4 to 5 minutes. A high temperature gives a good volume and texture, and nice, tender meringues. Just don't cool the pie in a draft, or the meringue will shrink. Browning meringues under the broiler, which is sometimes recommended, will toughen them. A lower temperature, about 350° for 10 to 15 minutes, is also used, but there is a risk of beading, which comes from too long cooking. Have the pie absolutely cold before cutting, so that the meringue will not spread.

Lime Meringue Pie. Substitute lime juice and grated lime rind for the lemon juice and rind in the preceding lemon meringue pie. Tint a light green with a very few drops of green vegetable coloring.

PEACH SURPRISE TART

- 6 *Elberta peach halves (fresh, canned,* or *frozen)*
- ½ *cup peach brandy* or *cognac*
- 1 *teaspoon almond extract*
- 1 *recipe flaky pie crust*
- ¾ *cup almonds* or *pecans*
- ½ *cup heavy cream, whipped*

Several hours before serving, place 6 drained peach halves in a bowl with ¼ cup of peach brandy or cognac, 2 drops of almond extract, and about ¼ cup of peach juice or syrup. Chill thoroughly in the refrigerator. Roll out the flaky pie crust about ¼ inch thick. Brush half of it with almond extract and sprinkle with ½ cup of nuts, finely chopped. Fold in half and roll out again. Cut into 6 rounds about 5 inches in diameter. Turn a 6-well muffin tin upside down and form the crust over the wells, pinching the lower edges to form pentagonals. Bake in a hot oven at 425° until a pale golden color, about 15 minutes. Remove and cool. To serve, place a peach half, cut side up, in the pastry cup. Put a spoonful of the brandy mixture in the center. Garnish with a rosette of whipped cream and a few nut meats in the form of a star. Serves 6.

SOUR CREAM RAISIN PIE

- 2 *eggs*
- 1 *cup sugar*
- 1 *cup sour cream*
- 2 *tablespoons flour*
- ½ *teaspoon salt*
- ½ *teaspoon cinnamon*
- ¼ *teaspoon nutmeg*
- ¼ *teaspoon ginger* or *cloves*
- ½ *cup chopped raisins*
- ½ *cup chopped butternuts*
- 1 *unbaked 9-inch pie crust*

Beat 2 eggs slightly. Add 1 cup of sugar and beat until blended. Gradually beat in 1 cup of sour cream. Sift together 2 tablespoons of flour, ½ teaspoon of salt, ½ teaspoon of cinnamon, ¼ teaspoon of nutmeg, and ¼ teaspoon of ginger or cloves. Add ½ cup of chopped raisins and ½ cup of chopped butternuts. Blend with the sour cream mixture. Fill into an unbaked pie crust and cook in a hot oven at 425° for 30 to 35 minutes, until the mixture is set and a knife inserted in the center comes out clean.

CHOCOLATE SUNDAE PIE

½ cup milk
½ teaspoon nutmeg
3 eggs
½ cup sugar
pinch of salt
¾ tablespoon gelatin
3 tablespoons cold water
½ teaspoon vanilla
1 cup heavy cream, whipped
½ cup grated dark sweet chocolate
baked 9-inch pie shell

Heat ½ cup of milk and ½ teaspoon of grated nutmeg in a double boiler. Beat 3 egg yolks with ½ cup of sugar and a pinch of salt until very light. Pour the hot milk slowly over the egg yolks, return to the double boiler, and stir until the custard thickens and coats the spoon. Meanwhile soften ¾ tablespoon of gelatin in 3 tablespoons of cold water. Remove the custard from the heat and stir in the gelatin, then ½ teaspoon of vanilla. Cool until the mixture stiffens. Beat it well, then fold in 3 stiffly beaten egg whites. Fill into the baked pie shell and place in the refrigerator until set and chilled. Before serving, garnish with slightly sweetened whipped cream and sprinkle the top with ½ cup of grated chocolate.

LEMON CREAM PIE

4 eggs
1 cup sugar
2 tablespoons cold water
dash of salt
juice and grated rind of 1 lemon
baked 9-inch pie shell

Put 4 egg yolks (unbeaten), ½ cup of sugar, 2 tablespoons of cold water, a dash of salt, and the juice and grated rind of 1 large lemon in the top of a double boiler. Cook, stirring constantly, until thickened. Remove from the fire. Beat 4 egg whites until stiff. Beat in the remaining ½ cup of sugar, a tablespoon at a time. Fold into the lemon mixture and put into the baked pie shell. Place under the broiler for 1 to 2 minutes to brown the top lightly; watch it every second, because it will brown quickly. Chill before serving.

BLACK BOTTOM PIE

14 *ginger cookies*
5 *tablespoons melted butter*
1¾ *cups milk*
1 *tablespoon gelatin*
¼ *cup cold water*
1 *cup sugar*
1 *tablespoon cornstarch*
pinch of salt
4 *eggs*
2 *squares chocolate, melted*
1 *teaspoon vanilla*
⅛ *teaspoon cream of tartar*
1 *tablespoon rum*
1 *cup heavy cream*
2 *tablespoons confectioners' sugar*
grated chocolate

Crust. Roll the cookies and put through a fine strainer. Blend with 5 tablespoons of melted butter. Line into a 9-inch pie plate, pressing the crumbs flat and firm. Bake in a slow oven at 325° for 10 minutes. Cool.

Basic Filling. Scald 1¾ cups of milk in the top of a double boiler over direct heat. Soak 1 tablespoon of gelatin in ¼ cup of cold water. Mix ½ cup of sugar with 1 tablespoon of cornstarch and a pinch of salt. Slowly pour the scalded milk over them, stirring all the while. Beat 4 egg yolks well, and add the milk mixture to them. Cook over boiling water until the custard thickens and coats the spoon. Remove from the fire, add the gelatin, and stir until it is dissolved. Divide the filling in half.

Chocolate Layer. To one half add 2 squares of melted chocolate and 1 teaspoon of vanilla. Place while still hot in the cooled crust, working carefully so as not to disturb the crust.

Rum-flavored Layer. Cool the remaining half of the filling. Beat 4 egg whites and ⅛ teaspoon of cream of tartar until stiff.

Beat in the other ½ cup of sugar, a tablespoon at a time. Fold into the cooled custard. Add 1 tablespoon of rum. Spread over the chocolate layer. Chill in the refrigerator several hours or overnight.

To serve, spread with 1 cup of heavy cream which has been whipped and sweetened with 2 tablespoons of confectioners' sugar. Sprinkle with grated dark sweet chocolate.

GRAHAM CRACKER CREAM PIE

16 *graham crackers, rolled fine*
1 *teaspoon flour*
1 *cup plus* 3 *tablespoons sugar*
½ *cup butter, softened*
1 *teaspoon cinnamon*
2 *tablespoons cornstarch*
¼ *teaspoon salt*
2 *cups milk, scalded*
3 *eggs*
1 *teaspoon vanilla*
⅛ *teaspoon cream of tartar*

Crust. Blend together the graham crackers, 1 teaspoon of flour, ½ cup of sugar, ½ cup of softened butter, and 1 teaspoon of cinnamon. Press ½ of this mixture firmly and evenly on the bottom and sides of a well-buttered 9-inch pie plate.

Filling. Mix 2 tablespoons of cornstarch, ¼ teaspoon of salt, and ¼ cup of sugar together. Scald 2 cups of milk with ¼ cup of sugar. Stir the milk into the cornstarch mixture. Cook over a low heat until the mixture thickens, stirring all the while. Beat 3 egg yolks well. Add a little of the hot cornstarch mixture to the yolks, stir, then stir the egg yolks into the cornstarch mixture. Stir over the fire until the mixture thickens. Remove from the fire, add 1 teaspoon of vanilla, and pour into the prepared crust.

Beat 3 egg whites with ⅛ teaspoon of cream of tartar until stiff. Beat in the remaining 3 tablespoons of sugar, a tablespoon at a time. Spread the meringue over the custard and sprinkle it with the remaining crumbs. Bake in a slow oven at 325° for about 15 minutes, or until lightly browned.

MARLBOROUGH PIE

6 *tart apples*	½ *teaspoon salt*
½ *cup water*	4 *eggs*
1 *cup sugar*	3 *tablespoons lemon juice*
3 *tablespoons butter*	1 *teaspoon grated lemon rind*

unbaked 9-inch pastry shell

Core and quarter the apples. Simmer with ½ cup of water until soft, about 15 minutes. Put through a strainer or food mill. While still hot, add 1 cup of sugar, 3 tablespoons of butter, and ½ teaspoon of salt. Cool. Beat 4 eggs. Stir in 3 tablespoons of lemon juice and 1 teaspoon of grated lemon rind. Add the applesauce and blend well. Put into the unbaked pie shell. Bake for 10 minutes in a hot oven at 450°. Reduce the heat to 300° and bake for about 1 hour longer, or until the crust is nicely browned and the filling set.

Marlborough Pudding. From handwritten recipe book, 1794: 6 apples, 6 spoonfuls rose water, 6 ounces butter, 6 ounces sugar, grate in 2 lemons and juice of 1, 6 eggs.

PUMPKIN PIE

2 *eggs*	½ *teaspoon nutmeg*
1½ *cups milk*	1 *teaspoon ginger*
1¾ *cups pumpkin*	½ *teaspoon salt*
1 *cup sugar (brown* or *white)*	1 *tablespoon melted butter*
2 *teaspoons cinnamon*	*unbaked 9-inch pastry shell*

Put 2 eggs into a large mixing bowl and beat slightly. Add 1½ cups of milk and beat until blended. Add 1¾ cups of cooked pumpkin, 1 cup of sugar, 2 teaspoons of cinnamon, ½ teaspoon of nutmeg, 1 teaspoon of ginger, ½ teaspoon of salt, and 1 tablespoon of melted butter (this is a Treadway Inn pastry cook's trick for browning the top). Stir until well blended. Pour into an unbaked pastry shell. Bake for 10 minutes at 450°, then lower the heat to 325° and cook another 30 to 40 minutes, until a silver knife inserted in the center comes out clean. The goodness of a pumpkin pie hinges on the freshness of the spices. This pie can be garnished with maple cream. Whip ½ pint of heavy cream until stiff. Slowly fold in ¼ cup of maple syrup. Make rosettes of maple cream around the edge of the pie or serve it separately.

PECAN PIE

- ⅓ *cup butter*
- ⅓ *cup brown sugar*
- 1 *tablespoon flour*
- 1 *cup dark corn syrup*
- 2 *tablespoons cool melted butter*
- 1 *cup small pecans* or *broken pieces*
- 4 *eggs*
- *unbaked 9-inch pastry shell*

Cream ⅓ cup of butter and ⅓ cup of brown sugar which has been mixed with 1 tablespoon of flour. Blend in a cup of corn syrup, 2 tablespoons of cool melted butter, and 1 cup of nuts. Slightly beat 4 eggs and fold in lastly. Fill into a 9-inch pastry shell and bake about 1¼ hours in a moderate oven at 350°, until the filling is set. Remove and cool on a cake rack before cutting.

Note. At some of the Treadway Inns maple syrup is used in place of corn syrup and gives the pie a fine flavor.

If you like seeing all the nuts on the top, bake the mixture without them for about 30 minutes, then cover the top with nuts and continue cooking until done.

DARK PECAN PIE

- 1½ *cups dark corn syrup*
- 1 *cup brown sugar*
- ½ *cup butter*
- 3 *eggs*
- ¼ *teaspoon salt*
- 1 *cup small pecans* or *broken pieces*
- ½ *teaspoon vanilla*
- *unbaked 9-inch pastry shell*

This pie has a dark, rather gooey filling with a delicious crisp crust. Bring 1½ cups of dark corn syrup and 1 cup of brown sugar slowly to a boil and simmer for 5 minutes, stirring all the while. Remove and cool. Melt and cool ½ cup of butter. Beat 3 eggs with ¼ teaspoon of salt until light. Slowly beat in the syrup. Fold in the butter, nuts, and ½ teaspoon of vanilla. Fill into the pastry shell and bake about 1¼ hours in a moderate oven at 350°, until the filling is set. Remove and cool on a cake rack before cutting. Both of these pecan pies will cut better if allowed to stand overnight.

MAPLE COCONUT PIE

3 *eggs*
1½ *cups maple syrup*
½ *cup sugar*
¼ *teaspoon salt*
¼ *cup cool melted butter*
3 *ounces shredded* or *flake coconut*
unbaked 9-inch pastry shell

Beat 3 eggs slightly. Blend in 1½ cups of maple syrup, ½ cup of sugar, ¼ teaspoon of salt, and ¼ cup of cool melted butter. Sprinkle 3 ounces of coconut on an unbaked 9-inch pastry shell. Pour on the filling. Bake about 30 to 40 minutes in a moderately hot oven at 400°, until the filling is set. Remove and cool on a cake rack before cutting. The pie will actually cut better if allowed to stand overnight.

CAKES

Cakes seem like a complicated subject because there are so many recipes for them. But basically they are quite simple. There are two main types: the so-called butter, or shortened, cakes; and unshortened cakes. In other words, some have fat in them and some don't. The majority of cakes are shortened – all the white and gold layer cakes and their many variations, such as chocolate, devil's food, spice, orange, and so on. The two standard unshortened cakes are angel food and sponge cake. (There are recipes for "butter" sponge cake, but it is not a true sponge cake.) A few years ago Betty Crocker introduced a third type, called chiffon cake, which resembles sponge cake but is made with an unflavored salad oil. The whole cake story really narrows down to this easy classification.

GENERAL RULES

Measure accurately, with standard measuring cups and spoons. All standard measurements are level. Cake recipes have been worked out after hundreds, if not thousands, of tests under rigid controls, and it is foolish to risk failure by tampering with them.

The baking powder in the cake recipes, as in all the other recipes in the book, is double-acting.

Cake flour is better than all-purpose flour because it will give the cake a more velvety crumb.

Use fine granulated sugar.

Before starting to make a cake, assemble all the ingredients.

Preheat the oven. The temperature is important. If it is too low, the volume of the cake will be small. If it is too high, it will burn the cake. For layer cakes, 350° to 375° is right, and not more than 360° for a chocolate cake. Thick cakes baked in deep tube pans are usually cooked at a lower temperature, around 325°.

Prepare the cake pans. Unshortened cakes are baked in ungreased pans so that they can cling to the sides while rising. Chiffon cakes are also baked in ungreased pans. For shortened cakes, the pans should be greased with vegetable shortening or unsalted butter (salt tends to make the cake stick). For an absolute guarantee against the cake's sticking, line the bottom of the pan with wax paper and grease the paper. Place the pan on wax paper and draw around the bottom with a pencil; then cut it out. The paper should fit exactly, not overlap the sides. The easiest way to grease pans is with a pastry brush.

The pan or pans should be placed as near the center of the oven as possible, to allow for free air circulation. If there is only one pan, place the oven rack in the middle of the oven, and the pan on the middle of the rack. If there are two pans, have one rack a third of the way from the top of the oven, and the other rack the same distance from the bottom. Stagger the pans so that one is not on top of the other; otherwise, the bottom one will not brown properly and the air will not circulate properly. Never have pans touch each other or the sides of the oven.

Overbaking will dry out a cake. To test whether it is done, see if the color is golden brown, the cake has started to shrink from the sides of the pan, and a toothpick inserted in the center comes out clean.

Leave a shortened cake in the pan at least 5 to 10 minutes before turning out, and it can stay in as long as 30 minutes. A warm cake is fragile and will crack easily. As it cools, the cell walls stiffen and the cake can be turned out without breaking. Turn out and cool on a cake rack, so that the bottom won't get soggy. Unshortened cakes are left in the pan until entirely cold.

Let cool before frosting.

SHORTENED CAKES

One of two shortenings can be used: butter or vegetable shortening. (There are a few cakes using cream or sour cream, but they are the exception rather than the rule, so will not be discussed here.) The advantage of butter is its flavor. Vegetable shortenings are plastic and therefore cream easily; and since they do not have as high a moisture content as butter, cakes made with them do not dry out as quickly. Both, however, are excellent.

There are two standard mixing methods: the conventional method and the one-bowl method. They are both described in detail in the following basic recipes. Here we will just say that they produce different kinds of cake. One-bowl cakes have a more vigorous blending and mixing, producing a cake with a very fine, close, velvety grain and large volume. They are also more foolproof. Conventional-method cakes have larger air spaces and cells, although this does not mean they are coarse. Many people prefer them. They are also more moist. I would suggest trying both to see which you prefer. Don't switch recipes, though, because the proportions differ, so should not be interchanged.

BASIC PLAIN CAKE
(Conventional method)

2¾ cups sifted cake flour
¾ teaspoon salt
3½ teaspoons baking powder
½ cup soft shortening
1 teaspoon vanilla
1½ cups sugar
3 eggs
1 cup milk

Have all the ingredients at room temperature. Preheat oven to 375°. Prepare 2 9-inch layer-cake tins.

Sift together 2¾ cups of sifted cake flour, ¾ teaspoon of salt, and 3½ teaspoons of baking powder. Cream ½ cup of soft butter or vegetable shortening thoroughly. Add 1 teaspoon of vanilla and blend well. Add 1½ cups of sugar, a tablespoon at a time, beating well after each addition. Continue beating after all the sugar is added until very light and fluffy. This step is the secret of success with this method. Beating air into the mixture makes the cake light and gives it a good texture. It is almost impossible to overbeat, quite easy to underbeat – and an electric mixer expedites matters considerably. Scrape the bowl often. Beat in 3 eggs, one at a time, again beating well. Add the dry ingredients alternately with 1 cup of milk, beginning and ending with the dry ingredients and adding about ¼ at a time, and ⅓ cup of milk. Use a low speed on the mixer for this step, or, better still, do it by hand with a large wooden spoon. Fill immediately into the cake pans. Drop the pans gently on a table or run a knife through the batter to break any large air bubbles. Bake about 30 to 35 minutes in a moderate oven at 375°, until a toothpick inserted in the center comes out dry. Let stand for at least 5 to 10 minutes, then turn out on a cake rack to cool. Frost when cool.

Note. The yolks and whites can be separated and the stiffly beaten whites folded in lastly to give the cake more volume.

VARIATIONS

Yellow. Substitute 6 egg yolks for the 3 whole eggs. Substitute 2 teaspoons of grated orange rind for 1 teaspoon of vanilla.

White. Substitute 6 egg whites for the 3 whole eggs. Stiffly beat them and fold them in lastly.

Orange. Substitute 1 tablespoon of lemon juice and the rest orange juice for 1 cup of milk. Substitute 1 teaspoon of grated orange rind and ½ teaspoon of grated lemon rind for 1 teaspoon of vanilla.

Spice. Sift 1 teaspoon of cinnamon, ½ teaspoon of ginger, and ¼ teaspoon of nutmeg or allspice with the dry ingredients.

Nut. Add ½ cup of chopped nuts to the last addition of flour.

Butternut. This is one of the famous Treadway Inn recipes. The nuts come from Vermont and have a distinctive, delicious flavor. If any readers want to try the recipe and cannot locate nuts – it isn't always easy even in Vermont – I will be glad to tell them a source. A cup of chopped butternuts is added to the above recipe, which is made with butter, and the cake is frosted with maple icing.

BASIC PLAIN CAKE
(One-bowl method)

2½ *cups sifted cake flour*
1½ *cups sugar*
3 *teaspoons baking powder*
1 *teaspoon salt*
½ *cup vegetable shortening*
1 *cup milk*
2 *unbeaten eggs*
1 *teaspoon vanilla*

Actually, the cake made the conventional way uses only one bowl these days, too; before the days of electric mixers the eggs were beaten before they were added to the creamed shortening and sugar. This method is quicker, though, since the creaming step is eliminated.

Have all the ingredients at room temperature. Preheat the oven to 375°. Prepare 2 9-inch layer-cake pans or 3 8-inch pans. Put 2½ cups of sifted cake flour, 1½ cups of sugar, 3 teaspoons of baking powder, and 1 teaspoon of salt into a large strainer or sifter. Stir and soften ½ cup of vegetable shortening in the mixing bowl of an electric mixer or in a large mixing bowl. Sift in the dry ingredients. Add ¾ cup of milk and stir until the flour is dampened. Beat for 2 minutes in the mixer at low speed or 300 vigorous strokes by hand with a large wooden spoon. Scrape the bowl. Add the other ¼ cup of milk, 2 eggs, and 1 teaspoon of vanilla. Beat 1 minute longer in the mixer or another 150 strokes. Fill immediately into the prepared pans. Bake at 375° for 20 to 25 minutes, or until a toothpick inserted in the center comes out clean. Let stand at least 5 to 10 minutes before turning out. Let cool before frosting.

Note. This cake may also be baked in a 13 x 9 x 2-inch pan at 350° for about 30 minutes, or as cupcakes at 375° for 20 to 25 minutes.

VARIATIONS

White. Substitute 3 unbeaten egg whites for the 2 whole eggs. Flavor with 1½ teaspoons of vanilla and ¼ teaspoon of almond extract.

Chocolate. Use only 2 cups of flour and 1⅓ cups of sugar. Substitute 1¼ teaspoons of soda for 3 teaspoons of baking powder. Add 3 squares of melted chocolate with the eggs.

Spice. Sift 1 teaspoon of cinnamon, ¼ teaspoon of cloves, and ¼ teaspoon of allspice or nutmeg with the dry ingredients.

Cherry. Substitute ½ teaspoon of lemon extract and 1 teaspoon of almond extract for the vanilla. Use half sweet cherry juice and half milk. Add 1 cup of chopped, pitted, drained sweet cherries at the end.

BASIC CHIFFON CAKE

2¼ *cups sifted cake flour*
1½ *cups sugar*
3 *teaspoons baking powder*
1 *teaspoon salt*
½ *cup salad oil*
5 *egg yolks*
¾ *cup cold water*
2 *teaspoons vanilla*
2 *teaspoons grated lemon rind*
1 *cup egg whites* (7 or 8)
½ *teaspoon cream of tartar*

Chiffon cakes use a flavorless salad oil, such as Wesson oil or Mazola, for the shortening, and the one-bowl mixing method. The result is a practically foolproof cake with a very tender, moist crumb and a fine, even texture.

Sift together into a mixing bowl 2¼ cups of sifted cake flour, 1½ cups of sugar, 3 teaspoons of baking powder, and 1 teaspoon of salt. Make a well in the center and in it put ½ cup of salad oil, 5 egg yolks, ¾ cup of cold water, 2 teaspoons of vanilla, and 2 teaspoons of grated lemon rind. Beat with a large wooden spoon until smooth. Beat 1 cup of egg whites with ½ teaspoon of cream of tartar until *very stiff* in a large mixing bowl. Pour the egg yolk mixture slowly over the whites, folding it in with a rubber scraper. Do not stir, but mix gently. Place in an ungreased 10-inch tube pan and bake for 65 minutes at 325°. Turn upside down and leave until the cake is cold, suspending the tube of the pan on a bottle or funnel if the pan does not have little legs as they often do.

VARIATIONS

Orange. Substitute 1 tablespoon of grated orange rind for the lemon rind, orange juice for the water, and omit the vanilla.

Spice. Omit lemon rind and vanilla. With the dry ingredients sift 1 teaspoon of cinnamon and ½ teaspoon each of nutmeg, allspice, and cloves.

Pineapple. Use pineapple juice instead of water. Blend in ½ cup of well-drained crushed pineapple with the oil, egg yolks, and so on.

Cocoa. Mix ¾ cup of boiling water and ½ cup of cocoa. Cool. Omit water and lemon rind. Increase sugar to 1¾ cups, egg yolks to 7. Mix cocoa mixture into the dry ingredients with the oil, egg yolks, and so on.

Butterscotch. Omit the sugar and lemon rind. Add 2 cups of sifted brown sugar to the sifted ingredients.

Chocolate Chip. Omit lemon rind. When the batter is finished, sprinkle 3 squares of grated chocolate over the top and gently fold it in with a few strokes.

Note. A smaller cake may be made in a 9-inch tube pan by halving all the ingredients except the egg yolks; use 2 of them. Bake at 350° for 50 to 55 minutes.

UNSHORTENED CAKES

SPONGE CAKE

- 1 *cup sifted cake flour*
- 1 *cup sugar*
- 6 *eggs, separated*
- ½ *teaspoon salt*
- 1 *tablespoon lemon juice*
- 1 *teaspoon grated lemon rind*

Have all the ingredients at room temperature. Add 4 tablespoons out of the 1 cup of sugar to 1 cup of sifted cake flour and sift them together 4 times. Beat 6 egg whites until foamy. Add ½ teaspoon of salt and beat until the egg whites stand in peaks but are not dry. Beat in the remaining ¾ cup of sugar, 2 tablespoons at a time. With the same beater beat the 6 yolks until very thick and lemon colored. Beat in 1 tablespoon of lemon juice and 1 teaspoon of grated lemon rind. Cut and fold the whites into the yolks. Sift about ¼ of the flour and sugar mixture over the top and gently fold it in. Repeat until all the flour and sugar mixture is blended in. Place carefully in an ungreased 9-inch tube pan and tap on the table once to break any large air bubbles. The pan is not greased, so that the cake can cling to the sides to rise. Bake in a moderate oven at 325° for about 1 hour. Remove, invert the pan, and let stand for 1 hour before removing the cake. Run a sharp knife around the edge to loosen the cake.

Note. The recipe for this sponge cake differs from the majority of sponge cake recipes in that the sugar is beaten into the whites rather than the yolks. It makes an excellent-textured, light, moist sponge cake that will stay that way for several days. It can also be baked in 2 loaf pans 3½ x 7½ x 3 inches, or in 2 9-inch cake tins lined with wax paper. Use a 350° oven, and bake about 20 to 30 minutes.

WAYS TO USE LEFTOVER SPONGE CAKE

Trifle. Fit slices of leftover sponge cake about 1 inch thick in the bottom of a large round dessert dish about 10 inches in diameter. Sprinkle with a generous half cup of brandy and sherry mixed and let stand for 1 to 2 hours. Spread thickly with raspberry or strawberry jam. Cover with hot custard sauce (*see* page 359) and chill in the refrigerator for several hours or overnight. To serve, spread with a thin layer of whipped cream and garnish with blanched, lightly browned almonds stuck in on end and a few fresh berries or candied cherries. Serves 10 to 12.

Swiss Chocolate Brick. Place 1½ ounces of bitter chocolate and 2 tablespoons of black coffee in the top of a double boiler over boiling water, and stir until melted and smooth. Let cool. Cream ½ cup of butter well, and add 1 egg yolk and 3 tablespoons of powdered sugar. Add the chocolate mixture gradually, stirring constantly. Place a layer of sponge cake cut in strips lengthwise in a 9 x 5 x 3-inch loaf pan. Spread about ¼ of the chocolate and butter mixture over the cake. Place another layer of cake strips crosswise on top and spread with chocolate. Repeat these two layers, ending with the chocolate mixture, and chill thoroughly. Just before serving, turn out on a plate and garnish with ¼ cup of heavy cream, whipped and sweetened. Serves 8.

Frozen Cup Cakes. Whip 2 cups of heavy cream medium stiff. Add ½ cup of sugar, ⅓ cup of chopped nuts, 2 tablespoons of maraschino cherry juice, 6 tablespoons of chopped maraschino cherries, ⅛ teaspoon of salt, 1 teaspoon of vanilla, and 3 cups of fine sponge cake crumbs. Mix well and fill into tortoni cups or small paper cups. Place the cups in an ice tray and freeze in the refrigerator. Garnish with cherries and small pieecs of ginger. Serves 8.

Banana Charlotte. Peel and mash or sieve 4 or 5 ripe bananas. Add a little lemon juice to each one as it is mashed to prevent it from darkening. Use about 2 tablespoons of lemon juice in all. Fold in ½ cup of heavy cream or evaporated milk, whipped. Soften ½ tablespoon of gelatin in 2 tablespoons of cold water, then stir over low heat until dissolved. Add the gelatin to the banana mixture with a dash of salt and sugar to taste. Butter a mold or loaf pan and line it with fingers of sponge cake. Fill with the banana mixture. Cut off the cake fingers level with the filling. Chill until set. To serve, unmold on a flat platter and serve plain or with heavy cream. Serves 6.

La Polonaise. Cut stale sponge cake into large rounds about 2½ inches in diameter, and place on a baking sheet. Beat 2 egg whites until stiff but not dry. Add 5 tablespoons of sugar, 1 tablespoon at a time, and ⅔ teaspoon of vanilla, continuing to beat until the whites stand in peaks. Fold in ½ cup of ground almonds. Place 1 tablespoon of heavy fruit jam on each cake round and top with the egg whites mounded into a dome. This recipe will be sufficient to cover 8 to 10 cake rounds. Sprinkle the tops with ½ cup of ground almonds and bake in a moderate oven at 350° for 15 to 20 minutes, until lightly browned.

Lemon Icebox Cake. Cream ½ cup of butter until it is softened and smooth. Add 1 cup of sugar gradually and cream until fluffy. Separate 4 eggs and beat the yolks until they are thick. Add to the creamed mixture and beat all together, adding the juice and grated rind of 1 lemon. Add ¼ teaspoon of salt to the 4 egg whites and beat them until they are stiff but not dry. Fold them gently into the other ingredients. Line an oblong loaf pan with thinly sliced sponge cake. Fill to the top with alternate layers of the lemon mixture and sponge cake slices, ending with the cake. The lemon layers should not be more than ½ inch thick. Cover with wax paper and chill in the refrigerator for at least 6 hours, overnight if possible. Slice and serve with whipped cream. Serves 6 to 8.

ANGEL FOOD CAKE

1½ *cups egg whites*
1 *cup sifted cake flour*
1½ *cups fine granulated sugar*
¼ *teaspoon salt*
1 *teaspoon cream of tartar*
1 *teaspoon vanilla*
¼ *teaspoon almond extract, optional*

Remove the eggs from the refrigerator an hour or so before you start making the cake, so that they will be at room temperature, and separate them. They are easier to separate when cold, produce a larger volume when warm.

Sift 1 cup of cake flour with ½ cup of sugar 4 times. Add ¼ teaspoon of salt to the egg whites and beat until foamy. Add 1 teaspoon of cream of tartar and beat until the whites stand up in peaks. Then beat in the remaining 1 cup of sugar, a tablespoon at a time. Fold in 1 teaspoon of vanilla and ¼ teaspoon of almond extract. Sift 3 tablespoons of the flour-sugar mixture lightly over the top and fold in gently with a large spoon. Continue doing this until all the flour is used up, with a minimum of gentle motions. Put into an ungreased 10-inch tube pan. Bake for about 1¼ hours in a moderately slow oven at 325°, or until the top is very lightly browned. Invert the pan on a cake rack and cool for at least an hour before removing the cake.

VARIATIONS

(*All will serve* 10 *to* 12.)

Chocolate Angel Food. Substitute ¼ cup of cocoa for ¼ cup of the flour in the preceding recipe. In other words, use ¾ cup of cake flour and ¼ cup of cocoa.

Toasted Angel Food à la Mode. Lightly toast sliced angel food cake under the broiler. Serve with ice cream and fudge, butterscotch, or strawberry sauce.

Coffee Cream Angel Food. Combine 2 cups of heavy cream, ⅔ cup of sugar, and 3 tablespoons of soluble coffee and chill for 1 hour. Whip until stiff. Cut an angel food cake into 4 horizontal layers. Add ½ cup of chopped walnuts to half the cream mixture and spread between the layers. Cover the top and sides with the rest of the cream. Chill several hours before serving.

Angel Food Waldorf. Whip 2 cups of heavy cream until it holds its shape but is not too stiff. Fold in 4 tablespoons of confectioners' sugar, 4 tablespoons of cocoa, a pinch of salt, and 1 tablespoon of brandy. When it is smooth, beat just a little to make sure the cocoa is evenly distributed. Chill in the refrigerator for 1 hour. Cut a top layer 1 inch thick off an angel food cake. Carefully scoop out the center part, leaving an outside and bottom layer about 1 inch thick. Fill the center with part of the whipped cream mixture combined with bits of the scooped-out cake. Replace the top and cover the top and sides thickly with the rest of the whipped cream mixture. Sprinkle ½ cup of blanched, shredded, browned almonds over the top. Chill at least 2 to 3 hours or overnight.

Strawberry Angel Food. Melt half a jar of red currant jelly with 1 tablespoon of water, strain, and cool. Cut an angel food cake in half horizontally. Whip 2 cups of heavy cream until it holds its shape. Add 2 tablespoons of confectioners' sugar and 1 teaspoon of vanilla and beat until it is stiff. Take about 1 pint of strawberries, leave half of them whole, and slice the rest. Spread the bottom half of the cake with whipped cream and cover with some of the sliced berries. Put the other half on top. Mix some of the currant jelly with the rest of the sliced berries and put in the center hole. Spread the top and sides with whipped cream, and garnish with rosettes of whipped cream and the whole berries dipped in the rest of the currant jelly.

CHEESE CAKE

1 *pound cream cheese*
¼ *cup cake flour*
½ *teaspoon salt*
1 *teaspoon vanilla*
1 *teaspoon grated lemon* or *orange rind*
4 *eggs*
1 *cup sweet* or *sour cream*
¾ *cup sugar*

Prepare an 8-inch spring-form pan with the crumb mixture given at the end of the recipe. Have all the above ingredients at room temperature. Cream 1 pound of cream cheese with ¼ cup of cake flour, ½ teaspoon of salt, 1 teaspoon of vanilla, and 1 teaspoon of grated lemon (or orange) rind. Beat in 4 egg yolks, one at a time. Blend in 1 cup of sweet or sour cream; sour cream gives the cake a nice cheesy flavor. Beat 4 egg whites until stiff but not dry. Beat in 3/4 cup of sugar, 1 tablespoon at a time, beating well after each addition. Continue beating until you are sure all the sugar is dissolved and the meringue has a shiny look. Fold into the cheese mixture with a slotted spoon, part at a time. Turn into the prepared pan. Bake about 1 hour in a slow oven at 325° for 1 hour. Leave in the oven with the heat off for another hour.

Note. Strained cottage cheese can be used instead of cream cheese and gives the cake a little coarser texture. Cream 2 ounces of softened butter with the cheese to make it a little richer.

CRUST

1 cup crushed zwieback crumbs
1/4 cup melted butter
1/4 cup powdered sugar

Blend together 1 cup of crushed zwieback crumbs, 1/4 cup of melted butter, and 1/4 cup of powdered sugar. Press into the bottom of a greased 8-inch spring pan.

PECAN DEVIL'S FOOD CAKE

1 1/2 cups sifted cake flour
1 teaspoon soda
1 teaspoon baking powder
1/2 teaspoon salt
1/3 cup shortening
1 1/4 cups light brown sugar
2 eggs, well beaten
2 squares chocolate
1/2 cup hot black coffee
1/2 cup buttermilk
1 teaspoon vanilla
3/4 cup chopped pecans

Sift together 1 1/2 cups of sifted cake flour, 1 teaspoon of soda, 1 teaspoon of baking powder, and 1/2 teaspoon of salt. Cream 1/3 cup of shortening and add 1 1/4 cups of light brown sugar gradually, creaming well after each addition. Add 2 well-beaten eggs and beat thoroughly. Meanwhile melt 2 squares of chocolate in 1/2 cup of hot black coffee and let cool slightly. Stir into the creamed mixture. Mix together 1/2 cup of buttermilk and 1 teaspoon of vanilla, and add alternately with the dry ingredients.

Stir in 3/4 cup of chopped pecans. Pour into a greased 8 x 8-inch cake pan, and bake in a moderate oven at 350° for 40 to 50 minutes. Let stand in the pan for 5 minutes, then turn out on a cake rack to cool. When thoroughly cooled, frost with fudge frosting (*see* page 335).

FUDGE UPSIDE DOWN CAKE

Combine melted butter, brown sugar, corn syrup, and nuts (as for pecan rolls, page 257) and spread over the bottom of a 10-inch skillet. Omit the pecans in the above recipe for pecan devil's food cake, and pour the cake into the skillet. Bake as above, and invert on a round platter to serve.

COCOA WHIPPED CREAM CAKE

- 5 *eggs*
- 1/2 *cup sugar*
- 1/4 *teaspoon vanilla*
- 1 *cup sifted cake flour*
- 1/4 *teaspoon baking powder*
- 2 *tablespoons cocoa*
- 1/2 *cup heavy cream, whipped*

Have 5 eggs at room temperature. Beat them with 1/2 cup of sugar and 1/4 teaspoon of vanilla until very thick and light. In the meantime sift together 2 or 3 times 1 cup of sifted cake flour, 1/4 teaspoon of baking powder, and 2 tablespoons of cocoa. Fold carefully into the egg mixture. Place in 2 greased and floured 9-inch cake pans. Bake about 20 minutes in a moderate oven at 375°. Remove from oven, let stand for 5 minutes, then turn out on cake racks. When cool, cut each layer in half horizontally. Sandwich the layers with a thin coating of whipped cream and the following chocolate cream filling. Frost the top and sides with chocolate butter cream frosting (*see* page 336) or fudge frosting (*see* page 335).

CHOCOLATE CREAM FILLING

- 2 *cups milk*
- 1/2 *cup sugar*
- 4 *eggs*
- 2 *tablespoons cornstarch*
- 2 *tablespoons butter*
- 1 *square chocolate, melted*

Bring slowly to a boil 2 cups of milk and ½ cup of sugar. Beat 4 eggs slightly. Dissolve 2 tablespoons of cornstarch in 2 tablespoons of cold water, and add to the eggs. Slowly pour the hot milk over this mixture, return to the fire, and stir over a brisk fire until the mixture thickens. Remove and blend in 2 tablespoons of butter and 1 square of melted chocolate. Let cool.

RUM CAKE

⅞ cup sifted cake flour
⅜ cup cornstarch
½ teaspoon salt
1 teaspoon baking powder
3 whole eggs
¾ cup sugar
3 egg yolks
1 teaspoon vanilla
¼ cup cool melted butter
about ⅓ cup rum

Sift ⅞ cup of sifted flour, ⅜ cup of cornstarch, ½ teaspoon of salt, and 1 teaspoon of baking powder together 3 times. Beat 3 egg whites until they hold their shape, then beat in 3 tablespoons of sugar, 1 at a time. Beat 6 egg yolks until thick and lemon colored, gradually beating in the remaining sugar. Add 1 teaspoon of vanilla. Add to the egg whites and fold in carefully. Sift about ⅓ of the flour mixture over the top at one time and fold it in. Blend in ¼ cup of cool melted butter. Place in 2 9-inch cake tins which have been greased, lined with wax paper, and greased again. Bake for 20 to 25 minutes in a moderately slow oven at 325°, until lightly browned. Remove, let stand for 5 minutes, then turn out on cake racks.

When cool, cut each layer in half crosswise and sprinkle both sides of each layer with rum. Generously frost each layer and the top and sides of the cake with the following rum frosting.

RUM FROSTING

3 tablespoons soluble coffee
1 tablespoon rum
½ pound (1 cup) butter
1 pound sifted confectioners' sugar

Dissolve 3 tablespoons of soluble coffee in 3 tablespoons of boiling water. Cool and add 1 tablespoon of rum. Cream ½ pound (1 cup) of butter until light and fluffy. Add 1 pound of sifted confectioners' sugar alternately with the coffee, beating well after each addition. Be sure the sugar is soft and fresh, and beat the frosting thoroughly for rich mellowness.

APPLESAUCE CAKE

2 *cups cake flour*
2 *teaspoons soda*
2 *teaspoons cornstarch*
1 *teaspoon cinnamon*
½ *teaspoon cloves*
½ *teaspoon nutmeg*
½ *teaspoon salt*
2 *teaspoons grated sweet chocolate*
1 *cup chopped walnuts*
1 *cup raisins*
½ *cup butter* or *vegetable shortening*
1 *cup sugar*
1 *egg*
1½ *cups applesauce*

Sift the following ingredients together 2 or 3 times: 2 cups cake flour, 2 teaspoons soda, 2 teaspoons cornstarch, 1 teaspoon cinnamon, ½ teaspoon cloves, ½ teaspoon nutmeg, and ½ teaspoon salt. Add 2 teaspoons of grated sweet chocolate (or ground sweetened chocolate if available), 1 cup of chopped walnuts, and 1 cup of raisins. Cream ½ cup of shortening and 1 cup of sugar. Add 1 egg and beat well. Add the dry ingredients and 1½ cups of applesauce and blend thoroughly. Place in a greased 9 x 13-inch pan. Bake about 40 minutes in a moderate oven at 350°. Cool and frost with the following mocha icing. Serves 20.

MOCHA ICING

2 *squares chocolate*
3 *tablespoons butter*
about ½ *cup hot coffee*
about 3 *cups sifted confectioners' sugar*
1 *teaspoon vanilla*

Melt 2 squares of chocolate with 3 tablespoons of butter. Cool slightly, then beat in about 3 cups of sifted confectioners' sugar and thin as you beat with hot coffee – less than ½ cup will be needed. Add 1 teaspoon of vanilla.

Brandied Applesauce Cake. Soak the raisins for ½ hour in ¼ cup of brandy before mixing with the dry ingredients.

WELLESLEY FUDGE CAKE

⅔ cup butter
2½ cups dark brown sugar
1 whole egg and 3 egg yolks
4 squares chocolate
⅔ cup boiling water
2½ cups sifted cake flour
1½ teaspoons baking powder
1 teaspoon salt
1¼ teaspoons soda
1 teaspoon vanilla
⅔ cup thick sour milk

Cream ⅔ cup butter and 2½ cups well-packed dark brown sugar. Add 1 whole egg and 3 egg yolks and beat thoroughly. Melt 4 squares of chocolate in ⅔ cup of boiling water, stir until dissolved and smooth, and add. Sift together 2½ cups of cake flour, 1½ teaspoons of baking powder, and 1 teaspoon of salt. Add 1¼ teaspoons of soda and 1 teaspoon of vanilla to ⅔ cup of sour milk. Add dry ingredients alternately with the milk. Bake in 2 greased 9-inch-square pans in a moderate oven at 350° for 30 to 40 minutes. Cool and frost with fudge frosting, and cover with chopped nuts. Serves 24.

PINEAPPLE UPSIDE DOWN CAKE

2 tablespoons butter, melted
¼ cup sifted light brown sugar
7 slices canned pineapple
7 cherries
2 cups sifted cake flour
2 teaspoons baking powder
1 cup sugar
½ teaspoon salt
2 egg whites, unbeaten
⅓ cup vegetable shortening
½ cup milk
1 teaspoon vanilla

Put the melted butter in a 9-inch round cake tin, rolling it around to cover the bottom and sides. Sprinkle the brown sugar over the butter, and cover it with the pineapple slices with a cherry in the center of each. Sift 2 cups of sifted cake flour, 2 teaspoons of baking powder, 1 cup of sugar, and ½ teaspoon of salt into the bowl of an electric mixer or into a large mixing bowl. Add 2 egg whites, ⅓ cup of vegetable shortening, and ½ cup of milk. Beat until the batter is smooth, using low speed on a mixer or a large spoon. Add 1 teaspoon of vanilla. Pour carefully over the pineapple rings and bake for 25 to 35 minutes in a moderate oven at 375°. Let stand in the pan for 5 to 10 minutes, then invert on a round platter. Serve with whipped cream. Serves 6 to 8.

CHOCOLATE ROLL

5 *eggs*
½ *cup sugar*
1 *teaspoon vanilla*
6 *tablespoons cocoa*
½ *teaspoon salt*
½ *cup flour*
2 *tablespoons cornstarch*

Beat 5 eggs and ½ cup of sugar until very thick and light, preferably in an electric mixer. Add 1 teaspoon of vanilla before you finish beating. Sift together 6 tablespoons of cocoa, ½ teaspoon of salt, ½ cup of flour, and 2 tablespoons of cornstarch. Fold into the egg mixture, about ¼ at a time, using a large wooden spoon. Tilt and revolve the bowl as you fold. Grease a jelly roll pan with vegetable shortening (shallow 12 x 18-inch baking sheet), line with wax paper, and grease again. Fill the mixture into the pan and smooth the top with a spatula. Drop the pan once to break the air bubbles. Bake in a hot oven at 450° for 8 to 10 minutes, until the top is very lightly browned. Wring a dish towel out in cold water and place it smoothly on a wooden board. Invert the chocolate roll on the towel, remove the wax paper, and fold the ends of the towel over the roll (they probably won't cover it all). Let stand until cool, about half an hour. Spread with the filling (*see* below). Securing the roll with the towel, make one fold lengthwise about 2 inches and press it down; then quickly roll it all up. Place on a cake rack and cover the top with fudge frosting, using half the recipe on page 335. To serve, cut into 1-inch slices slightly on the bias. Serves 14 to 16.

WHIPPED CREAM FILLING

Whip 1½ cups of heavy cream until it is stiff, then beat in 3 tablespoons of confectioners' sugar and 1 teaspoon of vanilla.

MARSHMALLOW FILLING

(*See* page 335.)

JELLY ROLL

5 eggs
½ cup sugar
½ teaspoon salt
¾ teaspoon water
½ teaspoon grated lemon rind
½ teaspoon vanilla
½ cup cake flour
1 tablespoon cornstarch
sifted confectioners' sugar

Beat together until very light and fluffy, preferably in an electric mixer, 5 eggs, ½ cup of sugar, ½ teaspoon of salt, ¾ teaspoon of water, and ½ teaspoon of grated lemon rind. Add ½ teaspoon of vanilla before the beating is finished. Sift ½ cup of cake flour and 1 tablespoon of cornstarch together 3 times. Fold the flour into the beaten eggs, about ¼ at a time, using a large wooden spoon. Now follow the directions in the preceding recipe for chocolate roll from "Tilt and revolve the bowl . . ." through "Place on a cake rack." Spread with one of the following fillings and dust the top well with sifted confectioners' sugar. To serve, cut into 1-inch slices slightly on the diagonal. Serves 14 to 16.

JELLY FILLING

Spread the roll with any jelly or marmalade, such as currant, raspberry, grape, strawberry, or orange.

LEMON ROLL

¾ cup sugar
2 tablespoons flour
¼ teaspoon salt
1 cup boiling water
¼ cup lemon juice
2 egg yolks
1 teaspoon butter

Spread with the following lemon filling: Blend together ¾ cup of sugar, 2 tablespoons of flour, and ¼ teaspoon of salt. Slowly add 1 cup of boiling water and ¼ cup of lemon juice. Stir over a slow fire until thick and transparent. Slightly beat 2 egg yolks. Pour a little of the hot lemon mixture over them and cook for another 1 to 2 minutes with constant stirring. Remove, add 1 teaspoon of butter, and cool before using.

COCONUT ROLL

Add 1 cup of grated moist coconut to the pastry cream recipe on page 296.

BOSTON CREAM PIE

Use the sponge cake recipe in the preceding jelly roll recipe. Bake it in 2 greased and floured 9-inch cake tins in a moderate oven at 350° for about 30 minutes, until lightly browned. Sandwich it with half the pastry cream recipe on page 296, and top with the fudge frosting on page 335, or with sifted confectioners' sugar.

WASHINGTON PIE

This is the same cake as Boston cream pie sandwiched with jelly and topped with sifted confectioners' sugar.

GINGERBREAD

2½ cups sifted flour
1½ teaspoons soda
1 teaspoon cinnamon
1 teaspoon ginger
½ teaspoon salt
¼ cup butter
¼ cup lard
½ cup sugar
1 egg, beaten
1 cup molasses
1 cup hot water

Sift together 2½ cups of sifted flour, 1½ teaspoons of soda, 1 teaspoon of cinnamon, 1 teaspoon of ginger, and ½ teaspoon of salt. Cream ¼ cup of butter, ¼ cup of lard, and ½ cup of sugar. When the mixture is light and fluffy, add 1 beaten egg and 1 cup of molasses. Stir in the sifted dry ingredients. Then add 1 cup of hot water, and beat until smooth. The batter will be thin. Pour into a greased shallow pan, and bake for 35 minutes in a moderate oven at 350°. Makes 15 generous portions. Serve with hot lemon sauce (*see* page 358), chocolate sauce (*see* page 352), whipped cream, or one of the following toppings.

CHOCOLATE MARSHMALLOW TOPPING

After the gingerbread is baked, place marshmallows over the top, so close together that they are almost touching. Place in a hot oven at 400° for about 15 minutes, or until the marshmallows are melted. Put a 7-ounce package of chocolate bits and 2 tablespoons of milk in a double boiler, and cook until the chocolate is melted. Pour this mixture over the melted marshmallows.

CREAM CHEESE TOPPING

1 cup cream cheese
1 teaspoon grated orange rind
2 teaspoons confectioners' sugar
pinch salt
3 tablespoons orange juice

Mash the cream cheese with a fork, and add 1 teaspoon of grated orange rind, 2 teaspoons of confectioners' sugar, and a pinch of salt. Add 3 tablespoons of orange juice slowly, creaming well. Spread on top of the cooled gingerbread.

FROSTINGS

UNCOOKED BUTTER FROSTING

4 tablespoons soft butter
2 cups sifted confectioners' sugar
¼ teaspoon salt
1 teaspoon vanilla
1 egg yolk
about 3 tablespoons cream

Cream 4 tablespoons of butter. Beat in ½ cup of sugar, ¼ teaspoon of salt, 1 teaspoon of vanilla, and 1 egg yolk. Beat in the remaining 1½ cups of sugar alternately with about 3 tablespoons of cream. The frosting should be quite creamy, since it stiffens on standing. Enough for 2 9-inch layers.

VARIATIONS

White Frosting. Substitute 1 egg white for the egg yolk.

Orange Frosting. Substitute 3 tablespoons of orange juice and 2 teaspoons of lemon juice for the cream. Add 1 to 2 teaspoons of grated orange rind.

Lemon Frosting. Substitute lemon juice for the cream. Add 1 teaspoon of grated lemon rind.

Chocolate Frosting. Melt 2 squares of chocolate in a double boiler with 2 tablespoons of boiling water. Cool and blend with the egg yolk. Add a little more salt and use about ¼ cup less sugar. **Mocha.** Substitute 1½ tablespoons of very strong coffee for 1½ tablespoons of cream.

FUDGE FROSTING

2 squares chocolate, cut up
2 cups sugar
2 tablespoons corn syrup
2/3 cup milk
dash of salt
2 tablespoons butter
1 teaspoon vanilla

Place 2 cut-up squares of chocolate, 2 cups of sugar, 2 tablespoons of corn syrup, 2/3 cup of milk, and a dash of salt in a saucepan. Bring slowly to a boil, stirring until the sugar is dissolved. Cook until 232°, or until a very soft ball will form in cold water, stirring occasionally. Remove, add 2 tablespoons of butter, and cool to lukewarm. Add 1 teaspoon of vanilla and beat until the frosting has a spreading consistency. Enough for 2 9-inch layers.

Caramel Frosting. Substitute brown sugar for white sugar in the preceding recipe, and omit the chocolate.

WHITE FROSTING

This has various names — marshmallow, 7-minute, White Mountain, and so on.

2 cups sugar
1 cup water
2 tablespoons light corn syrup
4 egg whites
dash of salt
1/2 teaspoon vanilla, optional

Put 2 cups of sugar, 1 cup of water, and 2 tablespoons of corn syrup in a saucepan and bring rapidly to a boil, stirring only until the sugar is dissolved. Cook quickly until it is 242°, brushing the sides of the pan occasionally to remove any sugar crystals. When the thermometer registers 220°, start beating 4 egg whites with a dash of salt, preferably in an electric mixer. Pour the hot syrup slowly over the stiffly beaten whites, beating all the while. Continue beating until the frosting is very thick and marshmallowlike and cool – it takes a lot of hard beating. May be flavored with ½ teaspoon of vanilla.

BUTTER CREAM FROSTING

Follow the preceding recipe, using 1 cup of sugar and ½ cup of water. Substitute 4 egg yolks for a yellow frosting, use egg whites for a white one; the yolks are the most usual frosting. When the mixture is thick and cool, beat in ½ to ¾ pound of butter which is solid but not too hard. Break the butter into small pieces and beat in gradually. Butter cream frosting may be flavored with coffee, chocolate, or rum.

MAPLE FROSTING

Cook 2½ cups of maple syrup to 242°. Pour slowly over ¾ cup of egg whites, stiffly beaten, and continue to beat until very thick and marshmallowlike.

COOKIES

SUGAR COOKIES

1 *cup butter (½ pound)*
1 *cup confectioners' sugar*
1 *teaspoon vanilla*
2½ *cups sifted flour*
1 *tablespoon milk*
1 *egg yolk*
2 *teaspoons cream*
granulated sugar

Soften the butter to room temperature. Cream it well. Blend in 1 cup of confectioners' sugar, a little at a time. Add 1 teaspoon of vanilla. Beat in the flour, about ½ cup at a time. Lastly add 1 tablespoon of milk. Knead the dough lightly for ½ minute or so on a floured board. Roll out ¼ inch thick and cut in any desired shape. Place on a slightly greased cookie sheet. Brush with egg wash made by beating together 1 egg yolk and 2 teaspoons of cream with a fork. Sprinkle with granulated sugar. Bake in a moderate oven at 350° for 20 to 25 minutes, until they just start to change color. Remove at once and cool on a cake rack. Makes from 2 to 3 dozen, depending on the size of the cutter.

Note. This is a good dough for Christmas cookies.

BUTTERSCOTCH REFRIGERATOR COOKIES

2 *cups flour*
½ *teaspoon cream of tartar*
½ *teaspoon baking soda*
pinch of salt
½ *cup butter*
1 *cup brown sugar*
2 *eggs*
1 *teaspoon vanilla*

Sift together twice 2 cups of flour, ½ teaspoon of cream of tartar, ½ teaspoon of soda, and a pinch of salt. Cream ½ cup of butter and 1 cup of brown sugar (firmly packed) until light and fluffy. Beat in 2 eggs. If not using an electric mixer, the eggs should be well beaten first. Blend in the dry ingredients, a little at a time. Add 1 teaspoon of vanilla. Divide the dough in half and form into 2 rolls 1½ inches in diameter. Wrap in wax paper. Chill in the refrigerator for at least 2 to 3 hours; the dough can stay there almost indefinitely. To bake, slice about ⅛ inch thick with a sharp knife, place on an ungreased cookie sheet, and cook at 350° for about 10 minutes, or until the tops are lightly browned. The cookies may be sprinkled with a few finely chopped nuts before baking. Makes about 3 dozen cookies.

Note. The great advantage of refrigerator cookies is that once you have a batch of dough, you can have fresh cookies in a few minutes; just slice off what you need and store the rest.

Plain Refrigerator Cookies. Substitute white sugar for brown sugar. Omit the cream of tartar and baking soda and use 2 teaspoons of baking powder.

Chocolate Cookies. Use the plain refrigerator cookie dough and substitute ½ cup of cocoa for ½ cup of flour.

Spice Cookies. Sift ½ teaspoon of ginger, 1 teaspoon of cinnamon, and ¼ teaspoon of cloves with the dry ingredients in either the butterscotch or plain cookies.

Lemon Cookies. Use the plain refrigerator cookie dough and add 1 teaspoon of grated lemon rind to the dry ingredients.

OATMEAL REFRIGERATOR COOKIES

1½ *cups sifted flour*
1 *teaspoon soda*
1 *teaspoon salt*
1 *cup shortening*
1 *cup brown sugar*
1 *cup white sugar*
2 *eggs, well beaten*
1 *teaspoon vanilla*
3 *cups quick-cooking oats*
½ *cup chopped walnuts*

Sift together 1½ cups of sifted flour, 1 teaspoon of soda, and 1 teaspoon of salt. Cream thoroughly 1 cup of shortening, 1 cup of brown sugar, and 1 cup of white sugar. Beat in 2 well-beaten eggs and 1 teaspoon of vanilla. Stir in the sifted dry ingredients. Mix in 3 cups of quick-cooking oats and ½ cup of chopped walnuts. Shape into rolls, and wrap tightly in wax paper. Chill thoroughly. Slice ¼ inch thick, and bake on an ungreased cookie sheet in a moderate oven at 350° for about 10 minutes, or until lightly browned. Makes about 5 dozen cookies.

CHOCOLATE CHIP COOKIES

1¼ *cups sifted cake flour*
½ *teaspoon soda*
½ *teaspoon salt*
½ *cup butter* or *vegetable shortening*
½ *cup sugar*
¼ *cup brown sugar*
1 *egg*
1 *package chocolate chips*
½ *cup chopped nuts*
1 *teaspoon vanilla*

Sift together 1¼ cups sifted cake flour, ½ teaspoon soda, and ½ teaspoon salt. Cream ½ cup butter or shortening. Gradually add ½ cup sugar and ¼ cup brown sugar, firmly packed. Continue beating until light and fluffy. Add 1 egg – previously well beaten if the mixing is done by hand, unbeaten if by machine. Add the sifted flour mixture in two parts, mixing well. Stir in the chocolate chips (semisweet), ½ cup of chopped nuts, and 1 teaspoon of vanilla. Drop by teaspoons 2 inches apart on a lightly greased cookie sheet. Bake about 10 minutes in a moderate oven at 375°, until lightly browned. Let stand for 2 to 3 minutes, then remove and cool on a cake rack. Makes about 3 dozen.

PEANUT CRESCENTS

½ *cup butter*
½ *cup sugar*
½ *cup brown sugar*
1 *egg*
¼ *cup heavy cream*
1 *teaspoon vanilla*
2½ *cups sifted flour*
1 *teaspoon baking powder*
½ *teaspoon salt*
2 *teaspoons cinnamon*
1 *cup finely chopped unsalted peanuts (½ pound)*

Let ½ cup of butter stand at room temperature for half an hour to soften. Cream it. Gradually add ½ cup of sugar and ½ cup of brown sugar (firmly packed) and beat well. Beat in 1 egg, then ¼ cup of cream and 1 teaspoon of vanilla. Sift together 2½ cups of sifted flour, 1 teaspoon of baking powder, ½ teaspoon of salt, and 2 teaspoons of cinnamon. Blend into the first mixture gently but thoroughly. Chill the dough for at least 2 hours. Roll the dough by scant teaspoons in your hands to form cylinders, then roll them well in the chopped peanuts, tapering the ends. Place on ungreased cookie sheets, curving to form crescents. Bake in a moderate oven at 375° for 8 to 10 minutes, until light golden brown. Makes 50 to 60.

HERMITS

1 *cup shortening*
2 *cups brown sugar*
3 *eggs*
3½ *cups flour*
1 *teaspoon baking powder*
1 *teaspoon soda*
½ *teaspoon salt*
2 *teaspoons cinnamon*
1 *teaspoon nutmeg*
½ *cup buttermilk*
1 *cup seedless raisins*
1 *cup coarsely chopped walnuts*

Cream the shortening and sugar thoroughly. Add 3 eggs and beat well. Sift together 3½ cups of flour, 1 teaspoon of baking powder, 1 teaspoon of soda, ½ teaspoon of salt, 2 teaspoons of cinnamon, and 1 teaspoon of nutmeg. Add alternately with ½ cup of buttermilk. Fold in the raisins and nuts. Drop by teaspoons on a greased cookie sheet. Bake in a moderate oven at 375° for 12 to 15 minutes, until nicely browned. Makes 4 to 5 dozen cookies.

JOE FROGGERS

- 7 *cups sifted flour*
- 1 *tablespoon salt*
- 1 *tablespoon ginger*
- 1 *teaspoon cloves*
- 1 *teaspoon nutmeg*
- ½ *teaspoon allspice*
- ¾ *cup water*
- ¼ *cup rum*
- 2 *teaspoons baking soda*
- 2 *cups dark molasses*
- 1 *cup shortening*
- 2 *cups sugar*

Sift together the flour, salt, ginger, cloves, nutmeg, and allspice. Combine ¾ cup of water and ¼ cup of rum. Add 2 teaspoons of soda to 2 cups of molasses. Thoroughly cream 1 cup of shortening and 2 cups of sugar. Add half the dry ingredients, half the water and rum, then half the molasses, blending well after each addition. Repeat. Chill dough for several hours or overnight. Roll ¼ inch thick and cut with a 4-inch cutter. Bake on a greased cookie sheet in a moderate oven at 375° for 10 to 12 minutes, until lightly browned; watch carefully so that they do not burn. Let stand a few minutes, then remove. Makes about 2 dozen cookies.

PECAN BALLS

- ¼ *pound butter*
- 1 *teaspoon vanilla*
- 2 *tablespoons sugar*
- 1 *cup sifted flour*
- 1 *cup pecans, chopped medium fine*
- ½ *cup sifted confectioners' sugar*

Soften ¼ pound of butter (1 stick) at room temperature for about half an hour. Cream with 1 teaspoon of vanilla until smooth. Combine 2 tablespoons of sugar, 1 cup of sifted flour, and 1 cup of chopped pecans. Blend with the creamed butter. Roll into small balls between the palms of your hands. Bake on an ungreased cookie sheet at 350° for about 15 minutes. Meanwhile sift ½ cup of confectioners' sugar and divide it into 2 piles. While the cookies are still hot, roll them first in 1 pile, then in the other. Makes about 25 cookies.

BROWNIES

- ⅔ *cup butter*
- 1½ *cups sugar*
- 3 *eggs*
- 3 *squares chocolate, melted*
- 1 *cup flour*
- ½ *teaspoon salt*
- 1 *teaspoon vanilla*
- ½ *cup chopped walnuts*

Have ⅔ cup of butter at room temperature. Cream it thoroughly with 1½ cups of sugar. Add 3 whole eggs, one at a time, beating well after each addition. Blend in 3 squares of melted chocolate, then 1 cup of flour, ½ teaspoon of salt, 1 teaspoon of vanilla, and ½ cup of chopped walnuts. Put into a greased 9 x 13-inch pan. Bake for exactly 20 minutes in a moderate oven at 350°. Remove from the oven, let stand for 5 minutes, then cut into squares. The mixture may not look done when you take it from the oven, but the heat of the pan will finish the cooking. Remove from the pan when cool. This makes a moist chewy brownie with a good crisp crust. Makes 24 brownies.

Note. Some additional chopped nuts may be sprinkled over the top before baking. Brownies may also be covered with fudge frosting (*see* page 335) and whole walnuts placed on each square.

BUTTERSCOTCH BROWNIES

- ½ *cup butter*
- 2 *cups brown sugar*
- 2 *teaspoons vanilla*
- 2 *eggs*
- 1 *cup sifted flour*
- 2 *teaspoons baking powder*
- 1 *teaspoon salt*
- 1½ *cups chopped pecans*

Thoroughly cream ½ cup of butter and 2 cups of well-packed brown sugar. Add 2 teaspoons of vanilla and 2 eggs. With an electric mixer, the eggs need not be previously beaten; by hand, they should be well beaten first. Sift together 1 cup of sifted flour, 2 teaspoons of baking powder, and 1 teaspoon of salt. Mix 1½ cups of chopped pecans with the dry ingredients. Stir into the creamed mixture – by hand for this step. Spread in a greased shallow 9 x 13-inch pan. Bake for 30 minutes in a moderate oven at 350°. Cut into squares while still warm.

NEW ENGLAND TEA DAINTIES

- 2 *eggs*
- 1 *cup light brown sugar*
- ⅔ *cup flour*
- ¼ *teaspoon baking powder*
- ½ *teaspoon salt*
- 1½ *cups chopped walnuts*

This old New England recipe makes nice, thin, crisp, well-flavored cookies.

Beat 2 eggs well. Add 1 cup of brown sugar and beat until the sugar is dissolved. Sift together ⅔ cup of flour, ¼ teaspoon of baking powder, and ½ teaspoon of salt. Add to the egg mixture and beat or stir until thoroughly blended. Add 1½ cups of chopped nuts. Drop by teaspoons on a greased cookie sheet about ½ inch apart. Bake in a moderate oven at 350° for 10 to 12 minutes. Makes about 40 cookies.

ORANGE NUT COOKIES

- 3½ *cups flour*
- 2 *teaspoons baking powder*
- 1 *teaspoon soda*
- ¼ *teaspoon salt*
- ¾ *cup vegetable shortening*
- ¼ *cup butter*
- 1½ *cups brown sugar*
- 2 *eggs*
- ¼ *cup orange juice*
- 1 *tablespoon grated orange peel*
- 1 *teaspoon vanilla*
- 1 *cup sour milk* or *buttermilk*
- 1 *cup chopped walnuts*

Sift together 3½ cups of flour, 2 teaspoons of baking powder, 1 teaspoon of soda, and ¼ teaspoon of salt. Thoroughly cream ¾ cup of vegetable shortening, ¼ cup of butter, and 1½ cups of brown sugar. Add 2 eggs and beat well; if not using an electric mixer, the eggs should be beaten before adding.

Blend in ¼ cup of orange juice, 1 tablespoon of grated orange peel, 1 teaspoon of vanilla, and 1 cup of sour milk or buttermilk, and mix well. Add the sifted dry ingredients. Lastly stir in the nuts. Drop by teaspoons on a greased cookie sheet. Bake about 15 minutes in a moderate oven at 350°. Makes about 60 cookies.

FRUIT AND COCONUT COOKIES

½ *cup butter*
¾ *cup sugar*
2 *eggs*
1 *cup flour*
1 *teaspoon baking powder*
½ *teaspoon salt*
1 *teaspoon cinnamon*
¼ *teaspoon nutmeg*
¼ *teaspoon ginger*
¼ *cup light cream*
½ *cup moist coconut*
½ *cup seedless raisins*
½ *cup chopped walnuts*

Soften ½ cup of butter at room temperature for half an hour or so. Cream it until soft. Add ¾ cup of sugar, a little at a time. Beat until light and fluffy. Then beat in 2 eggs; if you are not using an electric mixer, the eggs should be well beaten before adding them.

Sift together 1 cup of flour, 1 teaspoon of baking powder, ½ teaspoon of salt, 1 teaspoon of cinnamon, ¼ teaspoon of nutmeg, and ¼ teaspoon of ginger. Add alternately with ¼ cup of light cream. Fold in ½ cup of coconut, ½ cup of raisins, and ½ cup of chopped walnuts. Drop by teaspoons on a well-greased cookie sheet, at least an inch apart because they spread. Bake about 15 minutes in a moderate oven at 350°, until lightly browned. Makes about 3 dozen cookies.

WHISKEY BALLS

3 *cups vanilla wafer crumbs*	½ *cup cocoa*
1 *cup finely chopped pecans*	2 *cups confectioners' sugar*
3 *tablespoons light corn syrup*	½ *cup whiskey*

pinch of salt

Roll the vanilla wafers to a fine crumb and put them through a strainer (two 4¾-ounce packages will make 3 cups of crumbs). Chop the nuts rather than grind them – in a grinder you lose some of the oil and nuts. Blend thoroughly the crumbs, nuts, corn syrup, cocoa, 1 cup of the sugar, the whiskey, and a pinch of salt. Form into small balls. Roll each one twice in sifted confectioners' sugar. Makes about 3 dozen.

DATE BARS

8 *ounces dates*	1¾ *cups flour*
1 *cup sugar*	½ *teaspoon soda*
⅓ *cup water*	½ *teaspoon salt*
½ *teaspoon nutmeg*	1 *cup brown sugar*
1 *teaspoon vanilla*	1 *cup melted butter* or *vegetable shortening*
2 *tablespoons cornstarch*	
2 *cups rolled oats*	*confectioners' sugar, optional*

Cut the dates into small pieces. Put them in a saucepan with 1 cup of sugar, ⅓ cup of water, ½ teaspoon of nutmeg, and 1 teaspoon of vanilla. Cook over a slow fire for 20 minutes, stirring until the sugar is dissolved. Blend 2 tablespoons of cornstarch with 4 tablespoons of cold water, add to the date mixture, and cook until it thickens, stirring constantly. Remove and cool.

Mix together 2 cups of rolled oats, 1¾ cups of flour, ½ teaspoon of soda, ½ teaspoon of salt, and 1 cup of brown sugar. Add 1 cup of melted butter (or vegetable shortening), a little at a time, mixing it in well. Grease a 9 x 13-inch baking pan. Spread half the rolled-oat mixture on the bottom. Put the date filling over this and cover with the rest of the rolled-oat mixture. Bake for

20 minutes in a hot oven at 400°. Cool in the pan and cut into bars about 1 x 3 inches. Both sides can be sprinkled with confectioners' sugar if you wish. Makes about 40 cookies.

MACAROONS

1 *pound almond paste* 6 *unbeaten egg whites*
1 *pound sifted confectioners' sugar*

Put the almond paste on a marble slab preferably, or on a wooden board. Work in 3 egg whites with the heel of your hand, then work in about ¼ of the sugar. Work in the remaining egg whites, one at a time, alternately with the sugar. A heavy electric mixer may be used at low speed. When thoroughly blended, put the mixture into a pastry bag with a large plain tube and pipe out in circles about 1½ inches in diameter on an ungreased cookie sheet lined with ungreased brown paper. Pat the tops gently with a damp towel; this makes the macaroons shine and gives the tops professional-looking small cracks. Bake about 25 minutes in a slow oven at 250° to 300°, then raise the temperature to 400° to lightly color the tops. Remove, and slide the paper onto a marble slab or tabletop well moistened with lukewarm water. Let stand for 15 minutes, then carefully remove the macaroons with a spatula. Store in a tight container.

ICE CREAM DESSERTS

MERINGUES

Meringues are the bane of many a cook's existence. At one time I was associated with Dione Lucas, and on her audience-participation television show she was asked about meringues so often it became a stock studio joke.

As with all cooking, it is merely a matter of understanding the rules. Meringues are nothing but a combination of beaten egg whites and sugar. Cream of tartar is generally added to stabilize the beaten whites, and lemon juice or vinegar will bleach them. There are two types of meringues: soft and hard. Soft meringues have a marshmallowlike texture and a soft crust. Typical soft meringues are pie toppings like that for the lemon meringue pie on page 306 and the covering on the baked Alaska on page 349. Hard meringues, as the name implies, are much, much drier, both inside and out, than a soft meringue. The meringue shells which follow are typical hard meringues. To obtain a hard meringue, a very low heat is used, over a rather long period, to literally dry out the egg whites. Some pastry cooks use a temperature as low as 150°, and 250° to 275° is really the maximum; the lower temperature will also keep them white. A higher temperature is used with soft meringues so that they won't get dry. The actual temperature is discussed on page 347.

The standard proportions are 2 tablespoons of sugar for each egg white for a soft meringue and 4 tablespoons of sugar for each egg white for a hard meringue. If too little sugar is used, the meringues will be tough; if too much is used, they will be sugary. The sugar should be fine granulated sugar. The eggs should be at least a day old, but should be fresh. Old eggs have watery whites which do not work very well. The whites are beaten until stiff but not dry before any sugar is added. If it is added before they are stiff, the meringues will have a finer texture but smaller volume. The sugar should be beaten in a little at a time, and the mixture beaten a minute or so after each addition to dissolve the sugar. Dissolving the sugar is important for a smooth, dry meringue. The more the meringue is beaten, the drier it will be.

It is easier to separate eggs when they are cold. There will be a greater volume of beaten whites if they are beaten when they are at room temperature. So separate them at least 30 minutes before you make meringues, longer will not matter.

MERINGUE SHELLS

2 *egg whites*
dash of salt
¼ *teaspoon cream of tartar*
1 *teaspoon lemon juice*
½ *cup fine granulated sugar*
½ *teaspoon vanilla, optional*

Put 2 egg whites in an electric mixer; they can be beaten with a rotary beater, but it is an arduous job. Add a dash of salt and beat until frothy. Add ¼ teaspoon of cream of tartar and 1 teaspoon of lemon juice and beat until stiff but not dry. Beat in ½ cup of sugar, a tablespoon at a time, beating well after each addition. After all the sugar is added, continue beating for 5 to 10 minutes. Place heavy brown paper on an ungreased cookie sheet. Either pipe out the meringue with a pastry bag or arrange it by spoonfuls. It is stiff enough to handle easily and you can make it any shape you like. Place the cookie sheet on the bottom shelf of the oven. Either have it preheated to 150° to 250° – the lower the temperature, the drier the meringues – or start with a cold oven and set the temperature at 250°. Bake for about 50 to 60 minutes, until the meringues no longer feel soft. Turn off the heat and leave them in the oven another 10 minutes. Remove, let stand a minute or two, then take them off the paper while they are still hot to avoid cracking and sticking. They will keep indefinitely in an airtight container.

For less dry meringues with slightly softer insides, beat in 6 tablespoons of the sugar and fold in the rest after the beating is done. Or do not beat the mixture more than 3 or 4 minutes after all the sugar has been added. For chewier meringues, cook them at a little higher temperature, about 300°. They will color a little at this temperature. Half a teaspoon of vanilla may be beaten in at the end. This will make 12 to 18 large shells, and twice as many small ones.

Kisses. Drop the above mixture by teaspoons.

MERINGUE GLACÉE

Place a scoop of vanilla ice cream in a meringue shell. Spoon over a sauce of sweetened sliced strawberries, raspberries, chocolate, or butterscotch. The meringues can be colored with a few drops of red vegetable coloring for the red fruits, green for Saint Patrick's Day, or be beaten with a little cocoa for chocolate sauce. Garnish with a rosette of whipped cream. Meringues glacées are a glamorous dessert, pretty to look at and good to eat.

ANGEL PIE

- ½ *cup egg whites*
- ½ *teaspoon salt*
- ½ *teaspoon cream of tartar*
- 1 *teaspoon lemon juice*
- 1¼ *cups fine granulated sugar*
- 1 *teaspoon vanilla, optional*

Have the egg whites at room temperature. Beat them until frothy with ½ teaspoon of salt. Then beat in ½ teaspoon of cream of tartar and 1 teaspoon of lemon juice. Beat in ¾ cup of sugar, a tablespoon at a time, beating well after each addition. Beat for 5 to 10 minutes after the last addition. Fold in the remaining ½ cup of sugar. The meringue may be flavored with 1 teaspoon of vanilla. Cut a piece of brown paper to fit the bottom of a 9-inch aluminum pie plate. Sprinkle it with sugar. Fill with the meringue, taking care not to have it spread over the edge, or it will stick. With a rubber scraper pile the sides higher than the center. Or, using a pastry bag, pipe out a pie-shaped round on brown paper on a cookie sheet. Bake in slow oven at 275° for 1 hour, using the bottom rack of the oven. Remove, let stand for a few minutes, then take the pie off the paper to prevent sticking. Let cool. Fill with one of the following fillings.

LEMON FILLING

- 1 *cup heavy cream*
- 2 *tablespoons confectioners' sugar*
- 4 *egg yolks*
- ⅓ *cup sugar*
- ¼ *cup lemon juice*
- 2 *teaspoons grated lemon rind*

Whip 1 cup of heavy cream until stiff and beat in 2 tablespoons of confectioners' sugar. Spread half over the center of the pie. Cover with lemon filling and top with the rest of the whipped cream.

Lemon filling. Beat 4 egg yolks until thick. Gradually beat in ⅓ cup of sugar. Add ¼ cup of lemon juice and 2 teaspoons of grated lemon rind. Cook in a double boiler until thick, stirring constantly. Remove and cool.

FRUIT FILLING

Sandwich sweetened sliced fruit, such as strawberries or peaches, with whipped cream in the center of the pie.

BANANA FILLING

Fill the center of the pie with half the recipe for pastry cream on page 296. Cover with sliced bananas and a thin layer of sweetened whipped cream.

STRAWBERRY ICE CREAM PIE

Guests at the Treadway Inns love ice cream pies, and they are a good idea for any housewife to copy who has a freezer. At the inns they are served right from the freezer, and a batch can be made and frozen, ready for any sudden parties, unexpected guests, or impromptu children's festivities. Bake a thin pie crust. When cool, fill with a layer of vanilla or strawberry ice cream which has been softened to spreading consistency in a mixer or with a rotary beater. Place in the freezer until set. Remove and cover the ice cream with sliced sweetened strawberries. Cover with a soft meringue made with 3 egg whites and 6 tablespoons of sugar, following the directions on page 306. Bake in a hot oven at 450° for 4 to 5 minutes. Return to the freezer when cool. When serving, spoon a little strawberry juice over each piece.

BAKED ALASKA

This dessert has a reputation for sophistication which far outweighs its difficulty to achieve. The only real nuisance about it is that it takes a little last-minute preparation. Fill an oval-shaped mold with ice cream; it is usually vanilla but need not be. Freeze firm in a freezer. Cut a slice of sponge cake the same shape as the mold but a little larger. Just before serving, preheat the oven to 450°. Make a soft meringue, using 4 egg whites and 8 tablespoons of sugar, following the directions on page 306. Hollow out a cavity in the cake and fill it with a purée of fresh fruit. Unmold the ice cream on the cake, and cover the ice cream completely with meringue. Place in the oven for 4 to 5 minutes, until lightly browned. Serve immediately, and it is nice flamed with warm brandy or rum.

PEPPERMINT-STICK SNOWBALL

This dessert can be produced in no time at all at home, and is a special favorite at the Treadway Inns. Firm scoops of peppermint-stick ice cream are coated with chopped shredded coconut or coconut flakes and served with hot chocolate sauce (page 352) or hot fudge sauce (page 353). If the scoops of ice cream are placed on a cookie sheet and left in the freezer for half an hour or so, they will be firm enough to handle easily. Scoops of ice cream can also be rolled in rather soft, crushed meringues.

PARFAITS

Parfaits are a fine dessert, elegant to look at and to eat. The Treadway Inns serve about 15 different kinds, and the only limit really is what you have on hand or can get in the way of a sauce.

Parfaits are an ice cream concoction, really a sundae, but served in a special container called a parfait glass, which is a short-stemmed tall glass with an hour-glass figure. It is nearly filled with small scoops of ice cream, usually vanilla, leaving some small air spaces. Sauce is poured in and the top pressed down so that the sauce runs into the air spaces. A large rosette of whipped cream is piped over the top, which is garnished with a cherry or fresh fruit. Some good sauces are crushed sweetened fresh strawberries or raspberries, crushed pineapple, chocolate, fudge, butterscotch, Nesselrode, maple nut, and liqueurs such as crème de menthe, crème de cacao, Cointreau, and Grand Marnier.

PEACH MELBA

Poach fresh peeled peaches for about 10 minutes in a simple syrup made with 2 parts of sugar to 1 part of water and flavored with a small piece of vanilla bean. Drain and chill thoroughly. On individual dessert dishes place a scoop of vanilla ice cream, cover with half a peach, spoon raspberry purée over the peach, and sprinkle with a few slivered lightly browned almonds (sliced almonds can be purchased in tins). For the raspberry purée, bring a pint of fresh raspberries, ¼ to ½ cup of sugar, and ¼ cup of water slowly to a boil. Simmer about 5 minutes, then put through a strainer and chill.

ICE CREAM PUFFS

A very simple mixture to make and handle, called "choux paste," is the basis of cream puffs, profiteroles (small cream puffs), and éclairs. The only differences are the size and shape. Like popovers, cream puffs are leavened entirely by steam, so a hot oven is needed at first for steam to form quickly, causing the cream puffs to rise and "pop," leaving a hole in the center. The heat should then be reduced, so that the insides can dry out.

½ *cup butter*
1 *cup water*
½ *teaspoon salt*
1 *cup flour*
4 *eggs*

Bring ½ cup of butter, 1 cup of water, and ½ teaspoon of salt slowly to a boil, stirring occasionally. Turn up the heat, add 1 cup of flour all at once, and stir vigorously until the mixture forms a ball and clears the sides of the pan, a matter of seconds. Remove from the fire. Add 4 eggs, one at a time, beating after each addition until thoroughly mixed in; an electric mixer is preferable for this. The final mixture should be smooth and glossy. If time allows, let stand for ½ hour.

Pipe out into rounds 2 to 2½ inches in diameter, using a pastry bag and a large plain tube, or drop by rounded tablespoonfuls on an ungreased cookie sheet. Place them about 2 inches apart. They don't spread much, but will rise. Brush the tops lightly with egg wash. Bake for 15 minutes in a hot oven at 425°, then reduce the heat to 375° and continue cooking for another 20 minutes or so to dry them out. When done, they should be lightly browned and feel light. Remove and cool. Makes about 18 cream puffs.

Split the cream puffs in half, place a scoop of ice cream on the bottom half, and cover it with the top half. Spoon over butterscotch sauce (*see* page 353), chocolate sauce (*see* below), hot fudge sauce (*see* page 353), pineapple sauce, strawberry sauce, maple nut sauce – whatever you like.

Note. The above cream puffs may also be filled with sweetened whipped cream or pastry cream (*see* page 296).

SUNDAES

"Make your own sundaes" is a dessert that makes a hit with both the old and the young, and is a successful party dessert. You can serve either just vanilla ice cream or a choice of vanilla, chocolate, or coffee. Then have a tray with bowls of 3 or 4 sauces, chopped nuts, marshmallow whip, and coconut. The sauces can be sliced sweetened fresh or frozen strawberries, crushed pineapple, and any of the following butterscotch and chocolate sauces. Maple syrup is nice too.

CHOCOLATE SAUCE I

The easiest and perhaps best chocolate sauce is made with special baker's dark sweet chocolate, available at some candy stores and specialty shops. Just break it into small pieces and melt it with a little water or brandy in a double boiler over simmering water.

Another quick sauce is made as follows: Melt 2 squares of chocolate in a double boiler. Add 1 cup of light corn syrup and a little salt, and stir until well blended. Cook until thoroughly heated. Remove and add 1 teaspoon of vanilla. This sauce can be served hot or cold.

CHOCOLATE SAUCE II

1 *ounce chocolate*
¼ *cup light cream*
1 *cup sugar*
⅝ *cup light corn syrup*
generous dash of salt
½ *teaspoon vanilla, optional*

Melt 1 ounce (square) of chocolate in a double boiler over simmering water. In another saucepan bring ¼ cup of light cream, 1 cup of sugar, and ⅝ cup of light corn syrup to a boil, stirring constantly. Add to the chocolate with a dash of salt. Cook covered for at least 15 minutes or until ready to use if the sauce is to be served hot. Half a teaspoon of vanilla may be added.

FUDGE SAUCE

2 *ounces chocolate*
¾ *cup sugar*
1 *tablespoon cornstarch*
½ *teaspoon salt*
½ *cup milk*
½ *cup white corn syrup*
2 *tablespoons butter*
1 *teaspoon vanilla*

Melt 2 ounces (squares) of chocolate in a double boiler. Blend together ¾ cup of sugar, 1 tablespoon of cornstarch, and ½ teaspoon of salt. Add ½ cup of milk and stir until smooth, then add ½ cup of corn syrup. Blend with the chocolate and stir until the mixture thickens. Cook covered over gently boiling water for 15 minutes. Remove and add 2 tablespoons of butter. When the sauce has cooled a little, add 1 teaspoon of vanilla. The sauce thickens as it cools to a fine fudgy consistency.

CREAMY BUTTERSCOTCH SAUCE

1 *cup brown sugar*
6 *tablespoons light corn syrup*
3 *tablespoons butter*
¼ *cup water*
dash of salt
½ *cup light cream*
½ *teaspoon vanilla*

Put 1 cup of brown sugar, 6 tablespoons of light corn syrup, 3 tablespoons of butter, ¼ cup of water, and a dash of salt in a saucepan. Blend well. Cook over a moderate fire, stirring until the sugar is dissolved, until 230° is reached, or until the mixture forms a very soft ball in cold water. Remove and add ½ cup of light cream and ½ teaspoon of vanilla.

CLEAR BUTTERSCOTCH SAUCE

- ⅓ *cup brown sugar*
- ¾ *cup dark corn syrup*
- 1 *tablespoon butter*
- 1 *tablespoon water*
- *pinch of salt*

Put all the ingredients in a double boiler over gently boiling water, mix well, and forget about it. In 10 to 15 minutes the sauce will be hot and ready to serve. Or it can wait as much longer as you like. Serve hot, warm, or cold. If it is left covered at room temperature, this sauce will remain the same correct consistency for several days.

MISCELLANEOUS DESSERTS

BAKED INDIAN PUDDING

- 1 *quart milk*
- 5 *tablespoons yellow corn meal*
- 2 *tablespoons butter*
- ½ *cup brown* or *white sugar*
- ½ *cup dark molasses*
- 1 *teaspoon salt*
- ½ *teaspoon ginger*
- ½ *teaspoon cinnamon*
- ½ *teaspoon nutmeg*
- ½ *teaspoon mace*
- 2 *eggs, well beaten*
- 1 *cup light cream*

Bring the milk slowly to a boil in the top of a double boiler over direct heat. Slowly add 5 tablespoons of corn meal, stirring all the while. Put over boiling water and cook for 20 minutes, stirring occasionally. Add 2 tablespoons of butter, ½ cup of sugar, and ½ cup of molasses. Remove from the fire and add 1 teaspoon of salt and ½ teaspoon each of ginger, cinnamon, nutmeg, and mace. Blend in 2 well-beaten eggs. Put into a buttered baking dish. Bake uncovered in a slow oven at 300° for 2 to 2½ hours. Stir occasionally the first hour; then carefully pour 1 cup of cold cream over the top and finish baking without stirring. Serve hot or warm with cream or vanilla ice cream. Serves 8 to 10.

Note. Indian pudding is one of the truly authentic early American desserts and still a perennial favorite at the Treadway Inns. At the Publick House in Sturbridge, Mass., they sometimes add 1 teaspoon of grated orange rind, which gives a pleasant tang. The longer the pudding is cooked, the darker it gets, and therefore the better, according to traditional die-hard New Englanders.

MRS. L. G. TREADWAY'S BLUEBERRY PUDDING

4 *cups blueberries*
1 *cup sugar*
½ *cup water*
8 *thin slices white bread*
softened butter

This pudding is especially good when it is made with small ripe native blueberries rather than large cultivated ones. Bring the berries, sugar, and water slowly to a boil and simmer for 10 minutes. Remove the crusts from the bread and spread each slice with softened butter. If a small 9 x 4½-inch loaf pan is used, the bread will just fit, 2 pieces in each layer. Place the bread, buttered side down, in the pan, and cover with hot berries. Continue these layers, ending with berries. Let stand until cool, then chill in the refrigerator. To serve, unmold on a platter and slice. Serve with cream or ice cream. Serves 8 to 10.

BLUEBERRY GRUNT

- 1 *pint blueberries*
- ½ *cup water*
- *dash of cinnamon and ginger*
- ½ *cup brown sugar*
- 1 *cup flour*
- 1½ *teaspoons baking powder*
- ½ *teaspoon salt*
- 1 *tablespoon shortening*
- ⅓ *cup milk*
- *butter*

Use small native blueberries rather than the large cultivated ones if you can. Put them into a large heavy saucepan with ½ cup of water, a dash of cinnamon and ginger, and ½ cup of brown sugar. Let cook over a gentle fire while you prepare the dumplings. Sift 1 cup of flour, 1½ teaspoons of baking powder, and ½ teaspoon of salt into a mixing bowl. Cut in 1 tablespoon of shortening. Add ⅓ cup of milk and stir just until all the ingredients are blended. Drop by heaping teaspoons on top of the berries. Cover tightly and cook slowly without removing the cover for 20 minutes. Lift the dumplings out, break open with a fork, and drop a small piece of butter in each one. Pour the berries around them and serve with cream. Serve immediately. Serves 6.

Note. Any kind of berries can be used in this recipe.

BROWNIE FUDGE PUDDING

- 1 *cup sifted flour*
- 2 *teaspoons baking powder*
- ½ *teaspoon salt*
- ¾ *cup sugar*
- 2 *tablespoons cocoa*
- ½ *cup milk*
- 2 *tablespoons melted shortening*
- 1 *teaspoon vanilla*
- ¾ *cup chopped walnuts*
- ¾ *cup brown sugar*
- ¼ *cup cocoa*
- 1¾ *cups boiling water*

This is a rich but exceedingly good dessert, with a brownielike cake on top and a thick fudge sauce beneath.

Sift 1 cup of flour, 2 teaspoons of baking powder, ½ teaspoon of salt, ¾ cup of sugar, and 2 tablespoons of cocoa together into a large mixing bowl. Add ½ cup of milk, 2 tablespoons of melted shortening (it can be vegetable shortening), and 1 teaspoon of vanilla and mix until smooth. Stir in ¾ cup of chopped walnuts. Put into a greased 8-inch-square baking dish and smooth the top. Mix ¾ cup of brown sugar and ¼ cup of cocoa together and put through a coarse strainer if there are any lumps. Sprinkle evenly on top of the batter and pour 1¾ cups of boiling water over all. Bake for 30 to 40 minutes in a moderate oven at 350°, or until the cake starts to shrink from the edge of the pan. Serve warm or cold. Whipped cream or vanilla or coffee ice cream may top each serving, but none of these is necessary. Serves 8.

FRUIT FRITTERS

1 *cup sifted flour*
2 *teaspoons baking powder*
½ *teaspoon salt*
2 *tablespoons sugar*
1 *egg, well beaten*
½ *cup milk*
1 *tablespoon cool melted butter*
bananas, pineapple, or *apples*
2 *tablespoons lemon juice*
1 *tablespoon sugar*

Sift 1 cup of sifted flour, 2 teaspoons of baking powder, ½ teaspoon of salt, and 2 tablespoons of sugar into a mixing bowl. Beat 1 egg well. Blend in ½ cup of milk and 1 tablespoon of cool melted butter. Add to the dry ingredients and stir just until blended and smooth. Dip the prepared fruit into the batter, let the excess batter drip off if there is any, and fry in hot deep fat at 375° until nicely browned on both sides, turning once. Remove and drain on absorbent paper. If served as a dessert, sprinkle with confectioners' sugar and serve with the following hot lemon sauce or red currant jelly melted down with a little water. Enough batter for 15 to 20 fritters.

Banana Fritters. Cut ripe peeled bananas in half lengthwise, then cut in half crosswise. Sprinkle with lemon juice and sugar.

Pineapple Fritters. Drain sliced canned pineapple and cut each piece in half. Omit the lemon juice and sugar.

Apple Fritters. Cut peeled cored apples into eighths or into slices crosswise. Sprinkle with lemon juice and sugar.

HOT LEMON SAUCE

½ *cup sugar*
1 *tablespoon cornstarch*
⅛ *teaspoon salt*
⅛ *teaspoon nutmeg*
1 *cup boiling water*
2 *tablespoons butter*
1½ *tablespoons lemon juice*

Mix together in a saucepan ½ cup of sugar, 1 tablespoon of cornstarch, ⅛ teaspoon of salt, and ⅛ teaspoon of nutmeg. Gradually add 1 cup of boiling water, stirring constantly; cook over low heat until thick and clear. Add 2 tablespoons of butter and 1½ tablespoons of lemon juice, and stir until thoroughly blended. Can also be served with gingerbread or cottage pudding.

CHOCOLATE BREAD PUDDING

2 *cups bread crumbs made with stale white bread*
3 *squares chocolate*
1 *cup sugar*
3 *cups milk*
2 *eggs*
4 *tablespoons butter*
½ *teaspoon salt*
1 *teaspoon vanilla*

Put the bread crumbs, 3 squares of chocolate, 1 cup of sugar, and 2 cups of milk in the top of a double boiler. Cook for about 20 minutes over boiling water, stirring occasionally, or until a smooth paste is formed. Beat 2 eggs slightly. Add the other cup of milk, 4 tablespoons of butter, and ½ teaspoon of salt and stir into the chocolate mixture. Continue cooking until the mixture thickens, which will be in about 5 minutes, stirring constantly. Remove from the fire and add 1 teaspoon of vanilla. Turn into a

2-quart buttered baking dish and cook in a moderate oven at 350° for 20 minutes. Serve warm or cold with whipped cream, coffee cream sauce, custard sauce, or even plain. Serves 7 or 8.

COFFEE CREAM SAUCE

2 egg yolks
¼ cup sugar
pinch of salt
½ cup double-strength coffee
1 cup heavy cream, whipped

Beat 2 egg yolks until thick and lemon colored. Add ¼ cup of sugar and beat until the sugar is dissolved. Blend in a pinch of salt and ½ cup of double-strength coffee. Cook in the top of a double boiler over gently boiling water, stirring constantly, until it thickens. Remove from the fire and cool. Fold in 1 cup of heavy cream, whipped. Serves 7 or 8.

CUSTARD SAUCE

2 cups fresh milk
3 egg yolks
¼ cup fine granulated sugar
pinch of salt
1 teaspoon vanilla

Bring 2 cups of milk to a boil in the top of a double boiler over direct heat. Lightly beat 3 egg yolks. Add ¼ cup of sugar and a pinch of salt and blend. Pour the hot milk slowly over the egg yolks, stirring all the while. Put back into the double boiler and place over boiling water (boiling gently and not enough of it to touch the top). Cook, stirring constantly with a wooden spoon, until the custard coats the spoon. This will be before the boiling point is reached, and it is important not to let the custard boil, or it will curdle. Pour into a bowl and cool for 15 minutes, then add 1 teaspoon of vanilla. When the sauce has cooled to room temperature, place it in the refrigerator to chill. Serves 6 or 8.

BIRD'S NEST PUDDING
(Vermont apple dessert with cake crust)

6 to 8 tart cooking apples
1 cup sugar
1 teaspoon cinnamon
½ teaspoon nutmeg
3 tablespoons butter
1 cup flour
1 teaspoon baking powder
½ teaspoon salt
1 egg
½ cup milk

Peel, core, and slice the apples. Put into a buttered 9-inch pie plate. Sprinkle with ½ cup of sugar, 1 teaspoon of cinnamon, and ½ teaspoon of nutmeg; dot with 1 tablespoon of butter.

Crust. Sift together 1 cup of flour, 1 teaspoon of baking powder, and ½ teaspoon of salt. Cream 2 tablespoons of butter and ½ cup of sugar. Beat in 1 egg. Add the dry ingredients alternately with ½ cup of milk. Spread over the apples. Bake for 40 to 50 minutes in a moderate oven at 350°, until golden brown. Serve warm with vinegar sauce. Serves 6.

VINEGAR SAUCE

2 tablespoons butter
1 cup sugar
1 tablespoon flour
2 tablespoons cider vinegar
pinch of salt
about ¼ teaspoon nutmeg

Put into a saucepan 2 tablespoons of butter, 1 cup of sugar, 1 tablespoon of flour, 2 tablespoons of cider vinegar, a pinch of salt, and about ¼ teaspoon of nutmeg. Stir over a slow fire until the sugar is dissolved and the mixture comes to a boil; simmer for 4 to 5 minutes. If the sauce is to stand, keep it hot in a double boiler. Tastes much better than it probably sounds.

CHOCOLATE MOUSSE

- ½ *pound dark sweet chocolate*
- 6 *tablespoons water* or *coffee*
- *pinch of salt*
- 5 *eggs*
- 2 *tablespoons dark rum, optional*
- *whipped cream for garnish*

Break the chocolate into little pieces. Put into a medium-size saucepan with 6 tablespoons of water or coffee and a pinch of salt. Cook over a very low fire until the chocolate is melted and the mixture smooth, stirring constantly. Take the pan off the fire and add 5 unbeaten egg yolks, mixing until well blended. Stir in 2 tablespoons of dark rum. Stiffly beat the 5 egg whites and fold them in thoroughly. Pour into individual dessert dishes, and chill. This dessert sets quickly and can either be made half an hour or so before serving, or it can wait indefinitely in the refrigerator. Garnish with rosettes of whipped cream. Serves 6.

MAPLE MOUSSE

- 2 *tablespoons gelatin*
- ½ *cup cold water*
- 6 *eggs*
- 1 *cup pure maple syrup*
- *pinch of salt*
- ¼ *pound maple sugar*
- 2 *cups heavy cream*

Soak 2 tablespoons of gelatin in ½ cup of cold water. Beat 6 egg yolks until thick and lemon colored. Add 1 cup of maple syrup and a healthy pinch of salt. Stir over a slow fire until the mixture comes to a boil, then remove from the fire. Dissolve the gelatin over boiling water, add to the maple mixture, and let cool. Coarsely grate ¼ pound of maple sugar. Beat the 6 egg whites until stiff but still shiny. Beat 1 cup of heavy cream until stiff. Fold them all into the maple mixture. Put into a mold that has been rinsed in cold water or into individual molds. Chill in the refrigerator for at least 3 hours, or as long as you like. It will set in less time, but should get really cold. Garnish with rosettes of slightly sweetened whipped cream. Serves 10 to 12.

STRAWBERRY BAVARIAN CREAM

2 packages frozen sliced strawberries
3 tablespoons gelatin
½ cup sugar
1 tablespoon lemon juice
½ cup cold water
2 cups heavy cream

Defrost the berries and drain them, reserving the juice. Soften 1 tablespoon of gelatin in ½ cup of the juice for 5 minutes. Bring the rest of the juice (about 1 cup) to a boil, add the softened gelatin, and stir until it is dissolved. Pour into the bottom of a 2-quart mold that has either been lightly oiled with salad oil or rinsed in cold water – unmolding is easier if the mold is oiled. Chill until set.

Mix together the berries, ½ cup of sugar, and 1 tablespoon of lemon juice. Soften the remaining 2 tablespoons of gelatin in ½ cup of cold water. Stir over boiling water until the gelatin is melted and clarified. Add to the berries and blend well. Whip 2 cups of heavy cream until stiff and fold gently into the berries. Fill into the mold and place in the refrigerator for several hours to set and chill. To serve, unmold and, if you wish, garnish with additional whipped cream. Serves 8 to 10.

Note. If fresh berries are used, slice and simmer them for 2 to 3 minutes in ½ cup of water. Use ¾ cup of sugar.

Any fruit can be used. Strawberries, cherries, and raspberries are especially nice because of their color. The whipped cream may be tinted with a few drops of red vegetable coloring to accentuate the color.

CRANBERRY CRUNCH

1 cup uncooked rolled oats
½ cup flour
1 cup brown sugar
½ cup butter
1 1-pound can cranberry sauce

Mix together 1 cup of uncooked rolled oats, ½ cup of flour, and 1 cup of brown sugar. Cut in ½ cup of butter until crumbly. Spread half of this mixture in a greased 8 x 8-inch baking dish. Cover with a 1-pound can of cranberry sauce, either whole or jellied. Top with the rest of the mixture. Bake for 45 minutes in a moderate oven at 350°. Cut in squares and serve hot topped with vanilla ice cream. Serves 6 to 8.

GRAPES WITH SOUR CREAM

Blend together ½ cup of sour cream and 2 tablespoons of brown sugar. Toss with 1½ to 2 pounds of seedless white grapes and chill for several hours in the refrigerator. Serves 6.

CARAMEL CUSTARD

1 *cup sugar*
4 *cups milk* (1 *quart*)
4 *eggs*
4 *tablespoons sugar*
¼ *teaspoon salt*
1 *teaspoon vanilla*

Caramel. Put 1 cup of sugar into a heavy medium-size skillet. Heat very slowly, stirring occasionally, until the sugar is melted and turns golden brown. Caramelizing sugar isn't difficult, but it does require constant attention. As soon as it is the right color, pour into a 1½-quart baking dish, tilting the dish to cover the sides as well as the bottom. The caramel hardens quickly, but will dissolve again when it is baked.

Custard. Into a large mixing bowl put 4 cups of milk, 4 unbeaten eggs, 4 tablespoons of sugar, ¼ teaspoon of salt, and 1 teaspoon of vanilla. Beat with a rotary beater until just blended. Then strain several times – this cuts the air bubbles and gives a beautiful smooth custard. Strain lastly into the baking dish. Put into a pan with an inch of boiling water in the bottom. Bake about an hour in a moderate oven at 350°, until the custard is set and the top lightly browned. Remove from the oven and let stand at room temperature until cold. Then chill in the refrigerator. Serves 6 to 8.

Note. In this custard recipe the milk is not scalded and the eggs are not beaten separately – this is not an oversight; neither is necessary.

SHORTCAKES

Strawberry shortcake made with fresh ripe berries and a good crisp shortcake made with a baking powder biscuit dough is one of the best desserts in the world. The combination of the hot buttered biscuit and the luscious cold berries is almost unbeatable. The shortcake recipe is on page 270. Cut into individual 3-inch rounds. Several hours before serving, wash and hull fresh berries. Leave a few whole ones for garnish and slice the rest. Add brown or white sugar and place in the refrigerator to chill and for the juice to run a little. When serving, place berries between the biscuits and on top. Garnish with a large rosette of slightly sweetened whipped cream and top with a whole berry.

For a **peach** shortcake use sliced sweetened peaches. Allow about 1/4 cup of sugar for each cup of sliced peaches and add a little lemon juice to keep the peaches from turning brown. Half an hour or so is long enough in the refrigerator for peaches, so that they will not darken.

Frozen sliced strawberries or peaches may be used when fresh fruit is not available, and they are very good too.

JELLY DESSERTS

Fruit jellies are a plain dessert admittedly, but because they are both light and energy-giving – gelatin is a protein food – many restaurant guests enjoy them. They are simplicity itself to prepare, and the flavor is excellent if fresh fruit juices are used rather than package gelatins.

Gelatin should always be soaked in a cold liquid for a few minutes to get the full power. Allow 1 tablespoon of gelatin for each 1 3/4 cups of liquid for a jelly that is set but not too firm. Don't put any gelatin dessert in the freezer, all you get is ice. The method is the same for all jelly desserts:

1. Soften gelatin for 5 minutes in cold liquid.

2. Dissolve it by adding a boiling liquid.

3. Add flavoring and any other ingredients.

4. Pour into individual molds or dishes, or into one large container. If you are going to unmold it, first rinse the mold in cold water.

5. Let stand at room temperature until cold, then place in the refrigerator for several hours or overnight to set and chill.

6. Serve plain, with cream, custard sauce (*see* page 359), or rosettes of whipped cream.

FRUIT JELLY

2 *tablespoons gelatin*	½ *cup sugar*
1 *cup cold water*	*dash of salt*
2½ *cups boiling fruit juice*	1 *tablespoon lemon juice*

Soften 2 tablespoons of gelatin for 5 minutes in ½ cup of cold water. Pour on 2½ cups of boiling fruit juice. Add ½ cup of sugar and stir until it is dissolved. Add a dash of salt and 1 tablespoon of lemon juice. The fruit juice can be **orange, grape, grapefruit, loganberry, strawberry, raspberry** – in fact, juice from any fresh or frozen fruit.

For **lemon** jelly, use only ⅔ cup of lemon juice and water for the remaining liquid.

For **lime** jelly, proceed as for lemon, using lime juice.

For **coffee** jelly, all the liquid is strong coffee, and add 1 teaspoon of vanilla. Omit the lemon juice.

Serves 7 or 8.

Note. If cut-up fruit is added to any fruit jelly, wait until the jelly has reached a syrupy consistency.

GINGER ALE JELLY

2 *tablespoons gelatin*	½ *teaspoon ginger*
½ *cup cold water*	2 *cups ginger ale*
1 *cup boiling orange juice*	1 *tablespoon lemon juice*
2 *tablespoons sugar*	*pinch of salt*

Soften 2 tablespoons of gelatin in ½ cup of cold water for 5 minutes. Pour on 1 cup of boiling orange juice. Add 2 tablespoons of sugar and ½ teaspoon of ginger and stir until the sugar is dissolved. Add 2 cups of ginger ale, 1 tablespoon of lemon juice, and a pinch of salt.

HARBOR VIEW HOTEL

Edgartown, Martha's Vineyard, Massachusetts

THAT delightful island, Martha's Vineyard, lies south of the Falmouth end of Cape Cod. The oldest and largest town on the Vineyard is Edgartown, and there at the entrance to the beautiful harbor is the Harbor View Hotel, a Treadway Inn.

The hotel has a comfortable old-fashioned air, with two large wide-verandaed main buildings and cottages. They are situated on five acres of lawns and flower gardens, with swimming right at the front door.

Martha's Vineyard is a favorite vacation spot for thousands of people each summer, and understandably so. For anyone who wants a healthy, quiet vacation, with an abundance of sports, interesting historical associations, and things to see and do, the Vineyard is hard to beat.

The island is about twenty miles long and nine miles wide, and is famous for its miles of white sandy beaches, with smooth, quiet waters for swimming in the bay and harbor, and real surf where the "mighty Atlantic knocks unceasingly." This same contrast gives considerable variety to the fisherman, with surf casting, off-shore fishing for striped bass, scup, flounder, and mackerel, and deep-sea fishing for tuna and marlin. Safe harbors attract small craft. Boats of all types constantly come in and out of the Edgartown harbor, making it a fascinating place to watch from the Harbor View.

For sport lovers, in addition to swimming, fishing, and sailing, there are three excellent golf courses, horseback riding, tennis, bowling, dancing, and bicycling – which is pleasant, since there are comparatively few cars (the seventeen-dollar summer ferry toll for cars discourages short random car trips from the mainland).

Historically, Martha's Vineyard predates the *Mayflower*. In 1602 or 1603 it was visited by Englishmen in search of sassafras, an herb highly valued for its supposed medicinal effects. The main settlement was officially designated Edgar Town in 1671. At that time there was no other Edgar Town in England which it might have been named for, so, since the Duke of York had just taken over New York, it is supposed that it was named for his young and only son Edgar (who died when he was four years old).

In the nineteenth century Edgartown became one of the great whaling ports of the world, and the stately mansions the wealthy captains built still stand on main streets, tended with scrupulous pride. Every August there is an Open House Tour and also a Garden Club Tour.

Other summer entertainments are the annual agricultural fair in August; several of the biggest water events on the East Coast (one race, the annual Venona Trophy Race, one hundred miles around the island, is second only to the Bermuda Race for ocean sailing); band concerts; nondenominational community singing every Wednesday night at Oak Bluffs, and community singing on the Edgartown town dock on Thursday nights.

The Harbor View Hotel is five blocks from the center of Edgartown, within obviously easy walking distance of the tree-shaded narrow streets with the great old houses, antique shops, gardens, the Historical Museum, and a contemporary-art gallery.

Because the island is small, it is easy to see all of it, in all its variety. Its charm is genuine, stemming not from any superimposed attempts to create atmosphere, but from its natural inherent character. There are sand dunes and salt marshes, the picturesque fishing wharves, many small lakes, and softly rolling farmland. Six miles from Edgartown, in Oak Bluffs, are the Methodist Tabernacle Grounds – the seat of the original Methodist Camp Meeting – a unique collection of more than four hundred turn-of-the-century gingerbread cottages. On the annual Illumination Night these houses and surrounding trees are strung with hundreds of Japanese lanterns. God's Acre, the old burying ground, has gravestones which go back at least two hundred years, and some of the original diverting epitaphs can still be deciphered. At the far end of the island Gay Head, the former Indian reservation, is famous for its series of great chalk cliffs leading to the sea, variously and marvelously colored.

The practical aspects of reaching the Vineyard are simple. By car or train, the mainland point of departure is Woods Hole, just past Falmouth on Cape Cod. There, ferries go to either Vineyard Haven or Oak Bluffs, take less than an hour, and the summer service is frequent and on schedule. The New York, New Haven, and Hartford Railroad runs connecting trains from Boston, New York, and Providence to Woods Hole. There is also ferry service from New Bedford. Northeast Airlines has several daily trips from Boston and from New York.

One of the attractions of the Harbor View is an elaborate buffet supper every Sunday night, complete with handsome ice carvings. The hotel is run on the American plan and is open from about the middle of June until just after Labor Day. The innkeeper is John S. Packard, who has had many years' experience as a resort manager for the Treadways and is universally popular.

WINE

THAT good wine complements good food almost goes without saying, since it picks up and accentuates the flavor of the food. But Americans as a whole are not wine-drinking people the way most Europeans are. Maybe our drinking water has been too pure. We are slowly mending our ways, however, and wine consumption is steadily rising, and so is the production of sound American wines.

Maybe one of the reasons Americans distrust wines is that so much is written about them that sounds foolish to the uninitiated. Also, there is an alarming number of wines, so that making a selection can seem like a staggering problem. Rather than make a mistake, many people prefer forgoing the pleasure altogether.

The management of the Treadway Inns agrees that wine makes good food taste even better, and to encourage its use, offers carefully chosen domestic and imported wines at very low prices. The wine lists are not the same at each inn, but the same judicious selection applies everywhere. The wines which appear on most of the lists will be discussed briefly later, but before that, let's settle a few of the general questions about wine. Since it would take a long book to adequately cover the subject, this chapter will necessarily leave much unsaid.

Use. Wines fall into three categories: appetizers, table wines, and dessert wines. As **appetizers,** or apéritifs, they are a substitute for cocktails. The most commonly used are sherry, Dubonnet, Madeira, and either sweet or dry vermouth. Sherry used as an apéritif is usually a slightly chilled, dry, cocktail sherry rather than the sweet sherries which are more suitable as a dessert wine. **Table wines** form the vast majority of wines and are the ones we will discuss later on. **Dessert wines** are sweet, and may be a fortified wine, such as port or a sweet sherry, or a sweet table wine, such as sauternes or champagne.

Names. The name of a wine will tell you either where the wine comes from, or what the predominant grape is. To be more technical, the name is either generic or varietal. Varietal names are for the chief type of grape, such as Cabernet, Pinot, Riesling, Sauvignon, or Traminer, and most of the domestic wines have varietal names. The generic names apply predominantly to imported wines. In France, for example, there are two leading wine-producing areas, Bordeaux and Burgundy. In Bordeaux there are seven districts which have given their names to wines, such as Médoc, Graves, St. Émilion, and Sauternes. Each district has a number of vineyards, for which the wines may also be named, or the name of the vineyard may be tacked on to the name of the district. This accounts for the vast number of wine labels. For the amateur it is enough to know just a few leading wines, and only the connoisseur has the palate to make subtler distinctions.

What to Drink. For the average wine drinker, which takes in a lot of territory, an easy way to choose a wine is to decide whether it is to be red or white, dry or sweet, and then sample domestic, French, German, and Italian wines to see which you like best. If in doubt, have no hesitancy in asking an established wine seller or wine waiter – it is their business to know wines. Price, of course, is an indication of quality, but that doesn't mean you can't get a good drinkable wine at a low cost. With wine, age and scarcity are also factors that raise the price. But many plentiful young wines are good, with a correspondingly low price.

Service. White wines are customarily served with fish, shellfish, light meats, and poultry. Red wines are usually served with red meat, game, and cheese. Pink, or rosé, wines really go with anything, except possibly fish, since they are a little sweet. But there are no arbitrary laws about this; the main concern is to drink what you like.

Dry, by the way, when referring to wine, means not sweet.

The wine glasses are important. Traditionally there are different glasses for different types of wine. In practice, one type of glass does very nicely for home use. It should be plain, clear, round, and large, with a narrower rim than bowl to hold in the bouquet. Since the glass should be filled only ½ or ¾ full when the wine is poured, to allow it to "breathe," a rather large 6 to 9-ounce glass is best.

Frank Schoonmaker, a leading American wine authority, selected the following Treadway Inn wines, and the list should be an excellent guide for the novice.

WHITE WINES

All white wines should be served well chilled.

White Burgundies and white Bordeaux wines are in general more full-bodied than the lighter Rhine, Moselle, and Alsatian wines.

WHITE BURGUNDY

All the following wines are dry.

Mountain White. An inexpensive light, dry, fruity California wine; not as much body as the French wines, but with a nice fresh taste.

Almadén Pinot Blanc. Another California wine with a little more body than the Mountain White. Considered a good premium table wine.

Chablis. The name of a town in France. The wine is very dry, austere, with a delicate bouquet. Perhaps the best white wine with fish.

Pouilly-Fuissé. A French wine, named for two neighboring parishes. A dry pale-gold wine which is strong and vigorous, with a superb bouquet and flavor.

Meursault. Named for a vineyard of two hundred acres which supplies the world. One of the great white Burgundies, less dry than Chablis, delicate, full-bodied, softer and less powerful than Montrachet.

Montrachet. Called the "divine Montrachet," authorities class this as the greatest of the white Burgundies and one of the greatest white wines in the world. It is full-bodied and velvety, with an exceptional mellow quality and lightness.

WHITE BORDEAUX

The white Bordeaux wines, with the exception of Graves, are all sweet. Even a so-called dry French sauternes will be on the sweet side; the American ones are drier.

Almadén Dry Semillon and **Almadén Sweet Semillon.** The Semillon is the predominating grape, and this is a California sauternes-type wine, smooth, golden, medium- to full-bodied, with a flowerlike bouquet. The dry will be drier than a French sauternes. Also, in this country there is a tendency to drop the final *s* in sauternes.

Sauternes. A town in the Bordeaux area. The wine is heavy and characteristically medium sweet to sweet. A dry sauternes is a poor sauternes.

Barsac. In the Sauternes district but called by the parish name. It is less sweet than sauternes, with a gentle, nutty flavor.

Graves. A district in the Bordeaux area with gravelly soil, hence the name. A popular all-around table wine, pleasant, mellow, never bone dry, never sweet.

There is no official classification of the white Bordeaux wines as there is with the reds. The following are two fine vintage wines.

Château Olivier. A fine vintage Graves.

Château d'Yquem. One of the outstanding sweet wines of the world. Very rich, sweet, and expensive. Use as a dessert wine for very special occasions.

RHINE-MOSELLE-ALSATIAN

In general these wines are light, delicate, and fragrant.

Almadén Sylvaner. Sylvaner is an early maturing white grape, and the wine is fresh and fruity. It is the principal California-type Rhine wine, lighter than Riesling, with a delicate fragrance.

Almadén Riesling. Frank Schoonmaker calls the Riesling "one of the two incomparable white-wine grapes of the world." This is a good premium California wine, with a rich flavor and fragrant bouquet.

Livermore Grey Riesling. A soft and pleasing wine, with a mild spicy flavor. From California.

Liebfraumilch. The literal translation is "milk of the Blessed Virgin." It is now a general name given to many Rhine wines, typically light and pleasant.

Berncasteler or **Bernkasteler.** The most celebrated name of the Moselles, this is a delightful, inexpensive, fresh light wine. Berncasteler-Doktor is the most famous.

Traminer and **Gewurtztraminer.** The Traminer is a grape. This is an excellent, rather aromatic wine with a pronounced bouquet. Gewurtz means spicy.

Hochheimer. Hochheim is a town of the Rhinegau in Germany; a pleasant, soft, mild wine.

Johannisberger Klaus. An outstanding German wine, elegant, with wonderful finesse and bouquet.

RED WINES

All red wines should be served at room temperature. They should also be opened about half an hour before they are served to allow the wine to "breathe"; when it is exposed to the air, it begins to release its bouquet.

RED BORDEAUX

The red Bordeaux wines are more commonly known as clarets. They are in general lighter and less full-bodied than the red Burgundy wines.

Mountain Red. An inexpensive but good California claret.

Almadén Cabernet. The Cabernet is the premier claret grape of the world, and this is one of the best premium American red wines, light and soft.

Haut Médoc and **Grand Médoc.** The Médoc is a narrow strip of land north of Bordeaux in France which is known for its clarets, which are medium-bodied and have a nice delicacy.

St. Émilion. A district in the Bordeaux area which produces a wine which has less body and more bouquet than Médoc and a deep ruby color.

In 1855 there was an official classification of the wines of Médoc which is still followed. About four thousand wine-producing estates were involved, and the top classifications are called "growths"; there are five of them, covering sixty wines in all. All the following wines are in this classification.

Château Talbot. A fourth growth, and a good vintage.

Château Pontet-Canet. Although a fifth growth, this is an excellent, very popular wine, considered by many to be better than any second, third, or fourth growth.

Château Margaux. A first-growth claret (there are only four) and one of the great ones.

Château Lafite-Rothschild. Another first growth, and one of the four or five greatest clarets.

RED BURGUNDY

Red Burgundy wines as a general rule have more body and bouquet than the red Bordeaux wines, are a deeper color and are more assertive.

Almadén Burgundy. A California Burgundy-type wine, typically dry and full-bodied.

Almadén Pinot Noir. The Pinot Noir grape is the famous one from which most Burgundies are made. This California wine is one of the finest domestic Burgundies, with a velvet softness.

Beaujolais. A district in Burgundy where the wine is one of the best bargains in Burgundies. The wines are not of the great quality of the finer Burgundies, but they are clean, refreshing, fruity wines which are best drunk young, and they are relatively inexpensive.

Pommard and **Beaune** are both lovely wines, soft and light.

There is no official classification of red Burgundies as there is of red Bordeaux wines, but an unofficial classification by experts rates eight wines as first growths. Two of them are:

Chambertin. This famous wine is on the wine list at most of the Treadway Inns. It is a deep red, full-flavored, fragrant wine.

Musigny. This is one of the finest red Burgundies with a glorious perfume.

RHÔNE WINES

The Rhône wines in general are lighter with less body than the wines of Burgundy and Bordeaux. They are famous for their rosé wines, which are light and refreshing, with a fruity flavor and very pretty color. Rosés should be served chilled.

ROSÉ

Almadén Grenache Rosé. Grenache is the determining grape in this outstanding, very popular American rosé.

Tavel Rosé. Tavel is the district in France which produces this rosé, which is considered one of the best, if not the best, of the French rosés. It is a delightful wine, and a pretty pink, like the Almadén Grenache Rosé, with none of the orange tints some rosés have.

RED

Côte Rôtie. A major wine-producing section. The wine is a fine, full-bodied, deep red wine, one of the best of the Rhônes.

Châteauneuf-du-Pape. Another wine-producing area in France. A very popular wine, with a high alcoholic strength. It is full-flavored, medium-bodied, and soft, lighter than the Côte Rôtie. This wine is good even when young.

WHITE

Hermitage Blanc. Hermitage is a wine-producing area which has both red and white wines. The white is a well-flavored wine with body, and is a good companion to highly seasoned foods.

SPARKLING WINES

All sparkling wines should be served chilled.

The chief sparkling wine is of course champagne. The descriptive terms are sometimes confusing. **Sec,** or **dry, champagne,** which you would expect to be dry, is actually sweet. **Extra dry** is medium sweet, and **brut** is dry. The Treadway Inns list both domestic and imported champagnes; great care has been taken with the domestic ones and they are excellent. Choose a dry champagne as a table wine, and a sweet one as a dessert wine.

Sparkling Burgundy is another popular sparkling wine in this country. It is a bit on the sweet side, but good. The inns list domestic brands and **Chauvenet Red Cap,** one of the finest French sparkling Burgundies.

Asti Spumante. An Italian wine and one of the most famous sparkling wines in the world, with a sweet muscat flavor.

ITALIAN WINES

Chianti is a world-famous Italian wine sold in characteristic straw-covered bottles. Good Chianti is a very pleasant wine and the inns – some of them – list Chianti Red, Brolio, which many consider the finest red, and Chianti White, M & R.

Index